Praise for *Liars, Sai*

"Don't let the title fool you; this is not a shallow story of heroes and villains. In fact, *Liars, Saints, and Sinners* takes the black and white threads that bind families together—the bad and the good in life—and constructs a fabulous grey plaid. The triumphs and struggles of relatable characters include hard work, bad luck, choices based on lies, searches for meaning, longing for love, and unexpectedly beautiful moments of grace. Stevenson's intergenerational story grabs you from the start. Once I finished, I was even more certain that our shared humanity is what gets us through."

—HOLLIE PETTERSSON, Ph.D., psychologist, Salt Lake City, UT

"*Liars, Saints, and Sinners* is an intimate account of self-discovery, at times gut-wrenching but always with a thread of humor.

This is one of those can't-put-the-book-down stories. The author takes us through her life with vivid detail and realism, guiding us through her mother's five marriages, the loss of her father when she was very young and the mysteries surrounding his death, to reflections on her Mormon background and the need to always be 'okay.' She marries; divorces; struggles with family relationships; leaves her faith; achieves professional success; discovers sisters, her father's biological family and his hit-man brother; finds her soul-mate and marries again; and ultimately claims peace for her soul.

Ms. Stevenson's debut book is powerful, written with brutal honesty, and leaves the reader craving more."

—J.C. BRINTON, marketing consultant, Venice, FL

Liars, Saint, and Sinners takes the reader on a trip through not only Ms. Stevenson's remarkable life but also through the many aspects of the small-town society that shaped her. Her book is a testament to both her spirit of perseverance and to the community that shaped it."

—S. BUCK, coach and strategist, Salt Lake City, UT

"*Liars, Saints, and Sinners* is an incredible memoir of Ms. Stevenson's life and her very complicated family. She weaves together multiple fascinating stories with writing that is gripping, well researched, entertaining and in many cases, painfully honest. We are given much insight into what is like to grow up in Utah in a predominantly LDS (Mormon) and rural culture. I am impressed with Stevenson's intelligence, grit, humor, guile, and courage to persevere through abuse, strict religious teachings, multiple stepfathers, several husbands, and physical injuries all while developing into a strong mother, wife, and leader with a mind of her own."

—LORI JONES, M.S. Education, Principal, Counselor and Educator (retired), Salt Lake City, UT

"No biblical begats here! The vivid characters populating Dawn LaRue Stevenson's *Liars, Saints, and Sinners* appear naturally in the narrative, not on a skeletal family tree. Chapter 1, 'Momma's Eyes Are Green,' introduces Dawn, her sister, 3 half-brothers, 2 step-sisters, and 3 step-brothers planning Momma's funeral. The memories, the choices, the venue, reveal a large, robust and loving three-generation rural family celebrating the long life of an intensely devoted mother.

In subsequent chapters, her mother's multiple marriages, the death of her father early in her fourth year, a childhood sexual encounter, and the disappointment of her own marriage and church life lead Dawn on a series of truth-seeking adventures to find the missing pieces of her story—including, via Ancestry.com, a whole new set of half-siblings, an aunt, cousins, and a notorious uncle half a continent away.

Dawn also builds an upbeat, loving, and fulfilling life. Great reading!"

—DIANA MAJOR SPENCER, Ph.D., Purveyor of Truth, Beauty, and Independent Thinking, Mayfield, UT

"The tale is so compelling, so real, so accessible that anyone anywhere can identify with it, even if one has not been raised in the strict Mormon Church, as she was growing up."

— CLINT PALMER, fimmaker and writer, Pasadena, CA

LIARS, SAINTS, AND SINNERS

CRIME,
MYSTERY,
AND
FAMILY
HISTORY

DAWN LARUE STEVENSON

Foreword by Tom Curley, Former President and CEO of Associated Press

CANAL HILL

Louise,
With my greatest respect!
Dawn Ste—

CONTENTS

Dedication

To Russell and Ethel for unending love and stability
and
Woody and LaRue, both of whom have everything
to do with who I am

St Louis Family Player Card

Harry Alvin Dean (1867–unk.) *married (1899)* **Bertha Denison Snyder** (1875–1928)

Children:

(Nell) Margaret Dean (1900–1987) *married (1920)* **Charles Hall** (1889–1969)

Children:

Dean Hall (1921–2002) *married (1947)* Shirley Pallardy (1925–2002)
Children: John, Kathleen, Kevin (1950–2018), and Richard
Marion Hall (1924–2015) *married (1947)* Charles Brewster (1920–1992)
Joan *married (2009)* Ken
Anne

Ethel Dean (1902–1988) *married (unknown)* **John Hewitt**

Children: Gene Ellen (1927–) and Jacqueline (1928–2008)

Rolla Spencer Dean aka Blackie (1905–1954)

married (1925, divorced 1936) **Ethel Vollmer** (1903–unknown)

No children
married (1936, divorced 1940–45) **Bernice Douglas** (1905–1987)

Her daughter: Daisy Eileen
married (1946) **Catherine Moriarity** (1916–1980) m. 1946

Children: Mary Joan (1946–1946) and unnamed daughter

Sara Romaine (1909–1987) *married (1929)* **Roy Herschel** (1901–1976)

Children: Andrew and Paul

Mary Jane Dean (1913–2002) *married (1930)* **Albert Prack** (1907–1992)

Children: Albert Jr (1931–1931), Albert Jr (1933–2008), Nancy,
Donald, and James (1945–1983)

Woodrow Wilson Dean (1917–1952) *married (1939)* **Jane Evelyn Miller** (1919–2007)

Judith and Ken Ayster (1935–1995) m. 1961 div. 1977
Four children and Barry Wallraven *(married 1980 with one child)*,
Nancy

Woodrow Wilson Dean *(aka Don Stevenson)* *married* **Ethel LaRue Yard**

Children: Dawn LaRue
Debra Sue

Utah Family Player Card

homas Russell Yardley (1848–1921) *married (1871)* **Joana Isabel Keyes** (1853–1892)

Children:
Thomas William (1871–1873), James Gilbert (1873–1943), Tessa Estella (1875–1899), Alice Minerva (1877–1956), Celia Isabel (1879–1959), Irvin Elisha (1881–1936), Sarah Emma (1883–1899), Joanna Marietta (1885–1946), Leslie Clinton (1887–1933), Raymond (1889–1889),
Russell Samuel (1892–1962)

ussell S. Yardley (1891–1962) *married (1914)* **Ethel Gill Yardley** (1889–1972)

Children:
Thomas Rodchell (1914–1993), Birdell Russell (1917–1993), Howard Melvin (1919–1978), *Ethel LaRue (1921–2010)*, Ruth Althea (1923–2019), Beth NaDene (1927–2018), Gill LaVar (1929–2016)

aRue (1921–2010)

married (1944, divorced 1947) **Frank Powers (unk.)**

> *Children:* Russ, David

married (1948) **Woody/Don** (1917–1952)

> *Children:* Dawn, Debra

married (1953) **Gene Anderson** (1928–1956)

> *Son:* Nick

married (1964) **Arlo Kump** (1921–1993)

> *[Arlo Kump] married (1942)* **Vivian Burgon** (1925–1964)
>
> > Kathy (1943–1984), Kerry (1945–2003), Penni (1949–2019), Rick, Scott, David (1956–2010)

married (1993) **John Hone** (1927–2013)

> No children

)awn LaRue Stevenson (1949–)

married (1968) **Ernest** (1944–2020)

> Luna, Dora, Ox, Trina, CC

married (1995) **Herbert Nielsen** (1939–) *[no children]*

married (2013) **Robert J. Wasser** (1948–) *[no children]*

> *married (1986)* Sherryl H. *[Four children]*

FOREWORD

I met Dawn at a pizzeria in Easton, Pa. She was "from away"—a western woman who had married a high school classmate of mine and joined him for a weekend-long 50th reunion. She asked me to read a story she had written about an uncle who likely was a notorious St. Louis gangster.

Over the years I had come to dread such requests. New authors often lack the courage to reveal the juiciest secrets in family closets or the ability to tell a good tale. But Dawn sparked with energy. In a few minutes' conversation, she described a life story both startling and fascinating. Most important, she exuded the desire to share that story.

In describing the gangster connection, Dawn fessed up to having written three chapters about her mother's Utah pioneer family. I told her she was halfway to a book and to get writing. When she said she might need a year, I admonished her for giving herself too generous a deadline. Four years later she delivered a manuscript that turns out to be a page-turner.

Most family stories are as flat as an ancestor tree - blocks of names, dates, and relationship lines. They lack insight into the personalities and motives that drive outcomes, and, in some cases, affect history. Few offer glimpses into the historical forces—booms, busts, wars, technologies, calamities—that constrain or enable possibility.

Dawn collects eyewitness accounts. She finds a grandfather's autobiography, pecked out on his old Smith-Corona, mistakes and all. She uncovers biographies on a great-grandfather and another on her mother, both written by granddaughters. She also displays a scholar's ability to find buried documents or newspaper clips to put personal stories into historic and cultural context.

In tracing her father's journey, she sifts through a thousand newspaper articles and insightfully captures the sordid crime life of 1940s Los Angeles. Articles from St. Louis newspapers provide the details on Uncle Blackie, the most arrested gangster in St. Louis from 1926 until his death in 1954. In a twist with ironic overtones, this alleged hit-man is killed by his third wife after a domestic violence incident.

But the tour de force of "Liars, Saints, & Sinners" turns out to be Dawn's own journey. This book traces the saga of a girl who loses her father at age three in a mysterious traffic accident, needs five decades to discover he had a second family, is raped three times by age 15, painfully watches her mother descend through five marriages and suffers abuse at the hands of authority figures at school and work.

This is the story of a woman who summons the courage and strength to hurdle extraordinary turmoil. At crucial moments she enlists help from family, friends, colleagues, and therapists to keep going. Over six decades she hones a pioneering spirit of her own—one of self-determination and accomplishment no matter the barrier. In the process of shedding her Mormon underwear, Dawn completes a metamorphosis into a confident, secure woman who celebrates her humanity and gender as an equal.

As a girl, Dawn embraces Mormon doctrine. When confronted with contradictions, she neither blindly accepts nor casually rejects them. As a woman she digs deeper into history and scripture to understand. She questions elders and challenges those who take offense or move to dismiss her.

Dawn studies other religions. She immerses herself in Native culture. She becomes enchanted by Natives' reverence for ancestors, their struggles, and their enshrinement and knowledge of the land that sustains them. A journey of self-discovery evolves into something grander and seemingly timeless. These revelations to a non-Mormon or non-Utahan help explain so much about the land and culture it cradles.

Dawn documents her trail in journals both penetrating and searing. Through these journal "confessions," she puts earlier versions of herself in context—making sense of nightmares as well as dreams. There she battles demons from misguided clergy and guardians to even a few monsters who preyed on her. The journals became her path to a safer and eventually more tranquil place. Through this soul-searching, she evolves a personal spirituality that helps her leave behind the confining and often discriminating dogma of traditional church teachings or societal place-cast.

Dawn connects her own march to the historical backdrop of women's steps toward fairness and justice. She reflects on the struggles of others seeking fulfillment and respect, poignantly of Native people, and, more recently, on matters of sexual orientation and expression. She displays a generous gift of being able to forgive her trespassers and a refreshing ability to laugh at what life has thrown at her.

"Liars, Saints, & Sinners" captures stories of hardship, setback, struggle, and redemption across seven generations. It shows how the quintessential pioneer spirit can inspire a new generation of American explorers. It tempts readers to summon the courage to embrace that same spirit. You, too, may find it the trail worth taking.

Tom Curley
President and CEO (Retired)
The Associated Press

INTRODUCTION AND ACKNOWLEDGMENTS

I took the title for this memoir from a conversation with the mother of my book group friend, Sarah. Her Mom told me, "I learned to lie in the Mormon Church when my husband died and left me with five young children to raise. Everyone in Idaho expected me to be fine, so, I was fine." Her observation parallels my experience growing up in rural Utah. My father was dead. I was sexually abused. I had stepfathers. Everyone in my little Mormon community expected me to be fine. So, I was fine. Until I wasn't.

For most of my life, my biological father has been little more than a ghost, shadowy memories, and little detail. Since my late twenties, I have felt compelled to search for him, hoping for answers to the mystery of him. How and why did he change his identity, and, after some searching, how and why did he die? My half-sister, Judy, nearly a decade older than I, felt the same compulsion, also beginning her search in her late twenties. And my cousin Joan, the person responsible for bringing us all together, wanted to answer the family mystery of what happened to her Uncle Woody. It took decades for us to meet and begin to piece together the puzzle. Joan's years of searching and research inspired me to write our story. Joan says she felt compelled to keep looking. Woody was working on her. I am beyond grateful for my St. Louis family, Joan and Judy.

My husband, Mr. Wasser, is my stabilizing genius—the man with more common sense than anyone I know. His support for this project has been unending. I am cherished, and I know it.

My children have been my best and longest term teachers. They are less than enthusiastic about having their family story, some of which is very painful for them, spread about. I have changed their names in an effort to provide them some measure of anonymity. In my first drafts I called them Daughter #1, #2, #3, and #4 and my son. They were not fans of the no-name strategy, so I made a play on uno, dos, tres, and cuattro and came up with: Luna, the moon goddess; Dora, Greek for gift; Trina, short for Caterina which means pure; and CC, short for "blind to her own beauty." Each name fits the bearer. I planned to use Eric the Red for my son as a tribute to our Scandinavian and Irish heritage, but he prefers Ox, a nickname given to him by his co-workers— a tribute to his strength and his Oxford brain. One of my favorite parts of life has been talking and laughing with each of them. I am grateful to be their mother.

Whenever I felt discouraged or overwhelmed in completing this story, my son-in-law Winston kept me going. Winston is a Navy vet. Two months short of his 40th birthday, he collapsed with a seizure in the middle of a store on an ordinary Saturday morning. Within six days he had a diagnosis and brain surgery for what turned out to be anaplastic astrocytoma grade 3. After six weeks of proton radiation and a year of chemo, his life returned to mostly normal. Brain cancer never goes into remission. The best we can hope for is no active cancer confirmed by an MRI every six months. After each clean report, Winston makes remarkable posts about taking advantage of every day and every opportunity. He has been clear for six years now. His inspiration often kept me at the computer writing away.

I am grateful for my big alcoholic, incestuous, Mormon family, all my brothers, two of whom have passed now, my two sisters who have passed and most particularly for my sister, Debra. Many years in my life she has been my best friend. We did a good job for Momma. And I appreciate growing up around my Yardley family, most of whom are talkers; they are clever with words and funny. I have used their real names as much as possible. The family tree only shows relatives I have identified by name.

I have changed the names of my dating partners in later life, trying to give them a measure of anonymity. The stories I share are prototypical for each of them.

I am so happy I attended Marilyn Larson's British Lit class and her workshop "A Woman's Place." She introduced me to beautiful language in beautiful texts. Darryl Spencer, Honors Intensive Writing and Creative Writing, taught me how to write and how to care about writing. Tom Curley, President and CEO (retired) of *Associated Press*, helped me believe in my writing.

Anyone who writes knows how hard it is to get readers. Therefore, I am very grateful to Dora and her daughter, my oldest granddaughter, for their years of interest, reading, and feedback. My friend Nicole has been faithful and encouraging. My colleague Tom provided critical insights. And Tom Curley gave me more feedback on my writing than anyone, ever. Thank you all.

My women friends have seen me through life's toughest moments. Thank you to Jenny, Suzanne, Jackie, Bobbie, Dory, Hollie, Cindy, and Nicole who is my soul-sister and Sundance Film Festival partner in crime. My niece, Michelle, has been a friend and advisor all these years. My Bookies, the bright and accomplished women in my book club, have kept me reading and writing. They also served as my dating advisory board: Ellen, Jeanie, Kismet, Kris, Rose, Sarah, and Vicki.

I am grateful for professional colleagues Lynn Jensen, Dory Walker, Hollie Pettersson, Julie Mootz, Heidi Mathie, Amber Landward, Sandy Ameel, Tom Sachse, and Syd Davies plus Norm Gysbers, Pat Martin, Nicole Cobb, Ian Martin, Jay Carey, Trish Hatch, Judy Bowers, Donna Hoffman, Richard Wong, and Eric Sparks, all of whom moved me forward professionally. Thanks also to the many professional school counselors, classroom teachers, and dedicated educators who have collaborated with me over the years. I am also grateful to my hundreds of graduate students.

I am lucky I met Tiffany Papageorge, actor, author, mentor, and friend who introduced me to Michael Rohani who guided me through this whole process from manuscript preparation, to editing, to design, and all that goes into the production and publishing of a book.

I appreciate attorney David C. Reymann and his fine eye for detail. His insights and sage advice have been so helpful.

And I am so grateful for my editor, Trista Emmer, who helped me negotiate the tricky balance of writing a memoir in the present tense. She also kept me focused, in line, and on track. Her insights for Mormon and Utah culture along with her many other questions and suggestions have been invaluable. She is a wonderful person, kind and generous of spirit, and a pioneer in her own right.

Thank you all!

1

MOMMA'S EYES ARE GREEN

Momma's eyes are green, soft, greyed, rheumy with old age. The color of the distant foothills in early spring with light filtered by the late winter snow of the Rockies. Her skin is fine-grained and supple, wrinkled at the corners of her mouth and eyes. She is nearly 90. Her cheeks are smooth and tan from years outdoors—on the farm, in the mountains, in the garden, on the water. My daughter, the esthetician, assures me that we all tan up as our skin thins. After a brief flirtation with chubbiness in her seventies, Momma is back to 120 pounds on her five 5'6" frame. Restored to her lifetime tendency for leanness, willowy even into her sixties, she is thin again, but not agile enough for willowy. After Sunday dinner at the assisted living center, we walk the hallways, talking and laughing. Some Sundays the residents are entertained by a piano player at the center lobby. Momma and I sing snippets of "Take Me Out to the Ballgame," "Autumn Leaves," "Deck the Halls," or "April Showers," depending on the season or the holiday. Neither of us is a particularly good singer.

I have older, fonder memories of my Momma, Ethel LaRue Yardley Powers Stevenson Anderson at that point, singing in the car as we drive to Grandma and Grandpa Yardley's or Grandma and Grandpa Anderson's or to Salt Lake to see Aunt Beth. In those days she sings, "You are My Sunshine," my favorite, and "Hey Good Lookin.'" On the trip home we got "Goodnight Irene," but only the chorus and one verse; "Last Saturday night I got married. Me and my wife settled down. Now me and my wife have parted. I'm gonna take another stroll downtown." These honky-tonk songs feel like psalms of melancholy for my dead father. They may be the only grief Momma allows herself.

🖋

During one of our hallway conversations, Momma makes a quarter turn toward me and confesses, "I can't stand for John touch me. Of course, I can't stand to touch myself. I'm all skin and bones. It's kind of creepy really." Each sentence punctuated by a moment of thought. Momma makes me laugh.

And now Momma is dead. I like to tell people that I come from a great big, alcoholic, incestuous Mormon family. Mostly, I like to say that for the shock value; even so, it is true. We, most of her surviving children, are gathered to plan her funeral. Where once there were eleven of us, now there are eight. One stepsister and two stepbrothers are dead. My half-brothers Russ and Dave are here as are my stepbrothers, Rick and Scott. For me, half- and stepsibling are artificial distinctions that I only use when explaining my family to those who do not know us. In our family, a brother is a brother. We meet at the home of my only full-blood sibling, my sister Debra.

Before we even have plans to meet about Momma's funeral, our eldest brother, Russ, calls to ask if I think we can get away with having Momma's funeral in Salt Lake City, closer to where most of us live. I assure Russ I have no intention of going against Momma's wishes. I know she will haunt me to my grave.

Momma raises us in a small town, more like a village, in central Utah, near the farm where she was born. In the microcosm of blue-eyed blonds and light-eyed brunettes of our youth, my sister Debra is the dark-haired beauty, big brown eyes and long dark, dark brown hair with mahogany highlights. She irons her hair starting in junior high school. About the same height as me and Momma, in her youth Deb is slim and well-proportioned with real breasts, her clothes and personal style incredibly hip. She may be the coolest girl in town. In a family of smart people, Deb is likely the smartest—a measured IQ well above 135, likely above 140. I occasionally remind her that she does not have to know everything. As a nontraditional student, she earned a degree in accounting and then an MBA, going on to be an underwriter and middle management worker in a local HMO. In her entry position with the company, she found she could do the job in 30 hours per week rather than 40—she received permission to do so from her bosses and then used the extra hours for a part-time job as a baggage handler for Western Airlines before they merged with Delta. She was most interested in the travel benefits. In our decidedly middle-class family, Deb is the rich one, retired and the sole occupant of a 4,000-square-foot condo. Ten-foot ceilings, maple floors and cabinets, commanding view of the Great Salt Lake and Antelope Island, fabulous Western sunsets. Her master bath is covered floor to ceiling in black granite with white and peach veins. She has black toilets and basins and peach toilets and basins, all the walls painted a subdued peach, the custom furniture an equally subdued peach leather. The objets d'art come from her years of travel. Deb has been a life-long golfer and active in the Utah Women's Golf Association. Momma once tells me, "I hope I don't die during the summer. Debra will never take time to come to my funeral." Deb's ex-husband, a realtor and developer, paid off the condo in the settlement of their particularly long and difficult divorce, leaving her with enough hard cash for a long and comfortable life. The years have not been kind to Debra, but Debra has not been kind to Debra. Astrologically, she is a Scorpio rising. Every time she stings me with that tongue, I remind myself that all the harsh words she says to me and others, and about me and others, also rain down on her own head. Starting in our twenties, I often say, "the last person you want on your case is my sister Debra." Like most of us, as the years pile on so does the weight. I send her occasional e-mails with attached tips and articles on health, until the day she tells me, "You say one more thing about my weight, and I will bitch slap you." She does not actually slap me. I do not actually tell her that no one I know talks that way. The added pounds eventually take a predictable toll on her health. Growing up, she and I were close, best friends even, especially in our early years. She was often an awesome back-up mom for my children, taking in one of them for months after high school graduation. As adults, we have our best time together during the four years that we partner up to care for Momma and her fifth husband, John, while they are in assisted living. Otherwise, the time between speaking can stretch as long as a year and a half.

As the funeral planning begins, Russ, the self-appointed spokesman, tells us that our brothers' way of honoring our years of service to Momma and John is that they decide to let us plan the funeral exactly the way we want. "Us" means Debra and me. Deb and I do not look at one another and roll our eyes, but we are thinking the same thing: Russ' tendency toward being pompous is exceeded only by his tendency toward being an asshole.

John, Momma's fifth and last husband, is a Mormon Son-of-a-Bitch. He has all the trappings of religious piety, attending church regularly, praying often, reading his scriptures daily, and paying his tithing monthly. Yet, he remains small of spirit, not generous, stingy even, and self-righteous. John thinks he is the only good man Momma has ever known which is why we list the last name of each of her five husbands in the heading of her obituary. It costs us, costs John, an extra $100 per name. We come to better understand John's nature about 6 months in at the assisted living center. Momma mentions to Debra that she is running out of money. Deb, with her accounting background and MBA, can read and create elegant Excel files. When Deb investigates the situation with Momma's money, she discovers that all of the expenses for assisted living for both Momma and John have been taken out of Momma's account, an oversight that John is apparently happy to let slide. Momma gets a Social Security check and a small pension. John has his Social Security and a generous pension from his years of work at a steel mill. John's sister tells us that John has "every nickel he ever made." Now we know why. Nevertheless, John is generally pleasant and merry—he makes Momma laugh. However, Momma admits, "He is not as easy to get along with as Arlo." Daddy Arlo is our stepfather—really the only father we have ever known. Deb adjusts the finances for Momma and John to be more equitable.

For the past four years, Deb is at Apple Tree, the assisted living center, every Tuesday or Wednesday. She does laundry for Momma and John, monitors their bills and money, manages all their prescriptions, and takes them to many of their doctor's appointments. I am there most every Sunday with a home-cooked meal. I eat with them at the home often enough to know the food is not up to much, and Momma is a good cook. She feeds us well for years and years. I try to keep her connected to her good cooking by bringing in suppers that she taught me to make. In four years, I miss maybe ten Sundays. Occasionally, at their request, we go out for Burger King or pizza. But mostly, it is Momma's recipes that I serve: roast beef and mashed potatoes with gravy; pork chops with mushroom gravy made from Campbell's soup; corn-crisped chicken, cooked to fall-off-the-bone perfection with Daddy Arlo's warm mashed potato salad. I also make coq au vin and gratin dauphinoise from my new French cookbooks. And sometimes a Tex-Mex dish to honor our time in New Mexico. I occasionally write out checks for them. Once per month I cut their toenails, telling myself that cutting toenails on old people secures my place in heaven. I worry that I might die of fungus.

For the funeral planning, Russ, wiry even in his late sixties, continues as the self-appointed spokesman. His average height makes him short in our family of tall, lean men. He looks vaguely like Woody Harrelson; his two sons could be doubles for Woody. Russ has the dry Yardley skin, which does not age well. Failure to use sunscreen leaves him wrinkled to the top of his bald head. Within the decade I will have a fight with him on social media over which of us is better looking. His ego will never admit it, but I win because I actually am pretty. He isn't. Make no mistake, I love the man, and have at last made peace with him, but he is the first person over whom I ever muttered, "God save me from a repentant sinner." I was 15 at the time. In fairness, he can be funny and fun, and yet difficult. Russ has master's degrees in public health and public administration, but, in these last years, he works as a long-haul trucker because he never does figure out how to get along with people.

Also present for the planning is our brother Big Dave, a Marine veteran—Vietnam, right after the Tet Offensive. He is tall and no longer lanky, his skin ruddied by years in the sun as a manager at Uncle Tom's dairy farm, the ruddiness worsened by years of smoking. Dave is wryly funny, self-deprecating, and a genuinely good man. His post-Vietnam battle with alcoholism has been over for more than 30 years. With relish, Big David recounts a recent conversation with a doctor at the VA.

"Doc, when I was in my treatment program, they told me that, after some years, I could even have an occasional drink. What do you think?"

"Well Dave," the doctor replies, "I think after thirty years sober you could try an occasional drink. If something goes wrong and you wake up three days later in Vegas, you'll know it wasn't a good idea." Subsequently, Dave satisfies an infrequent yearning for some Johnny Walker Black Label.

Big Dave, who once wanted to be a history teacher, could likely also have been a very good professional writer, but, post-Vietnam, the girls at the community college drive him out of academia with accusations of baby killer, to which he responds, "You are all upset about war and casualties, but I promise you, I know more about death and dying than you ever will." He remains well-read and politically astute. We are on opposite ends of the political spectrum. I am the token liberal in our conservative family. I avoid arguing with Dave because he knows more than I do and will whoop me every time, nevertheless, we occasionally get into it over his overload of information from Fox News. All of us love Sharon, Big Dave's wife, who is upbeat and full of smiles and laughter. She has the rounded body typical of a woman who has spent her life as a waitress at Mom's Café.

Rick and Scott are here with their wives, both named Julie. Rick is the older of these two brothers who are, technically, our stepbrothers. As a 19-year-old, our brother Rick gives up his teenage practices of smoking and drinking to serve an LDS mission to England for two years. In his teens, Rick has several appearances before the juvenile court judge. At Momma's 80th birthday party, Rick stands to tell all present that at the end of every court appearance the judge would ask if anyone had anything else to say? Momma always stood and said, "Your honor, I want you to know that he is a really good boy." Sometime after his LDS mission, Rick returns to his teenage habits of smoking and drinking. When he marries his third wife, Julie, he converts to Catholicism. He is a good Dad to three good kids. Rick is a hard-drinking, community-minded man who serves as the Utah President of the Knights of Columbus. Rick's Julie is pretty, dark-haired and soft-spoken, mostly concerned about family and relationships.

Scott, the quiet one of the family, is sweet, uncomplicated, and good-hearted. He is only 15, when 16-year-old Julie comes to the pink house in Gunnison with her parents who want to talk about what is to become of their pregnant daughter. Scott is handsome—shorter than his brothers but muscular with curly hair and light eyes. Julie with the beautiful lissome body is also painfully plain, and Scott is totally smitten. They marry within weeks of that "what to do" conversation and make it successfully with lots of support from Julie's parents. Scott graduates high school and becomes a machinist. They have two boys and eventually raise their own granddaughter. Scott battles depression and alcoholism through most of his life, attempting officer-assisted suicide at least once. Julie's solution to his mental health problems is the Mormon magic cure—read your scriptures, say your prayers, pay your tithing, and go to church. The Mormons believe they have this salvation thing all figured out. Follow all the rules and you are home free. This works for some church members, but, by and large, a meta rule among Mormons is that it is more important to look good than be honest. During our funeral planning for Momma, Julie's big concern surfaces almost immediately. With all the delicacy of a bull moose, she wonders, "Now that Momma is dead, can I move ahead with sealing her to our Daddy Arlo in an LDS Temple?" A sealing means that the couple are married for "time and all eternity" as compared with "until death do us part." Everyone looks to me for a response.

"Julie, you and Scott had that conversation with Momma several times," I respond. She nods in confirmation of the conversation.

"Momma told you no."

Still bent on checking off all the requirements, Julie says, "We just want to be sure that everything is taken care of."

"You know she is sealed to my father Don Stevenson," I respond.

Julie replies, "Well, we don't know if Don will accept his temple work, and we just want to be sure." The Mormons believe that every soul who ever walked the face of the earth must eventually be baptized, ordained to the priesthood if male, and sealed in eternal marriage. It is your only ticket to the Celestial Kingdom, one of three degrees of glory in the hereafter. The Terrestrial Kingdom, the lowest of the three, is much like this earth life, full of life happenings and good and bad people. The Telestial Kingdom, the middle kingdom, is for "good people who were nevertheless deceived," which includes anyone who does not embrace Mormonism during this mortal life or accept the work for the dead performed by proxy by faithful Mormons who go to Mormon Temples to do Mormon Temple Work. These poor Telestial souls are likely destined to be winged (say wing-ed) seraphim and attendants to Gods and Goddesses. The Celestial Kingdom is for the glory and exaltation of faithful Mormons, the place where we become Gods and Goddesses, with eternal increase. I think that means we create children eternally. I am not sure I am in for this one; it sounds like I might to be pregnant eternally.

In resolution, I tell Julie, "I guess you are going to have to do what you have to do." Acquiescing for Scott, not for her. I consider it a lack of maturity on my part that a decade later I am still mad as hell about that conversation. I am probably angrier with myself that I did not just let Momma's "No" lie.

Our brother Nick, technically half-brother, lives in Idaho and will be here in time for the open casket viewing in three days. Nick, a life-long rebel, grew his hair past his shoulders in high school. This was the early 70s. The school administration and the Board of Education want his hair cut above his ears. Rather than comply, he wears a wig to school every day of his senior year, which he pulls off every day as walks through the parking lot, shaking out his dark blonde hair that grows past his shoulders. Nick, tall and lean, has one green eye and one brown eye and does his asanas every day. Entirely self-educated, he remodels homes by reading about it, including major additions and replacing all the roof trusses. He passes all his certifications for a licensed fire-sprinkler engineer by reading about it. He counts among his clients the Sony Theater in San Francisco. Nick, also a recovered high-functioning alcoholic, has an FBI top-secret clearance, required for his stint as the fire safety specialist for the Idaho National Laboratories. Nick tells me that during his 8-hour interview with the FBI agent, he suddenly realizes, "this guy knows stuff about me that I have forgotten." Some weeks later, on completion of the clearance, the FBI agent tells Nick, "You are the biggest screw-up I have ever investigated for whom everyone in your past has nothing but good wishes." His wife, Royleen, thick blonde curly hair, and heavy set, serves for years on her local school board. She is jovial and energetic, an avid do-it yourselfer and a good right hand for my project-oriented brother. She is a Mormon stalwart, but not a stiff with the blind obedience of Scott's Julie. Nick and Royleen lose their first child to SIDS. Subsequently, Nick works out of his home, so he is always available to his second daughter and his son. He is also a life-long musician who builds his own drum kit, including a custom lacquer, for which he creates a rotating paint and finishing device to avoid runs on the rounding surfaces.

The planning for the funeral proper is easy. Mom has the whole program written out. Opening hymn, closing hymn, intermediate hymn. Nick's Uncle, Lee, is supposed to give the opening prayer, but he dies the month or two before Momma, so Nick's son, also named Lee, takes that role. Momma wants Dr. Stewart, who has been our family physician and the LDS Stake President, a local LDS church leader for all the small towns in southern Sanpete County, to be the main speaker. Dr. Stewart dies the year previously, so that will have to change. Momma wants to include a song from Deb's ex-husband accompanied by guitar, Van Morrison's "Have I Told You Lately That I Love You?" Deb's ex played the same song at the funeral of our stepfather, our Daddy Arlo, who died 17 years to the day prior to Momma's death on New Year's Eve. Julie, Scott's wife, the Mormon stiff, reiterates at least three times that guitar accompaniment is verboten in LDS services, and a funeral is most assuredly an LDS church service. Such accompaniment is specifically forbidden in the General Manual of Instruction which indicates that funerals and all other meetings should include instruction in LDS doctrine. We choose the Mayfield Church mostly because of its small size, its proximity to Grandpa Yardley's farm to the west and the mountains to the east, and the fact that our cousin, once removed, is the LDS bishop and will let us do what we want. Our apologies to Cousin Russell, the bishop.

We finish planning the funeral, and, three nights later, we are in that Mayfield LDS Ward Church. In the end, we are here because of Momma's strong sense of place. My Grandpa Yardley's house and farm, some 3 miles west of the church, has been the geographic center of the universe for Momma's entire life and for all of my growing up years. Sanpete County has been her home, the nearby mountains a central feature in her life and the life of her family, the surrounding land where her father and brothers farm. This land, at the base of the foothills of the Wasatch Plateau, is arable, but never lush. The beauty is stark. Twice in my lifetime Momma tries to leave Sanpete County. The first time moving north to Brigham City for a better job, more anonymity, closer to her lover. She lasts from March to August and then moves back to Sanpete County. The second time, a new marriage takes her, takes us, to southern New Mexico. Multiple factors—lack of employment for her, two unhappy children, and her own homesickness—influence her decision. We only stay in New Mexico from September to February and then it is back to the pink house in Gunnison.

We move into the pink house at the end of my kindergarten year. I remember Momma working on the clean-up prior to our moving in. She is hugely pregnant with my younger brother, Nick, her last child, who is born at the end of May. The house exterior is cheap pink gypsum siding—the kind that can be easily broken with an errant baseball. The overall design is 1950s bungalow with an over-sized galley kitchen and a bump out for the laundry/mud room on the east. The remaining first floor is comprised of the living room, a bathroom, and a bedroom at the northwest corner, and another bedroom in the northeast corner, all connected by a central hallway with a linen closet on one side and a coat closet opposite. Originally, the living room is a deep coral—back in the day, I am present when one of Mom's dates looks around and says, "Gee, LaRue, for a nickel more you could have had red." When Momma and Daddy Arlo update the exterior, the gypsum siding is replaced with pink slump block, making the house eternally pink. In her last years, Momma makes us promise at least three times that we will bury her in Sanpete County, next to my father, her second husband, in the same county with the pink house and near Grandpa Yardley's farm.

Cousin Russell presides as the bishop, or local parish leader, of the Mayfield LDS Ward Meetinghouse, completed in the late 1930s, at the end of the Great Depression. LDS policy requires that local members fund a percentage of the construction costs. Because of the depression, local members cannot pay off their portion of the Mayfield Church until 1942 when the building was finally dedicated to the Lord and approved as an official LDS meetinghouse. The fact that the building is used for nearly ten years and not dedicated because of the unpaid debt remains a secret source of shame for the members in Mayfield. The building is small by LDS standards, the chapel proper holds a mere 200 souls. The sturdy little church is exactly the color brick-red, the heavy wooden double doors, as well as eaves and window casings, are covered with decades of white paint. In a typical floor plan for the time, the church has a split entry with a half flight of stairs down to the basement level classrooms and offices and a half flight of stairs up to the chapel and the cultural hall.

Note bene: Cultural Hall—a half-size basketball court with a highly-varnished hardwood floor often with a stage and a kitchen attached, used for everything from basketball games to Christmas programs to wedding receptions. I never could figure out how to make an elegant reception spot out of a basketball gymnasium, so I find locations other than the local church for such celebrations for me and for my own children—a sign of a slight rebellious streak in me. The faithful are thrilled to have their wedding reception in the cultural hall basketball court.

We have Momma's viewing in the cultural hall the evening prior to the funeral. When all is said and done, we spend a whopping $13,000 for the whole shebang. Four grand just for the obituaries, which must be run in four different newspapers—at John's insistence—with all six of her last names in the heading, at our insistence. John tells us that several of his family think the obituary Deb and I wrote is morbid. Oh, well. Momma has a $10,000 funeral policy, and John has plenty of money, so we have no qualms about him paying for everything. Momma has a beautiful metal coffin with brushed orchid finish, another favorite color for her. We have plenty of flowers. Mostly we want to make sure she has a nice party.

Following the funeral, I talk with Kent, one of my former colleagues at Gunnison High School, where I started my career as an educator, teaching four preps over a seven-period day that first year. Kent says he is sorry for missing the viewing, "I heard it was fun," he tells me. It was fun. We all see many of our old high school friends, each of us as happy to see the friend of a sibling as we are to see a friend of our own. Some of that fun also comes in seeing many of the older people, those who have known us since we were children: Marian, our neighbor of fifty years who lived just down the street, mother of Tim, my best friend from junior high school; Doris, our next-door neighbor, who we, in our youth, thought was a terrible gossip. When we grow older, we learn of her generosity toward so many of the people whose business she minds. When asked about taking care of Mom and John, Debra tells people at the funeral, "At first we thought we did it for them. Then we realized that we did it for us."

This little LDS church, the only denomination represented in a physical structure in the little town of Mayfield, is the cultural center of the community, population 496, that nestles at the foothills of the mountains at the north end of the Manti-LaSal National Forest. The heart of the Rockies. During our growing up years, and the growing up years of Momma and her brothers and sisters, these foothills and the surrounding mountains are a central part of life. Momma goes on many late-spring and early-fall cattle drives, moving the red Herefords up these mountains to summer forage and back down for marketing at the cattle auction. Heading east from Mayfield, a 40-minute drive up a gravel road will get you to Twelve-Mile Flats, an open meadow in the shadow of Mt. Baldy—named for the lack of vegetation demarcating the elevation at which the forest of Engelman spruce and alpine fir and accompanying underbrush cannot survive. On the way to the Flats, we pass The Forks, forested with gambrel oak and cedar, tick laden, good only for a brief supper cooked over an open fire. More than a few hours spent at this lower elevation will cost you a thorough search of your naked body to rid yourself of the little critters. If the tick head is buried in flesh, a hot match will be required. I have several ticks so removed during my life. Shudder.

Above The Forks, the aspens begin to flourish, Coffee Camp appears as a widened spot along the road, ideal for the traditional morning break for the Yardley family after a pre-dawn start of driving the cattle from the farm up the mountain for summer grazing. I never went on any of the drives; my brothers went on a few. Beyond Coffee Camp, the quakies give way to the spruce and fir forest surrounding the open meadow of The Flats, the location of The Russell and Ethel Yardley family reunions, a three-day camping affair initiated by Momma a quarter-century prior.

Though the true definition of canyon is a deep narrow gorge, usually made by a river, as in the Grand Canyon, we always called these mountains, the Forks, The Six Mile Ponds, and the Twelve Mile Flats, "the canyon." As in "Let's go up the canyon." And we do. During our growing years, we often spend a week camping with at least one family of cousins in old canvas tents with heavy wooden supports at the Six Mile Ponds, built as a WPA project during the Great Depression. Not that we are highly supervised down in the valley; in the mountains we kids enjoy even more freedom. We walk the edges of the ponds, exploring the forests. We squish our toes in the cool mud. We balance on the logs gnawed down by the local beaver population. In the safety of these forests, we know that the most dangerous critter out there is our fellow man, evidenced when one of the boy cousins get a fishhook in his toe. With morbid curiosity, we watch Uncle Miles push the fishhook out through the opposite side of the toe, clip off the barb with his always ready side-cuts, and then pull the hook back through the original pathway. For the rest of that summer, we have to wear shoes.

Food is especially delicious in the cool mountain air. Many meals are cooked or heated over the open fire, but the buttermilk or sour dough pancake breakfasts are always cooked by Uncle Miles on his new Coleman stove. Evenings we spend around the campfire listening to stories of our parents growing up. Even in the light of the campfire, the stars in the dark mountains are a never-ending fascination. We all rest better sleeping in the high elevation, a welcome respite from the summer heat in the valleys below. The Six Mile Ponds, our most frequent destination for our week of summer camping, are restored to their "natural" state in the early 1970s—that is, the dam destroyed and the depressions for the shallow ponds filled—a naturalization process initiated by the United States Forest Service that also includes the removal of a truly beautiful white clapboard mission-style USFS Ranger station located at the low end of Cabbage Flats, a broad expanse of wet meadow filled with skunk cabbage that emerges in early spring. The smell lingers year-round. By mid-summer the meadow fills with an abundance of Western cone flower, also known as black-eyed Susans, with a protruding dark center that provides ample ammo for warring, rowdy, boy cousins. Susan's black eyes are not characteristic of domestic violence. They are an ethnic characteristic—beautiful and exotic.

These canyons, mostly Willow Creek to the south of the Flats, are the location for the annual Yardley family deer hunt. Momma, much to her brother's chagrin, goes on her first deer hunt when she is 15. My brothers and my cousins report that they are between 14 and 16 when they go on their first deer hunt. By the time I was their age, I was more interested in washing my hair. But for most of the Yardleys, the late October deer hunt is the highlight of the year, a chance to relax after a year of planting, irrigating, and harvesting—not to mention branding, de-horning, and twice-daily milking. And, of course, the cattle-drives up the mountain and back down. My brother, Big Dave, even at age 70, says rapturously, "the deer hunt was unbelievable—the highlight of my youth." The Yardley's have more dedication to the enterprise than many other local families. Early on, Grandpa Yardley is always there with his three older sons: Tom, Howard, and Birdell. Momma and her younger sister, Beth, eagerly join the hunt as soon as they are old enough. Momma's younger siblings seem less enthusiastic.

The Brown boys, cousins from Salt Lake City, are welcome at the campsite. The California cousins less so—my Cousin Mary Ann reports seeing Grandpa Yardley, who never does anything mean, stir ashes into their pot of stew warming on the campfire, but perhaps that is meant to be a dash of camp seasoning. The tents used by the Yardley campers are Army surplus, white or khaki canvas, some large enough to sleep a dozen people on cots, supported by heavy wooden poles, heavily staked around the outside. They often have a cooking stove inside the tent. One year, the road to Willow Creek is so rutted and washed out, Grandpa Yardley uses a tractor to pull the wagon loaded with camping gear to their usual camp site. As Momma's siblings grow and marry, the number of tents grow. Uncle Tom brings his oldest son, Gene, and eventually his daughter Mary Ann and her husband Doug. Uncle Howard brings his boys, Mel and Michael. Uncle Birdell comes with his four sons: Rod, Gary, Clyde, and LeOr. Momma, a single woman, camps with Beth and her husband Miles, and their son Lee. My brother David, best friend of Lee, is always there with Momma. Around the camp perimeter, poles are suspended between trees, to hold the hanging carcasses that soon appear. In those days anything smaller than a four-point buck is not to be taken. The Yardleys always thoroughly field dress a buck, teaching each successive generation how to do it right. For the new male hunters this learning becomes a kind of initiation, making the young hunter who shoots his first buck crawl right up into the carcass to cut out the stomach and the scent bags. Big Dave says, "It is a bloody mess that includes lots of good-natured ribbing."

Cousin Gene, who is only 15 years younger than Momma, says that Momma was, "a pretty good deer hunter, . . . who did more than her share of cooking in camp. And [she] was also fun to be with." In a message written in honor of her 80th birthday, Gene goes on to tell Mom, "I remember you sitting under a pine tree at Lone Pine Point, and I remember some pretty NICE deer you got." For most of my growing up years, Momma is a single mother who works full-time, but she rarely misses a week of camping with her brothers, uncles, cousins, and their families for the annual fall deer hunt. Momma spends a week baking and preparing for the excursion. She cooks pots of chili or stew or sloppy joes along with sour-cream cookies, made with real sour cream that spoils in our fridge—stinky, but worth it. Also, carrot cookies and dozens of home-made rolls, all packed up in the biggest Tupperware containers she can buy.

Momma is a great camp cook, but she climbs, rides, and hunts with the best of them. She gets her buck nearly every year. For a few years, she saves up her hide credits to procure a fringed buckskin jacket with a zipper front that she wears for more than a decade. After she marries my stepdad, Arlo, Momma bags the biggest buck of the season, which she describes as "a pretty big buck, and it had 14 points and a 30" spread between points." Another deer hunter further up the ridge comes by and offers her $100 for the rack. She tells him, "No. No, thank you. I want to keep them." The deer head with the large rack is mounted and stands guard over our family carport for more than thirty years until we move Momma to assisted living. Momma tells her own story about shooting a buck.

"One [deer] we shot was the same place on the hill where I shot the big one. We were up there, and Beth said she'd be the dog, and she went down and

went through the bushes, and she drove out this last
buck, and I shot it. And then we said to each other,
'What in the world are we going to do with it now
that we've shot it?' 'Cause you like to clean them out
as soon as you shoot them, and none of the menfolk
were around at all. It was just Beth and me together
there. We finally dressed it out ourselves. Beth knew
a little more about it than I did. She'd watched her
husband, Miles, clean them out quite a few times.
We finally got it done and then it was so heavy that
we couldn't lift it up in the tree. We couldn't get it
clear off the ground. We were huffing and puffing
and trying so hard to lift this deer up. My cousin's
son, Keith Brown, came and helped us lift it up in
the tree to keep it off the ground to keep the meat
good and let it drain out and air out."

Momma and her brothers all hunt to add to their family
food resources. At least one year, my uncle Howard bags
his deer so he can make mincemeat in the bathtub of his
extra bathroom. I suppose you can get a bathtub as clean as
you can get a cooking pot; however, this seems sketchy. The
mincemeat, though, is actually good. He gifts each family
with a quart or two for Christmas. I honor the work that
goes into the preparation.

I am in junior high before I ask Momma why some
roast meat tastes different than other roast meat, failing
to consider that some was beef and some was venison.
Once, after the hunt, Momma cooks a stuffed venison
heart—delicious. Another year Momma and Daddy Arlo
decide to do the butchering themselves so they can save
the price of processing the meat. I am used to having a deer

carcass hang in the tree out back for a day or two, but it is something else to see that carcass laid out on the Formica kitchen table. I always thought a deer was a small animal, compared to a cow, but lying out on the Formica table it looks huge. Daddy, well-muscled from long years of physical labor, really struggles to make those first big cuts, separating the legs from the body, struggling in turning over the carcass to access those big cuts on the stomach and the back. The grizzly sound of the saw, rasping away on the bones, drives me out of the room. I am surprised that they do not press us older kids into service during what turns out to be a night-long ordeal that they only attempt once.

For six years or so during my thirties, I leave my younger children at home so I can shepherd adolescent females the ages of my older daughters through an annual week-long girl's camp at The Flats for our church ward, a unit similar to a parish. I am not an avid outdoors woman, but I know how to choose a tent site, how to put up and stake a spring bar tent, and why there should be a little trench and a bank of dirt around the tent on the three uphill sides. I can cook several meals over an open fire. As the leader of the 12- and 13-year-old girls, I become an expert at digging out and setting up a nice clean latrine with a log seat and a lovely enclosure made of old bed sheets. That latrine assignment only lasts four years until the USFS requires the use of portable outhouses—much less enjoyable than my open-air latrine. But you know the drill: carry it in and carry it out. Better for the land.

As a leader, I go on the overnight hike with the older girls, twice, backpacking three miles, cooking two meals over an open fire, and sleeping under the stars. At 10,000 feet on top of a mountain, I can almost touch the Milky Way. Sleeping here is a natural progression from sleeping out in Momma's back yard. Momma and Grandpa Yardley don't get around to planting grass at the pink house until the summer after fourth grade. By the next summer I am old enough and the lawn is thick enough we can sleep out at night, escaping the house with no AC. Often our daytime pals sleep out with us. Our relationships seem different talking in the dark before we drift off. Sleeping under the stars and under the trees with the mountain outlines in the distance feels bigger than I. At the same time, lying eye-level with the grass, held by the earth, feels very connected. I do admit that my fear of the multitudinous earwigs in Aunt Beth's backyard requires a modified sleeping posture: one ear pressed firmly into my pillow and the other ear covered by my hand.

Nearly as disturbing as the thought of an earwig, is the fact of waking up on the mountaintop to the sound of a foraging cow munching grass within 10 feet of my head. I wonder if the threat is proportional to the size. Cows are kept out of the camp sites at The Flats by the full-log, zig-zag fences, similar in pattern to split rail, surrounding the actual campground, which is located on the hill above the meadow. It is along those full-log fences that my mother and her cousins, my cousins and I, and my children and their cousins master the balance walk atop the fence— brothers, sisters, cousins, friends—all competing for the longest run of zigs and zags. No doubt, some child some-where has fallen off and broken something. We get bumps, but never breaks.

The power of a thunderstorm becomes magical while sheltered in a tent at this 10,000-foot elevation, truly in the clouds, counting on the trees being ever so much taller than the tent to attract the lightning, the bolts startlingly close, and the noise reverberating through my body more

than any rock concert. I have seen a snowstorm with the
intensity experienced in a tent. My last year of camping at
The Flats was a mid-June Girl's Camp, early in the season to
be on the mountain. Unfortunately, our first night, we have
a late spring snow that hits the mountain as darkness falls.
Just as we are settling girls and leaders into their tents, we
discover that one 14-year-old is missing. A half-dozen of us
leaders pair up for a search, clad in summer camping gear,
the lucky ones with rain ponchos. A dark forest can be an
awesome and a fearsome thing, especially in a world where
children are abducted. After 90 minutes of looking and calling through the dark, we use the satellite radio to call the
sheriff's department. Within the hour, we have another ten
bodies, and after another two hours, we find our runaway,
sound asleep, safely tucked into a stranger's camp trailer
parked for the summer about a half-mile outside the campground. We learn later that she threatens to run during
dinner. This is my first experience with a drama queen. It is
also the coldest I have ever been. We settle into our tents
near midnight, snow falling in flurries. I have a mummy bag
lined with a blanket, but the air moves insistently through
the tent and through my sleeping bag, my feet and legs feel
frozen. In desperation I crawl out of my cold sleeping bag,
searching in the dark for my rubberized poncho which I
wrap securely around the sleeping bag. The wind no longer
blowing directly on me, I pull the mummy bag up to my
eyes, tucking my nose and mouth into my sleeping space
and, with the promise of warmth, I finally drift off to sleep.
After a mere five hours of sleep, we arise in the morning to
several inches of snow on the ground. Most of our campers already have one soaked pair of shoes. Many have wet
bedding. We leaders huddle for a brief conversation and

announce to the disappointed girls that we are cancelling the rest of the week of Girls' Camp. We call the valley for our rides home, gather personal belongings, and leave the camp intact for dismantling on a drier day.

As my own children grow, we go several times each summer to The Flats to cook dinner over an open fire in a cast iron Dutch oven and large cast iron frying pan. Usually, it is breakfast for dinner. There are few things that smell as good as bacon with onions and potatoes mixed with the scent of fresh pine and wood smoke. Otherwise, my kid's father and I are not big campers. Our children often stay overnight in the trailer with Momma and Grandpa Arlo for the Yardley reunion at The Flats. Momma and Daddy also make sure that each set of grandkids goes on at least one fishing trip each summer, usually to a reservoir on the east side on the mountain, over the ridge from the Flats. Their favorite fishing spot, Wrigley's Reservoir, appears to hang off the side of the east-facing mountain, surrounded by aspens and greenery, a stark contrast to the ashen valley below, the beginnings of the San Raphael swell, dry and grey, but laden with natural geological beauty and archaeological treasures. These are Our Mountains. I always rather resent it when city people come down to use Our Mountains, especially when they bring four-wheelers and dirt bikes. And then after a while, my cousins and their children bring four-wheelers and dirt bikes to the Yardley Reunion.

Sitting in the shadow of our mountains, Mayfield itself is a sweet little village, filled with memories for me, more so for those who live there. Because of a shrinking population, the town's elementary school closes in 1952 and is converted to a "rest home." My former father-in-law notes that his spinster sister, Aunt Va, and her friend wander the halls of the Mayfield Manor Rest Home like a couple of lonely old heifers. Mayfield's main street echoes the zig-zag course of the log fences in the mountains above. Coming from the west, on the two-lane highway from Gunnison, the first fork veers right, away from the road north to Manti, the next left turn passes the house of my cousin Mary Anne and her husband Doug, then passes the house of my brother Dave and his wife, Sharon, before another right turn, the Mayfield LDS Ward Church on the outside corner, one more left-hand turn and the road heads east into the mountains. There is a small store, with a hot-food counter, between Dave's house and the church. A gravel road between the store and the church descends to the old riverbed and the city park with two pavilions built by members of the Lion's Club where we now have the annual lunch that is the remnant of the Russell and Ethel Yardley Family Reunion, a bit degraded from the original three-day camping trip.

West of Mayfield is Christianburg, an unincorporated collection of a dozen or so houses and farms. Along the north fork of the two gravel roads that snake through the Burg, is the home of Grandpa and Grandma Yardley. Set back from the road about 100 feet, the little white farmhouse is surrounded by a U-shaped driveway, a small pasture at the north between the house and the road, often filled with lambs, an old-fashioned, wild, yellow rose bush at the northeast corner. The U-shaped driveway separates the house from the farm outbuildings. In September 1906, Grandpa and Grandma Yardley, along with his father, Thomas Russell Yardley, trade their failing peach orchard in Utah county for 35 acres and $3,000 dollars of debt, building the original house, which still stands, of adobe brick.

Wood siding is eventually added, the white paint applied many years later. South of the house are livestock sheds open to the south fields. There is a granary at the southeast corner of the surrounding driveway, chicken coops to the right of the granary and a horse corral between the granary and the pens for the Holsteins connected to the dairy barn at the east of the house. Further east of the dairy barn lies the deep irrigation pond where we ice skate in the winter directly under the base of the canal hill.

Grass surrounds the house on the south, east, and north sides, Grandma's lilacs line the north side of the flagstone walk that connects the dairy barn to the house. The huge old cottonwood trees at the southwest and southeast corners of the lawn, plus others at the south and east, started as fence posts. Grandpa cuts the post-size saplings growing around the irrigation pond, sticks them in the ground to support the field fencing around the lawn, and the posts begin to grow, four or five of them surviving as adult trees—the field fencing still wrapped on the side of the trees that face the surrounding driveway. To the west is Grandpa's garage with tall poplars on the north side. Further west of the garage is the abandoned brick honey house, one of Grandpa's cash crops. Further west still are the canal and the road across the bridge to the south fields.

Christianburg, The Burg, nestles among the dry shale foothills. Farming here is arduous and accomplished only with irrigation. Nevertheless, it is a picturesque setting: gray, coral, and purple foothills at the north, east, and south, yellow cliffs that rise to a bluff at the west. On the cliff north of Highway 89, Don Louis—we say all say it with a country pronunciation, "Don Lu-ee" rather than the sophisticated "Don Lu-ees" that is his given name—hangs off the face of

the yellow cliff to paint a large black Thunderbird sometime in the 70s. He must have been in his late fifties at the
time. Don Louis, slightly taller than average with a muscular build, is a remarkable character who survives falling
through the ice on a pond one winter when he is skating
with his young children. He beats his way back through the
ice with his fists. He forms up and casts his own rock and
concrete fence posts. He starts raising Appaloosas in the
60s. When I am 14, I get my first job, recommended by my
cousin Phyllis, working for Don Louis's exotic Spanish wife,
Emogene. I do ironing and light housework, interesting
because they have a daughter just a year older than I. Their
son, the same age as Deb, and his younger sister remain
Deb's life-long friends.

Travelling east along Highway 89 from the house of
Don Louis Larson, son of Judge Larson, the Voorhees
house nestles beside a coral and yellow bluff. Mr. Voorhees
is one of the few neighbors with whom Grandpa has an
occasional disagreement, usually centered on Grandpa's
German shepherd, Pal. Momma gives Pal to Grandpa Yardley because her third husband, Gene, makes an unbearable
fuss about her spending so much money on a pedigreed
German shepherd. So, Pal spends some early weeks of his
life in our house then he moves on to Grandpa's. When
Pal reaches adult size, he develops a habit of climbing up
onto the bluff east above the Voorhees house that overlooks the right-hand turn onto the gravel road towards
Grandpa's. More often than not, Pal is on the bluff searching for us as we come up the highway. We figure he knows
we are coming through some kind of dog radar—channel-
ing Rin-Tin-Tin or Lassie: Timmie's in the well. Pal invariably scrambles down the bluff, crosses the highway, and

then races through the fields, jumping livestock fences, and crossing the railroad track, making it back to Grandpa's house so that he is waiting in the driveway when we pull in. We love Pal, and he loves us. One day, Mr. Voorhees shoots Pal three times with his rifle, as the dog stands on that bluff, claiming that Pal has been in his sheep. Pal never bothers Grandpa's sheep; it is unlikely he bothers Mr. Voorhees' sheep. The beautiful dog makes it back to Grandpa's, clinging to life for three painful days before he finally dies. I always hate Mr. Voorhees. I don't think Grandpa does.

Grandpa's house is along the east fork of the of the gravel roads through the Burg. Uncle Howard's house, similar to Momma's pink house but white and more plain, sits across the road; Uncle Tom's slightly larger red brick house, typical of a prosperous farmer, is a mile or so up the canal hill; Cousin Gene's larger, more modern, and champagne colored brick home sits just below and across the street from his father, Tom. Back toward the west is the abandoned Jensen house at the corner near the south fork that heads to the Mayfield highway with the Nielsen's, Madsen's, Christensen's, and then the Gregerson's homes along the paved road to Mayfield. I may have missed a few, even though all these houses are standing and occupied in my memory.

Grandpa and Grandma Yardley, along with his father Thomas Russell Yardley, make the adobe bricks for the house with 18" walls, keeping it cool in the summer and warm in the winter. My Aunt Althea, Mom's younger sister, says, "We were about half-grown, I think, when Dad "raised the roof." He removed part of the roof and built three upstairs bedrooms onto what had been our one-story house. Then he dug a basement under the house." Althea continues, "while Dad was building the basement, Mother put all the food she was canning in an upstairs bedroom. I don't know how much food (fruit, vegetables, meat) she canned that year, but we counted it one year—900 quarts, enough to last our family of nine all winter." Althea continues her story:

> The basement Dad built contained a furnace room wherein he installed our brand-new coal-burning furnace. Hooray, now we could have heat throughout the house, even in our bedrooms. The basement also contained a "fruit room" where Mother could store all those hundreds of jars of canned food.
>
> So, guess what? When Dad finished that basement, Mother told LaRue and me to go upstairs and carry all the canned goods down to the basement and store it away. "Groannn!" We didn't relish the idea. We were not the least bit enthused: hundreds and hundreds of jars of fruit and food down two flights of stairs. Ugh!
>
> However, LaRue, bless her heart, came up with a perfectly wonderful idea. I stood at the top of those bedroom stairs and she stood at the bottom. One by one, I tossed each of those glass jars down to her. And one by one she caught them. All except one, that is. It hit the floor by her feet. Fortunately, it didn't break. But LaRue did take the time out to go into a downstairs bedroom and get several pillows. She placed them on the floor at her feet. Then our game of toss and catch continued. Hey! That job turned out to be fun after all. And we got all the fruit down into the basement without breaking anything!

I don't know if Mother ever found out how we got that fruit down there or not."

Momma loves growing up on the farm. Most of all she loves being outside working alongside her dad and her three older brothers. Momma says, "I was a tomboy. I wanted to be outside. I'd go out when my dad was harnessing the horses and help him. Then, before we could get away to go out into the field, [my] Mom would come out on the porch and call [me]. I wouldn't answer. Finally, Dad would say, "LaRue, isn't your mother calling you?" Mom said Grandpa Yardley reminded her every day to go into the house and help her mother with her two younger sisters and baby brother. Even before she was old enough to be a help, Momma preferred to be outside. Mom tells us how she loves horses. According to her, "My first memory of [loving horses] was my being 3 or 4, maybe older. I had one of the work horses out in the yard. I was on [the horse] and I put my [bare feet] on each side of its backbone and stood up and was waving at the neighbor. The neighbor about had a fit; she thought I was going to get hurt. And this other time with this horse—he was the best work horse we had— there was a stream of water that went down through the yard. This was after they had been working, and they had unharnessed the horses, and [the horse] was over there drinking out of the stream. I was right by his front legs petting its legs and a dog started chasing a cat, and the cat ran right across the horse's back heels. My Mother thought sure the horse was going to go forward and step on me. But that horse didn't move a muscle; otherwise, he may have jumped. He was a smart horse. They could take this horse and hook him to the [plow] that made furrows down the beet rows—this was a one-horse outfit—and they would hook him on there and get him started, and he would walk putting one foot ahead of the other right down the water row so he wouldn't mess up the fields or the beets."

Aunt Beth tells the second most-famous of the LaRue Horse Stories. "LaRue always loved to be out of doors . . . with Dad. One day, she got old Kit and started down the road to meet her dad. [Mom tells me she is standing barefoot on the horse, as usual.] Dad was driving the team up from the field down by the railroad tracks and when LaRue was about half there, Dad yelled, 'LaRue, get off that horse.' Well, she didn't see why she should get off . . . she had ridden down to meet him other times. He yelled again, 'LaRue, get off that horse!' But when her father stopped his horses, jumped down off the rig and started running toward her, she decided she had better mind him. The instant she slid off; the poor old sick mare collapsed." Momma said the horse went down near the honey house. The sick horse lay in the middle of the road for several days while Grandpa nurses her back to health. Aunt Beth was likely only a toddler when this happens, but she has learned the story from family oral tradition.

Momma tells her version of the most famous of the LaRue Horse Stories. "We had this one particular horse [Prince] that was very spry that liked to run and liked to go. One day I was with a whole bunch of my friends, and they dared me to ride that horse, and I said, "Well, I'll ride him." And, of course, I rode him bareback. I rode him up to the top of the canal hill, and then headed back down the hill toward the house and Prince was running pretty hard, and I got to the driveway to the house, and I knew I couldn't make the turn with him, that it would throw me. So, I held him on the road till I thought we were plenty far past the turn, but when I relaxed the reins, he spun around and stopped dead still at the fence. I went over his head and came right down into a rosebush. I had stickers all over me. It took a couple of hours to pull them all out, and I was scratched. It was my Junior Prom that night and I wanted to go. I was upset because I didn't want to go the way I was, and I had nobody to go with. My cousin Bob Brown, who would come down every summer to visit us, was there. And he said, "I'll take you to the dance." I had a black jacket, and I put this black jacket on over my prom dress and about roasted to death, but at least my scratches didn't show up." Momma tells this story many times as we grow up and when we are grown. She always thinks it is sure proof that she is a dumb little country girl. After the funeral, when I tell my kids Mom's conclusion, they say, "Oh no, this is sure proof of how cool Grammie is or was."

✐

On January 4, 2011, our cousin Russell, the Latter-day Saint (LDS, Mormon) bishop, conducts Momma's funeral. His wife, Cindy, plays the organ. My nephew, Lee, offers the opening prayer. We sing a hymn, "Because I Have Been Given Much." My brother Rick reads the obituary. He omits the phrase "appropriate—hey?" that follows the line "Momma became active in The Church of Jesus Christ of Latter-day Saints later in life—. "I wonder if he skips the phrase "appropriate—hey?" because of his conversion to Catholicism. I never do ask him.

After Rick, I deliver my tribute to Mom, a eulogy of sorts, but Mormons do not eulogize. I want to talk at her funeral, but I know the only way I will get through it is to write out every word. I do. My talk begins:

The Timpanogos Storytelling Festival often features Donald Davis, a former minister and a gifted storyteller. Donald Davis was presenting a workshop on family stories when a woman asks him what to do with another family member who "didn't tell the truth" or who "didn't get it right." Davis replies that family stories are not photographs that are either focused or blurry, but are rather more like portraits, very much influenced by the artist. So, with that disclaimer, I present to you some of my perspectives of Ethel LaRue Yardley Powers Stevenson Anderson Kump Hone.

I base most of my talk on a journal entry dated April 2, 2008, and titled "What I want to Say at Mom's funeral." It begins:

My Mother taught me four things. And like all good teachers she taught me by example.

- Stick by your children

- Be faithful to your spouse

- Go to church if you can

- Believe in true love

And then in my journal I go on for about 6 more pages with my pithy examples that in retrospect seem didactic and preachy. As my talk continues, I make another disclaimer: before I share my stories, I acknowledge that we, Momma's children, keep a few stories to ourselves. I do not mention her lover of five years, nor the many "boyfriends." Nothing about the miracle ring on her hand the night Momma dies. I learned this lesson on the Navajo Reservation from my friend, Frances. I do mention the influence Frances had on my life and on my relationship with Momma.

One of the joys of my life has been working with Navajo people and educators trying to improve outcomes for our Native students. The first year I start this work I stay for several days in the home of Frances and Stanley Holiday in Monument Valley, Utah. Frances and I form a great bond, in part because we both lost our fathers when we were 3 years old. Frances is a remarkable Navajo woman, especially for her generation. She completes high school through her junior year and then drops out when her sister dies unexpectedly, leaving behind 3 children. Frances raises those 3 children and has 5 more natural children. Frances says that her mother did not teach her much of the traditional Native ways and not any of the stories, so when she is older, she learns some of the traditions and stories on her own from reading. Other stories and traditions she learns from her husband Stanley as he trains to be a medicine man, or traditional healer. My last morning staying with Frances, she and I are up before 6:00 a.m. feeding and watering the animals, throwing two bales of hay in her small pickup, and driving the mile or so out to a little box canyon where she and Stanley run 13 head of horses. We feed the horses and then sit on the tailgate and talk for more than an hour. She tells me of how she works to encourage her children to do well in school and also to learn the traditional ways. She says to me "I taught them the stories." And then she pauses and says, "But some of the stories I have kept for myself."

As my talk continues, I acknowledge that Momma's many last names give evidence that she had lived many lives; she lived many stories. Momma learned through a long life of living and learning how to pick herself up and go on despite what came her way. When Momma married Arlo Z. Kump she was determined to build a stable life for herself and her children. Momma had only known Daddy for a week when they went to Elko to be married by Daddy's brother Jay, the bishop. Such a hasty courtship could have been a disaster, but their 29 years of marriage and the family they created tells me it was a smashing success. Momma and Daddy stuck together through good times and bad, through work and play. In their last years together, they sat by each other's bedside through every hospital stay.

My talk continues: "One of my favorite memories is dinner time and the fun we had there. But more than the good conversations, I remember Momma carefully preparing a plate for any one of us who was off working or participating in some activity. She took food from the first of the meal for every absent child, covered it in foil, and placed the plate in the warm oven. It was waiting for us no matter what time we came home." Sharing food is important to me because it was important to Momma. She told us many times, "We grew up during the Great Depression. We went without many things, but we never went without food," meaning she knew people who did.

Note Bene: I tell everyone for years that I have a very poorly tuned sense of decorum. I will go for a laugh over dignity every time. Even my poorly tuned sense of decorum will not allow me to share the following anecdote at the funeral. Nevertheless, I include it here as an illustration of the kind of fun we have around the kitchen table. This favorite dinner-time story comes out of a usual happening, sharing ordinary and interesting events in our school day. It is the first days of a new school year. Nick has just started junior high school and mentions his PE class. He tells us how goofy he feels in his uniform. Deb, who is now a sophisticated freshman, asks, somewhat brutally, "Oh and did you get a jock-strap?" He ducks his head and makes an embarrassed affirmation. Not quite finished with him, Deb continues, "And what size is it?" Before he can respond, she speculates, "Teeny weeny?" We all laugh uproariously, much to Nick's discomfort. But one of the older brothers comes to his rescue, noting that they all went through the same thing.

I go on to say aloud, "It is interesting to me that in the latter part of her life Momma chooses to go to church." At this point in my life, I am no longer going to church. I will give Momma her Mormon funeral, but I do not want to make this an over-the-top-Mormon event. My Momma was earthy and I loved her earthiness. I make my point, "I think I was 15 when big Dave baptized Mom before going off to Vietnam. For you grandchildren and for our brothers and sisters who became our family as teenagers, I want you to know Momma was a firecracker. She was a pistol. She loved life in spite of its often-apparent harshness. She liked to have fun. I remember sitting in the kitchen when Deb and I were probably 14 and 16 and Momma asks us if we like her. We say, "yes of course." And she says, "No, really, if I weren't your Momma would you like me?" I remember telling her yes, because she was fun, and she liked to laugh, and she loved making us happy. And the point of all this may be that she was a bit more fun before she went to Church."

It is later reported to me that at this point our Cousin Russell's shoulders are shaking in silent laughter. Presenting my last lesson from Momma, I say, "Finally, always believe in true love. Heavens, Momma marries five times—she never gives up on you men, even when she was deserted, and widowed, and widowed, and widowed, and endured long years of ill health. During her years at Apple Tree, Momma and I would walk the halls, and she would tell me her stories. One day she said that she kept marrying because she needed someone to love her. I found that little confession sweet, innocent, and hopeful. Lucky for her she found many men who loved her. Always believe in true love."

I focus my gaze on John as I thank him for the years he spent with Momma. I am only mildly surprised that John is dozing off. Not enough doctrine from me for him.

And then I make my conclusion, "As Momma and I walked the hallways of Apple Tree, she would often stop in her tracks if she had something important to say. She would turn slightly toward me and deliver comments that ranged from hilarious to heart wrenching. A week or two before Thanksgiving, we had one of those hallway moments. Momma stops her somewhat unsteady pace, turns toward me and says, 'I've decided the only thing that really matters is love.' Remember Momma. Remember Grandma. Remember LaRue. Stick by your children. Be faithful to your partner. Go to church if you can. And always, always believe in true love."

The next speaker is my niece, Terilyn, whom I have always called T.L. I love T.L. I always have, but this will be the most Mormon moment of the service. The intention of Deb and me was that T.L. would speak as a representative of all the grandchildren. I am not sure that Russ communicated that to her. She shares a very personal experience. While well-intentioned, it feels off the mark. She first tells of the time her grandma, LaRue, bailed her out on a tax problem with $700. I promise you that every other grand-child in that room could have used a $700 bail out from grandma at one time or another. None of the rest of them get the cash. I am kind of irritated. T.L. also assures the audience that her grandma has a testimony of Jesus Christ. I feel like she is correcting my more casual admonition to "go to church if you can." For T.L.'s assertion that Mom has a strong testimony of Jesus Christ and the Mormon Church, I would play the Judge Judy card and declare, "Hearsay." I think T.L. needs to say these things for herself and for Mom's husband John.

After T.L. we have the guitar song by the former brother-in-law. He makes a few opening remarks about how much it has meant to him to be a part of this family. His foot beats out a heavy rhythm as he sings "Have I told You Lately That I Love You?" All of Mom's kids remember him singing this song at Daddy Arlo's funeral. My sister, Debra, his ex-wife, tells us that the heavy foot rhythm is for managing his emo-tions. The words still ring true.

My cousin, Gene, the father of Cousin Russell and a former LDS bishop in his own right, is the last speaker at this typically Mormon funeral. Gene is a weather-worn dairy farmer, 15 years my senior with the wry Yardley sense of humor—just like Mom. Gene and I have been bantering back and forth since I was a teenager. I finally get the best of him when he appears on the front of Utah Farmer maga-zine, and I can forever call him Cover Girl Yardley. Gene is some nine years into a Parkinson's diagnosis. He says he would never have retired so soon if he had realized how slow the progression would be. Now he suffers noticeably as he describes the story of Momma and Kit, the sick horse, noting how much love and trust she put in the horses on Grandpa's farm. Then he segues to one of his favorite stories about his favorite aunt, his Aunt LaRue, the spry horse, the rose bush, and the Prom. Gene was not yet two at the time, so he has learned this story through family oral tradition. Then Gene tells how he comes to know and trust his Aunt LaRue. "My friend, Kent Mellor, and I rode my bicycle the mile down the canal hill road to Grandpa's house. We were on our way to catch the school bus. We were loaded pretty heavy on one bike. I was pumping, and Kent was sitting on the front handlebar holding all our books. While going down the canal hill, my dog ran in front of us. The front tire went up over his tail and onto his body; we went over him, and fast into the gravel road. We had a lot more gravel in our hands than skin. We had also skinned our faces, arms, and knees. We gathered up our books, but not our composure, and walked down to Grandpa's house. [LaRue] became our nurse. [She] was very good and nice to us. She cleaned the dirt and gravel out of our wounds. Then she sterilized and bandaged us up. Finally, she pampered our feelings and drove us to school. She was so careful, understanding and kind."

Gene finishes with a story of how Momma clenched favorite Aunt status in 1955. Some of his friends talk him into running for high school student body president. Gene reports, "I was a bashful, freckle-faced farm boy running against the school basketball star, who had nearly every girl after him." Gene says he didn't get much encouragement from his own parents who were worried about losing his help on the farm. He says that Mom was the only adult who encouraged him to give it a try. It was Mom saying, "I think you can beat him." Mom also helped him make campaign signs. Gene says, "I don't know if I would have tried it" if it hadn't been for Aunt LaRue. Gene becomes student body president at the high school. He goes on to become student body president at Snow College and was active in student government at Utah State University.

Cousin Russell, as the bishop and the presiding clergyman, has the opportunity to make final remarks. This is his chance to interject doctrine. He comes to the podium, "I think there is nothing more to say than Amen." And he sits down. We begin the process of making our way out of the church, into the procession, and on to the cemetery. Consistent with her desires, Mom will be buried in Manti, next to Don Stevenson, the biological father of Debra and me. When Debra and I are at the motel getting ready for the funeral earlier in the morning, I look out the window and groan at the heavily overcast sky and the solitary snowflake that floats downward. Debra asks, "What?" I reply, "Just the kind of day I hate for burying people."

Yet, by the time we arrive at the cemetery, the sky has cleared and the sun shines strong, even though it is still a very cold twenty-something degrees. Cousin Russell brings us together by noting, "Wow, Aunt LaRue must have some pull. We have not had a beautiful clear day like this in Sanpete County in two weeks." I make a mental note about the possibility of Mom being the Goddess of Weather. Final prayers are said. Goodbyes are made. And most of the mourners return to the Mayfield Ward cultural hall for a lunch prepared by my cousin Arlene and her children as well as Gene and Anita's children. Ham, funeral potatoes— at least four different versions—green salad, several varieties of Jell-O and fruit salads—the one with home canned cherries and real whip cream is our favorite of the day.

Arlene, a long-time elementary school teacher, tells me that after hearing my talk she thinks I need to write a book. "Write anything," she says. I hug her, thank her, and tell her I will think about it.

⚘

We, meaning us kids, but mostly Debra and I, move Momma and John into Apple Tree on Jan. 20th, four years before her death. It's funny how some dates stick in your head. We talk among all of us kids for three years about the possibility of assisted living and with Momma and John for nearly as long. We worry about their health, one or the other of them has been hospitalized two or three times each year for the last few years. We worry about their nutrition. We worry about their medications. The last straw for me comes in the November prior to our moving them into assisted living. I have been on an overnight trip visiting schools in the south-central part of the state. I come back through Gunnison.

I pull up to Momma's pretty pink house. We have a photo of the house from the years when Mom is completely retired and still healthy enough to dote on her gardening. The place looks like Snow White's cottage, flowers every-where, tidy green lawn. All that is missing are the little blue birds. I park in the driveway that Daddy Arlo puts in when he and Mom marry, go to the side door, ring the bell, and enter—the door is rarely locked until bedtime. John is in the living room. We chat for a few minutes as I look over the cultured marble fireplace with the gold-veined smoked mirror tiles above. The definite 70s décor has been the same for more than 40 years. The only change is the walls, now painted off-white with wainscoting and wallpaper. At one point the walls were gilt—paint that contained real gold—honest—$30 per quart even that many years ago. Mom grew up during the Great Depression, and she likes fancy decorating. John tells me that Mom is in bed. She has been sick for several days. I go to the bedroom to see her. She is huddled up in her terrible red plaid, polyester plush robe under a pile of quilts. I stay with her for a quarter of an hour or so. Then I go back to the living room and ask John what I can do to help him. He asks if I could clean the bathroom. I tell him absolutely, no problem.

I check the bathroom to see what is needed. Mom has had diarrhea for three days. There is shit on the toilet, shit on the tub, shit on the sink, shit on the carpet. I go to the local grocery for cleaning supplies and rubber gloves. It takes me about an hour to scrub the 50s blue bathroom fixtures. I do my best on the patterned carpet. Consistent with Mom's fancy decorating, the tile on the walls and the tub surround is patterned. The wallpaper is flocked and patterned. The carpet is patterned. At least all of the patterns are blue. The curtain is a white sheer with blue fringe. This shit-covered bathroom situation is completely beneath my mother's dignity.

After I leave Momma and John's, I drive up the street and around the corner to see Kent, their LDS bishop. I explain the scene I have just left. I talk about our concerns. And I tell him I am going to be a mean daughter and insist that Mom and John move to assisted living. Kent tells me that at church and as neighbors they have the same concerns. One of the local physicians has been going by on Sundays. He also worries about their health, their nutrition, their medications. I call Debra the next morning. We make plans.

Deb and I drive the 130 miles to Gunnison every weekend for the next seven weeks. On one of those weekend visits I tell Momma that I actually am willing to change her diapers, but she has to live close enough for me to be able to do it. Not a big deal. I have five children, and I figure I have changed on the order of thirty-five thousand diapers in my lifetime. Human fecal matter is part of existence. One weekend we take Momma and John to look at four possible assisted living facilities. Momma and John are very resistant. Just after New Year's, I ask Momma what she would do if I told her that we made a deposit on a room at Apple Tree, their favorite of the possibilities. Momma says she guesses they would have to try it, for at least a few months, maybe through winter. Debra and I move fast. We get a truck. We call Kent, who will help us load up their bedroom furniture, their Lazy Boys, and the loveseat.

🍃

Within days Russ, our brother, calls me. "Our Mother has called all of my children to tell them she is going to Kaysville to die."

I giggle.

"It is not funny," he says.

"Oh c'mon, Russ. You know our mother. She is the Queen of Guilt."

"Well, you and Debra have been lying to old people," he parries.

"We have not lied," I defend.

"You two told them you had made a deposit on a room."

I equivocate, "What I said was, 'What would you say if I told you that we had made a deposit on a room?' And then Momma said she thought that they should try it."

"You should have been more cautious. You should have taken more time." He storms and thunders.

"Well, it is damn convenient for you that you were out of town working your truck route for those weeks and weeks when we were trying to be careful and take time," I clash back.

"If our mother wants to die on the top of Mary's Nipple, I will carry her there on my back," he says piously.

"Easy cowboy," I say. "Put down the six guns. This is not a shootout," I continue mockingly.

Note Bene: Mary's Nipple is a peak south of Mount Baldy which we can easily see from Momma's kitchen. It is distant, but visible from the entire valley. Looking quite breast like, it is equally bare of vegetation. "Mary who?" we always wonder.

My mocking triggers further righteous wrath as Russ goes on and on about what he thinks. At the end of my patience, I borrow a line from Rod Steiger and *Crazy in Alabama*. "I do not give a good Goddamn what you think," I tell him. And I hang up. I am still going to Church and Goddamn is not a regular part of my vocabulary.

🪶

On January 20th, Deb is there with the truck. The bishop and the neighbors have Momma and John loaded up by noon. Debra packs their clothes and personal items the day before. I join our brother, Rick, and his son, Chris, at the assisted living center to help them unload. The day we move Momma in, Deb and I meet Harriet, age 92, who moves herself into Apple Tree when she is in her mid-eighties. We tell her Momma is pretty sad. She replies, "Well, you can be about as happy here as you decide to be." I come by on Sunday to eat dinner with them. On my first visits, I think I need to be the entertainment committee. A few months in,

I learn from Pema Chodron that the best I can do for them is just spend time doing what they like to do. You know, parallel play. I eat in the dining room with them several times and realize the food is adequate, but not delicious. At least I get to know their table partners.

Momma cries for weeks. By early March, she and I have started our routine of walking around all three Apple Tree hallways: red apple, yellow apple, and green apple. Each hallway and individual apartment door bear the color-coded apple icon along with the room number, helping the residents find their way home. Red Apple hallway is the nature walk with two "naturalized" Koi ponds with tree-size schefflera, corn plants, and rubber plants. Several bird cages, left behind by departed residents, line the low concrete walls that surround the ponds and the planters. The birds make me melancholy. The ceiling in Red Apple is painted like a pale sky with clouds. Skylights feed sunshine to the plants and the residents. The wing chairs and settees in Red Apple, upholstered in a small-flower tapestry of green and mauve, look like a grandmotherly living room. Green Apple Hallway has Adirondack chairs and settees with cushions of wide green and white stripes, brightened by pillows of polished cotton printed with water-color flowers. Green Apple also has planters and skylights, no fish. Yellow Apple has an Asian Tropical feel, bamboo-look furniture and brown and orange batik cushions. Also, planters, skylights, and no fish. The artwork in each hallway mirrors the decorating motif. As we walk, Momma tearfully tells me how much she misses her house, her view of the mountains in the east, and her friends and neighbors. Spring is coming. She misses her garden. I ask her if we need to take her back home.

"Oh, I can't go back home," she says.

"Why not?" I ask.

"I am losing my mind," she confesses. My own heart breaks a little.

For Momma's birthday in mid-March, Deb and I make plans to meet at a restaurant near my work so we can have lunch together. Deb will pick up Momma and John and drive them to downtown Salt Lake City. After Momma's losing my mind statement, Deb and I began to make plans for cleaning out Momma's house. Debra has owned Momma's house for more than 20 years, having bailed Momma and Daddy Arlo out when they decide, at age 60 something, to mortgage the paid-off house and invest the money in my cousin's dairy, where Momma is keeping the books for the store. Within a year the dairy and the store are bankrupt; apparently my uncle Tom along with the elder brother, Gene, have been bankrolling the operation for this youngest son. Deb pays off the mortgage, puts her only child in an after-school program and goes back to work several years earlier than she planned. When Daddy Arlo dies, Momma wants Debra to agree to split any profits on the house with the rest of her children and stepchildren. Deb refuses. When Momma is planning to marry John, Momma wants Debra to sign an agreement that allows John to stay in the house until he dies—he is six years younger than Momma. Deb agrees. Now Deb is divorced, and she could use the money. The day before Momma's birthday, Deb calls me to say that she can get a dumpster delivered that same day. We plan to talk with Momma about the dumpster when we have lunch on her birthday.

The next day, Momma's birthday, I am in the parking lot heading to my car to drive to the restaurant when Russ calls to give me another piece of his mind. Apparently, his ex-wife, the snoopy old bitch, has been watering Momma's house plants. After she sees the dumpster in the driveway, she calls Momma to wish her a Happy Birthday and to quiz her about the 15-foot dumpster. Russ tells me, "You two are trying to ruin Momma's birthday."

"Russ, Deb and I are the only ones here with Momma to celebrate her birthday. If anyone has tried to ruin her birthday, it is your busybody old wife." When it comes to dishing out guilt, I have learned a few tricks from Momma.

Even though it is a 30-minute drive from Apple Tree to downtown, Momma does not mention the phone call from Connie, Russ's ex, until Deb is exiting the freeway. I meet Momma and John at the curb and walk them into the restaurant while Deb parks her car. My youngest daughter, who also works nearby, joins us for lunch. I rise to greet Deb as she enters, quickly advising her I am aware of the situation. Before we even order drinks, voices at our table become elevated. Great. We are sitting at the very front of the restaurant, near the entrance and in full view of everyone. We are making a scene. Momma accuses,

"You two are trying to ruin my birthday."

"Momma, Deb and I are the ones here with you trying to celebrate your birthday."

I also tell her that I think it was wrong for Russ's ex to say anything to her about the dumpster. Momma worries that we are going to throw out everything. We remind her that for the past two years she has been asking Deb and me to come down and help her clean out her house. We ask her what she wants done first. Eventually we turn it around. Agreeing that we will consult with her before getting rid of anything major. My youngest daughter tells me she is embarrassed to tears at the restaurant. She is twenty-something. I nod my head and tell her I understand.

Deb goes down to Gunnison alone to begin the work of cleaning out Momma's house. I join her on Saturdays. We start on the fruit room—hundreds of jars of home-bottled goods, tomato everything, green beans, peaches. And cans of food. With no small amount of guilt, we dump it all. I am appalled at the number of little knick-knacks that have passed as gifts to Momma over the years. After the knick-knacks, my siblings start giving gift cards. I end up doing the shopping for the gift cards. After two years, I beg my siblings to please just give Momma and John their time. If you want to give aging parents a gift, give them your time. Go for a long visit. Play cards. Take them to dinner. Just do whatever it is they like to do. A gift card is not a gift for people who cannot or do not go shopping.

We find the cache of afghans that Momma has crocheted. She does beautiful work with many complicated patterns. Each of us kids, all of our children, and many of our grandchildren receive a crocheted afghan made specifically for the individual. We sort these that have not been gifted, choosing one for each sibling. When Momma was at her crocheting prime, her late fifties and early sixties, she crocheted seat covers for her 1978 Ford LTD. The car is white with a burgundy vinyl roof. She chooses the Navajo Diamond crochet pattern, using white, black, and burgundy yarns with turquoise accents. She makes covers for the front bucket seats—including both sides of the seatbacks, and for the bench seat and back rest of the back seat as well as covers for the front arm rests. In retrospect, they were a thing of beauty, a homemade masterpiece. At the time, we take them for granted, much like we do Momma. Wish we had a photo. During the years that Momma drives the LTD she also has a car-dog—her Schnauzer, Bo Peep, who goes with her everywhere. Bo Peep waits in the car while Momma gets her hair done on Fridays. She waits while Momma runs into the post-office, the bank, the power company, even the grocery store. In those days, the car was never locked, and the windows were properly ventilated. Momma would never abuse an animal. She is the best dog trainer I know. My Momma may have been an animal whisperer. Did I mention that the photo on the front of the program for her funeral shows her feeding a pet deer she raises for the family? They find the apparently abandoned fawn wandering the foothills and take it home where Momma is the primary caretaker. There is Momma, looking very chic in her fitted 40s suit and heels, with the deer standing on his back legs reaching for the treat in her hand.

Deb and I also begin to sort out housekeeping items for Russ, who is about to embark on a new round of bachelorhood. We sort out years of school photos. We try to identify sources of gifts, hoping to return them to the givers, especially the higher priced items. The house is eventually emptied. Deb comments that it is the first time she appreciates that sentiment often expressed, that "it was only yesterday." By early fall Momma's pink house is sold to a stranger.

*

As we are growing up, we are close to Momma's sisters, Althea and Beth, who are two-and-a-half and six years younger, respectively. Althea, a spinster, is a retired schoolteacher who lives most of her professional life and her retirement in the Phoenix area. When I am in elementary school, I ask my Momma why Aunt Althea never married.

She tells me, "Because Jesus' hair is too long." After I say, "What?" she repeats her reasoning and then explains what she means. It makes sense to me. I remember several young men that Althea brings home to the farm to meet Grandma and Grandpa Yardley. I like them all, particularly the young veterinarian. In our mostly Mormon family, Aunt Al is the odd-Christian-out. She meets most of her beaus through the Church of Christ that she attends nearly 100 miles away from the farm. Some of the men come from connections she made at the Christian College she attends somewhere in the East. Truth be told, Aunt Althea is an independent soul. During World War II she works as a radio repair technician, the only woman on a team of twelve based in New York City. The men live in a dormitory. Al has to find her own housing and her own food—the men also eat at the dormitory. The experience no doubt enables her to attend college on the east coast and travel cross-country in her own car, driving by herself. Perhaps she never meets a man who could support that. Perhaps she wants a woman. Who knows? Nevertheless, Al is a cheery and encouraging aunt, always interested in our activities and our thoughts. For more than a decade, while Momma is still alive, Aunty Al calls each of us Yardley cousins to find out what is happening and what is new. She compiles these details into an annual quiz which she delivers in a folder to each individual cousin, thus keeping us informed and connected to one another.

By the end of her life, I realize that Althea is one of the finest people I know, perhaps the off-spring most like my beloved Grandpa Yardley. After she teaches a few years in a small elementary school in southern Utah, she moves to Chandler, AZ where she establishes herself as an exemplary educator. She wins accolades in her education program and in the district with her master's thesis on teaching reading. When I am in fourth grade, Grandma and Grandpa Yardley begin spending the winter months with her in her little pink house on Dublin Street—the bricks a slightly darker shade than Momma's. Momma generally drives us to the Phoenix area at Thanksgiving and Easter to visit Althea, Grandma, and Grandpa. When we arrive a little after dark on one early spring evening, Al, Grandma, and Grandpa are gathered around her small black and white television, watching a local program about learning to speak Spanish. I learn my first phrase in Spanish that evening: el muchacho wapo, "the handsome man." Aunty Al is learning to speak Spanish so she can better serve the handful of Latinx students she has in those early classrooms. By the time she retires, her classrooms are filled with Latinx children, she knows all of their names, and she knows all of their parents, many of whom are former students themselves.

When Big Dave returns from Vietnam and struggles to find his footing, Al opens her home to him. We do not realize at the time that he likely suffers from PTSD. She encourages him to enroll in community college, and she pays for his tuition. With Al's help and encouragement, he gets a grip on the rest of his life. More than a decade later, when Little Dave also leaves the military, she does the same for him, opening her home, encouraging education, paying for tuition. We never acknowledge aloud that she likely saved the lives of both nephews.

Aunt Beth, hands down my favorite aunt as I am growing up, is married for 20 years or so, divorces, and then remarries some 20 years later for a very short time to a very rich and very mean man. Her second marriage also ends in divorce. During the years following the death of Momma's third husband, Gene—Nick's father—we spent a lot of time with Beth and her family. We camp with them in the summer and drive to Salt Lake for visits at least quarterly, sometimes monthly. My Auntie Beth is pretty, witty, and creative. Aunt Beth makes fabulous Halloween costumes for her daughter, NaDene, who is just a year older than I— Rapunzel with a yellow yarn wig and braids 10 feet long; a Geisha with kimono, obi, and an elaborate black wig. You get the idea. Bethy or Bethus, as we often call her, always tells us jokes—many of them very corny. She hands us a paper with "TERRIFY TISSUE" printed in block letters. She says, "Read this aloud." We do, several times, and when we get a bit of a question in our voices, she replies, "Not at all" and presents her cheek for a kiss. Or there's this one, "Two rabbits are in the garden munching away on Farmer John's vegetables. One little rabbit plucks out a vegetable and declares, "Eeew, this radish tastes pithy. To which the other little rabbit replies, 'Of courth it doth; I just pithed there.'" When we roll our eyes and groan, she inevitably responds, "'Et tu, Brute'?" Then Bethy has to explain Brute' to us, and she does. Thanks to her we know the rudiments of Julius Caesar when we are still in elementary school.

Back at the assisted living center, the weeks and months and years roll by. We have our ups and downs—Momma has her ups and downs. Although Momma is usually even tempered, she is frequently angry with Althea and Beth. Momma is mostly angry because they are always going off to do things together without her. Deb, John, and I all prevail on Momma to use her Christian sensibilities and be forgiving of her sisters. In my mind, Beth and Althea stick together because they are mostly single, and Momma is mostly married. To indicate just how done she is with her sisters, Momma often gestures with her wrists crossed at hip level, making a sweeping gesture that she will eventually use to cut off sex with John. She is very angry when Beth and Althea go off to Washington, D.C. to visit nephew Gene and his wife, Anita, while they are LDS Missionaries in D.C. Realistically, the only way Momma could go with them at that time and keep up would be in a wheelchair. And she would not tolerate that. For a short time, Momma has difficulty walking. She declines enough that she can barely get around the apartment. The not walking starts with a bout of flu during which she is confined to her easy chair or to her bed for several weeks. Nevertheless, through her own grit and determination she regains her ability to walk. Twice daily she goes out into the hallway at the assisted living center, holds onto the rails that run along the walls on each side, and walks as far as she can. When I am there, she leans on me. She builds back up to two 1-mile walks most days. Momma's attitude improves when Beth and Althea invite Momma to visit at Beth's house in Manti during Althea's Christmas and summer visits from Arizona. Either Deb or I drive Momma down to Manti. She stays a couple of nights and the other of us goes down to drive her back. She discovers that after a few days she is ready to be off on her own and back in her own space, anyway.

Deb and I often run out of patience with the demands and the challenges of dealing with aging parents. Debra gets particularly frustrated over Momma's demands and idiosyncrasies. I was mad as hell at Momma from the time I was twenty until I was a little over forty. I was angry for all her mistakes and all the things she didn't do. One day I just decide to get over it. And I start to appreciate her for who she was and the things that she did do. In the years that Debra and I helped care for Momma and John at the assisted living center, whenever Deb is overwrought with something Momma says or does, I offer my best advice, "expect less." I repeat this advice often, and I repeat it to myself. I mean this seriously. A bit of Taoist wisdom. Accept what is and you will be less disappointed. Momma's vision is diminishing, and she cannot read the historical romances that she has loved so well. Momma is bored watching television with John. Deb takes Momma to buy yarn so she can crochet again. She uses a simple stitch, creating variations only in color. She crochets some three dozen afghans during her time at Apple Tree, giving all of them away. None of them are square—I own two of the crooked afghans. The recipients do not seem to mind.

One Sunday evening after a difficult night of failing memories, repeated stories, and cutting toenails, I call Deb and leave this message on her voice mail. "Hi Deb, this is Dawn. I just left Momma and John. Here is the plan. You and I get together. We take hemlock. This will have three distinct advantages. 1) We no longer have to take care of Momma and John. 2) We do not have to go through this ourselves. 3) Our children will not have to go through this with us. Perhaps this message is too dark for a Sunday night. Call me." I think I am so brilliant I write this memory down on a yellow pad during staff meeting the next morning. Some three years later, after Momma's death, our office manager finds my note folded and tucked into the back of a yellow legal pad. We read it and laugh about the challenges and heartaches of aging parents.

For her 89th birthday Momma wants to go to Mayfield, to Big Dave and Sharon's house, for a roast beef dinner, "like we always used to do." Two problems: one, we never all went to Mayfield to David and Sharon's house for roast beef dinner. More likely we all went to Momma's house for roast beef, or corn-crisped chicken, or pork chops. The other problem: none of us who live in Salt Lake are much interested in driving to Mayfield for roast beef dinner. In retrospect, maybe we should have been interested. Deb and I are in the Yellow Apple hallway with Momma, tropical chairs and batik cushions in the background, when Momma once again makes this request, which to us feels like a demand. We have determined that the answer is no. When we tell Momma no, she pitches a fit, clenching her fists and stalking off with her arms stiff at her sides. She looks and sounds like a small child, yelling at us from 15 feet away. We hold steady. We have birthday dinner at Debra's house. Russ is there. So are Big David and Sharon, Rick and Julie, Scott and Julie, Nick and Roylene. I am there with Robert. It is the first time he is meeting my family. I coach him on names on the drive up. We have to help John out of Russ's pickup—It takes four grown men to hoist him out and hoist him back in when the party is over. Before the day ends Momma commits us all, once again, to burying her in Sanpete County, next to my biological father, in the same county as the pink house.

~

In February, before Momma's birthday, we learn that our youngest brother, David, has terminal cancer. There is nothing to be done. A little chemo will slow the progression slightly. He has less than a year. Deb and I make plans to take Mom to Phoenix for a last visit. Little Dave and his wife make plans to move to San Diego—that has been their retirement plan. Dave is taking medical retirement from the VA where he worked for 25 years. They are walking away from the house with an upside-down mortgage.

Little Dave is called Little to differentiate him from Big Dave. When Momma and Daddy Arlo marry, she has an 18-year-old son named David, and he has a 9-year-old son named David. We call them big and little because of their ages. It makes sense until Big Dave grows to 6'2" and Little Dave grows to 6'4". For the most part, it needs explaining only to younger generations inside our family. But I do feel a little like the Bob Newhart Show, "This is my brother Darryl, and this is my other brother, Darryl."

To say that Momma and Little Dave had a troubled relationship is more than an understatement. When Momma and Arlo marry, Momma and I, Debra, and Nick, pack up and move to New Mexico. Big Dave is in his senior year of high school and stays behind, living with Gene and Anita and their family of five children. Russ is leaving for his LDS mission within weeks. The summer just prior to Momma and Daddy Arlo marrying, the summer Little Dave turns nine, his mother kills herself. By late September his father, Arlo, finds and marries Momma. Momma and David's mother, Vee for Vivian, look physically similar, tall and lean, with dark red hair. Little Dave is understandably a needy young boy. He clings a bit too much, is a bit effeminate, and a bit too formal, calling Momma "Mother." All of this sets Momma's teeth on edge.

Momma has almost always been a working mother, but she is not able to find a job as a bookkeeper in our tiny company town or anywhere in the area around Silver City.

We have a family with seven children. Money is a big concern. At Christmas, Momma and Daddy ask Deb, Penny—our stepsister—and I if we will forego Christmas presents, so they can spend more on the young boys. We easily agree.

I love living in New Mexico. I have a new sister who is my age and eases my entry into a new and much larger high school. Also, I am free of my brother, Russ, for the first time in my life. Debra and Nick are much less happy. Debra hates her public junior high school so much that Momma and Dad enroll her in Catholic school even though she has to take Catechism daily. To the end of her days Momma worries that the reason Debra no longer goes to the Mormon church is the result of her time at Catholic School. Nick also does not like school. And he is not so comfortable going from youngest spoiled son to one of four preadolescent boys. By February, Momma decides to go back to Utah. Daddy Arlo and his kids stay in New Mexico for the rest of the school year while he arranges a transfer with United States Smelting and Refining to a Utah facility. Momma and Daddy see each other once a month for the remainder of that school year. One or the other of them makes the 12-hour drive, one-way, over a 4-day extended weekend.

By the beginning of the next school year, we have four of Momma's kids and four of Daddy's kids living in the pink house in Gunnison. Daddy works in the Salt Lake area and drives the two hours home on Wednesday with a return to Salt Lake Thursday morning, repeating the circuit on Friday evening and Monday morning. In Salt Lake Daddy lives with his mom, Grandma Hiatt, in her tiny house. Daddy is good to us stepkids. He lets us take his big ol' Mercury out to drag main or drive to dances. I return the kindness of Penny by integrating her into my large group of high school friends. We have our Junior Prom. Momma has her dress-maker sew custom prom dresses for Penny and me. All is well, but Debra feels left out, not because she has always been included with all my friends, but because Penny always is. Momma is back at work in her bookkeeping job at the car dealer. Dinner and food are more demanding just in sheer numbers, but for me it is very fun—kind of like having a sleepover every night. Penny works as a waitress her last summer in New Mexico. She brings an infusion of new clothes for our wardrobes. I start working at the Gunnison Rexall Drug with the beginning of our junior year, so I provide make-up and nylon stockings for all three of us girls. The year passes quickly. By the end of our junior year, Penny has a serious boyfriend who is a year older.

Mostly we all get along well, at least it seems so to me. At Christmas of our senior year, Momma and Arlo have a great big fight—doors open and doors slam. The fight spills out into the yard. I remember two specific statements: Momma says to whomever is present, "I don't have to have sex if I don't want to have sex," and Penny, running back and forth from her boyfriend's car to the house, declaring, "It is all my fault. It is my fault that my mother is dead." By the end of Christmas break, all seems well again. In January, Penny announces she is pregnant. After many conversations, she decides on a small family wedding in the basement of the church. LDS practice does not allow for weddings in the chapel. I sew a pretty, street length, pale blue brocade dress for her. I know she is disappointed with her wedding. Then she moves in with her husband, Theldon, and his parents.

Things seem even more normal. I go off to college, following my boyfriend, Ernie, to BYU, driving home together on many weekends. In April we are engaged, planning to marry in the summer. Marrying at 18 or 19 is accepted and common social practice for girls in Mormon culture, especially for my generation. After our marriage, Ernie and I move to Los Angeles where he attends UCLA Dental School. The next summer our first child is born, also usual practice among my Utah peers. We go home for three days at Christmas before the baby and return home again the summer and the Christmas after her birth. The following summer we are home for a week. My baby is almost 2 years old. I am visiting with Momma when she tells me, "You have to see what I have done to David." She calls him in from the back yard, has him lift his shirt and shows me David's back. It is covered with black and blue bruises, really covered, not just a bruise here and there. I am aghast. I am nearly speechless. After David leaves, I ask her how this happened? Has it happened before? Apparently, she has been beating him for years, but this is by far the worst episode. I tell her she must stop. I tell her I should report this to the county. I go back to Ernie's parents' house where we are sleeping—they have much more room for us—I tell Ernie that we need to get David out of that house. We talk about taking him back to L.A. with us. Neither of us can conceive how to raise a 13-year-old boy on his own in L.A. I now know that David likely would have been better off with us than leaving him in my mother's home.

David leaves home at age 15, landing first with his oldest brother, Kerry, and his wife, Earlene, who live some 40 miles away. David works at a gas station and convenience store owned by Kerry's father-in-law. Money goes missing at the store. David is accused. He runs away. Daddy Arlo calls Kathy, David's oldest sister, to warn her and her husband, Richard, that David might be heading their way. A day or two later, he does show up at their door in southern New Mexico, having hitchhiked from Central Utah. David begs Kathy to let him live with her. Richard agrees, but Kathy refuses to expose her children to his history of his drug experimentation. Daddy Arlo and Momma drive to New Mexico to pick David up. They have determined that David will live in Northern Utah with Penny and Theldon. David goes to night school, gets a GED, and joins the U.S. Navy at age 17. Daddy Arlo was in the Navy in WW II. David's oldest brother Kerry was in the Navy for eight years. My brother Russ was in the Navy at that time. It seems a reasonable choice. David is stationed in San Diego. In early summer, when David is home from the Navy, he comes by my house to see my newest baby, my fourth. We are sitting on the floor talking after playing with the kids. Penny calls: she is looking for David. She has moved back to Gunnison, so I invite her to come over. The three of us are sitting on the floor when Penny begins to quiz David about his status in the Navy. He admits that he has been discharged. Penny is distraught. She knows before the words are out of his mouth that the dishonorable discharge is for homosexual activity. Penny, who has converted to Evangelical Christianity, continues to agonize. I know nothing about this aspect of his life, but I am neither surprised nor alarmed. If ever a kid needed love, Dave is that kid. David spends several weeks in Gunnison and then, with Momma's help, he makes a plan to go to Arizona to live with Aunt Althea.

Kathy's daughter, Chrissy, has been living with Penny for the summer. Kathy and Richard are trying to keep Chrissy away from her boyfriend, but now her parents are letting her return to New Mexico by way of Aunt Althea's house. David drives his car, with Chrissy as a passenger, back to Chandler to begin his new life. Althea follows them in her car. They stay overnight in Sedona. Al pays for meals and hotels. Chrissy reports that the road trip is one of the highlights of her teenage years. When they get to Chandler, David begs Chrissy to go with him to visit his former lover. He wants an escort because he does not want anything to happen. Chrissy reports that she meets this "crazy, cranked-out hippie" who was much older than David. Dave returns some items to the lover, and they part without emotion. David might see him one more time years later.

David would be an attractive partner for anyone. 6'4" and lean with clear olive skin that is almost always nicely tanned. Full lips with strong teeth, an engaging smile, and, of course, dimples. Great cheekbones. Heavily lashed pale eyes and thick hair. He has never been vain about his good looks, probably was never convinced of his good looks. He keeps that lean frame and those looks to the end of his life, getting ever more handsome as he gains wisdom along with graying hair at the temples.

At community college, as long as David gets good grades, Al pays for tuition and expenses. He does well for a semester or two until a suicide attempt with cut wrists lands him in a psych ward. I think there are several more suicide attempts and several more periods of institutionalization—that is the word we use in the school counselor's office when we cannot say a student is in detention or the psych ward. For a time, David cannot be released without the signature of a parent—maybe because he is still not twenty-one. Some of his treatment includes electroshock therapy. It is about this time David meets Diane, another patient at the institution. They make a pact with each other: they will never again be crazy or attempt suicide; they will earn their release; and they will be together forever. Years later, David, with his great sense of humor, often laughs that he meets his wife in the crazy house.

On April 10, 1978, David and Diane are married in the living room of Arlo and Momma's pink house. I think the entire arrangement is so weird. I want them to have something nicer. I am disturbed that Diane is older than David and that she had two kids, ages 7 and 9. I think Diane is mean. I think David is prettier than she. In spite of all my concerns, the marriage proceeds. They survive and thrive, living in Utah for nearly 10 years. David completes a bachelor's degree and, later, a master's degree in public administration. Diane completes her bachelor's degree. They move back to Arizona. Diane's son, Michael, moves with them. Her daughter, Tammy, is married with a life of her own.

After Arlo dies on New Year's Eve, 17 years to the day before Momma's death, Dave moves back to Arizona. He does not speak to Momma for 10 years. During those years, I meet David for dinner three times when I am in Phoenix for conferences. I tell David that I do not blame him for not speaking to Momma. I tell him how terribly sorry I am for not rescuing him from his abusive childhood. Then one day, out of the blue, Dave and Diane make the 10-hour drive from their house in Arizona to Momma's pink house in Gunnison. David tells Momma that he forgives her completely. After that, we see him once or twice a year at family gatherings.

Occasionally, when Momma and I walk the halls at Apple Tree she cries about David. The conversation usually goes like this:

Momma says, "I have no idea what I was thinking."

"Momma, I have no idea what you were thinking, either."

Her response is usually more crying.

I respond, "All I know is that David says that he forgives you completely." Then I add, "I think you should follow his example and forgive yourself, too." She declares she doesn't know how.

I tell Momma I think the key is to accept his forgiveness and forgive herself. We have this conversation four or five times during her four years at Apple Tree. They seem to cluster. I cannot detect a precipitating event.

David receives his cancer diagnosis after consulting the doctor about chronic pain in his back. A life-long smoker, he has the lung cancer not caused by smoking; it has metastasized to his bones. He is terminal the day of his diagnosis. Debra and I do take Momma to Arizona to see him. We arrive at David's home on a Friday in March. We plan to stay in a hotel, but David wants us to sleep at his house. Our niece, Chrissy, who lives nearby, joins us later in the day. On Saturday Aunt Althea comes by to visit. Momma begins to get agitated. She makes a couple of snide comments to Debra and me about Althea interfering with her time with her son. David's house is filled with peace, and I am sure that grace abides within. Debra and I do not want to interrupt this calm. We take Momma out to the garage for a talk. We tell her we do not want anything to disturb the peace in David's home. She begins a tirade against her sister. She has a litany of complaints, both real and imagined. We tell her that she will, nevertheless, say nothing that is rude or inflammatory. What we do not discuss is that Aunt Althea helped raise David and provided him a safe haven for launching his life. Momma is mad. She stomps out of the garage. I follow her on a silent walk, a silent stomp, around the block. We remind her of her frequent admonition: "if you can't say anything nice, don't say anything at all." We go back inside. Eventually, Momma actually does a good job of making kind and friendly conversation, even warming up to her sister. After dinner and after Althea leaves and Momma goes to bed, Debra, Chrissy, and I join David out at the swimming pool as he smokes. Our conversation eventually turns to growing up as stepbrothers and sisters. Deb and I acknowledge how Momma heavily favored her son, Nick, over her stepsons. We do not acknowledge that favoritism extended to Debra, too. Maybe that is just my perspective. Debra and I do acknowledge how much we each regret not saving David from Momma's abuse. He reminds us that he has forgiven her completely.

A month later, I have another conference in Phoenix. I arrange to spend another weekend with David. Chrissy also comes over. We have a lovely Friday evening and Saturday together. After dinner, when everyone else is asleep, Chrissy and I are sitting out by the pool as David smokes. Diane still hopes that David will stop smoking. His doctors ask "Why?" As the conversation goes on, I bring up the subject of David's abuse again, admitting that I likely had no idea what that was like for him. He asks me, "Do you really want to know how bad it was?"

I assure him that I do.

He says, "Are you sure?"

"If you had to live through it, I think I can listen to it."

Before he begins, he reminds me that he has forgiven Momma completely. Then he tells me of the day my mother cuts off the end of his finger. Shocking? Unbelievably so. The story begins with David making some infraction that I do not recall, whether he didn't say or I forgot or he forgot. It hardly matters.

Momma says to David, "You make me feel so bad. You hurt me so much." And she continues, "I will show you how bad you hurt me."

I have called Momma the Queen of Guilt. She used to do this all the time to us, even as grown-ups. It made me so God damn mad, even in the days when I didn't say God damn. After threatening David, she pulls out the cutting board and her big chopping knife. She takes time to use the sharpening steel. Then she tells David to put his hand on the cutting board. And he does. She cuts off the pad of his little finger. Just the tip of the pad. She cuts off the end of his little finger.

"I was home that summer. I saw that bandage." I manage to choke out.

He agrees.

"You covered for her?" We cry together for a few minutes. I hug him, murmuring I'm sorries. We talk until we all settle down. I fly out the next morning, giving David a final hug before I leave.

In May, Debra flies to Phoenix, helps David and Diane load the U-Haul, and drives it to San Diego. They move into an apartment two blocks from the beach. Even when his bones hurt so much that he is in a wheelchair, he makes it to the beach nearly every day.

When I am back at home, back at work, I feel slightly less sane for having heard David's story. I am bothered so much that I email my friend Bill, who teaches psychology at the University. "How is it," I ask, "that a parent who is largely adequate for most of her children can be a monster for just one of them?" I relate the circumstances leading to my question. Bill, of course, says that it is hard to tell from a distance, but it could be that Momma resented Arlo for leaving her in Gunnison to raise kids while he went off to work in Salt Lake. He says that often the child who is most needy is most likely to be abused. This explanation makes sense to me. Momma tells me more than once how hard it is after she marries Arlo to find herself still alone in a house with even more kids to raise.

I reach out to a second source, Burt, who is the cousin of my kid's dad, Ernie. Burt is the administrator of a mental hospital in Texas. I ask Burt the same question, "How is it that a parent who is largely adequate for most of her children can be a monster for just one of them?" I relate the circumstances leading to my question. Burt responds that after thirty years of experience in the mental health field, he has no idea what goes wrong with some minds and some relationships. "I do, however, know one thing. I am firmly convinced that after age forty, our job is to forgive our parents for everything we think they did to screw us up." Then he says, "the lucky ones do."

I ask David that night by the pool how he could forgive my mother completely. He tells me that he had to, for his own good. He says that his psychiatrist helps him see that those aversive childhood experiences may have helped him become the strong person that he is. I think the peace I felt in his home came from that strength of character. I have to remind myself more than once that if David has forgiven her, I, too, should forgive my Momma.

🖋

We get the call that David dies in September on a Sunday evening while I am at the assisted living center. Momma has gone to bed. I lie down beside her and hold her while we cry. She tells me several times, "I wish it were me. I wish it were me." Finally, I tell her, if she really wants it, I can get her a release blessing.

"Really?" she asks.

"Really," I assure. I tell her I can call my friend Syd.

Syd and I have worked together for nearly three years. The week before David dies, I am in a car with Syd making the nearly 4-hour drive to Ruby's Inn, the rural location at the mouth of Bryce Canyon of an annual fall meeting with educators from around the state. Diane calls while I am in the car, saying that they think David might not make it through the week. I share David's story with Syd who is half Māori. He tells me of the Māori traditions of his father's family around death and dying. He has an extended family of more than 2000 members in four generations. Syd is the first person to complete college and the only person with a PhD. He tells a group of graduate students that he is an "exemplar in his tribe." He is remarkable in his own right. Syd is also a practicing Mormon. He tells me that he is so good at giving release blessings that his girl cousins cry and wail if he arrives when an elder is ailing. A release blessing is simply a blessing for the failing person that they can let their body and their soul separate so they can be released from this physical world. In the right circumstances it is a lovely thought.

When I call, Syd says he will be happy to come to the assisted living center even though it is more than an hour's drive from his home. He brings his wife, Maureen, and his son, a young priesthood bearer. You need two Mormon priesthood bearers for an authentic blessing. Syd gives Momma a beautiful blessing about a life well-lived. He gives John a blessing of comfort and strength. He gives me a blessing that I will be a wise and loving matriarch for my siblings. Syd is a wonderful friend.

On Wednesday of the week following the blessing, Momma calls my cell phone. I am walking past the cubicles toward my corner office. Momma says, "You remember that thing we were talking about on Sunday night."

"The blessing?" I query.

She confirms.

"Yes, I remember."

"Well, I changed my mind," she says.

I hold back from laughing out loud, imagining Momma as Emily Latella, telling God, "Never mind."

This is one of my favorite Momma stories. I giggle all the way back to my office. There is Momma all caught up in the moment and then she stops to think about it and changes her mind, looking heavenward and telling God, never mind.

I share this story with my friend, Cassidy. She tells me about her cousin, we'll call him Chase, who lives a pretty rough street life. Chase is handsome and charming all his life. He and Cassidy are both cousins of Cheryl Ladd, blonde, blue eyed, and attractive as all get out—you get the picture. According to Cassidy, Chase is dying of cancer. He has two sisters with large and lovely homes who would gladly care for him. He chooses to spend the end of his days in a cheap hotel near his street friends. One day his uncle comes by for a last visit. He finds Chase unconscious. The uncle administers a release blessing for him. As he finishes, Chase opens one eye and asks, "Are you trying to kill me?" Cassidy and I think that in the end we all cling to this life. Think of John Travolta in Michael, looking over the fallow field and lamenting that his will be his last trip to Earth.

🖋

In October, Momma tells me that she heard her father call to her in the night. He said to her, "LaRue, it is time for us to go." She grabs her robe and makes it to the outside door, which is down the hallway next to their apartment before she realizes that Grandpa is probably not really waiting for her outside. Lacking her key, she goes to the desk, asking them to let her back into her apartment.

I am surprised at how quickly Momma begins to deteriorate. Before fall is half gone, she is noticeably slower, noticeably less alert. One Sunday in early November she and I are heading back to her apartment after our walk. We pass that hallway that goes to the nearest outside door, which is some thirty feet away, when I see a small water snake, maybe 10 inches long, slithering along on the carpet. Not a fan of snakes under any circumstances, I am determined not to let the little critter cross my mother's path. I try to step on it. I bend over to pick it up. No luck. It slithers right in front of Momma and under the door into her apartment. A snake crossing your path is a portent of death according to Navajo tradition. I say nothing to Momma. Within half an hour, one of the male attendants has recovered the slippery little devil from the back of the coat closet just inside the apartment door.

🖋

Robert and I have lunch with Momma and John on Christmas Day, a Saturday. On Monday, I return to Apple Tree, planning to take Momma to see her sisters. Visiting for an hour or two and making the 280-mile round trip will take the entire day. When I enter the apartment, I find Momma sitting in her Mormon underwear, hovering between dressed and naked. John tells me that she has not eaten since Saturday and that she has fallen twice. I tell Momma that I think this is not a good day to go visiting. I get her to drink a can of Ensure and get her back to bed. I go down to the office to speak with Teresa, the nurse. After giving her an update, I say, "I think it is time for hospice." She says she has been thinking likewise for two weeks, but she was trying to get us through Christmas. I call Aunt Beth and Aunt Althea and tell them we are not able to visit today. I tell them the truth—we are going to put Momma on hospice. I call Debra. We make an appointment with Momma's physician. We see him Tuesday at 2:00. He tells us we did not need to come in person. We tell him, "Yes, we did."

Tuesday evening at 9:30 Momma falls and breaks her hip. I meet Debra at the emergency room close to 10:30 p.m. Momma is in and out of consciousness and in considerable pain. I adjust her leg, hoping to ease her suffering. The physician comes by to confirm the broken hip. He tells us that without surgery she will not walk again. We tell him we reached the same conclusion. Debra assures the doctor that Momma will not likely survive the surgery as she nearly bled-out from her last surgery, years earlier. A very busy night at the hospital, it is after 1:30 when we get her into a room. The attending physician, Dr. Jimmy Stewart, is very kind as he reviews the hospice orders, supporting us in our decision to provide palliative care only.

The next day I pick up John at the assisted living center. When we get to the hospital, Momma thinks she is going home. She cannot return to the assisted living center. They are not a multilevel facility, and she must be mobile. The hospital can only keep her for 48 hours, we must find a new care facility. Debra arranges for a new facility by the next morning. We will transport Momma the following evening at 5:00. The day of the transport, we have lunch with Momma and John at the hospital. I take John back to Apple Tree and then return to the hospital for the transport. Before they move her to a stretcher, they give Momma a good dose of her new pain medication, Methadone. John, the ambulance driver, carefully explains to us that he will cover her face with her blanket to protect her from the storm that is bearing down on us while he moves her out of the hospital and into the ambulance.

We arrive at the new care facility, and they clothe Momma in a fresh gown and settle her into a bed with clean sheets. It reminds me of her putting us to bed on summer nights. Fresh sheets and clean PJs are two of my favorite things. Her new room has a definite Mediterranean feel, sage green floors, accents of Tuscan gold and dark red. Momma rouses briefly in these new surroundings and then drifts off on a happy cloud. Deb and I hurry for home. This is the worst winter storm we have had in years. The roads are terrible. My car needs new tires.

The drive back to my house usually takes 40 minutes, but this drive lasts nearly 2 hours. By the time I get home it is past eight. Scrambled eggs for dinner and some relaxing music. I read some and wash my face. I am drifting off when the phone rings at 12:20. Momma died at 12:15. Debra is going back to the care facility. I am going back, too. The roads are still terrible, my tires are still bald, but most of the cars are gone. Deb is in the hallway on the phone with the mortuary when I arrive. I have a few minutes alone with Momma. I hug her deeply. She is still warm. I can see the massive bruising on her back from the fall and the blood settling in her body. Her jaw hangs open in a most disturbing way. Otherwise, they have cleaned her up before we arrive. I wish they had not crossed her hands under the blanket.

Sandy, the hospice worker, arrives. We have a laugh about her French last name and the French perfume that I am wearing. The driver from the mortuary arrives. We must inventory Momma's jewelry and belongings. We explain that Momma arrived at the hospital wearing nothing but her Mormon underwear and had absolutely nothing with her. Nevertheless, we must check her for jewelry. We pull back the blankets that the nurse placed over her crossed hands. Debra and I look in amazement at her hands; we see a slim gold band on the ring finger of her left hand. Debra exclaims, "What is this?" I respond, "I think it's a small miracle." For me the gold band seems a part of Momma's hand as if covered by a transparent layer of skin, almost surreal. Debra touches it. The ring is real. We list it on the inventory for the mortuary driver. Deb and I go back to her house and stay up all night writing Momma's obituary. By the time Momma arrives at the funeral home the little gold ring is gone.

🖋

The day after Momma's funeral, Debra and I go to Apple Tree to clear out Momma's belongings. John's children are moving him to Utah County, closer to where they live. We decide who will get what furniture. In the afternoon Rick and his son Chris come by with a truck to move the couches and the grandfather clock. Deb and I take Mom's clothes and jewelry. We save a pair of earrings for each daughter and granddaughter. We help John make final payments for the funeral, not realizing this is the last day we will ever see him. For the most part we are glad to be done with the burden of taking care of him. Momma was right. John is a lot harder to get along with than Daddy Arlo.

🖋

At the monthly board meeting of our professional organization, a colleague brings a copy of Momma's obituary and reads it aloud. She says that her grandmother read it to her on the previous Sunday, noting that, "These kids loved their mother." Everyone is very kind.

When I get back to work, I see that Cassidy has included me in a group message with Momma's obituary as an attachment. Cassidy says, "I love this woman and do not even know her. What a pioneer." I email back, telling her "It has been an amazing three days. I have quite a story to share." Six weeks later Robert and I meet Cassidy for dinner. I mention something about Momma dying.

Cassidy says, "I didn't know your mother died."

"Cassidy, you sent me a copy of her obituary."

"That was your mother?"

"My name was in there."

"Ohmigosh," she declares, "I'm still not used to your maiden name."

We laugh and laugh. That was my Momma.

2

THE JERRY LETTER

The Letter: three pale green sheets, a cursive crawl covers one side of each page. "Dear Red, I am writing to close our chapter, but really, I feel like I am closing the book of my life." Momma's affair with Jerry ended a year earlier. Momma marries five times. This is the story of the one that got away, the man she did not marry.

Her first husband, Frank, deserts her and their two sons shortly after the end of WW II. They have moved back to Appalachia, near his family. After a fight he storms out. When he fails to return after two weeks and Momma is out of money and out of food, she phones her parents on the farm in Utah. They wire the money. Seven months pregnant with her second child, she travels home with her young son. Frank shows up at her parent's door more than a year after he walks out on her. Momma tells about their conversation:

"I guess you divorced me?" he says.

"I guess I did."

"Well, if you change my sons' names, I will kill you."

Momma changes their son's names when she marries my dad, Don Stevenson. I am named for my father and my

mother, Dawn LaRue Stevenson. When I get to be a teenager, I think it is an awkward name. Everyone calls me Dawn
LaRue, except my cousin, Phyllis, who calls me Dawny. Don
Stevenson dies in a car accident in June before I would turn
three in October.

Momma's third husband, Gene will always be the man
who killed my dog, a cocker spaniel named Lady, of course.
To my younger brother Nick, this father, his father, is a hero,
a veteran of the Korean War. Nick sleeps with Gene's Army
blanket for most of his life. Gene tells Momma after less than
two years of marriage that she needs to divorce him.

"On what grounds?"

"You name it, I've done it." He responds.

In less than a year, before she can bring herself to sign
the papers, Gene dies of an accidental gunshot while on
coyote watch at his family's sheep camp. This sheep camp
is a run-down woodshed with a door, rather than the traditional Western sheep camp, a wood wagon with four wood
and iron wheels and an arched roof, usually painted John
Deer green. His sister-in-law contends that Gene's death
is suicide, but an accidental gunshot through the cheek as
a result of a slip on a rickety step is a more likely explanation. His death is ruled an accident. His parents are heart
broken. Momma is in a daze. She has five young children,
two husbands dead, and another long since run-away.

✦

After Gene's death, Momma works nights and weekends at the Cowboy Café as a cook and a waitress with her
friends, Elaine and Lorene. Elaine is petite, dark curly hair,
olive skin and divorced. Her daughters, Susan and Linda,
are best friends with Deb and me. They live a block west of

our pink house, between us and main street. One afternoon, on the way home from elementary school, I see Elaine's husband beat her in the front seat of their car. Susan wants me to stay, but I am too frightened. Lorene is voluptuous, blonde, and still married, the mother of some of our other neighbors and friends. They live between our house and Elaine. Her husband seems dark and mysterious, reminding me slightly of the grainy photo of my dead father.

Momma is the slender red head, not a natural red, but a nice tribute to her English and Irish ancestry. She is generally thought of as a widow, beautiful, thirty-something with five young children to raise. Momma works hard, but we are not poverty-stricken. My father leaves her a $50,000 life insurance policy—a chunk of change in 1952. She also has Social Security Survivor's benefits. So, she builds a house, plants a lawn, raises a garden, and works for extra money—and for her sanity. Momma can butcher a chicken, shoot a buck, and cook like nobody's business. She tells me when I am a young mother myself that after my dad died, she determined that she would cook a full dinner every night even though she knew she, "could get by with soup and sandwiches." She does cook every night. And we have cooked breakfasts every morning. Some of our best memories are around that kitchen table.

Our neighbor, Jimmy, tells me that for him Momma is as glamorous as Jane Russell. Momma is practically the only working single mom that any of us know; the only one who dresses up every day. Jimmy tells me how Momma saves his life when he is in high school. He sneaks out of church and runs all the way home to sit in her kitchen and drink coffee. He says she accepts him completely, treating him like a grown-up. The second son, Jimmy has been pressed into man's work on the family farm since he was twelve. Momma helps Jimmy accept a gawky 6'11" frame that is all knees and elbows. He loves sports but has not yet grown into his body. She helps him feel good about himself. After her funeral, my not-yet-husband, Robert, who only knew Momma as an old woman, sees a photo of her lying on my dining table.

"Who is this?"

"My Momma in her late twenties or early thirties, "I tell him.

"Your Mom was the prettiest girl in the West?" he questions, and then he looks at me again.

Another neighbor, Dixie, says that she, too, thought Momma was glamorous. She was glamorous by our small-town standards, and accepting, and mostly shy. Any misstep she ever made she took as proof positive that she was just a dumb little country girl.

During the years that she works at the Cowboy Café, Momma also works days as a part-time clerk, sitting at the City Hall two days every other week to collect water payments.

Momma meets Jerry Thompson at the café when I am in fifth grade. Jerry and his friends, Jay (who looks old and gray) and Butch, a very handsome younger guy who reminds me of Ed Burns, come to Gunnison as part of a crew, linemen installing a border-to-border electrical line to serve the growing populations of the West in the early 60s. The guys live at the Gunnison Motel and eat at the Cowboy Café, where the food is good and the women are fun. They are lonely, far from wives and home, and here are women who need something to look forward to. Momma and Jerry fall into an easy liaison.

One Sunday Momma says to us all,

"Put on your Sunday clothes."

We almost respond in unison, "Aw, heck, do we have to go to church?"

"No, we are going to the café."

"For what?"

"I am going to teach you how to eat a steak." True enough most of our evening meals were meat and potatoes, generally a beef or venison roast. Sometimes ground beef. In retrospect, I think Momma probably didn't know about medium rare steak until the appearance of Jerry and the line crew. At the café, she and Lorene cook up five good size steaks, all medium rare. This is our first steak ever. We are skittish about the size of the portion and about the redness of the juice on our plates. Momma prevails—now we all eat our steaks medium rare. After Momma dies, Debra and I go out for steak dinner on her birthday.

Let me tell you the good parts about Jerry.

He is good to my Momma—as good as an adulterous lover can be. He buys her great clothes for her birthday and Christmas. My favorite is a double-knit wool suit, classic Chanel styling, an amazing pumpkin color. Jerry encourages Momma to buy Jantzen skirts and sweaters. Momma has a great sense of style. Maybe all women of the 40s have a great sense of style. Momma's beautiful Persian Lamb coat, a remnant of those 40s fashions, falls apart as it hangs in the coat closet of the laundry/mud room. The slow deterioration has been oddly heartbreaking to me. Jerry buying her beautiful clothes feels like someone is caring for her once again.

Later, when I can nearly wear her same size, she lets me borrow the skirts and sweaters—my favorite is the pale lime, cable front, short sleeve sweater with the off-white, burgundy, and pale lime plaid pencil skirt. I have to roll the waistband to keep it up, but that makes the length better. When I am still in junior high, Momma sews a green plaid pencil skirt for me with a coordinating pale yellow weskit top that picks up a color in the plaid. The kick pleat has three pleats and a tab with buttons on either side at the top of the pleats.

The Christmas that I am in sixth grade, Jerry asks what Deb and I want. He fulfills our request when he brings an Easy Bake Oven. The thing about Jerry is that he is the first person, or maybe the first male, in my life who seems remotely interested in making my wishes come true. At least, he is the first man who does so on a regular basis. The next fall he asks me what I want for my birthday. I am ready for this one. I want a black, button-front cardigan. He double checks my request. Sure, I have just started 7th grade, but I am only 4'8" and weigh 72 pounds—so kind of a grown-up request for a pip-squeak. He does not make that observation. He simply agrees to try. I hold out hope. I assure him that my friend Peggy is even smaller than I, and she has such a cardigan. The weekend before my birthday, Jerry brings the black, button-front cardigan.

That same weekend, Jerry also brings a 6-week-old German shepherd puppy, very tiny and very black. Those first days I have a hard time distinguishing between my new black sweater and our new black puppy. One day I reach out to pick up my new sweater off the arm of the couch, and, to my surprise, I grab a puppy. Thanks to Aunt Bethey, we all know what to name him. A very annoying boxer lives two doors down the street. A teenage tough guy is the owner of this dog named Caesar. Certainly, if we name our German shepherd Brutus, he will eventually take care of this out-of-control Caesar. Jerry giving us our beloved Brutus only adds to our good will toward him. Jerry revels with us as the awkward little puppy grows ever larger and ever smarter. When Brutus is about 19 months old, I, Deb, and Nick, are walking past the house where Caesar lives. It is early spring and still cool for us to be out walking in our light jackets. We are young: eighth, sixth, and third grade, respectively. Caesar, up to his usual shenanigans, comes racing around the side of the house from the backyard, barking his way across the front yard, and standing aggressively on the park strip with that wide-legged boxer stance, his chest thrown out. Brutus, newly aware of his strength and agility, looks at Caesar and throws his ears back slightly. Caesar throws his ears back and growls. Brutus, never on a leash and always as obedient as Momma has trained him to be, walks companionably by our side. When he hears the growl from Caesar, he is off like a shot, hurling his full large-size German shepherd weight at Caesar's average-size boxer body. There is a considerable amount of growling and snarling, but within four or five moves, Brutus has Caesar on his back, standing over him. Injury is not the point of this interaction. Brutus gives Caesar two hefty "harwoofs" from deep in that big chest of his, as if to say, "Look shorty, these are my kids. Don't mess with them." Then he trots over to our side, and we continue our walk. From that day on, Caesar never bothers us. He may notice us as we walk by, but he is never again aggressive. No doubt, there were other kids in our neighborhood who were a bit afraid of Brutus and his big bark, but any of us kids, his kids, can call him down. All it takes is a sharp, "Brutus," followed by a firm, "Here boy," and he is calmly standing at our side, sitting at our feet, or, if one of us is sitting on the porch, tucked under our arm, leaning against us in a big dog hug. He is our dog, and we are his kids. Not that it ever happened, but each of us lives sure that if we are in trouble across the street or across town, Brutus will be at our side to guide us to safety. If I had to, I would say that Brutus is the alpha male for the entire small town of Gunnison. He trots alongside us as we walk to the homes of friends or to the swimming pool, curling patiently under a tree, waiting for us. In public spaces he never bothers anyone. At home, his domain is Momma's over-size galley kitchen. He stays in the laundry room for mealtimes and sleeps there for most of his life. Brutus ventures into the living room only around the time we kids should be returning from school, sticking his nose behind the drapes to watch for us through the big picture window. When we kids are at the kitchen table doing our homework, he is under it, warming our feet and licking the wounds on our skinny legs.

Momma tries to get pedigree papers on Brutus. The American Kennel Club will have no part of it. Momma fails to follow naming conventions. There is no way that AKC will pedigree a German shepherd, no matter how beautiful, that has been known from his first days of paper training as Brutus Paderewski, the Great Pianist.

As we grow older and separate off with our friends, Brutus becomes the constant companion for Nick, keeping pace with him as he races around on his 10-speed. Nick lives at home until he is 20. After Nick leaves home, Brutus waits on the corner of the lawn every Friday night for his weekend return. While Nick is still at home, Brutus runs for miles every day for more than 13 years. I think this active life lets him live to be 17 years old. Brutus knows all of my babies, except the last one. My oldest daughter, Luna, reports that he was her constant companion when she was at Momma's house, sitting with his nose nestled on her shoulder watching whatever she was doing. Brutus was there when Deb and her young son move in with Momma for a couple of years. I am sure that he is the best dog that ever lived. Momma never will talk with us about having to put him down.

It helps that Momma is the best dog trainer I have ever known. She does it intuitively, like she is connected to the sentient being. And while Momma loves her dogs, beginning with Brutus, she does not confuse them with her children. Momma knows full well that animals inhabit their own powerful realm that we are allowed to share with them. Momma's rapport with animals is built on her respect for the nature of animals.

After a year or so, Jerry stays some weekends at our house. The frequency increases with each passing year. I am 14 the day I sit on Jerry's knee and tell him that, if it makes any difference to him, I would love for him to marry my Momma and come live with us full-time. His tears well-up, and he tells me he knows this to be true, but he cannot leave his kids to grow up without a father. By those last years, he is at our house every other weekend. I wonder how his kids like that. For us, other than the awkwardness with the neighbors, which in a tiny rural town in Utah is considerable, the arrangement is comfortable, or at least familiar.

The summer before my 10th grade year, Jerry is working in Las Vegas. He gets up one morning at 2:00 am to stand in line to buy tickets for the Beatles concert. On a

long-distance phone call from Vegas, he reveals this surprise for Deb and me and our cousin, NaDene, our Aunt
Beth's daughter. I am pretty sure that Jerry pays for most of
our trip to Vegas for the concert. We have a great time—
not great seats, middle balcony, lots of screaming—but a
great time. I sit in my seat and watch a wave of girls move
in unison toward the front of the balcony. The news reports
are true—girls go wild. Great is an insufficient descriptor
for this experience. It is unbelievable to see the Beatles
during those early years. My best friend Vickie is so jealous
she can hardly see straight. The next summer she tells me
that she is sending my yearbook off to be signed by the Beatles. My yearbook is gone for weeks, then she forges their
signatures, and returns the book to me, finally confessing
her deception weeks later. Other than Deb and NaDene, I
am still the only person I know who ever saw the Beatles in
person: August 20, 1964, Las Vegas Convention Center, my
first concert ever. Jackie de Shannon opens, singing, "What
the World Needs Now." The internet says the song was not
recorded until 1965, but she sang it that night.

The Beatles run onto the stage, a bit late, in their collar-
less red suits. They launch into "Twist and Shout." Within
the first measure, Paul whaps himself in the mouth with
the microphone, cutting his lip and delaying the show until
they stop the bleeding. After the concert, we hang out on
the sidewalk near the Las Vegas Hilton, hoping to catch a
glimpse of the Fab Four. I still remember the tomato-red
sleeveless sheath dress I wore. One problem with the evening, we cannot mention Jerry during the concert because
we are sitting right next to his daughter and two of her
friends. I know it is her because she has his tight curly hair.
Failure to plan. Momma and Aunt Beth warn us about the

dilemma as we leave our motel for the concert. It is even more difficult when we notice that she has mini binoculars. We want those binoculars. We say nothing.

🪶

Let me tell you the not-so-good parts about Jerry.

Truthfully, it is hard to come up with the not-so-good parts. The deal is that I love him, wholeheartedly. He has a lot to do with what attracts me in a man—barrel chest, some good height, and a sure sense of manliness. Before we ever even find Jerry's goodbye letter, I consider trying to find him. I tell my best friend, Carrie Ann, the family therapy major, that I don't want to fuck with his life. "Why not?" she asks. "He fucked with yours." And that, I guess, is the not-so-good part. One of my therapists says that is exactly the problem. He screws with my life.

Something happens between Momma and Jerry on the Vegas trip. After the concert, the grown-ups drop us off at our motel in North Las Vegas and go back out on the town. I am not sure, but I think Aunt Beth comes in before Momma. Momma comes in very late, maybe five in the morning. Beth and Momma take us to breakfast and then we head to a clothing store—an apparently desperate mission to buy women's black western-style dress pants, very similar to a pair Momma already owns. Back at the motel, as we are packing, I pick up Momma's original pair of black pants and find they are torn open, entirely shredded along the inseam. I ask Momma what happened? Of course, she says, "Nothing." I have no idea who attacked her. Like many emotional events in Momma's life, we never speak of the incident.

We don't see Jerry for weeks after the concert. Maybe because he is still working in Vegas. By the time he shows up at our door, some six weeks later, Momma is married. We each spend a few minutes with him in the cab of his pickup saying a tearful goodbye. He tells me, "Get out of this damn town. Go be a stewardess. Find someone who can take care of you."

Before Jerry, and even during Jerry, Momma dates a bit. The summer before I start sixth grade she goes so far as to get engaged to a man who brings her flowers, boxes of chocolates, and Mantovani records. He gives her a diamond ring. He takes Deb and me shopping for school clothes, driving us 90 miles to Provo so we can go to JC Penney and Sears. He buys us shoes and two dresses. While we are trying on the second dresses, he tries to come into the dressing room, which creeps me out completely. We insist that he leave. After the purchase of the second dresses, we insist that he take us home. I am pretty sure that I tell my Momma. She breaks off the engagement and refuses to give him back his ring.

In mid-September 1964, right after The Beatles concert, a resident of our little town calls Momma to set her up on a date with his nephew who is visiting from New Mexico, a recent widower who lost his wife in June. All of us kids meet Arlo. We like him well enough, but we are in shock and awe when, within a week, Momma runs off to Elko and marries Arlo on September 22, 1964, little more than a month after the concert. Our lives are turned upside down. It could be a disaster. Within days after my birthday the first week of October, Debra, Nick, and I and our beloved Brutus are living in Vanadium, New Mexico, a company town for United States Smelting and Refining. David and Russ stay in Utah, David to finish his senior year of high school and Russ to leave on his LDS mission. We live in a three-bedroom house with a new stepsister and three new stepbrothers. Another stepbrother is away in the Navy and an older stepsister is married with two children, living a few doors over in the company town. Stepsister Kathy has a daughter 3 years old. She and I bond instantly. She visits our house. We go by Kathy's to see if this niece can ride along on our errands. In stores I carry her on my hip. It seems effortless.

I love living in New Mexico, partially because my stepsister is my age, likes me, and includes me in her social world. I learn how to negotiate a new, much larger school— Cobre High School, Bayard, New Mexico, 700 students, 70 White students. This is a life-changing experience for me with a permanent impact on my perspective. These few months give me a strong sense of social justice that carries through my entire professional life. One pivotal experience involves a student named Monster Holguin. At Cobre High, the Latino students divide themselves in to two groups, Mexican and Spanish, depending on the ancestry of their family. In my home economics class, the White girls are stiff, uninteresting, and I can sew better than all of them. I can actually sew better than the teacher who does not even know how to put in a zipper with a lapped application. Eye roll. So, I sit with the Spanish and Mexican girls who also sew better than the teacher and who are always laughing. I ask them to teach me Spanish. They talk amongst themselves in Spanish and then, in agreement, they tell me that they will teach me Mexican wedding songs, naughty Mexican wedding songs.

Some days after this new arrangement in home economics I am heading to my locker down the West hallway near the end of lunch period. I leave the cafeteria where the students are eating, listening to music and dancing some, rocking the entire room whenever Roy Orbison sings "Pretty Woman." I see a group of boys off to my right. I dread walking past all of them, but also seeing no alternative, I proceed. As I am passing, a big strong hand grabs my arm, pulls me into the circle of boys, and I am suddenly staring into the face of Monster Holguin. We call him Monster, but not to his face, because of his size and his pock marked face. I look into his eyes, and he looks into mine. It is difficult to say how much time passes; it seems like a long time. I realize my vulnerability. At one point I start to tear up, and I give Monster a half-smile, but steadily meet his gaze. After several more moments, seconds or minutes, who knows, he lets go of my arm and says for all to hear, "This one is okay. Leave her alone." I pass some kind of test. I think I needed to realize my own vulnerability and to offer the proper respect. Decades later I tell my niece, Chrissy, the 3-year-old on my hip during our few months in New Mexico, about this experience.

She says, "Oh, yeah, Monster Holguin."

"You know him?"

"Yes," she acknowledges. "We served on the school board together in Silver City."

We laugh and remark, "Once an activist, always an activist."

A dozen years ago, I am at a conference in Boston in late winter. Some colleagues want to ride the MBTA out to the coast, just for a look. On our return into town, a large group of Latina girls board at one of the stops. They are talking and laughing, eventually breaking into song. I do not remember so much the words, but I recognize the melody and the rhythm of one of those naughty Mexican wedding songs. I go over to the girls and introduce myself, telling them about my experience in home ec. so many years ago. I thank them for the memory. They are kind and laugh with me, leaving us a few stops later. My one guy friend from the conference, another school counselor, laughs at my experience. He and I get off two stops later. We go to Filene's Basement to buy shoes, one pair for me and one pair for his wife.

🖋

Living in New Mexico, money is short. Momma cannot find a job, even with years of experience as a bookkeeper for several car dealers. The hardest part of this Christmas when we older girls forgo presents is that we were not able to buy little exchange gifts for our friends. Lack of money is not the only reason that Momma, Deb, Nick, and I are back in Utah by mid-February. There have been many closed-door, whispered conversations. I am not sure what most of those were about. One huge crisis is that Sherene, the six-month-old baby of Daddy Arlo's oldest daughter, Kathy, dies of crib death, SIDS. It is a confusing and tragic time for all of us. Nevertheless, Momma is rehired back at her old job at the car dealership, and before you know it, we are back in Gunnison. That spring and through the summer, Momma, Debra, Nick, I, and Brutus live in a little rented duplex behind the car dealership because Momma has leased out the four-bedroom pink house. I am back at school in Gunnison by the time spring dance season rolls around.

By the end of summer, Daddy Arlo, whom I call Pops for the first year or so, and his four younger children have moved to Utah. Pops takes a considerable pay cut to transfer to USSR in Salt Lake. He keeps up the rigorous schedule of the twice per week drive from Gunnison to Salt Lake City for four years. He can often make the 2-hour drive in an hour and a half. Finally, Daddy retires from USSR, moves to Gunnison, and manages a dairy farm in which Momma's brother has invested.

So, for most of the week, we have eight kids and a mostly single mom living in one house. For the most part we kids get along. For the most part Momma and Daddy make a good marriage for each other. They take us on vacations to Arizona and Idaho to visit aunts, uncles, and cousins. We go camping, fishing, and picnicking. Where there was once only a narrow gravel drive, Daddy puts in a concrete driveway wide enough for Momma's car and Daddy's pick-up. They extend the eaves and face the house with pink slump block. Daddy builds a pink slump block storage shed, and he adds a carport. Daddy often cooks when he is home. Momma and Daddy often cook together: his famous warm mashed potato salad to go with Momma's corn-crisped chicken, his mashed potatoes with Momma's pork chops and mushroom gravy. Our favorite was Daddy's specialty, "the twenty-pound enchilada," stacked in a 9x13 pan, New Mexico style. Our Daddy Arlo never leaves the kitchen until all the dishes are done, regardless of a full day of work and a 2-hour drive. In addition to taking each set of grandkids fishing every year, Momma and Daddy drive up the mountain to the forests every fall to cut firewood, enough for everyone's wood-burning stove. They go out to the west hills every year to gather bags and bags of pine nuts to roast and share all winter long.

Daddy Arlo dies on New Year's Eve, 1993, from complications of a quadruple bypass. At Daddy's funeral there are ten of us children still living. We decide not to include spouses in the receiving line, so we line up with no particular plan. I look down the line and there is a kid from Momma and a kid from Dad alternating through the whole group, not in age order. Momma and Daddy do a good job for each other, and we kids do a good job for them. We kids get along. We stick together in hard times and difficult situations. And there were plenty of those.

🖋

About 20 years into her marriage to Arlo, Momma confesses to me that is a good 10 years before she does not think of Jerry every day. When we are living in New Mexico, right after Momma and Daddy Arlo's marriage, I know Momma has a post-office box where Jerry sends letters. She sends him school photos of us kids that year. She reads most of the letters to me. He sends Deb and me little diamond chip necklaces for Christmas—the Christmas with no presents. We have to sneak them into the house and keep them hidden. I am certain that during those months that Momma is back in Gunnison without Arlo she never goes to Salt Lake by herself. She never leaves for a mystery weekend. Momma says that she did not love Arlo when they married, but she came to love him as they built a life together. She says when Arlo proposed marriage, she was determined to make a better and more stable life for her children and herself. I think she had to cut out part of her heart to do it.

🖋

One week in late spring, after Momma and John have moved into assisted living, Deb is working alone cleaning out Momma's house; she finds the goodbye letter from Jerry. Deb reads it and cries. I read it and cry. Big David reads it. He does not cry, but he asks, "with all of her husbands and this long-term lover, I wonder who was the love of her life?"

The weekend before Mother's Day, Deb and I take Momma to lunch and then shopping. Deb buys her an outfit. I buy her another. She buys one for herself. After lunch, we are sitting in the car when Deb shows Momma the letter.

Momma says, "Oh, I don't remember the letter."

Debra asks David's question. "Momma, you have been loved by a lot of good men. Who was the love of your life?"

"It was your father, Don," She assures us.

We take Momma back to Apple Tree. She is so excited to show John her new clothes. The old tight wad barely says a word, even though he knows the new clothes did not cost him a penny. As we make our goodbye hugs, Momma whispers in Deb's ear. "Take care of that letter. I think I may need it."

Within a week or two of Debra and I reading Momma the Jerry letter, Deb calls me in a panic. Momma wants Deb to bring the letter to her.

"What should I do?" she asks.

"Well, it is her letter. I guess you should give it to her."

"Really?"

"Sure. But first, make a copy for us." Deb does make a copy for us. I was thinking she would take it to Kinko's. She uses her shitty little home copier. Oh, well.

In June Momma confesses to me that Don Stevenson has been so much on her mind she often calls John, Don.

She says he does not hear well enough to notice. She feels like she is so emotionally disconnected that she does not care. During these early summer walks, Momma tells me a few of the stories about my dad that I have not heard. When they go on their first camping trip together, they are so poor they can only buy one sleeping bag. If they need to turn over, they do it in unison. When my dad buys a little camp trailer to take to the oil fields, he cleans the outside and sings, "Ta-ra-ra Boom de-ray, Ta-ra-ra Boom de-ray, Ta-ra-ra Boom de-ray, did you get yours today? Ta-ra-ra Boom de-ray."

One year Momma cannot go on the Yardley deer hunt, so my dad goes without her. He comes home with a black eye, which he does not explain, and my Momma does not question. The next week she learns the story from her sisters. My dad and my uncle Birdell, who was likely with the OSS in World War II and used to a fair amount of authority, fight over where Dad shoots his buck. My dad tells his story, describing his location. Uncle Birdell counters that he must have been in some other spot. My dad sticks with his story. They argue back and forth. I am pretty sure Uncle Birdell throws the first punch. Momma reports that he can be a hot head. Then Momma delivers her biggest insult, "And Birdell was no kind of farmer either." She tells me she thought it was very gentlemanly of my dad to not rat out her brother.

*

By late summer, I become, to my surprise, Momma's sexual confessor. The first time, we are walking the halls at Apple Tree after an early dinner from my kitchen: meatloaf and gratin Dauphinois with asparagus and a salad. I rarely make dessert. Momma has little appetite for sweets. John is easily satisfied with generic chocolate chip cookies. Or occasionally, generic rainbow crisps. He keeps the bag by the side of his easy chair with the lift seat. He always has cookie crumbs all around his chair. For this first sexual confession, we are still in Red Apple hallway at the beginning of our walk. Momma pauses, turns slightly toward me, and says, out of the blue, "I hate it after John and I have sex." Pause. "He just lays there between my legs and falls asleep." I am aghast, not only at the content, but at this new aspect of my relationship with Momma. On one hand, it is kind of sweet that a couple in their eighties can have a sexual relationship. On the other hand, it would be good if it were sweet for both of the partners. On the other hand, I do not want to hear about my mother's sex life. On the other hand, it is cool that she trusts me with this information. On the other hand, I am not sure what to say. Am I out of hands yet? Wait, there's more.

Just before Christmas, my new role of sexual confessor pops up again. Momma says, "I can't stand to have John touch me." We both giggle a bit.

This time I actually respond, "Momma, do you really not like sex? Or do you just not like sex with John." Apparently, it is sex with John.

I tell her, "Well, you do not have to have sex with John if you do not want to."

"What?" She seems incredulous.

"If you really do not want to have sex with John, you do not have to. Just because you are married does not mean you have to have sex with him. Just tell him no." I explain to her that many women her age decide that they are done with sex.

There is considerable giggling on both sides of this conversation. Momma is nearly giddy with this new power. I practice with her, "Just tell him, 'No, I am not interested.'" She happily mutters to herself.

I call Debra. Momma is not having these discussions with her. We giggle over the content and agree that Momma should "Just Say No." Some weeks later Deb reports that John has managed to get assistance with his showers. Momma tells me he just stands there and lets the young female attendants scrub him down. She relates this detail with an air of disgust. Deb and I speculate that John is getting his jollies at the hands of the young attendants, so to speak.

Momma does not bring up the subject of sex again until March. She and John are starting their second year at Apple Tree. We finish dinner, and we are walking the halls. We do not get far when Momma stops, makes a quarter turn toward me as she always does with something important to say.

She begins, "Well, we had a really big fight last night."

"You did? What did you fight about?"

"John wanted to have sex and I told him, 'No, I told you I was done with that.'" In emphasis, Momma crosses her wrists at the level of her uterus and makes a sweeping gesture with her hands out to the sides. Clearly that reproductive system is off limits.

"What did he say?" I ask.

"He asked me to rub him."

I lose it completely. I nearly whoop with laughter. I laugh so hard I tear up. I hug Momma. She is giggling. We laugh some more.

Finally, I catch my breath and ask her, "Did you tell him he can rub himself?"

"No," she says, somewhat embarrassed.

"Well, tell him that he can rub himself. Tell him Deb and I will buy him magazines and everything," I snort.

I am still laughing. She is, too. I am nearly bubbling with laughter the rest of the evening. We go back to their room and settle in to watch Andy Griffith and Perry Mason. I am grateful to Pema Chodron for her advice to just "do what they do." We have a good routine.

On my way home, I call Deb to tell her this story. We laugh again. I do not stop there. Later in the week I am at the Bone Marrow Transplant Unit at the Huntsman Cancer Institute visiting my son-in-law who has acute myeloblastic leukemia, very rare in patients under age 40. He is 39. We are waiting for a donor match. He has been at Huntsman nearly a month. He needs some cheering up. I tell him not just the "rub me story." I regale him with all of Momma's sexual revelations. We laugh until we cry. Later in the year, the son-in-law tells me that he calls John "Rub Me." I feel marginally guilty. Poor John. He cannot, in fact, rub himself. Masturbation in any form is forbidden by the Mormon religion. And John is very Mormon.

⚘

Interwoven with Momma's sexual revelations, she tells me that she reads the letter from Jerry several times every day. I ask her how she arranges to do that. She pulls the letter out of her pocket. The envelope is beginning to tatter, the edges fuzzy with small tears. It is clear to me that Momma keeps the letter in her pocket during her waking moments. As soon as she dresses it goes into her pocket. And apparently comes out multiple times daily. She admits to me that she walks three or four times daily. In demonstration of her new habit, she sits down in the nearest chair and reads it again. She asks if we can find Jerry. I tell her we will try. I call Deb to discuss the possibility of finding Jerry. Debra tells me that some 20 years earlier she looks in the phone book and finds a woman who she thinks has the same name as Jerry's wife. She even drives to the house, parks across the street, and watches for several hours. I tell her that around that same time I call Eileen, Butch's wife. Butch, Jerry's younger friend, and Eileen move to Gunnison in the late 70s. Momma tells me that they are in town because Butch is dying of cancer. He sits on the porch of his old house on Main Street. I notice him there when I drive by, taking my children back and forth to school and activities. Butch looks old and tired. By the time I get around to calling Eileen, Butch has long since passed. I introduce myself only as LaRue's daughter. She pauses only slightly when I tell her I want to find Jerry. She tells me that the last she heard, he was living in the Sahara Motor Park in Las Vegas and drinking himself to death. I thank her. She wishes me luck. I do not take it any further. I keep the note with his name and location on a piece of paper in the back of my 1987 journal. I never do anything about trying to find Jerry. I am not sure how it would go.

"Maybe we could ask Eileen again," Deb suggests.

"That won't work," I respond.

"Why?"

"I saw her headstone when I was in the Gunnison cemetery on Memorial Day."

We discuss hiring a private investigator. Secretly we hope this idea of Momma's passes. The next week Momma says that Jerry's letter mentions going by Aunt Beth's.

"Maybe Beth knows where Jerry is" Momma suggests as she pulls the letter out of her pocket.

"Momma, the postmark on this envelope is dated September 1965. That is more than 40 years ago." Her eyes well with tears. I can feel her heart breaking. I drive to Manti to visit Aunt Beth to see if she knows where Jerry is. Aunt Beth says she does even not remember Jerry. I am glad I didn't try having that conversation by telephone.

🖋

Deb calls again. She thinks Momma is losing her mind.

"What's going on?"

"Momma says if we find Jerry, she wants to run off with him," she tells me.

"Momma isn't crazy," I assure her. "She is just very unhappy. A fantasy life looks so much better to her than her current reality."

The following Sunday, Momma tells me the same thing. She says, "I have definitely made up my mind. If Jerry shows up, I will just get in his truck and drive off with him. I don't care what anyone thinks."

"Where will you go?" I ask her.

"We will drive up into the mountains and listen to Jim Reeves like we always used to do." She tells me she has reconsidered; Jerry might be the love of her life.

I tell her that we have checked phone books and internet sources. I tell her about Debra driving by his wife's house decades ago. I tell her about my conversation with Eileen those years ago. I tell her we have considered hiring a private investigator. I tell her we will keep trying.

By the end of summer Momma tells John about the letter in her pocket and about her affair with Jerry. She tells me that John asks her if she had sex with Jerry?

"Did you tell him 'Lots and lots'?" I ask her. John's question seems a bit naïve, but John is a Mormon stalwart and sex outside of marriage is strictly forbidden. I think John probably starts praying for Momma's mortal soul.

As it turns out, Momma uses the letter to leverage John into improving his hygiene. He ups his shower schedule from once per week to every other day. I am pretty sure Momma still refrains from having sex with John. At least I do not get anymore sex updates. We speak less and less often of Jerry.

During those months of looking for Jerry, I go to an apartment building in downtown Salt Lake to see my daughter and her husband who are staying with a friend for a few weeks while they wait for a condo to open up. In the lobby I encounter two workmen. One of them is tall, broad-shouldered, curly hair to his shoulders with a tool belt around his waist. He instantly reminds me of Jerry. I say nothing, not sure how it would turn out. I still wish I had not kept silent.

I am not sure how much longer Momma carries the letter with her. I suspect until it falls apart. After she dies, Deb and I find three or four fragments of the letter in her wallet, small squares with frayed edges. I wish we had kept the pieces.

3

WOODY AND ME

PART I

My father writes me a letter when I am about 6 months old. It reads: "Hello my Bonnie Blue Eyes. How's Daddy's little darling Dawn LaRue? Are you still keeping those big boys standing back? Well, keep them back just a little bit longer. Love, Daddy." I keep the letter for years in my diary or, later, inside a framed photograph of him. Before I leave for L.A., I steal that photograph from the hall closet at Momma's house, telling myself that "she no longer cares about him anyway." Then when I move from L.A. back to Gunnison, I lose it. In doing so, I lose the only photograph we have of him, a blurry enlargement of a small snapshot that Momma made after he dies.

My memories of my father seem as blurry as my recollection of the photograph. I am two or so and standing in my crib in the single bedroom we all share in the living quarters behind our little roadside café, The San Pitch Inn. I call, "Daddy, Daddy. Bed bugs. Bed bugs." He comes in from the kitchen that serves both the Inn and our family quarters and moves me to the big bed he shares with my mother. A few minutes later, I call, "Daddy, Daddy. Bed bugs. Bed bugs." He comes in and moves me back to the crib. Some minutes later, I call a third time. He comes in and says, "No more."

I remember him giving me my weekly "allowance" of a candy bar and a soda. I feel his big hand on my tummy as he holds me over the commercial soda cooler that looks like a giant red ice chest filled with water and emblazoned with Coca-Cola logos that stands in the main room of the roadside café. My brother Russ later tells me the café was more like a honky-tonk. I choose the Orange Nehi and a candy bar, probably Three Musketeers or Baby Ruth. I remember swinging in the wooden chair swing that he makes for me. It has a seat, a back, arms, and a horizontal front piece that crosses my chest to hold me in it, one of three swings suspended from a cross post lashed to two of the mature trees in the front yard. Years later, Russ tells me how he helps my dad make my chair swing, cutting and sanding the wood, back braiding the ropes that hold it together, a technique used by sailors, and then back braiding the ropes that hold all three swings to the cross beam in front of the San Pitch Inn.

I remember my father in his casket. I am in the arms of a someone I do not know. I ask her, "Why won't my daddy wake up?" She tells me he has gone to heaven. "Won't I ever see him again?" I do not clearly recall her answer. I remember them closing the lid and taking my daddy away, out of the shadowed living room, onto the porch, down the steep stairs, into the sunlight, down the sidewalk, and out of my sight.

I am 8 years old. My mother is in the kitchen, at the stove, preparing dinner. I am around the corner in the hallway, lying on my back, my legs up the wall. I ask her, "How old was I when my father died?"

"Three," she says. "You were almost three."

"And three and five make eight. Right?"

"Right?"

"So, this is the year I get to see my dad?"

"What?"

"This is the year I get to see my dad?"

"You never get to see your dad."

By this time, I am in the kitchen, next to the stove, glaring at her when I ask, again, "What?"

"Your dad is dead. You never get to see him again," she says, glaring back.

Her words are final. We never talk about him. I know that she will not bring this up again. Even at age 8 I am good at concealing my feelings. Days later I go to my Grandpa Yardley's farm, climb the big cottonwood tree at the west corner of his lawn, find the broad branch I can lie back on, and then I let the tears slip silently from my eyes, rolling off my face to the ground. I see the dark green of the leaves, watch the filtered light dancing around me, refracting in my tears. Some minutes into my private grief, I hear Grandpa asking from below, "Dawny, are you okay?

"Yes, Grandpa, I'm okay." I respond. And I am, but just okay.

Through all of my growing up years, from the death of my father until I am well into adulthood, I have two recurring nightmares. The first dream, the most frequent, we are driving from Gunnison to Manti in Momma's blue and white '53 Chevy. We are rounding the curve by Nine-Mile Reservoir when the water overflows the shallow banks, flooding the road and flowing around the car. Eventually we

are stranded with water up to the running boards. Everyone in the car—Momma and my two older brothers—know
how to get to dry land. I am always left behind. Afraid and
angry. The second dream I am at my uncle Tom's, up the
canal hill from Grandpa Yardley's, in the calf barn walking
along the top of the narrow fences that separate the pens.
All of the pens are filled with baby bulls, miniatures of the
giant bull that occupies the large corral with the heavy
fence that dominates the farmyard. Stuck balancing on the
fences surrounded by the baby bulls, I can find no way out.

As I am growing up, we rarely talk about my father, not
Momma and I, not my sister and I, not my brothers and I. I
am in my forties when Momma tells me that it hurt her so
much to talk about him that she just locked her memories
away. I know that my dad dies in a car accident on a Friday
night. During the week, he works in the oil fields to make
money to carry us through the winter and spring until the
café gets off the ground. Momma tells him to wait until Saturday morning to come home, but he leaves as soon as the
work week is done. She tells us that he dozes at the wheel
and collides with a lumber truck. At least that is the story I
repeat to myself so that it becomes my memory.

I know that Momma meets my dad in late spring when
she is working at JC Penney's in Gunnison. She comes back
to Grandpa Yardley's farm to live with her two little boys
when their father abandons them. My father comes into the
store to buy a blanket. He has just signed on as a hired hand
for Mr. Pickett. Momma's co-worker, Barbara, flirts openly

with the handsome stranger. The next day, my dad comes into Penney's to ask Momma to go to a dance at Snow College on the coming weekend.

Mom asks, "Why didn't you ask Barbara?"

"She asks too many questions," he responds. His response will become increasingly significant.

Momma and this new man catch a ride to Snow College with Dr. Reese, common practice in small towns post-WW II. They spend the evening dancing to the music of Les Brown and His Band of Renown. My dad is a dancer. At the end of each song, he spins Momma around until her feet come off the ground. Not to worry, he has a firm grip. On their second date, he borrows Mr. Pickett's truck and takes Momma and her little boys into the mountains for a picnic. They have gone dancing several times before they go to a dance in Gunnison. A few songs in, my future dad says to my future mom,

"Hey babe, loosen up."

Momma explains her anxiety. People she knows are watching her. What must they think?

"Doesn't matter," he responds. "It just doesn't matter." Momma tells me this story when I am struggling with my membership in the Mormon church. They date all spring and summer and in November go to Evanston, WY, to marry.

After my father dies and we are living in the pink house, Momma has her uncle Jackie make a bear skin rug from the pelt of a bear my dad shot. That story goes like this: We are in the mountains camping with Momma's family. Momma is carrying me in her arms, heading back to camp. Dad is walking toward her about 100 feet away. He says to her calmly, "LaRue, don't look back. Calmly move over to the other side of the road." She does as he requests, then my dad kneels, takes aim, and shoots the female bear that has been following her back to camp. We don't have the bear skin rug out all the time, just occasionally to pet and play on. Russ puts it over his head and shoulders and scares the daylights out of a baby-sitter one night when we are playing hide and seek in the house.

That's it—all the stories of my dad that I grew up with. I have to wait until I am an adult to learn more stories about my father. Momma is in assisted living when I get the detail about Barbara asking too many questions.

🖋

On my way to growing up I am sexually abused between the ages of 9 and 14 by a series of three teenage boys who should have known better: a relative, a neighbor, and a relative. The abuse ranges from full intercourse—I am 9 years old; to threatened intercourse—I am 12 years old; to a hand in my pants—I am 14 years old. The last two abusers I simply hate to the end of their days. Both die in middle adulthood. I run into the hand-in-the-pants guy at the Gunnison Hospital. I hear he is dying of throat cancer. He has a white rag tied around his neck. His skin is green. When he dies three days later, I am that song from Chorus Line, "I Felt Nothing." My first abuser, the most brutal, I have, for the sake of my well-being, forgiven. One thing that saves me is my desire to be normal.

My best friend, the family therapy major, says by all rights I should be crazy. The death of my dad, the sexual abuse, and a string of alcoholic stepfathers nearly overwhelms me. That I am not crazy is a lucky combination of factors: my constant desire to be normal, a loving and supportive extended family, and a relatively safe community.

In elementary school, my teachers tell my mother, "Dawn is a good student, but she talks too much." I am very social, and very distracted, but wanting more than anything to be normal; I do my best to approximate normal. As an adult I come to call it my normal dance. I develop social skills up the gazoo. I also know when I am growing up that I am, in my own words, boy crazy.

In fourth grade I have my first date. Richard Larson takes me to the Saturday Matinee at the Star Theater. His mother drives us. He gives me a pink pearl necklace while we are riding in the back seat. I wear it to the movie theater. In sixth grade, my best friend, Marsha V. Beck, and I decide to crash an all-boy birthday party. It is a beautiful autumn day when we make one pass by the house of the birthday boy, who lives through the block from Momma's pink house. On our second pass, the boys are ready. They come charging across the street toward us. Marsha, much faster than I, slips by the charging hoard. In an effort to avoid them, I ride my bike off the road and into the pea gravel shoulder. My bike hits a large rock, comes to an abrupt stop, and I fly over the handlebars, landing face first in the gravel. Richard Larson, who is by now the biggest boy in our class, carries me across the street and into Richard Jensen's house. In spite of my protests, Richard J's mother, Thelma, insists on calling my mother at work. Momma takes me to the hospital. The physician on duty is Dr. Reese, a tough, stogie smokin' old Army doctor, who spent his early professional years in a field hospital during World War II. Dr. Reese scrubs out the scrapes and lacerations on my face with a wire brush.

I whimper.

He says, "I'm sorry, sweetheart."

A few seconds pass. I whimper again.

He says, "Shut up, dammit." And so, we continue, me whimpering, him alternating sorrys and shut-ups. Finally, the wounds are clean enough that he can put stitches in the deep gouge in my upper lip and the flap in my lower lip made by my teeth. I have a concussion and must stay overnight in the hospital.

The following afternoon Dr. Reese comes in to check on me. I am at the window of my room on the second floor, waving to people on the lawn below. Dr. Reese approaches me from behind. As he draws near, he asks,

"Who are you waving at?"

"My little brother and sister."

"Are they alone?" he asks.

"No, they are with my Grandpa Yardley."

Dr. Reese comes up close to look out the window. He puts his hand lightly on my shoulder as he says, "Your Grandpa Yardley is the best Mormon I know."

I look at him and say, "My Grandpa Yardley is not a Mormon."

He says, "I know." Then he finishes checking my wounds, checking my joints and limbs, looking in my eyes, checking my heart, taking my temperature. A slight fever means another night in the hospital. I have something big to think about after my conversation with Dr. Reese.

The second night, an older neighbor, whom we all know as Dixie, never using her given name of Sydney Kay Snow, visits. Dixie lives across the street from our pink house. She spends an hour or more giving me thrilling rides in a wheelchair through the two-story hospital. Dr. Reese converted that large, old late 1800s home into a hospital when he came to town. The old hospital sets a precedence in establishing Gunnison as a health care center for much of central and southern Utah, attracting good doctors, and patients from 100 miles away, and, eventually, a new built-to-order hospital.

The following afternoon Dr. Reese comes by to give me a final check before discharging me from the hospital. When he is finishes, I ask him to sit in a chair. I sit gingerly on his knee and put my hand up on his shoulder. "Thanks, Doc, for fixing me up," I say. I think he has tears in his eyes. It is two more weeks before he can take out the stitches. I am left with a scar on my upper lip that looks very much like a repair on a cleft pallet. I choose to not worry about it over much.

🖋

Like most kids growing up in the 50s, we have a lot of liberty. We ride bikes all over town. We meet up in friend's yards. We go exploring. There are abandoned houses to investigate. We have an anti-aircraft gun with some working parts installed in the city park—it rotates on its base and the aiming controls can still be cranked. We have a city pool that occupies our time in summer. Marsha, my most adventurous friend, teaches me how to wiggle in and out of the wind-sculpted sandstone hat holes east of the irrigation canal. She talks me into wriggling under the Indian Princess' rock, nearly room-size, marked with a few petroglyphs, located at the curve west of town just before the straightaway known as the farmer's freeway. It is a miracle that we don't encounter a rattlesnake. And Marsha is even smaller than I—it is a wonder I don't get stuck.

My horse friend, Jackie, teaches me the few horse skills I have. We ride horses at her house and at her grandparents'.

Jackie and her family—mom, dad, and brother—have a passion for the Mustang. Often called wild, they are more accu-
rately feral animals; they escaped domestication. We ride
many of the spry little horses all over her neighborhood and
all over her grandpa's farm. We have sleepovers in her dad's
sheep camp with the traditional rounded roof, painted the
traditional green color, sleeping under heavy, dust covered
camp quilts. We cook flapjacks on the wood-burning stove
with a fire we start. We are in elementary school.

My walking-home-from-elemetary-school friend is Meredith. Her Dad owns the bank. Her mother has a degree
in social work. They are elegant and lovely people who
welcome me into their home where Christmas trees are
splendorous and wrapped gifts a work of art. The family is
Presbyterian. Most Sundays they drive 40 miles to Mount
Pleasant to attend services adjacent to Wasatch Academy,
a private school, where Meredith and her older sister,
Marsha, will complete high school. Meredith is my best
social friend through elementary and junior high. We sleep
out in the summer and ice skate in the winter. She has a
pretty sorrel in her backyard. She and Jackie go to Western
Riding Club together.

At Grandpa Yardley's we play outside for hours, climbing on the chicken coops where we move stealthily so as
not to disturb the laying chickens. We sit on the roof and
tell stories. NaDene teaches us show tunes, including, "I'm
Getting Married in the Morning," and "A-Tisket-A-Tasket."
We share poems we memorize with Grandma. When cousins Carol and Arlene are on the roof with us, they teach us
to sing rounds of "Sippin' Cider Through a Straw" and "I
Love the Weiny Man." One summer, NaDene, Debra, and
I spend hours trying to understand horse language so we

can talk with Grandpa's beautiful sorrel gelding, Red Wing. We must have been younger than eight to have such trust in our magical thinking.

🪶

One afternoon in late summer, Grandpa calls us kids down off the sheds and in from the fields. He tells us we need to go into the house with Grandma for a while. I ask him why?

"I have to do something," he tells me.

"What do you have to do?"

He explains to me that he needs to slaughter the big black steer in the pasture south of the sheds. I come to understand that he has to kill the animal.

"I want to watch," I say.

"You want to watch? Are you sure?" I assure him, then he instructs me to stand near the sheds, which are about 200 feet away from the steer. And he tells me,

"If anything happens, you run for the house."

"What could happen?"

"If anything seems wrong, head for the house." The house is about equidistant from me as the steer.

Then I watch my beloved Grandpa walk calmly across the pasture toward the steer, casually holding a large knife at the side of his leg. When he is alongside the steer, he puts his left hand gently on the critter's shoulder and makes a quick move with the knife along the animal's neck. Then he just stands there calmly. Grandpa takes a step back as the animal weakens. After a few minutes, the steer buckles and sinks to the ground. Grandpa walks calmly back to where I am standing.

"We need to go in the house now."

"Why?"

"We need to leave the animal alone."

This was one of the most powerful experiences of my life. I do not see it as brutal. I merely see my gentle Grandpa do what needs to be done in terms of life and death. We leave for home before Grandpa even begins the arduous task of butchering. I am sure some of that beef ends up in our freezer.

≈

In the winter, we ice skate on Grandpa's irrigation pond. They drive a tractor out onto the ice to make sure it is safe for us. Most Christmas mornings we cousins—five of us from Momma, four from Uncle Howard, seven eventually from Uncle Tom—meet at Grandma and Grandpa Yardley's to share our favorite present, then we all walk a quarter mile up the hill to the pond to skate while the grown-ups prepare dinner. Grandma Yardley has a miracle table with multiple legs and multiple leaves that expands through both rooms of the living room and parlor. Nevertheless, there is still a kids' table for the youngest among us. Most Christmases someone gets ice skates. We have a dozen pair in various sizes hanging on nails in Momma's basement furnace room, white for the girls, black for the boys, figure skates, not hockey skates that are often traded back and forth between families. On rare occasions we cousins are joined by two more cousins from Aunt Beth, four from Uncle Birdell, and even rarer, two from Uncle Gill.

Up the gravel road, past canal hill, at Uncle Tom's farm, we ride horses. Cousin Carol is the chief rider. She saddles up Molly, describing her as "our old sway-back, corral-bockey mare." Molly is big, black, and beautiful, with white stockings and a white blaze. Carol cannot be older than eighth grade, probably seventh grade initially. That means NaDene is in fifth grade, Arlene and I are in fourth grade, and Debra is in second grade. We load up Molly with Carol in front and her sister Arlene behind in the seat of the black and white saddle. Debra, who is tiny, goes up front on Carol's lap. When NaDene is in town, she sits behind the saddle, and I get the rump with nothing to hold on to but the long tassels at the back of the saddle. And off we go—down the lane, over the San Pitch River, usually more of a creek or dry bed, and out to the south fields. We ride around the edge of the crops. Sometimes old Molly will gallop, which is easier than when she trots. It is hard to get in the rhythm of a trot with so many jouncing little girls clustered together.

Uncle Tom's farmyard is dominated by a big hay derrick constructed of massive pine logs, worn smooth and grey with age. The square base is two logs high, each corner supporting an angled upright, all four meeting at a point creating a fulcrum topped by an irregular log triangle with a rotating center pole anchored in the base that swings freely above the barn yard to facilitate loading and unloading of hay. On lucky days, our oldest cousin, Gene, gives us thrilling rides high above the barnyard. There is a rope suspended from the long arm of the top triangle that holds an old chair rung. All the knots are checked and then double checked. And we each clamber up onto Uncle Tom's tack shed with the corrugated metal roof. Little kids straddle the chair rung. Big kids hang on with their hands. The natural motion of the derrick creates a dipping and soaring ride over the roof of the calf barn, past the corrals for the dairy herd and then high again over the bull pen with the heavy,

heavy fence. We each get two rounds, landing in a short sprint that ends at the cushy end of the depleted haystack. Years later I ask Momma how she could calmly sit at Aunt Loa's kitchen table and drink coffee while we are flying above the barnyard. She replies, "The derrick we played on was bigger."

In later winters, Cousin Gene and then later brother Russ, contrive to give us all group sleigh rides, tying an old car hood behind a tractor. We pad the contraption with camp quilts then load on a dozen cousins and fly over the rolling land and through the sagebrush at the base of the shale foothills.

At Easter we take our baskets and scramble through those same shale hills up to the abandoned salt mine. Rolling eggs down a hill long and raggedy enough to render the colored eggs inedible if not completely destroyed. During one of our summer days at Uncle Tom's farm, his ranch hand, John Henry, comes down with hepatitis. All seventeen of us cousins who are on the farm that day are loaded into cars and driven into town to Dr. Stewart's office for a preventative injection of hemoglobulin, all of us in a line that snakes through his waiting room. Only our cousin Lee contracts hepatitis which eventually leads to a liver transplant as one of the first patients at the University of Pennsylvania. But first he works for years as a U.S. Forest Service smoke jumper and leader of pack-mule trips into the rugged mountains of Idaho and Montana. He and his son both become champion bow hunters. He teaches his son to pray over their kill in the manner of the Native Americans. After his liver transplant, we are at the Yardley Reunion at the Flats when he tells me, "Before I got sick, I thought I was 8 feet tall and could catch bullets with my teeth." We all thought so, too.

Grandpa Yardley dies when I am in seventh grade. We have his viewing and his funeral at our pink house. His death is very hard on Momma, who has now lost two good and important men in her life—my dad and her father, plus the runaway husband and a near divorce that ended with death. Before they close the casket, Grandma Yardley kisses her husband goodbye. Momma gasps, almost shrieking.

When I am in eighth grade, after Grandpa's death, Fred Mellor, my favorite bus driver also tells me, "Your Grandpa Yardley was the best Mormon I know."

I tell Fred, "My Grandpa Yardley was not a Mormon."

"I know," he says. I have now heard this report on my Grandpa from two highly reliable sources: I have more to think about.

Grandpa Yardley is the youngest of eleven children born to Joanna Isabelle and Thomas Russell Yardley. Their first child dies at 18 months and the tenth child dies in infancy. The parents of great-grandpa Thomas Russell are baptized in Manchester, England as part of the early Mormon missionary program. These parents along with 3-year-old Thomas Russell emigrate to join the Saints in their westward migration, arriving in Upper Alton, IL, in late spring 1851. The father of young Thomas dies of cholera in St. Louis in July 1851 and his mother dies of congestive chills in October 1851. Young Thomas, 3 years old and an orphan, is taken in by his uncle, William Marsden and family, who finally leave for Utah Territory on April 29, 1855, settling first in the Provo area. By 1861, Uncle William is called by Brigham Young to establish a cotton mill in Parowan, UT.

Uncle William, a very proud man, eventually owns a store in Parowan, enabling him to wear a stiff white shirt, a stove pipe hat, and swallow-tail coat, carrying a cane all the remaining days of his life. Life for great-grandpa Thomas was a bit more hard-scrabble. His biographer, my Grandpa Yardley's cousin Bertha, relates that Great-Grandpa Thomas tells of wrapping his feet in burlap to gather winter wood for the family and going barefoot in the summer. When Thomas is old enough, middle teens, he goes to work in the cotton mill as a carpenter where he excels, eventually outfitting himself with a full set of clothes and his first pair of grown-up shoes. When Thomas is barely 20 years old, he walks back to Oquawka, IL to assist his aunt, recently widowed, and her children in their migration to Parowan. Young Thomas, walking all the way out and all the way back, brings back lawn, flower, and vegetable seeds and watercress, which he plants in all of the springs and streams in the surrounding towns. When I notice watercress in the springs in Zion National Park, I speculate that the efforts of Thomas Russell Yardley helped it get a start.

By the time great-grandpa Thomas meets 17-year-old Joanna Isabelle, he is 22. He has moved out of his Uncle William's home and built a comfortable adobe home, with excellent carpentry, across the street. Handsome, square-jawed Thomas marries the young and beautiful Joanna Isabelle in late January 1871. Then they make a 2-week trip by horse and wagon to Salt Lake City in the dead of winter to be sealed for "time and all eternity" in the endowment house in early February 1871, returning after the month-long journey to their lovely and fully furnished home. Great-grandpa Thomas builds a grocery store, and then a liquor store, which he subsequently turns into a blacksmith shop, the first one in Parowan. He becomes a skillful blacksmith, creating another successful business. One day a group of U.S. Soldiers come through Parowan with a twelve span, or twenty-four mules. They must have them shod before continuing their journey to California the next day. Hearing that Thomas Yardley is an expert, they hire him to shoe all twenty-four mules in 24 hours. Mules are harder to work on than horses, so Thomas works the most strenuous day of his life. The soldiers praise his work and pay him 25 cents per shoe, a dollar per mule.

Nevertheless, Thomas wants more for his family, so he sells his house in town and homesteads 160 acres northwest of Parowan. He is the first in Parowan to homestead. The family lives in a two-room log cabin for two years, until he finishes another, larger adobe home with four rooms downstairs, and two large bedrooms upstairs, one for the boys and one for the girls. He also builds a most unusual barn, very large with an open span and no inner posts to support the broad roof. Grandpa Thomas can drive in a load of hay, unload it, and turn the team of horses around inside the barn. In the four corners are pens, three for animals and one for machinery. He makes all the tools he needs on the farm. In the winter everything is under one roof—feed, animals, and machinery.

Around the births of their fifth or sixth child, Thomas and Joanna Isabelle have a falling out with the local Mormon bishop and are excommunicated from the church. Research by my cousin indicates that they enjoy inviting several couples to their home for dancing in the large downstairs rooms. The local bishop finds this behavior far too light-minded, not focused enough on working out their eternal salvation. So, after ex-communication, Great-Grandpa and

Great-Grandma take their children to the Presbyterian
Church.

Grandpa Yardley, the last of the children, is just 3 months
old, when tragedy strikes—his mother dies. Margaret Mead
would likely note that the cause of death for Joanna was
exhaustion from childbirth. It was a hard season for the
Yardley family that winter of 1892. Great Grandpa Thomas
is in bed for forty-eight days with pneumonia. His son James
is recovering from a mashed foot. Three of the children have
measles. The older daughters, ages 17 and 15, care for the
family and begin to raise Grandpa Russell. They are the only
mothers he will ever know, but both older girls are married
by the time Russell is 4 years old. Great-Grandpa Thomas
Russell lasts another year and half on the farm, then sells his
large and successful farm, returns to Parowan, and buys back
his previous home, adding on additional rooms and runs
it as a hotel. Both the house in town and the house at the
farm are surrounded by lawns, flowers, and trees, including
orchards and mulberries. Great-Grandpa planted the first
trees around houses in Parowan. Neighbors come to him
for seeds of every kind. As the older daughters marry and
move away, Thomas Russell again becomes discontented.
He sells the hotel and moves to the Provo area, where my
grandpa Russell meets and marries my grandma Ethel May
Gill, who is no stranger to tragedy herself. Grandma Yardley is two weeks short of her 12th birthday when her father
dies at age 51. My great-Grandma, Mary Jane Bargery Gill,
his widow, beautiful even by today's standards and 10 years
his junior, is left with nine surviving children, ages 25 to 5.
All the children are still living at home. Two other of Mary
Jane's children died in infancy and another set of twins was
stillborn. I come from a line of hardy women.

For most of my growing up years, I regard my Grandma Yardley as a grouch. We are all a bit afraid of her. We spend a lot of time in warm weather at her home, mostly so we can spend a lot of time with our cousins, Howard's kids across the gravel road, Tom's kids up the canal hill, Beth's kids when they come from Salt Lake, and Birdell's kids who came rarely from even further north. Mostly Grandma chases us out of her house. One warm summer afternoon, we are running around in the yard. We take a break in the shade of the row of lilac bushes. One, or maybe all, of us decides we are hungry. We all tell my brother David, "Go ask Grandma Yardley for a sugar sandwich." We all know he is her favorite. We don't realize it as children, but likely this favored status comes from the years she cared for him when he was an infant and Momma was working in town at JC Penny's. I think we each get a half slice of Grandma's homemade white bread with real butter and a sprinkling of sugar, no oleo or lard for us. We are dairy farmers, but we mustn't spoil our dinner.

Grandma Yardley shows us a few outside tricks, teaching us how to fold a lilac leaf and make a whistle of sorts. One day, she makes Hollyhock dolls for all the little girl cousins. On another day, Grandma has Deb, Nick, and I at her house when seemingly out of the blue, she takes us by the hand out to the chicken coop where we gather several dozen large, white chicken feathers. Then Grandma sews strips of old white muslin sheets into bands with pockets for a dozen or so feathers, tied at the back, a custom fit Indian headdress of sorts for each of us.

When we are not outside, all of the action at Grandma's house happens in the kitchen. We sit at the grey Formica table on the green Naugahyde-covered chairs and talk to her while she scurries about. I am reading Good Housekeeping magazine one afternoon when she wonders aloud about dessert. I show her the photo of a chocolate pie. Miracle of miracles—we have chocolate pie for dessert, complete with Dream Whip, a real surprise considering that fresh milk and cream are available daily from the dairy barn.

Nearly every visit Grandma breaks into a performance there in her kitchen. She has dozens of readings memorized. My favorite is "When Mother Upped Her Hair," but a variation of "I Am My Own Grandpa" is also good. She often recites every stanza of The Cremation of Sam McGee, frequently by request. There in her kitchen, while we are doing dishes, she helps me memorize a poem.

> *I met a little elf-man once*
> *Down where the lilies blow.*
> *I asked him why he was so small*
> *And why he didn't grow.*
> *He slightly frowned and with his eye*
> *He looked me through and through.*
> *I'm quite as big for me said he*
> *As you are big for you.*
>
> —John Kendrick Bangs 1862–1922

And then she helps me understand it. Grandma Ethel is no slacker. She is a member of the Women's Literary Society and the Garden Club. The year she is Garden Club officer she writes a monthly gardening advice column, "Over the Garden Fence," for the Gunnison Valley News, the words of wisdom delivered through conversations among her imaginary friends: Sue, Vee, and Kay. I wonder if some of her interest in gardening comes from the 10 years that great-grandpa Thomas lives with them on the farm. Maybe it is genetic. My Momma was a gardener. I am a gardener. My kids are gardeners. Like my Grandpa Yardley, Grandma is always a reader, and she loves to write. Words were magic for my Grandma Yardley.

Most days at Grandma's we are rarely allowed into her bedroom at the southwest corner of the house. It has long, elegant windows on the east and on the south with lots of sunshine, the design of Great-Grandpa Thomas. One day I am in Grandma's bedroom alone with her. Debra and Nick may be napping. She tells me she has something to show me. She searches around on the top shelf of her wardrobe with the carved oak doors and pulls out a bundle wrapped in white muslin, tied with a torn strip of muslin. She unwraps the bundle on her bed. Inside the muslin wrapper is a mostly red cotton square which she tells me is from a bag of Turkey Red Wheat from the roller mill in Lehi. The mill commonly uses squares of bright colored cotton to hold a bag of wheat, giving the family that purchases the bag a kind of bonus. This particular square of fabric has a red print border with a light ivory oval printed in shades of grey, a drawing of a young man and young woman, and titled at the bottom, "The Catcher in the Rye." After she explains this origin, Grandma sings the song for me, more than once. Inside the red scarf are two smaller muslin bundles. Inside the smallest of the two is a carved wooden doll about the size of my hand. She has moveable shoulders, elbows, hips, and knees. Her cute little face is enameled with simple features. Her upped hair is part of the carving. Except for the painted face, the little doll is raw wood.

Grandma tells me that her mother is about 6 years old when, in 1860, her parents sell every possession to finance their immigration to America to join the westward migration of the Saints to Salt Lake City. According to Grandma Yardley, Great-Grandma Mary Jane is the only child on the boat. One of the sailors finds a block of wood and carves the little doll. Mary Jane carries that doll in her pocket as her family makes the long journey by ship from England to New York, then by train from New York to St. Louis, and then by wagon train, walking many long miles across the plains to our home in the mountains. The larger of the small bundles has another larger doll. Not porcelain—more likely stoneware or paper mâché—head, arms, and lower legs with a fabric body, her face and her proportions not nearly as beautiful as the little wooden marvel. I think Grandma Yardley shows me the tiny doll one other time, explaining to me, "I have not yet decided who should get this doll—you, as the oldest daughter of my oldest daughter, or your cousin Dorothy, as my oldest granddaughter."

When I am in my twenties and Grandma and Grandpa Yardley are long since gone. I ask Aunt Althea if she knows what became of the dolls in the muslin bundle. She does not recall ever seeing them. More than a decade later, Althea calls me during her summer visit from Phoenix to Utah, telling me she has something she thinks belongs to me. When I see her at Momma's pink house, she presents me with a little bundle wrapped in white muslin, tied with a torn muslin strip. Inside is the red, ivory, and gray cotton square and the two little bundles of dolls. I had asked Althea about a doll "the size of my hand," so 6 inches or so. The little doll before me is not even 4 inches tall. I realize how small my child-size hand must have been. I ask Althea,

"What about my cousin Dorothy?" Al tells me, "You are the only person who ever asked about the dolls. I did not even know about them. Mother wanted them to go to you." In the end, we agree that Momma will keep the dolls, and then they will go to me when she dies, but first I hand-stitch a grey silk dress, with an open-front ivory and grey stripe pinafore for the wood doll and a red cotton pin-dot dress for the little stoneware doll. Then I have them all framed and shadow-boxed for Momma for her Christmas present. Included in the project is a fringed handkerchief, with grey stripes around the edges and a little cotton pincushion that both daughters recognize as their mother's.

Another decade later, Mom and Aunt Beth are cleaning out the attic at Grandma and Grandpa's house recently purchased by Cousin Russell and his wife Cindy. In a beautiful old trunk, they find another doll. This one about 10 inches tall, fine porcelain face, arms, and legs with a kidskin body. Her eyes no longer open and close and her blonde hair has been loved off. They also give this doll to me. I take her to Melba, the mother of Peggy, my friend since childhood. Melba repairs the eye mechanism, makes her a new blond wig, and freshens up the simple ivory muslin dress, sewing a small piece of tatting found in the bundle around the waist as a peplum. Melba tells me that this lovely porcelain doll with the open smile and exposed teeth is likely valuable. For the next year Debra bitches at me so much about giving at least one of the dolls to David—I check, he does not want any—that I give the lovely porcelain doll to her. At least she puts it under glass and keeps it on the dresser in her bedroom

🍂

My cousin NaDene's daughter, Gaidry—short for Galadriel—tells me, "Aunt LaRue scared the bejeebers out of me
when I was little." For much of my life I, too, am more than
a little afraid of my Momma. She has all the power. The fear
seems to resolve as I deal with my childhood issues. Both
women, my mother and my grandmother, are formidable.
In French we say "for-me-dahbl." *These women are formidable in their capabilities. Cettes femmes sont formidable.*

My Grandma Yardley bakes bread every week, mixing
the sponge and letting the dough rise in a round aluminum wash pan. She balances the pan on her kitchen stool
when she kneads the bread, the pan thumping and spin-
ning as she sings or recites, the old pan severely dented
from the years of use. My Momma bakes bread every week,
first using an aluminum wash pan, like Grandma, and later
a bread maker. When Grandma comes to live at the pink
house, she frequently gets after us for eating our mother
out of house and home. Every day after school we have
two or three thick cut slices with real butter and Momma's
homemade strawberry jam. Hiding outside with my third
slice, Grandma comes around the corner of the house and
catches me red-handed, if you will.

When my children are growing, I grind wheat and bake
five loaves of molasses whole-wheat bread every week. They
like it with homemade strawberry jam. We have a pretty
tender/funny video of my oldest daughter, age 16, pitching
a fit, complete with tears, over a call from the bishop of our
ward asking her to give a 5-minute talk to the congregation
on Mother's Day, some two weeks hence. In spite of the fit,
she delivers a well-crafted speech of her own making that

begins, "Have you ever come home from school hoping for home-made bread with strawberry jam and instead you find a witch in your kitchen?" Her premise is that even mothers need care and feeding—one of the best Mother's Day talks ever, in my humble opinion.

I keep Grandma's and Momma's dented aluminum wash pans on the counter in my laundry room.

Of the move from Provo to Christianburg, my Grandpa Yardley writes, "it took three trips with the team to move all of our stuff down from Provo, for by that time we owned a cow, three calves, about 50 chickens, and three horses. By the way, the old mare we called Kit [the same horse that buckles in the road when Momma slips off her back] is one we brought from Parowan before I was married. The last trip I made to Provo with the team, I had just five dollars, and at that time I didn't know where any more was coming from."

Great-Grandpa Thomas lives on the farm with Grandma and Grandpa Yardley for eleven years, helping them build the adobe home that still stands today, constructing outbuildings, and establishing sheep ranching, dairy farming, and beekeeping. Great-Grandpa Thomas must have touched the cottonwood sapling fenceposts that sprang to life on the Christianburg farm. He is the first person to make my Momma smile. Momma is just three-and-a-half-months old when he dies, refusing to have his diabetic leg amputated. Never remarrying, he remains faithful to beautiful Joanna Isabell for 28 years. Stubborn to the end.

Grandpa Yardley's cousin, Bertha, writes of Great-Grandpa Yardley, "[He] was a wonderful man. He was

Jack-of-all-trades and MASTER OF THEM ALL. I don't know of anything he couldn't do that he tried. His trades were: Farmer, blacksmith, carpenter, mechanic, brick layer, stock raiser. He introduced the first pure bred cattle into this county. As a boy he helped to build many homes in Parowan. He was one of the men to help guard against the Indians in Parowan. He had many colonies of bees. He started the first fruit trees to this county. Grandpa made all his tools he used on the farm, his plows, etc., and built his own wagons and a buggy."

In his own autobiography, my beloved Grandpa Yardley has a less exultant view of his father, mentioning that, "One way or another, Father went broke in the sheep business . . . When [he] went broke in the sheep business, he left a $600.00 debt, which I managed to pay off in two years by working for a dollar a day, plus my room and board." This kind of work ethic helped my Grandpa Yardley pay off the Christianburg farm in twelve years, adding an additional 318 acres. Grandpa Yardley also purchases another sixty-eight acres just before the Great Depression, admitting, "A year or so later I found I could not keep up with the payments of the sixty-eight-acre farm, so I let it go back." Momma tells me about this episode when I ask her about Grandpa Yardley "being the best Mormon I know," noting that Grandpa Yardley had bought the sixty-eight acres on a handshake, asking the seller if he wanted to go to the bank to sign a note. The seller tells Grandpa Yardley that with him, the handshake is sufficient. Momma also tells me that Grandpa Yardley almost never loses his temper and seldom cusses, and then only at a stubborn cow.

In his own words, Grandpa Yardley reveals a bit about how he established such a good reputation. He writes, "sometime before we paid off that original mortgage, I and about a dozen other farmers purchased an iron-wheeled tractor and a threshing machine. I was elected to operate the thresher as well as to be secretary and treasurer. Well, I operated the thresher for about 15 years. It was a small machine, but we used it to thresh as much as 60,000 bushels of grain in one season—made good wages for those days, about $10 for 12 hours of work. We also made a good dividend on our investment. I used to start work at 6:00 am and work until 6:00 pm. Then after I got home at night and before I left in the morning, I had anywhere from two to ten cows to milk by hand, a few pigs, sheep, and horses to care for. Also, I had some irrigating to do in order to have the ground ready for fall plowing."

Grandpa Yardley says of his life in Christianburg, "I have done a lot of hard work on the farm and most of the time I have enjoyed it. We have raised a family of seven children and sent them through high school. Those that have had college schooling have done so on their own. We have always tried to help them help themselves. We are very proud of our family. I think their mother has done a very fine job, too. She lived in the city most of the time until we were married. Not long after we married, we moved out on this farm. Even though she didn't know much about farming, she did a lot of hard work and seldom if ever complained. For years she did all of the washing on the old-fashioned washboard and carried water from the ditch, did all the heating and cooking with wood, and all of the ironing with an old-style flat-iron."

My Grandpa was a worker and an adventurer his entire life. He leaves formal education before the end of fifth grade, in some ways driven out by the bullying of the Mormon boys because he is not Mormon. Also, winter was coming, and he had no shoes. Grandpa reads books and newspapers every day of his life, never ceasing to learn. Grandma and Grandpa travel by boat to Hawaii twice during the 50s, as well as two sea excursions to Alaska. One of Grandpa's most memorable encounters was with an Inuit elder. And that is some of the story of how my Grandpa Yardley lives to the be "the best Mormon I know." I guess Momma and I thought all men would ever be thus.

☞

In Gunnison all secondary students, grades seven through twelve, use the same building. By eighth grade, I am class reporter. Roland and Ira, two junior boys who work with Momma at the Chevy dealership tease me unmercifully, dragging me into the boy's bathroom, threatening to hang me up on a coat hook, and generalized hallway torment. Their teasing is good natured. They make me feel cool. In ninth grade, I am junior high student body president. I choose to run for president because at least one of my friends is running for each of the other elected offices. My best friend from junior high, Tim, is student body president the year ahead of me. My cousin, MaryAnn, who is six years my senior, was the first female student body president of the senior high, so we have a family tradition. Bruce, the boy I run against, becomes my boyfriend for the next year and a half. He is tall, athletic, and rides his Honda 150 without a shirt, and illegally. The principal of the junior high, Payton H. Alexander, who is also the head coach, scares the beejeebers out of me, but we build a trusting relationship. Pate, as we call him, is a feminist, the father of an only daughter and the husband of a lovely and formidable woman. He lets us officers do lots of activities as long as they are well-planned and well-organized. By the end of the year, I can see affection in his eyes. And, by the end of the school year, I am okay with consulting him in his office without Vickie, who serves with me as secretary and wingman.

In tenth grade, when Momma precipitously marries Daddy Arlo, I spend part of the year in New Mexico and come away with another set of skills. By the time I return, Bruce, my boyfriend from ninth grade has switched to my cousin, Arlene. It is just as well. They eventually marry and are together to this day. In the spring of this sophomore year, I make a serious social error by going to the Junior Prom with the junior class stud—the guy who notches his boot heel for each of his sexual conquests. My mother warns me of my folly. I assure her that I know what I am doing. The boy's mother, whom we call Stella Honey because she calls everyone Honey, stops me on the street to tell me how glad she is that her son is taking "a nice girl" to the biggest dance of our high school years. At the post-Prom party, we are at a house with no adults present. My date, the stud, asks me if I am going to the bedroom with him. I tell him no. He goes to the beverage table, chugs half a jug of beer and passes out, or fakes passing out. An older guy, who is out of high school and yet lingers at the party, who has been accused of rape by a girl not at the party, offers me a ride home. I am trying to figure out how to avoid this trap, when Theldon, who eventually becomes my brother-in law, intervenes and gives me a ride home. Back at school on Monday, it becomes obvious to me that my date tells a different story. During lunchtime in the gym, which doubles as a cafeteria after the trays are cleared, we have 20 minutes or so for dancing. During that Monday lunch, every bad boy in school asks me to dance, each of them holding me in embarrassingly tight embraces. The worst of the bunch bends me over backward so far that I think I will fall and drag him over on top of me. Before the week is out, I realize that the only way to save myself is to give up dating for a long time. I do not date any town boys for more than a year. One of my guy friends actually writes in my yearbook, "Dawn, I have heard terrible things about you this year, but you have a pretty good head on your shoulders." There are several other scrawling epithets reading, "Stay a virgin" scattered through the autograph pages. Because of my own sexual abuse, I have all of the guilt and none of the deed.

The problem persists into the summer. I am at the pool on my own, that is with no friends and no brother or sister. I am at the deep end doing casual crosswise laps. It is nearly closing time, so the pool is deserted except for me and the assistant lifeguard who jumps in way too close to me. As I am treading water, he asks me for a date—he is a confederate of the bad boys—three years older than I. When I tell him no, he dunks me under water. He asks again. No again. He dunks me again. This continues for another ten rounds. I am having such a hard time catching my breath, I start to think he might drown me. I am not sure why he eventually stops. I do not go to the pool on my own again that summer.

Just before school starts for my junior year, I get a phone call from Don Buchanan, the owner/manager of the Gunnison Rexall Drug. He wants me to come to work this afternoon at four o'clock. I tell him I will be there, but I am confused. I call Momma at work.

"Momma, I just had a call from Don Buchanan. He wants me to come to work this afternoon. Are you okay with that?"

"Oh, Dawn. I mentioned to him a couple of times over the summer that you would sure like to work at the drug store. I forgot to tell you." She laughs. "Of course, you can go."

The deal is that working at the drug store is the most coveted job for high school girls in town. My friend Vickie has been telling me for half a year how she has been working with one of the older cheerleaders to get her recommendation for one of the two positions they hire every other year. But, I get to work at the drugstore. We have a 15-foot-long stainless-steel soda fountain. I make everything from hand-packed cones to ice cream sodas to fresh-lime drinks in the summer, and iron-port anytime. I brew and serve coffee to Dr. Reese and Frank the hospital administrator, and wash dishes while they talk and smoke cigars. In addition, I help at the pharmacy, sometimes counting out pills, and provide customer assistance throughout the store. Norma, who is married to Clyde, one of my best friends, says that her mother, Margery, always says, "why can't you be like Dawn? She is always nice to me when I want to buy red lipstick, not pink." Momma gets my first formal job for me.

Junior year I am program co-chair—everything but the prom—for my class. Vickie, the Prom co-chair, and I sell our ideas for theme and decorations to the class—La Mer, Beyond the Sea, with a Japanese motif, including a 20-foot-tall Buddha. My junior year, I date a boy from a town 15 miles away, the younger brother of Chiyo, my 4-H teacher. When we were in eighth grade and on our way back to Gunnison from a 4-H activity at Snow College, we convince Chiyo to stop at her mother's house and introduce us to her younger brother whom we have all heard about. For me that meeting on the front porch is a magic moment, the closest I come to love at first sight. He is tall, dark, handsome, funny, smart, and poor. His father, a teacher, dies when he is 5, so we share that bond. He rides his bicycle the 15 miles to Gunnison weekly to see me. One night he runs into a parked car, so injured he nearly dies. He writes me romantic letters. When he goes to Boy's State, he leaves me with his stereo system for the week. He plans our entire life. I will grow out my hair—I have a Sassoon cut—he will go on his mission. We will go to school. We will marry. The plan fills me with panic. I break up with him the night we attend his Junior Prom. I forget to buy him a boutonniere for the dance.

During my junior year, I am friends with many Senior boys. I tell them dirty jokes and make them laugh. In one of the last issues of the school newspaper for that year, Eric and Curtis, both Senior boys, write a short article recognizing their favorite junior girls: Best Figure—Vickie Faatz; Best Clothes—Peggy Lund; Best Personality—Dawn Stevenson; Best All-around—Dawn Stevenson. This is one of the high points of high school for me. I never do get nominated for queen of anything, a result, no doubt, of my failure as a virgin, and also likely the scar on my lip, plus a gold capped front tooth—well half-gold, which I obtained during a run-in with the merry-go-round in elementary school. At Washington Elementary, only three of us in my class dared to get in the middle of the merry-go-round and push. All of us, Steve, Paul, and I lose our footing, fall, and fracture a front tooth, not all on the same day, but within weeks of each other. Yes, I always do feel a bit like Madame Ruth— you know, "the Gypsy with the gold-capped tooth."

The summer between junior and senior year I drive my mom's car a lot—a '63 gold Chevy Impala with a great big engine. Mom works full-time as a bookkeeper at the Chevy dealer, so she gets this car used from a supervisor in the Highway Patrol. The car is recognized by other Highway Patrolmen. It gets her out of at least one speeding ticket. One night, late, I take that car and five boys—juniors and seniors—out on the Farmer's Freeway, a 6-mile straight-away west of town. I drive 120 miles per hour. The boys love it. They want to do it again.

"Uh, no," I say.

"Let us drive it, then," they say.

"Uh, no." I realize at that speed; one wrong move and we are all history.

Of course, Deb and I take Driver's Ed, but, before Driver's Ed, when Deb and I are just 15 and 13-and-a-half, we teach ourselves to drive our brother Russ's '55 Ford while he is at work on our uncle's farm. Straight-H shift on the column, we master the clutch, driving forward to the back of our property, a city-size lot, turning left to travel across the back of the lot that faces Woodrow Beck's alfalfa field, and then putting it in reverse to do it all over again. When we are confident in our shifting and steering skills, we take our little brother Nick and head out on the graveled back roads to get raw milk at the dairy about 5 miles away. These roads cross culverts for many irrigation ditches. We quickly learn which culvert bumps can get us airborne and how fast we have to go to get air. In our minds, we make up for abusing the '55 Ford by washing it whenever Russ demands. Once Mom starts working for car dealers, she always has cool cars, a cute dark red and white Buick, a '58 Chevy Impala coupe—pearl white, the '63 gold Impala, and then a '66 and a half Chevy Caprice in Royal Plum. When Momma and Daddy Arlo buy the Caprice, they put in an extra $100, to buy Deb and I a red and white '59 Rambler

Metropolitan. We learn to do donuts in the snow in that car. It has guillotine windows that drop unexpectedly, and the trunk is latched with bailing wire. So much fun.

My senior year, I am president of the French Club—there are only five of us in second year French—and President of the drill team. I make or oversee the making of the drill team uniforms. The vests, which I sew, are a hit; the pleated skirts are a disaster. The budget was too tight, and I tried to do too much. I should have consulted more with Momma, who actually knew how to make a pleated skirt. Realistically, we should have bought the skirts. Sewing is easy for me, and I love it. By the time I finish high school I have made most of my school clothes, made several dresses for Momma, made five bridesmaid dresses for one cousin, made three bridesmaid dresses for another cousin, and won the district Make-It-With-Wool contest with a white wool dress coat, accessorized with a white fur hat, very Jackie Kennedy. I tell myself it is my only talent. I am not a cheerleader. I do not sing, and I am not a trained dancer. I am in a one-act play and in the American Legion Oratory Contest. I place at the district level in both competitions. I am named the Betty Crocker Homemaker of Tomorrow for my school. That honor comes from taking a national test that is some measure of social health and psychological functioning. I know I think differently than most of the girls my age, but I thought I was the one who was off.

The summer before my senior year I start dating a 22-year-old. I will be 17 in October. I cannot imagine what my mother is thinking. I guess she is thinking he is my brother's best friend and a returned LDS missionary. I cannot imagine what he is thinking. I guess he is thinking he will always have a young and malleable girl on his hands. I am thinking he is a really good-looking college boy, a student at BYU. I remember the first time I see Ernie. I am on the upper landing of the entrance to the Gunnison church. He has just returned from his mission, handsome as all get out in his grey herringbone sport coat, blue button-down shirt, and stripe tie. I catch my breath when he walks through the front door and step back into the shadows. I do not want him to see me; I am not sure why. I always wonder if that was an omen. In the spring of my senior year, I see my school counselor about signing my application for BYU. He tells me that people from my family are better off at Snow College, meaning that I am not the type of girl who belongs at BYU. He also tells most of my brothers not to bother going to college; they just won't make it. Half of them ignore him and make it anyway. I tell him I am going to BYU because that is where my boyfriend is.

Before my first year at BYU ends, before we are engaged in April, Ernie and I are deeply involved in heavy petting, behavior that could result in our expulsion from the strict religious institution. I would have gone all the way. Ernie would not. We are one more cheating couple at BYU, hoping against hope that we will not be caught and released. Fish on a hook is an appropriate image.

The following summer, in preparation for our marriage in the Manti LDS temple, we have separate interviews with our home bishop. Ernie confesses our indiscretion and gets his temple recommend. I do not confess, due in no small part to the way this bishop looks at me in my bikini at the Gunnison pool. I am sure not wanting to talk about the childhood abuse plays a part in my not confessing. I also get my temple recommend. It is not the last time I will be a cheat.

We have our wedding reception in the backyard of Momma's pink house with two apple trees in the background.

Close by is Daddy Arlo's shanty, a repurposed shed of aged wood that he moves intact from Grandpa Yardley's farm to be used for backyard garden storge. Of course, I sew my wedding dress, silk organza that I custom tucked into a one-of-a-kind fabric. I also sew the six bridesmaid dresses in six different pastels of silk dupioni, and dresses for both mothers. It is a labor of love.

~

Not unexpectedly, the unresolved grief over the death of my father and the sexual abuse takes a toll. The first indicator comes when Ernie and I are living in L.A. He attends dental school at UCLA, and I work at UCLA, first at the student placement center and later in student loan collections. One evening, on the way back to married student housing, we are rear-ended on Wilshire Boulevard near the Federal Building. I get whiplash. My injury is moderate but will plague me the rest of my life. The orthopedist at UCLA suggests that there may be a psychological element to my lingering headaches, suggesting that I take some time off work.

"We cannot afford my quitting work."

"Perhaps your parents can help?" he wonders.

"Are you kidding? They have eight kids at home. They are glad to have one out of the way." I respond.

I have a mad crush on the Orthopedist. He drives a Jaguar XKE. Thank God, I never throw myself at him. I do think about it.

4

WOODY AND ME

PART II

By the time I am twenty-six and a half I have four children. The oldest is six and half. I am so angry at Ernie that I am torn between "cutting out his black heart with a knife" and "torching the absolute mess on his desk." These are the words I use in my head—too many romance novels. I am suicidal, post-partem depression a likely unrecognized factor. One day, the man who lives across the street blows his brains out with a shotgun. My older brother, Dave, works with the victim on the dairy farm. The suicide shakes Dave, a Vietnam vet, to his core. Everyone is shocked. They say, "I cannot imagine what he was thinking." I can imagine. I want to run away someplace and sleep. I will come home when I am lonely. I tell Ernie I am crazy. He tells me, "If you think you are crazy, then you aren't." I am, in fact, crazy.

I convince Ernie to try counseling. On Deb's recommendation we find a counselor in Utah County. We stay overnight in Provo the night before our first appointment. When we are entering a restaurant for dinner, I see Mike, a student from Snow College, who I also dated surreptitiously while I dated Ernie back in those college days. I pretend not to recognize him. I am afraid that I will upset Ernie and he will not go to counseling.

Henry, the counselor, is the older brother of one of my teachers from high school. We have plenty to talk about. Mostly we work on my problems. I have plenty. One of my assignments is to take one day off every week. I am to get out of town. Go do something. Go see someone. This is a much more effective strategy than me calling Ernie at the dental office, telling him I cannot take one more minute trapped in an inadequate house with four young children, leaving my 7-year-old daughter alone with her siblings before he drives into the driveway. Vivienne in Divine Secrets of the Ya-Ya Sisterhood comes to mind. Like Vivienne, I keep a thread of violence running through my family. I spank my kids with an open hand on the bum. When I cannot catch them, I throw a shoe—my aim is very bad; I clip the thermostat right off the wall in the central hallway. Several times, I do in fact hit my kids with a belt. I have also beaten them with a pillow. I do not use drugs and alcohol, but I do run away. Not for days, but for hours. In the new coping strategy, I work out babysitting with friends and family. During the summer I get a junior high student to stay with the kids. The day off a week literally saves my life. Ernie expects me to come home by dark. I usually stay in Provo until the stores close at nine. I am always home by midnight. My children grow up with abandonment issues. Ernie also feels abandoned.

One of our older babysitters is Afton, a high school girl with a huge crush on my younger brother, Nick, who is considerably older than she. One night I am driving Afton home when she tells me that I have spirits in my house. She says she does not want to scare me, assuring me it is a friendly spirit. She tells me the spirits of her grandparents are at her house and watch over her. Afton is much younger than her siblings and has grown up almost an only child.

Later that same night I am lying in bed thinking about what Afton said, wondering if it could be true. I try to clear my mind to see if I sense anything. I think I feel the presence of my dad in the L-shaped space in our bedroom that is around the corner from the king-size bed I share with Ernie and usually one or more children—that's why we have king-size bed, right? I find the potential presence of my dad comforting. After this, I feel his presence occasionally. One afternoon, I am standing in the kitchen when I am about to lose it and start the kind of yelling at my kids that will end with me driving away. Suddenly, I become strongly aware that my father is present. I know exactly where he is standing. He says to me, not in words I can hear, but clearly in my mind, "Dawn you can do this." It makes a difference for me.

I try talking to Henry about the sexual abuse. He sends Ernie out of the room and asks me if I enjoyed it? I am extremely uncomfortable with the course of this conversation and feel completely misunderstood. I will need to find someone else to help with this issue. Nevertheless, Henry helps me learn how to talk about my feelings, even recognize them and feel them rather than intellectualize them. I learn the importance of self-care. I take time to exercise and play. I get more stable. I am happier. Ernie and I build a new house. Life is better. I become calmer and more confident.

🖋

The summer before I turn 30, I call Momma to tell her I want to start doing my father's genealogy. She says I will have to come see her; she has something important she must tell me. We live in the same town, going to her house for a special chat is puzzling. When we meet, she tells me that after my father dies, she has a hard time getting his Social Security. She shows me an array of documents: two Social Security cards with two different numbers, two different names, and two different signatures, a California commercial driver's license and two small notebooks. The Social Security Administration tells her that the man she knew as Don Stevenson was born Woodrow Wilson Dean. The California driver's license for Woodrow says he was born in Birmingham, AL. Of the two small notebooks, one has names and addresses, about twenty pages torn out, another has what looks like a mileage log between distant cities, some Bible references and scriptures, and notes about religious issues. Momma tells me that my father was married before he marries her. He has two daughters with his first wife. Somewhere in California I have two half-sisters. The man I come to call Woody tells her that he has not seen his children in years, that he is divorced and that he doesn't pay child support He claims that he leaves his wife a duplex in Long Beach to help with the child support. Woody tells Momma he was in the U.S. Coast Guard during World War II. Momma assumes he changes his name over the child support. She feels like my dad's secret identity, undiscovered by her until his death, is further proof of how dumb she is. She feels so embarrassed.

I write a letter to the SSA to confirm the Don/Woody identity issue. Six months go by. I get no response. I call and talk with a regional senior administrator who tells me he will be glad to help me try to recover records for my father. Months later, he writes to tell me that Woody's records have been destroyed due to age. He confirms the names of his parents: Bertha M. Snyder and Harry N. Dean. I call Union Electric Company in St. Joseph, MO, who issues Woody his first SS card, explaining my efforts to find information on my father's birth family. The woman says she will be happy to help. She writes back saying that their legal counsel says there are privacy issues and no information will be forthcoming. I write to U.S. Military Records. They tell me Woody's records would have been stored in the part of the St. Louis facility that was destroyed by fire. I write to Alabama for his birth certificate. Twice. They find nothing. I write letters to all of the names with addresses in his notebook. Two letters are returned, undeliverable. Two letters are not returned, but there are no replies. I joke with family and friends that my father was a Mafia hit man who left no trail.

I think Ernie and I are going to make it. We have another baby. By the time CC is one and a half, I have contacted a divorce attorney. I am ready to file papers. I ride my 10-speed to my Momma's house to make the phone calls to the attorney because Ernie has a toggle on his phone at the office that lets him switch from his office line to our home phone. He listens to my phone conversations all the time. I talk to my LDS bishop. I tell him I will take some time to think about the divorce. I talk to Henry. He tells me that if I ask for half a loaf, as I am planning to do, I will end up with crumbs. When I describe to Henry how I felt about seeing my Manti boyfriend at a recent wedding reception, Henry asks me, "Do you know how vulnerable you are to an affair? All someone has to do is speak kindly to you and touch you on the shoulder." I tell him, "I do not need that kind of trouble. My life is complicated enough already."

Instead, I use the Mormon approach of fasting and praying to get a confirmation about leaving. One evening, Ernie
hauls me over to Dr. Stewart's office to talk about this folly
of a divorce. Dr. Stewart is our stake president, so a local
authority in Mormon culture. With the exception of Dr.
Reese caring for me after the bicycle accident, Dr. Stewart
has been my physician since elementary school. He cares for
my broken collar bone, twice, takes out my tonsils, gives me
my first gynecological check, delivers my last three babies,
and gives me all of my gynecological checks up to the point
when I decide to get an IUD, then I drive to Provo to see an
Ob/Gyn who will not give me a bad time about birth control. Ernie's mom, who works as a CNA at the hospital, tells
me how dangerous IUDs are. In my mind I tell her, "You
have no idea how dangerous another pregnancy is." I tell Dr.
Stewart that Ernie breathes his nitrous oxide for an hour or
more every day, that codeine is his drug of choice and that he
often writes prescriptions in my name or in his grandmother's name until I scream at him to "leave me out of your drug
schemes." He tells Ernie to cut it out, then he literally shakes
a bony finger at me telling me to cut it out with the divorce,
too. He admonishes both of us to read our scriptures and
pray, the magic Mormon cure for every problem.

In retrospect, I see Ernie as an early adopter in the
opioid crisis. Drug salesmen come by and leave hundreds
of samples of Tylenol with codeine. I am not sure how many
of these samples make it into the hands of his patients. He
writes prescriptions for Percodan and Percocet. In my more
judgmental moments I say to myself, "Ernie had every gift,
and he pissed it all away." Perhaps it is kinder to say that
"Ernie had every gift and let it all slip through his fingers."
Even now I work to find empathy for the illness that is the

reality of opioid abuse rather than condemning it as a character flaw.

When Ernie and I see Henry the counselor, Henry tells me that mostly Ernie has a bad day every day and that his first impulse is to make sure I have a bad day too. The Austrian therapist that my oldest daughter, Luna, and I see in California tells me the two of us give him a similar picture of Ernie; on a day-to-day basis he is kind of hard to live with and then every-once in a while he is a real asshole. Herbert observes that I tend to wait until I am at a breaking point and then I pitch an emotional fit leading Ernie to concede more than he is willing. Herbert gives me tips on how to interact more effectively. Years earlier, Ernie tells one of his assistants that he did everything his parents wanted him to do. He was a good student. He served an LDS mission. He finished college and went to dental school. He married and had children. And still he was not happy, and I knew it.

Ernie, though most often grumpy, can be lots of fun for our kids. If one of them wakes early, he sneaks off with them to the Quick Stop to share half a Hostess Cherry Pie—he calls it a fast one. Ernie also likes to make big meals for church groups and fundraisers, most often south Texas tostadas—crisp flat tortilla with refried beans, chili meat, cheese, and finely shredded cabbage. So delicious. When Ernie is the leader for the Explorer Scouts, he works with them on fundraisers to bring fireworks back to Gunnison for the Fourth of July. For more than a decade he oversees the annual display until the Lions and the volunteer fire departments take over the project.

We take our children on regular family vacations driving in our big station wagon and then in the Ford van to

Ernie's two favorite destinations: Southern California and South Texas. We spend days at the ocean in Redondo Beach between Avenue I and J and on the shores of Padre Island. We are all a bit happier on those long drives and under the warm sun.

After my first serious consideration of divorce, I decide to stay. I realize that I am not prepared to be the single mother of five young children. Ernie and I need to do some work. We go back for semimonthly sessions with Henry. While I am sorting out plans, I run into my sister, Penny, on Main Street in Gunnison. Penny is estranged from the family because she has accused Arlo of sexually abusing her. None of my siblings believe her. Momma does not believe her. I believe her. For one thing it explains some of what happened during that big Christmas fight. It also explains why Penny blames herself for her mother's suicide. We talk for more than an hour standing on the sidewalk on Main Street as she shares her story with me. The more detail she gives, the more I believe she is telling the truth. Because of my own abuse, I understand why she remembers what she remembers and why she describes things as she does. I feel so badly for her and for the stepfather I have loved.

Within days I find myself breaking into tears at odd moments—in the bathtub, in the car. At our next appointment with Henry, I tell him about the conversation with Penny. He asks me how I feel about it. I tell him I feel like someone has died. He says, "Talk to me more about that." I say, "I feel as if the only father I have ever known has died." And then I really cry. Henry explains to me and to Ernie that I need to mourn the death of my father and the heartbreak of the situation with my stepfather. Ernie says he does not want this to ruin a relationship with Arlo. Henry explains that it does not have to ruin it, but it has to be taken into consideration. He tells me:

"Go home. Take the time to cry. Get rid of your church assignments, at least for a while. I want you to let yourself sit, a lot. Get a rocking chair." I have five children; I have a rocking chair.

I follow his advice. I am surprised by how resistant others are to let me say no. I am firm in my resolve. I let myself feel all the sadness in me. I explain to my children, who are old enough to notice, that I am finally letting go of the sadness I have felt about the death of my father. I sit in my rocking chair and cry. I sit out on the deck under the stars and cry. I lie in my bed and cry. I wake in the night with tears running out of the corners of my eyes and onto my pillow. I think I may be a bottomless pit of tears. Late one night I say to the stars, "this is more grief than I can bear." The heavens reply back, "Then let it go." I do. I feel the angels groan. The overt grief lasts about 6 weeks.

I talk with my sister Penny about my own abuse. She has a counselor who has been very helpful for her. I decide to see her counselor whom I will come to know as Lankford. I like him a lot. He works with many victims of sexual abuse. On my first visit, I am skeptical about the use and usefulness of hypnosis. He does a simple demonstration by teaching me deep breathing and an eye roll, then he tells me he is going to tie a helium balloon to my wrist. I can feel the string and the gentle tug of the balloon lifting my arm. Then he tells me to go to a favorite safe or peaceful place. I go immediately to Grandpa Yardley's big cottonwood tree. I see the sun filtering through the leaves. I smell the warm, soft earthiness of the tree. When he brings me out, I am sure that the color of the green is too dark. After our session, I drive the 80 miles home and then go the extra 6 miles to Grandpa's farmhouse, where my cousin Russell and his wife Cindy now live. The green of the cottonwood is exactly right.

I talk with Ernie, and we decide to switch counselors. I call Henry to tell him we are switching counselors. He insists that I come to talk with him because he thinks Lankford is trying to poach clients. I decide I can see him in person; I figure it will be good for me to stand up to an authority figure. During our interview I remind Henry of his inept handling of my first attempt to talk about my sexual abuse. I assure him that I am switching to a counselor with much more experience in dealing with sexual abuse.

Lankford helps me understand that looking at all the elements of the sexual abuse is like cleaning out a wound. If the wound is bandaged without cleaning, it will only continue to fester. Lankford teaches me self-hypnosis so that I can get to deep relaxation, helping me access what I describe to myself as the "deep pockets of calm" that I carry inside. I do a lot of bibliotherapy, starting with John Powell's Why Am I Afraid to Tell You Who I Am? I read to Lankford a passage about being tossed to and fro on an ocean of emotions. He tells me, "You have been the tiniest little tugboat on that ocean. We will make you into an ocean liner." I attend weekly sessions on my own for several months. I have a difficult time calendaring the events of my abuse.

I tell Lankford, "It is as if they took place in a different house from where I live."

He tells me, "It is the ability of your mind to make that separation that has kept you sane."

Using various techniques, we build a calendar of sorts, connecting the abuse to my real life. I realize that the abuse started when I was 9 and ended about 14. When we have

spent many months looking at the events and the consequences, Lankford tells me, "You can keep these movies in
your head, if you want, but it will be easier on you if you
wrap them up and put them on a shelf somewhere. You can
take them out to look at them when you need to, but don't
look too often. You can put this behind you."

Ernie joins me for couples counseling twice per month.
Similar to our time with Henry, Ernie is content to attend
counseling sessions as long as we are working on my problems. When it is time for me to confront my abuser, I beg
Ernie to stay with me while I talk. I sincerely fear that my
abuser might kill me. In the PBS Series John Bradshaw:
On the Family, Bradshaw says that a sexual abuser has
the power of life or death over their victim. Abuse is soul
threatening. Bradshaw also warns against making abusers
into monsters, separating them, and us, from our humanity. It is only through our humanity that we can heal. Ernie
refuses to stay with me. I decide to face my abuser on my
own. I have nothing to lose—I am dying inside anyway.
At least, I have been crucifying myself over the abuse for
years. I tell my abuser firmly how I felt at his hands and
some of the life consequences I have suffered. He tells me,
"If you won't accuse me of raping you, I won't accuse you of
seducing me." I remind him I was 9 years old; he was much
older. I play the broken record and firmly tell him again
how I felt at his hands and some of the life consequences.
He describes for me in detail how attractive he found my
little girl body. I feel like retching. I use the broken record
again. After the third time through, he says, "Well, you will
never get an apology from me. I can't apologize."

The following spring, I apply for a position in student loan collections at Snow College. It is exactly the work I did at UCLA. I am so surprised when I do not get the job even though it is clear in the interview that they have someone else in mind. As an alternate plan, I enroll in summer classes at Snow College, taking biology and psychology. Before I start classes I call Robin, another young mom who goes back to college to complete her degree in elementary education. I tell her I am scared. She tells me, "Don't worry Dawn. They're all jocks and potential cheerleaders." I find that there is nothing about my work as a mom that detracts from my ability to do college work. After the Fourth of July weekend, one of my young friends in psychology says, "Wow, I just did not have time to do my homework with the holiday and all." I smile, silently acknowledging that I did all my homework, all the laundry, attended a potluck dinner and hosted a family party. I can do this work.

In the fall I enroll in British Literature. I have to consult with the instructor before our first paper is due to make sure I remember what a thesis sentence looks like. I get an A on my paper. On our first exam, I am thrilled to realize that I know everything down cold. My instructor returns my paper with these comments, "100% A+ Stunning—exceptional—a tribute to returned students everywhere." This is the good news. The bad news is that the instructor, Marilyn Larson, is about my age, maybe a bit younger and she knows so much more than I do. Fortunately, I am thirsty for knowledge. I have an equally successful quarter in all my other courses. Second quarter I am invited into the small honors program at Snow College. Our course, titled "Intellectual Traditions of the West," includes literature, music, art history, and historical context. I see my first opera, *Lucia di Lammermoor*. I am hooked on learning. I want a degree. I will be happy to contribute to the family income, but mostly I want to be educated. I go on to take geography, microbiology, conceptual physics, and honors math— Calculus without Tears—I cry—and every literature course that Marilyn Larson teaches. I declare an English major. I love physics enough that I actually think about switching my major, but my math skills are so deficient, it would take two years to catch up.

I continue through three quarters my first year and the first quarter of my second year without actually picking up my grade reports. The comments on my papers and tests are enough for me. I realize that I am smart, something I did not know in high school. Back then, I had no idea that my grades were in my control. At the time, I think my grades only relate to whether or not I like the class and like the teacher—then it is easy. If I don't like the course or the teacher, then it is not so easy. A few weeks into the second quarter of my second year, I walk into the lobby of the LDS Institute. My cousin Roy, son of Cousin Gene and younger brother of future Bishop Russell says to me, "How does it feel to be in the running for valedictorian?"

I say, "Oh right, Roy. Me and everyone else on this campus. We all have a chance, hey?"

"No, seriously. It's you, Keith, and John," he responds.

Nota bene: An LDS Institute is a building located near colleges and universities where students can take college level courses in LDS scriptures and theology. I take one course every quarter, including genealogy. I do not find out anything about my father, but I learn how to use the LDS genealogy library and resources. I learn that the release of the 1930 Census data may be important. I may find birth information on Woody. I will have to wait until 2002.

After Institute class, I go see my friend Cless, the geography instructor, and one of the college counselors. He confirms what Roy said. I am in the running with Keith, the son of the institute instructor, and John, the son of my cousin Mary Ann. We are each separated by .01 GPA points. I am in the lead. I am also registered for 22 credit hours. I want to finish my associate's degree by summer so I had registered for 18 credit hours. Then one of the instructors in the education program puts huge pressure on me to join an education class so it will carry—that gets me to 22 hours. I join the class, but I resent the instructor. It is right here in this space that I discover I have ambition. I want to be valedictorian. I want to be smart. I want to be successful. My prayer goes like this, "Please God if there is any way that being valedictorian will fit into your plans for me, let me have it." I decide to fast one day a week as a sign of commitment. If nothing else, I am really grateful for every meal I do get to eat.

Nota bene: An LDS fast means 24 hours without food and water. Seriously, no food or water for 24 hours.

I also find out that my cousin John, MaryAnn's son, has been talking to professors trying to get his grades changed. John is ratted out to me by one of his roommates, the son of a friend of mine. In my coursework at Snow College, I have only one grade that is not an A, an A- in microbiology. I talk to the microbiology professor, reminding him that he promised a straight A to the person in our class who had the highest overall score. That was me. He tells me I was six points off an A. I tell him what is going on with John and him changing grades. The instructor changes my grade to an A. I hear later that John is furious. I talk to Marilyn, the English instructor. She says she was hoping I was in the running for valedictorian. She says John is smart enough, but I am far brighter. The thing is that in the Yardley family, my mother and her children have been the outliers, the rebels, the odd ones out especially during the years of her affair with Jerry. The children of my uncle Tom, including his daughter Mary Ann and her son John, have always been the good kids, the exemplars. So, beating John would be very cool for me. And very cool for Momma.

In the end, I am the Snow College valedictorian for the class of 1986. My address is on entropy and the importance of paying attention to and caring for educational institutions. I get my 15 minutes of fame. My photo is on the front page of the Gunnison News. I stop at the market the day the weekly paper comes out. I am buying frozen pizza for dinner. A woman who is in my LDS ward sees me, holds up her copy of the paper and says, "Oh, this is how you do it! Frozen food for dinner." There is more than a slight edge in her voice. I just smile as I think to myself, "Yeah, frozen pizza. That is the secret to my success." In reality, I follow closely the two to one rule, for every hour in class I spend two hours studying. I do most of my homework after the kids are in bed at 8:30 or 9:00 pm and on Sunday afternoons. Most weeks, on one or two nights, I stay up until 2 or 3 am studying, sitting on the bathroom floor which is cold enough to keep me awake. The morning the announcement appears in the paper, I leave my house at 7:30, travelling 20 miles to Snow College to take two final exams. Then I drive my friend Anne, one of the returning women students at Snow, to Provo to see Lankford. Anne is married to a man who thinks he is Godzilla. He rules his family with absolute terror and anger. Anne reports that her physician tells her, "Women like you have three choices. You can get sick and go to bed. You can get an education and a career. Or you can have an affair." I choose option B, and eventually C.

Ernie appears in the valedictorian photo with me that is published on the front page of the B Section in the *Salt Lake Tribune*. The caption says he "poses" with me which is exactly true. He poses as a supportive husband for the photo. After my first fall quarter at Snow, Ernie says,

"I don't think I should have to support you or pay for you going to school."

"Why not? I supported you going to dental school."

"What?"

"I quit college, went to work, and supported you through dental school."

"Well, that was different," he says.

"Yeah," I say. "I will tell you how different it was. That was you and this is me. That is how different it is."

I so need Ernie's support. I do not think he knows how to give it. Perhaps I am so different from what he hoped for. In my attempts to lighten the toll on my family, on Saturdays I cook three meals to be used during the week. Ernie eats some of all three on the day they are cooked and then complains during the week about having to eat leftovers. The truth is, with Ernie, I can never be enough or do enough. I beg him for help. I beg him to be a friend to me—he is a good friend to both of the women who work in his dental office. My last quarter at Snow College, I have to take a class at 8:00 a.m. So far, I have been able to keep my classes mostly during the hours that the kids are at school and the youngest is at preschool. I ask him if he can delay his first appointment of the day to be home until the kids are on the bus at 8:00? Instead, he starts going to the office before I leave for class at 7:30 a.m. The situation only gets worse when he understands that I am going to drive 90 miles, one way, to finish a bachelor's degree at BYU. He tells me on a regular basis that as soon as I have my degree he is quitting. I take this threat seriously. I really am afraid that he will burn out before I graduate.

With the valedictorian thing, I get a full-ride scholarship at BYU. Of course, the president, the registrar and two of my professors at Snow College have to write letters to BYU to make that happen. At first, BYU averages my freshman grades—a 3.06 from 20 years earlier—with my straight 4.0 from Snow College, making me "unqualified." With sufficient protest, the powers that be at BYU change their minds and offer me a "Y" scholarship, covering full tuition for up to 4 years as long as I maintain a 3.5 GPA. So, with tuition covered, I only have to pay for books and gas. For my second year at BYU, I am awarded one of ten Orea B. Tanner Scholarships, the highest award in the English Department—$1500, so books and gas will be covered. I never get to use the Tanner money.

I put off attending BYU during my oldest daughter's senior year of high school. I take second year French classes at Snow College, but that is all. I start at BYU in the fall of '87, 20 years after I entered as a freshman. In the spring of 1988, an orthodontist friend of Ernie's has found a dental practice looking to expand in Arroyo Grande, CA. I am actually supportive of this opportunity. Ernie dreams of practicing dentistry in California. Here is the way my logic goes: If Ernie is happier, then we all can be happier. The summer after I am valedictorian at Snow College, we are in the car with all of the children when Ernie says to me, "You have really become a sassy little bitch since this valedictorian thing."

"Yeah? Well, I have to be."

"Why?"

"Because you are an asshole," I explain.

"I am not an asshole," he retorts.

"Yes, you are. But you are my asshole, so maybe that's okay." I have stolen the gist of this conversation from some movie I do not recall. I am pretty sure the line is delivered by Jeff Goldblum, or maybe Martin Mull.

In July, after Snow College graduation, I have lunch with Marilyn Larson. She tells me again how wonderful it is that I was valedictorian.

I tell her, "You know what's the greatest thing about being valedictorian?"

"What?"

"The greatest thing is that I finally have the credentials to argue with Dr. Ernie."

Ernie tells me for years that I am not logical, that I cannot possibly know how a real family should work, coming from a screwed-up home like mine. In a couple of years, when I am in graduate school, I will get further exoneration, when all graduate students, including PhD. candidates, take an assessment of logic. The professors tell the group that one of us has a score 10 percentile points higher than the next closest student. I have the highest score.

Nevertheless, I am supportive of the move to California. They have schools, and I am smart. I can get into college in California, too. Before we move to California, while we are still trying to decide what to do, we have a house fire. Our only son, Ox, having grown up with four sisters, has to prove every day that he is a boy. He is smart, funny, and full of energy. He can speak so fast that he talks while he inhales. By the time he is 11 or 12 he often sneaks home during the last two hours of our 3-hour block of time at church. Once, when he goes home in the early spring, he finds that Mr. Hansen is picking wild asparagus off the ditch bank across the street from our house. His grandma, Shadow, tells him some weeks earlier to "keep his eye on the asparagus and tell me when it is ready." In his mind, Mr. Hansen is picking Shadow's asparagus. Ox goes in the house, gets the pellet gun, and shoots out three windows in Mr. Hansen's Bronco. Then he locks himself in the house and does not say word one about the incident when we come home. At 5:00 pm a city police officer shows up at our door to report what happened. We are talking on the front porch when he says, "I do not want to scare the hell out of him." We assure the officer that we want him to scare the hell out of him. We make Ox earn money to help pay for the Bronco windows.

Some years later, when Ox is 14 or so, he sneaks home from church early in June and tees up a golf ball in the front yard. He puts one ball right through the center window on the second floor. This incident he tells us about. On Monday, I call the insurance agent to make a claim and discover that our homeowner's insurance has lapsed. The next week, I take our second-oldest daughter, Dora, to the Salt Lake airport to pick up her best friend, who moved from Gunnison to Bellevue, WA. When we arrive back in Gunnison we turn west onto our street, but I can only drive to within a block of our house. The street is so full of people I have to pull over to the side of the road. I get out of the car and see that the fire engine and the ambulance are parked in front of our house. There are clusters of people on the front lawn. I run that last block. I am so relieved when I see that one of the clusters of people is Ernie and our other children. One of the volunteer firemen, Blake the insurance man, approaches me and says, "Please tell me you renewed your house insurance." I did. I switched to the other insurance agent. In a small town everything gets political, and we try to spread our business around to everyone. So, we have insurance, but our house is absolutely unlivable. In a matter of minutes, we have no useable clothes, no useable beds, not a comb nor a toothbrush.

Ernie tells me how the fire begins. He and the other kids had been out in the yard and just came in for lunch when they hear a loud crash of breaking glass upstairs. Thinking a neighbor has put a ball through the window, again, Ernie runs upstairs to find the east bedroom is on fire. He goes downstairs, tells our son to call the fire department and get his younger sisters out of the house. He grabs a bucket of water and heads back upstairs. By the time he gets to the top of the stairs, the smoke is down to his waist. He knows he must get out, too. While they are waiting for the fire truck, Ox grabs a big sprinkler out of the orchard and aims it through the broken window. When the volunteer firemen arrive, they go upstairs, sense the heat and retreat just in time to avoid a flashover on the second floor. They pour some 40,000 gallons of water into our house in less than 2 minutes. I carry my youngest daughter on my hip as we all hold hands and survey the damage. The youngest daughter cringes at every new revelation, clinging to me at every turn. My son keeps his bedroom door closed. The smoke damage is minimal in his room. The east bedroom is mostly consumed by the fire, melted Barbie dolls lying everywhere, a shelf full of warped Cabbage Patch dolls in the closet. The west bedroom is in perfect order, but everything is still covered with smoke and ash, as is the master bedroom. Everything from keepsakes to post-it notes are equally abused. The firemen cannot immediately determine the cause of the fire. The state fire marshals will have to make an inspection.

We are lucky. Ernie's parents have two empty bedrooms and room for us to sleep. Before we have dinner, friends have rounded up clothes for all of the kids and for me and Ernie. We are well cared for. One of my neighbors sews two new sets of play clothes for the two younger girls before the end of the week. Ernie's assistant brings me a bag of clothes and a hairbrush. My favorite item is a long cotton summer-weight robe, white with a strawberry print. No matter how filthy I get sorting through damaged items during the day, every evening I get a shower and the lovely robe.

A week later two State Fire Marshals examine the damage. After spending several hours looking through the house and questioning Ernie and I about furniture loca-tions and household details, the fire marshals tell us one of our children is keeping a terrible secret. The fire started with a candle in the wooden Barbie doll house that I had built for the kids a decade earlier. They tell us we are lucky one of the kids did not discover the fire. Children tend to hide from fire rather than flee; that is why so many children die hiding under a bed or in a closet.

We sit on the deck to talk with the kids about the fire, telling them what the fire marshals said about the candle in the Barbie doll house.

"Did any of you use a candle in the last few days?"

"Yes," said our third daughter, Trina. Telling us that Dora had been in the bath the evening before the fire, before we went to the airport. Trina said to Dora, "It's kind of dark in here. Do you want the light on?"

"No, go downstairs and get me one of those big candles off the top shelf."

"Did anyone else use the candle?"

"Yes, I used it the next morning when I had a bath," says Trina.

"And then?"

"I used it for my bath, too," said the youngest, CC.

"What did you do with the candle when you were done with it?" We ask.

"I put it back in the cabinet."

We check. The candle is not there. We tell the children the candle is missing. The face of our youngest crumples as she confesses, "I took the candle from the bathroom to the bedroom and put it in the Barbie doll house. I forgot." We all cry with her.

We tell her that is why it is called an accident. Ernie, surprisingly, does a really good job not laying on the guilt and blaming this little 8-year-old for what is clearly an accident. Years later, a counselor will ask me what is the significance of this young daughter burning down the Barbie doll house? "It was her defiance." I respond. On a cosmic psycho-babble level, that was my interpretation though clearly no intention on her part. More significantly, I eventually defied a house and a family system that was completely unworkable.

The next week, we decide to drive down to the Central Coast of California to look at the dental practice. We get a motel on the beach, listening to the surf as we drift off to sleep each night. We all have a moment of silence when a fire truck, lights flashing and sirens blaring, passes in front of us. Our son observes, "I guess we know how they feel." The California practice looks good. We now know that our house in Gunnison will not be habitable for 6 months. I find a house to rent. We stay through the week and drive home to begin packing. I drive the 90 miles to BYU one afternoon to resign my two scholarships. I talk with the chair of the Tanner Scholarship. He also caused a house fire when he was only 3. I happen to see my intensive writing professor. I say to him, "I don't know why everything happens to me." He said, "Perhaps God means for you to be a writer." I fantasize about it, but never actually work on it.

California is good for us. Ernie relaxes into the new dental practice, travelling back to Gunnison one week per month to keep that practice going while he grows a new practice. Our oldest, Luna, stays in Salt Lake City to work and go to school. Dora makes the high school volleyball team and the girl's track team in California. Our son falls in with a family of boys who integrate him into school and teach him to surf. We ship a surfboard to Gunnison to surprise him while we are home in the mountains for Christmas. It is a custom made Xaxias (say-shus) surfboard. The name becomes useful for at least one future dog. Our fourth child, Trina, makes the junior high cheerleading squad. She has a great school that teaches the students to track all assignments and deadlines. The schools in this district of the Central Coast of California have open air hallways and outdoor lockers. In the district, they have closed campuses, meaning that students cannot step one foot off the curb, even when Mom is dropping something off at lunchtime. Elementary school is not as much fun for our youngest. CC is in a mixed third-fourth grade and her teacher is harsh. I work hard, visiting the school and the teacher often, to make sure our daughter is not labeled in the school, or in her mind, as a bad kid. Ernie and I have more sex. For the years that I was at Snow College and BYU, he did not even sleep upstairs in our bed with me. He slept on the couch. He comes to bed with me only one night during those years. When I ask him to turn off the television so I can sleep, he becomes angry and storms off downstairs for the rest of the night.

In California, we are much more stable and much happier for that first year. After 6 months the little house across the street from our equally small rental comes up for sale. We buy it as a second home, adding an illegal bedroom in the garage. So, four bedrooms and two baths. We are good. The California real estate boom is spreading north from L.A. and south from San Francisco. We are happy to be in the market.

By early fall, the California dental practice is not going so smoothly. Ernie's new partner suffers from bipolar disorder and is not staying on his meds. In one day, in a manic phase, he puts earnest money on eleven different properties. He tells our friend who works at the local bank that he has been called to prepare all of the dentists in southern California for the second coming of Christ. This sounds funny, hysterical, in fact, but it is heartbreaking to see him and his life fall apart. By the middle of December, he loses his building. It is bought by a recent graduate of dental school who has passed his California state board exam. The buyer is the youngest son of the family that owns the local grocery chain. While Ernie is looking for another place to practice, he is approached by the owner of the best dental practice in San Luis Obispo County, who wants to retire. Ernie's hang-up is that seller wants cash and Ernie is hesitant to get a loan from the bank. Ernie wants the seller to finance. Danny, his best friend from high school, who is a successful entrepreneur in L.A., visits over a weekend. He looks at all the numbers and advises Ernie that it is a good deal. Nevertheless, Ernie lets the deal slip through his fingers. That is the secular version. Let me tell you the Mormon version. The basic details are the same; the big difference is that after the building from the first practice is bought by the young graduate, Ernie and I go to the LDS Temple in L.A., fasting and praying for help and guidance from the Lord. By the time we complete the temple ritual and get to the Celestial Room it is about two o'clock. Generally, from a Mormon perspective, the Celestial Room is the place where insight or inspiration is gained, or prayers are answered. Neither of us have a clear idea of what to do. When we get back to our home in Arroyo Grande, we find a message on the answering machine from the seller of the best practice in San Luis. The message is left at two o'clock—the exact time when we were in the Celestial Room. In usual Mormon experience this would be seen as a message from God. Ernie remains unconvinced to buy the practice. I tell him that he is practically faithless. Neither God, nor his best friend, can convince him to move forward.

Just after Christmas, we learn that another young dentist has purchased the San Luis practice. We cannot afford to stay in CA without income. I tell Ernie and the kids we need to go back to Utah. They are all mad as hell at me. By the middle of February, we are back living in Gunnison. Our Dora stays in CA with friends. She wants to graduate from a CA high school; however, she is also back in Utah by the end of April. I work in the dental office in Gunnison to help Ernie get the dental practice back up to speed.

The following spring, Luna, who joined us in California after Christmas, becomes engaged to an LDS missionary she meets while we are living in California. The wedding is the first of August. I sew her silk, satin, and lace dress, very late-80s style, leg of lamb sleeves, fitted waist, bustle bow in the back—Alençon lace bodice, appliques, and hem. It is truly beautiful—the hardest, most fun sewing I have ever done. In September, I start classes back at BYU. Dora is a freshman there. She tells me, "If you see me on campus, don't wave unless I wave at you first." I actually never see her on campus. I have to go to the dorms and later her apartment to see her. I drive the 90 miles to BYU three days per week. For my Shakespeare class, I buy the unabridged audio tapes for the 14 or so plays, mostly the romantic comedies, that we study. I listen to a tape on the trip up and the trip back. When I get home, I listen to the tape as I follow along with the text. Then I listen to the tape again on the way up and back as I drive to BYU. I usually have at least one course per semester that lends itself to "car studying."

Before the opening of the Gunnison prison in 1990, townspeople are invited on guided tours. When we leave the public areas and enter the lock-up portion, our guide closes a big metal gate behind us. The heavy clink of the metal one is one of the most chilling sounds I ever heard. That same summer I am standing in the kitchen with Ernie. He is berating me for something. I look at him and think to myself, "We would be closer if we had sex more often." Then I think, "Why would I want to do that? Why would I want to be that close and that vulnerable with someone who treats me so poorly?" I answer my own question, "I don't." And that is that. I tell myself, "Wow, I am 41 and I think I have just given up my sex life." In my mind I hear the clink of that heavy metal gate.

🪶

I finish all of my course work for my English teaching major in two years and a summer. I use Cliff notes only for The Faerie Queen. It is summer semester. I am having trouble concentrating. What can I say? One day after classes I feel especially tired. I stop in south Provo at a convenience store for a giant Dr. Pepper. This location has the good little ice pellets that are so fun to crunch. I am increasingly drowsy during the 80-mile drive. I should have stopped for another Dr. Pepper when I turned off the freeway on to the two-lane highway for the last 40 miles to home. This is a dangerous road on which to be drowsy. I try all the things that do not work: turning up the AC, turning up the rock music station, slapping my face. The last 10 miles I follow a tractor trailer rig. When I finally reach the hill that drops down into my little town, I feel like I have made it. By the time I reach the city park, I am fully asleep. A voice in my head, "DAWN!" rouses me enough to slow down and make the turn to home at the south side of the park. I can feel the exact spot in my brain where I hear my name. I look in my psychology text, and I am so surprised that it is the intuition center. In the evening I tell Ernie what happened. He says, "Oh, the voice was probably your father." A couple of days later, I am chatting on the phone with Momma, and I tell her what happened. She says, "Oh, the voice was probably your father." On the weekend, when I tell Luna, she says, "Oh, the voice was probably your father."

In the fall I move from the Knight Humanities Building—the JKHB, home of most English courses, to the McKay Building—the MCKB, home of the Education Department with education courses that seem pedestrian compared to the high flights of discussion and creativity in the English Department. The Multicultural and Exceptional Education class is okay. My high school experience in New Mexico leaves me with a strong social justice agenda. I can pay attention here. Miss Joyce Nelson teaches Foundations of English Teaching. She is fabulous. She dresses up for every class, maintaining that we should dress at least one level above our students. One stunning outfit is a red wool jersey dress with a fitted waist and a circle skirt. She also has a dusky lavender jersey with the same styling and a sea-shell belt. She tells us when we dress up for our students to be sure to point that out them—it makes them feel special.

The instructor for one education class, Dr. Herbert Nielsen, has the best shirts and ties in the department. My teaching courses meet only twice per week in the afternoons and evenings. After class the second week, I am waiting outside the MCKB for my children who dropped me off and then went on to Salt Lake City for their monthly appointment with the orthodontist. Dr. Nielsen strolls by, and we have a brief exchange. I am not aware that his office window looks out on the grass and bench where I am sitting. Not many weeks later he invites me to his office after class to discuss astrology, especially as it pertains to me. He holds my hand. The second week of October I attend a training he is giving at a Provo area high school on his discipline and instructional strategies. After the training, we make out in his car for an hour or more before I go to the home of Carrie Ann for the night. She is expecting me.

"Where have you been?" she asks when I arrive after 10:00. "Getting felt up by the faculty," I reply. She is not shocked, or, if she is, she keeps it to herself. She is my best friend and very loyal. When she takes the California Personality Inventory, she is described by the interpretation guide as the Keeper of the Village Traditions, never judgmental, but knowing clearly what the expected behaviors are.

By the end of the semester, I am late for my Multicultural final because Herbert and I have just had sex at the motel at the south end of town where I have stayed during finals week for these last two semesters. During my first stay in August, I tell some of my classmates how wonderful it is to be at the Colonial Motel, $29.00 per night, entirely to myself without worrying about any agenda but mine. My creative writing professor overhears this conversation and says to me, "Better be careful. Soon someone will say, 'Where is Dawn?' and we will say, 'Oh, she went south.'" An apparently prophetic observation. Here I am once again, a cheating BYU student, hoping against hope to not get caught and released. A fish on a hook.

After both my Multicultural and English finals, Herb drives me back to the Colonial Motel. We stop on the way at Wendy's for a bowl of chicken soup. I am sick with a terrible cold, which is how he came be at the motel in the first place. I call him as soon as I check-in. He realizes how sick I am and offers to pick me up and drive me to the MCKB for my finals. I am relieved. The student parking lot that I use is on top of the bluff at the north side of campus. In the winter, especially when it snows—and it is snowing today, the wind howls around us students making our way down the hill. I often think during those wind gusts about Mormon pioneers out on the prairie with the wind howling, nothing more than a canvas covered wagon for protection. Sick and who knows how little there is to eat. I think I know why some of those pioneers just lay down and died.

Of course, when Herb takes me back to the motel, we have sex again. The plug has been pulled on that dam. And the plug has been pulled on that damnation, too. I could certainly be kicked out of BYU for this behavior. The Honor Code is very strict about sex outside of marriage. So, no premarital sex. No extramarital sex. No gay sex. No lesbian sex. No premarital touching of body parts. No masturbation. Mormons on the whole are pretty screwed on the sex availability front. The Honor Code is also very strict about many other behaviors: no smoking, no alcohol, no drugs. All of these no's drive some BYU students to a variety of bizarre behaviors. In this current time frame, a group of BYU girls and a group of BYU boys take a road trip to Las Vegas, get married, have sex for the weekend, and then try to get the marriages annulled without BYU, or their parents, getting wise. They are all dismissed from the University as a result of this happy adventure. At the high-school level, behaviors are equally bizarre. Kids tell themselves, "If it's oral, it's moral." Fellatio and cunnilingus are a go—they have no idea of these technical terms, of course. Anal sex does not really count as sex, no penile penetration of the vagina. And best of all, there is a practice called "floating," which does include penile penetration of the vagina, but as long as no one moves, it is, technically, not really sex. Yowzers. I know all these rules.

That night, when Herbert is leaving the motel, I am at the door in my long johns—it is cold outside. I am mostly hidden behind the door when I notice a familiar looking car pass through the parking lot. In the morning, when I am heading out to yet another final, I do not see anyone I know. On the weekend, at church, I hear Diane and Sharon mention that they were in Provo during the night of the snowstorm and managed to get rooms at the Colonial Motel. I tell them, "Oh, I was there, too. I have been staying there a night or two for the past two semesters during finals week. It was such a bad snowstorm. I am glad I didn't have to drive home." I am pretty sure the car I saw was Diane's green station wagon. I try to read their body language to see if they saw me in the doorway at the motel. I think they did, but my observations are inconclusive. I adopt this strategy of honesty because of a line from the Tamarind Seed. Omar Sharif says to Julie Andrews, "Tell the truth whenever you can. Then when you have to lie, people will believe you." This strategy will serve me well during the coming months.

I know these women fairly well. I lived next-door to Sharon for two years. And I have been a kind friend to Diane. I have their daughters, Christine and JoAnne, who are best friends, in one of my classes at church when they are 8 or 9. I call them the Whisper Sisters, because they whisper to one another almost incessantly all through church services. Both girls were quite shy. When JoAnne is a senior in high school, she lands the lead in the spring production of Giselle at the Central Utah Ballet where our daughters attend twice weekly classes. On the stage, when she is dancing, JoAnne blossoms. She needs a costume for Giselle. Diane approaches me about sewing the costume for her. I agree to do it but insist on no pay—the family cannot afford what it might actually be worth. So, I make Diane a list and send her off to the best fabric store in Salt Lake City. She scores—pale blue cotton lawn for the double layer skirt, linen just a shade darker for the weskit, and ivory voile for the peasant blouse underneath. When Ernie finds out I am not charging them, he is furious and demands a justification. I explain to him, "They have a need and I have skills. I am doing this because I can." Vivian, the owner of the ballet school, is a small woman, half-Puerto Rican and vivacious. She did some of her training at the London Royal Ballet. Her eyes sparkle when she tells me that JoAnne's Giselle dress is one of the most beautiful costumes she has seen for that role. I have my payment.

A further complication, or a contributing factor, of this situation with the BYU professor is the fact that I am planning to divorce Ernie. Before the start of each school year, every student at BYU must submit an ecclesiastical endorsement, signed by the local bishop, or head of the local ward that certifies their purity for the Honor Code. In August, when I see Allen, my bishop, before starting my education courses in the fall, I tell him, "Unless something changes big time, I will be divorced by next summer."

He says, "Oh, Dawn. You have to do whatever it takes to save your marriage."

"Well, I don't have to die," I think to myself. I do feel like I am losing myself; I am fading away. In the comments section of my ecclesiastical endorsement Allen writes, "No problems. Ever."

My impulse to divorce is further pushed to this breaking point by revelations from Luna about her terrible marriage to the missionary she met when we lived in California. I tell Ernie that we need to get her out of the situation. He says that she needs to get herself out. I should go get my dad's truck and move her myself. Daddy Arlo would help. I think to myself, "My Lord, I have stayed in my terrible marriage so long that my children may not even know what to look for."

The other thing that convinces me to pursue divorce is concern for my mental health. As Luna separates from her husband and begins divorce proceedings, Ernie slips into more noticeable depression. I suggest he go see Lankford and get some help. I know that he will not do anything to help himself. One night he says something about getting the gun, his pistol. I think to myself, "Oh, my Lord, let me get it for you. You can put yourself out of our misery." I can be so harsh with him, too. Over the following days and weeks, I find myself thinking increasingly often about the gun. Where is it? Where is the clip? Then I surprise myself when I question whether or not I know how to load the thing. I think, "Oh, Lord, I am becoming homicidal. I better take a good look at how angry I am, and what I am going to do about it." It is these alarming and dangerous thoughts that lead to my resolve that summer to finally divorce Ernie. But first we have to resolve Shadow's health issues.

~

In March, prior to the summer of my discontent and my decision to end my marriage, Ernie's Mom, Shadow, has a grapefruit-sized mass removed from her abdomen. It is benign, but she already has spots on her lungs. Prior to the surgery, when I first see Shadow lying in that hospital bed in Provo, I take one look at her and think, "Holy Crap, this is it." No one in the family talks about it, but I am sure she refuses chemo and radiation. She and LaMar, Ernie's dad, have spent much time and money on natural eating. She thinks she can beat this.

By early summer Shadow spends many of her days in
bed. I start insisting that Ernie and I, and the kids who want
to come along, walk down to see his parents every evening,
walking back home in the twilight, easing him into and out
of the discomfort and worry. In July, Aunt June calls me
from Texas to see how her sister, Shadow, is doing. She
reports that LaMar and Shadow are assuring them that she
can beat this cancer. June and Bob, and Ernie's cousin Burt,
their son, are planning to drive up from Corpus Christie
later in August. I tell her, "June, Shadow weighs less than
100 pounds. She spends most of her days in bed. If you
are going to come, come sooner." Aunt June and Uncle
Bob, along with Burt arrive by car the first week of August.
During most of their elementary school years, Burt and
Ernie spend summers together. My children's Papa, LaMar,
is a schoolteacher and during summers he drives his wife
and three sons to Corpus Christi, TX where he works as a
seasonal house painter while Shadow and the kids bask in
the indulgent love of their south Texas family.

Burt marries his high school sweetheart a year before
Ernie and I marry. Within a decade the marriage unravels over her affair with their church choir director. Over
the years Burt has several long-term girlfriends, living with
one or two of them, but he never remarries. My children
regard him as their eccentric, fun-loving, game-playing
single uncle with the laugh that starts deep in his belly.

Over the years I realize that Burt has a crush on me. It
is only fair—I have a crush on him. For most of the years I
have known Burt, at least once each day when he visits in
person he greets me with his warm baritone belting out,
"Delta Dawn, what's that flower you have on?" As with the
song, he answers the question with a question, "Could it

be a faded rose from days gone by?" Good natured ribbing from Burt and a nice tribute to his South Texas heritage. The significance of the remaining lyrics is not lost on me. When I am pregnant with my last baby, Burt calls Ernie drunk to tell him he is coming to Utah to steal his wife—I am so disgusted with both of them talking about me as if I were a suitcase that I hang up my phone extension before the conversation is finished.

Poor Ernie. Poor Burt. I am probably the Walter Mitty of romance, always looking for someone to fall in love with. For many years Burt was my enduring escape plan, but there were others. Remember my crush on the orthopedic surgeon at UCLA? Later, I often found a college professor to wrap my head around. I would sit on the front row and imagine I was sucking their brain. Seriously, just the brain. This was a combo effect of my search for knowledge and my search for romance. Ernie and I once admitted to each other that we would both like to fall in love again. Before we move to the Central Coast of California, I develop another crush, this time on an LDS missionary—he is older, 26, and I am 37. I talk with Lankford about this attraction. He tells me to go home and tell Ernie. I assure him that I will do no such thing. I know Ernie will just use it against me. During a counseling session on his own with Ernie, Lankford, forgetting my refusal to disclose, reveals my secret. Ernie, maybe scared witless, tells our children about their mother's folly. Several of my children tell me over the years that they often felt even when I was there, I wasn't there. Perhaps I was lost in a romantic or intellectual fantasy, or both. Or just simply daydreaming as I did for most of my childhood.

With her Texas family present, Shadow rallies. We have several lovely days and evenings visiting and eating with Bob, June, and Burt. When we are saying our goodbyes, Burt, perhaps realizing my precarious position with Ernie, whispers in my ear, "I love you." I whisper back a callow, I love you too, sweetie kind of response. I know from many past conversations that any future with Burt would require that I leave behind my children. He thinks that is a reasonable solution—a friend of his made just such a choice. He does not know me at all if he actually believes that would be an option.

When her sister leaves, Shadow retreats to her bed. Ernie and I continue our walks to her house most evenings. On the second of September, for the first time in over two years, Ernie drives the kids to Salt Lake to see the orthodontist. Shadow has been in the hospital for a couple of days. While Ernie is out of town, she slips away. His two brothers are there with their dad when she dies. I am convinced that she has to go when Ernie is not around. He would have kept her many more days with his longing. I learn from this experience that it is one thing to let go of a loved one who is ill and suffering. It is an entirely different thing to let go of the healthy, lively person they once were. Shadow dying of lung cancer when she has never been a smoker feels especially unfair to her three sons. Her death in September followed by my decision to divorce is brutal, but I have consciously worked very hard all spring and summer to get Ernie through at least Shadow's passing.

I will always be grateful for Shadow and Papa—I use the name my kids use for them—and the things I learn from them: healthier eating and political activism, although I gave up on their John Birching years earlier. I find the conspiracy theories exhausting, and I need a more positive outlook on life. In many ways they treat me like the daughter they never had, so thoughtful and charming in their gift giving. But I also spend many years mad as hell at them for screwing up their son until I finally realize that he is a grown-up and making his own choices. Shadow, Papa, and their boys are one of the most enmeshed families I have ever known, rolling down life's highway like one big ball of humanity. This was my mental image even before I had professional training in enmeshment.

Up to the point I engage in extramarital sex, I think I have this divorce thing all under control. Lankford's voice from years earlier tells me, "If you are going to get a divorce, it has to be the most unemotional decision you ever make." Here's the plan. I will get through fall semester, the second to last semester before I finish my bachelor's degree in English Teaching. I have talked with the principal at Gunnison High, and I am set to do my student teaching there during second semester. I will get my kids through the fall and Christmas, then wait until the end of January or the first of February to announce my intentions for divorce so the kids don't associate the divorce with the holidays. My son will be 19 in June and can go on his LDS mission. Dora will be 21 in September and can go on her LDS mission. In November, as I am making my plans, I tell my best neighbor-friend, Jackie, what I am thinking. She cries. I cry. Over the previous 10 years, I have spent many hours with Jackie as she works her way through her own divorce.

Over Thanksgiving weekend, Ernie and I attend my high school reunion. Some of my classmates congratulate me on the valedictorian thing and my educational success and then ask me about my future plans.

"I am considering graduate school for a degree in school counseling."

"But?"

"But Ernie says that he will divorce me if I go to graduate school."

"What are you going to do?"

"I am going to apply."

Ernie listens to this conversation. On our way home, he asks me if there is someone else. I tell him, "No." At this moment, this is still true. I have not taken that final step with Herbert; we have not yet had sex. I still could stay the course, but this marriage has failed of its own accord.

The first part of December, the principal at the high school calls me to offer an internship in place of my student teaching. One of the teachers has suffered a breakdown and will not be back for the remainder of the school year. I will get half salary for a half-year contract. Six thousand dollars—I am employed! When students come back to school after the Christmas break, I have taken over. I clean my new classroom and my new office. I create bulletin boards. I make lesson plans. I have four preps: 3 sections of English 10, one section of 8th grade Utah History, two sections of 10–12 World History, and Drama. Before the semester ends in mid-January, I have traded Drama with another teacher who actually has drama experience. In return I get a section of English 12.

My supervising teacher, Mr. Harward, is awesome. He tells me, "The minute you send a student to the office, you have lost control of your class." I actually know how to manage my classroom, thanks to my university class with Herb. The first day of teaching I begin each class by passing out 3 × 5 cards. I ask each student to write on the card, in a word or two, how they want to be treated in a classroom. For the most part, students want to be treated "fairly" or "with respect," except for one student who signed his name Bruno: "I want to be treated like a big piece of meat." Even this declaration gives us something to work with. I engage the students to operationalize what Fairness and Respect looks like in the classroom. Then I ask them about their expectations for me. They only have 4 or 5 hard requests. I repeat this process six times that first day. At the end of each class I say, "Well, you know your job, and I know mine." This is very similar to the approach used by LuAnn Johnson in her book *My Posse Don't Do Homework*, and brought to the screen with Michelle Pfeiffer in *Dangerous Minds*. It isn't simple, but it is doable. I am elated after my first week in the classroom, saying to myself several times, "I can do this work. I can do this work." If a student really acts out during class, I drop a prepared note on their desk that says, "Please see me in my office after class." Most of them would prefer to meet their mother in the principal's office. I do not yell or threaten, I simply explain that they created an embarrassing situation for me. We review the expectation, what they should have done, and I ask for a commitment for better behavior. I buy a gross of pencils so no one has an excuse to not engage. I insist that they engage with me.

At church, my calling, or volunteer assignment is with the Stake (regional) Young Women's Presidency. After our January meeting, Becky, the president, drives me home. I tell her that I need to be released as secretary. I explain my plans to divorce Ernie. She tells me she understands. I acknowledge that she has always liked Ernie. She tells me, "That does not mean I don't see him clearly." She hugs me and wishes me the best. I talk with the stake president, the male priesthood bearer of our region, telling him of some of Ernie's behaviors. Making assumptions not justified by my words, he tells me, "You need to get you and your kids into a safe situation. Move him out but use the divorce to leverage Ernie into counseling. It will cost $25,000 or $30,000, but you will have your celestial marriage back."

I respond, "We have tried counseling before. I finally have the wherewithal to take care of me and my children. I can no longer be responsible for Ernie. He will have to help himself." I do not tell Becky, nor the bishop, nor the stake president about Herbert even though these would be normal receivers of my confession.

At the end of January, on his Friday day off, I tell Ernie that I am planning to divorce him. We are alone in the house. He tells me several times I cannot do this. He even stands close to me and bumps me with his stomach. He is at least 60 pounds overweight. I ask him, "Considering our relationship, how did you think this would turn out?" The next morning, Dora is home from BYU. We gather all of the kids in the family room. I am standing at the edge of the kitchen when I tell them I am divorcing their father. In unison they rush to Ernie's side. I expect them to rally with him. They will not want the divorce either. It still stings when I see it happen.

It takes me more than 3 weeks to get Ernie to move out of our house. I finally tell him if he does not move out over the weekend, I will put all of his stuff out on the front porch for the neighbors to see. He finally moves in with his father who has been alone since Shadow died.

Back to the situation at hand. I am living in Gunnison doing my teaching internship. Herbert, who supervises student teachers for the music department, visits me at the high school on an "official visit." He does actually help me with some practical suggestions for my teaching, but that is not the focus of his visit. He tells me, while we are sitting on a bench in the commons of the high school, that, so far, he is not planning to divorce his wife. I tell him, "Well then, I guess I will just have to be your concubine," as if I learned nothing from my mother. After school is out, we drive out to a country road and have sex in his tiny little Integra. He has also been calling me weekly, on Wednesdays, after school. I see him when I go to Provo for my once per month check-in with my internship supervisor. By the end of February, I tell Herb I cannot see him for the next few months. I have to be clear about my reasons for divorcing Ernie. In March, I waver and then I decide firmly; I am going through with the divorce because the marriage I have had with Ernie is done. I tell myself that it may be possible to have a different marriage with Ernie, but the one we have is over.

Before we are completely clear that the divorce is happening, Ernie and I try sharing a lawyer and coming to an amicable resolution. By April, Ernie realizes that I am hoping to attend graduate school, he hires his own attorney, Andrew McCullough, who, for decades, runs for Attorney General in the state of Utah every four years on the Libertarian ticket. One day Byron, my attorney, calls me.

"Do you have a boyfriend?" he asks.

"No." I respond without hesitation. "Why?"

"Ernie's lawyer tells me that he keeps calling him in tears."

"Why?" I query.

"Are you still sleeping with him?"

"I have not had sex with Ernie for well over a year." And I then discuss with Byron my usual question. "Considering our relationship, how did Ernie think this would turn out?"

I am so angry about that conversation that over the weekend I finish ten lessons in a health course through BYU Extension that is required for my degree. During the following week, I also finish an extension course in adolescent literature that is required for my degree. When the anger cools a bit, I realize that I have used the fuel of my anger to complete both my associate's and bachelor's degrees. Rage has kept me going for years. After all that has been wrong with this marriage, I do not want the divorce to be about whether or not I have a boyfriend.

In April, I graduate from BYU with a BA in English Teaching. At the end of May I finish my teaching internship at the high school. I did apply for the master's degree program in school counseling at BYU and was accepted. In May Herbert receives permission to hire me as a graduate assistant. Starting with summer term, I will assist in teaching some of his classes and help with the revisions on a text he has been writing. I find a three-bedroom apartment near my best friend, Carrie Ann. Three bedrooms allows for Ox, if he chooses, to join Trina and CC and me when we move to the Orem-Provo area. In the end my son chooses to stay in Gunnison with his dad, at least for the summer.

Once school is out, I spend three days on the couch in my family room curled up in the fetal position with a phone in my hand, trying to summon the courage to actually move forward. I dial the number of one friend after another, hanging up before the first ring. I finally call my brother, Big Dave, and tell him how incapacitated I am. I am afraid I am screwing up my life. I am afraid I am screwing up the lives of my children. He listens to my dilemmas and then asks me, "What is going to be good for Dawn?" Getting out of Gunnison and going to graduate school will be good for Dawn. The other stuff I will figure out he tells me. He says he will help me load the heavy stuff in the truck early Saturday morning so we can arrive at the new apartment in Orem by early afternoon on Saturday. Members of the Elders Quorum—the LDS Priesthood group for males under age 40, maybe 45, are ready to help us unload. Trina and CC and I do not get out of Gunnison until late afternoon on Saturday, cresting the hill overlooking the lights of Utah County just at twilight. CC and I are in the truck. We have a brief exchange about the start of a new life. Trina, following with the car, mentioned that she, too, notices the moment.

By the time we drive to our new apartment at the northern half of the valley, it is too late for the church men to help us unload. I have been in touch throughout the day with Carrie Ann, who has arranged for the help. She reschedules them for Sunday at noon. The girls and I drag a couple of mattresses into the apartment, stock the refrigerator, and go to bed.

Apparently, I also keep Herb informed of our progress in arriving at the apartment. I do not remember that so much as I do remember the dumb ass showing up in his jeans and chambray shirt to help. I hiss at him, questioning, "What the hell do you think you are doing?" He is overly casual in replying that he will be my new boss and just came to help. I put him to work installing the washer and dryer. Even the church guys think it is awkward. My daughters are really put off. He stays about an hour.

Nevertheless, Trina and CC seem to enjoy the apartment, especially having the pool right next to our unit for the summer. They are a little nervous about starting at a new school in the fall and making new friends. In the fall they will also start classes at the best ballet school south of Salt Lake City. For Trina this has been sufficient motivation to move during her senior year of high school. For the summer, going to church and having Carrie Ann's sons just through the orchard seems to keep both of them going. Carrie's sons often come over for a swim after a long day of work with their dad in his construction business. I settle into a routine of going to work at Herb's office for half-days, staying late for his once-per-week night class. During my days in the office, I work with him on a text that he has self-published on classroom management and instructional strategies. The tone is too dry and clinical. I persuade him to take a more conversational approach. I work for him as a graduate assistant for summer and fall semesters only.

Trina and CC often go with Dora, who is staying in Provo at BYU for the summer, to Gunnison to see their dad on the weekends. Herb and I meet just as often at hotel rooms around the valley. One particular, ill-fated weekend, Herb gets a nice room, telling the clerk that he is having an anniversary getaway. That weekend CC decides not to go to Gunnison with her sisters. So, I spend all weekend dashing from my apartment to the hotel, then back to my apartment and back to the hotel, like a perverse scene from The Importance of Being Earnest, all the while trying not to smell like sex, of which there is plenty.

By late August, my classes have started, and the girls are in school. I help Ox with deposits and first month's rent on an apartment in Salt Lake with a group of boys. An LDS mission is not in the plans for him. He gets a job at Kinko's where he and his future brother-in-law specialize in creating fake IDs for the many young snowboarders he hangs out with. By late spring of the following year, he will have tired of the drinking and partying. The way he tells it is this: He has just come home from a perfect day of snowboarding. The powder was light, the skies were blue, and the sun was shining. By the time he gets to his apartment, several of his roommates and friends are already drunk. One is puking in the hallway. He thinks to himself, "I have to do more than this. I have to get myself into college. The only way that will happen is to move back to Gunnison, live with my dad, and go to Snow College." He eventually makes that better choice.

In early fall, Herb moves out of the house he shares with his wife and into an apartment. My classes for the master's degree in school counseling are well underway. For the most part, they are easier than the upper division English courses, much less reading and much less writing. I do my homework during the week so that on the weekends that Trina and CC are out of town I can go to Herb's apartment. I am often torn between guilt over my extramarital sex and the joy I have in my secret life. I treasure the complete privacy I have with Herb on these weekends. The sex is simple; we get naked and we make each other happy. I feel like Thelma, who just had sex with J.D. (Brad Pitt), "Oh, this is what all of the fuss is about?" I have two musical themes for this time with Herb. The first is Bruce Springsteen singing "I'm on Fire." As he sings the opening questions, I have the opening answers. No. Yes. And yes, I too "got a bad desire."

The conflict I feel between my desires and my religion aligns perfectly with the song. Honestly, sometimes I feel like I will break in two. I have "a six-inch valley through the middle of my soul." The other song playing for this time of my life is Bonnie Raitt singing "All at Once." So true. One or the other daughter flies off in a rage. I am like a woman possessed, part of me trying to find myself, or holding on to myself, looking for a place of solace and safety. Herb always says that a good healthy sex life can promote a lot of healing. I feel like I am connecting more with me.

Sex with Ernie had been so much more complicated. He was mad at me. I was mad at him. He had huge requirements for sex. He found Mormon underwear, called garments, extremely unsexy, which they are, but that is one of their purposes—to separate the wearer from their sexuality. Ernie often gave me a hug and a kiss and said, "You would be so much sexier if you were wearing fewer clothes." And I would take off the garments for a whole day, and we still did not have sex. He also wanted me to wear just the right lingerie—something ruffled and girlish. I fail on that front many times. One year for Christmas, I go to Juliette's, the lingerie store, and buy a red lace bustier with garters, matching bikini panties, and thigh-high red stockings. I put the entire outfit on for him several nights before Christmas, after the kids go to bed.

He takes one look at me and says, "That is not sexy."

I look at him and sigh, "Give me a raincoat and half an hour; I will be back with at least six men who will assure you that this is sexy." We do not have sex. The next week I toss a Juliette's catalogue in front of him and say, "If you find something sexy in there, go buy it, and I will wear it for you. Otherwise, I am done trying."

🪶

During our months of working with Henry the counselor, I finally get Ernie to talk with me about his involvement several years earlier with one of his assistants. Around the birth of Ox, our third child, I felt that something was going on. At the time, I thought that it was sexual. Within a year of his birth, I was pregnant again. During those years I had no time or energy to explore my concerns. When we finally do talk, some eight years have passed. Ernie tells me there was some sexual involvement, but no intercourse. I remain unconvinced that this is true for several reasons. 1) It felt different than that. 2) It was common among LDS bishops at the time to advise men who had been unfaithful to not reveal the full measure of their infidelity. During this conversation Ernie says aloud, "I don't think I should spend the rest of my life making up for it." I wonder to myself, "Why not?" And finally, when I am pursuing this divorce, Ernie says, "I can't believe you are divorcing me now, and you didn't leave me when you should have." I should have asked more questions.

Carlfred Broderick, a Mormon psychologist at University of Southern California and head of the marriage and family relations department, often found himself crosswise with LDS Church leadership by advocating for early and often teaching of sex and sexuality to children and youth. Broderick had an audio book titled It Came Out of the Blue, Like a Scheduled Airline: Guarding Against Adultery and Weathering Tribulation. He says that in fact the only way for a couple to survive adultery is to discuss it fully, each person sharing completely the full range of their thoughts and feelings. What drove the transgressor to cross that line? The betrayal? The loss of intimacy? Ernie and I both should have asked more questions.

~

I spend that first Christmas Day after the divorce from Ernie at the Gunnison Hospital. My Daddy Arlo is dying. In July, he suffers a mild heart attack with a subsequent quadruple bypass. The postoperative stage does not go well. He has used so many drugs for arthritis management for so long that his body does not hold together. He literally oozes. After a week he is released from ICU to a regular room. By August, still in the Provo hospital, a super-bug invades his harvest leg. The first of September, having run out of antibiotic options, the doctors consider amputating that harvest leg. Daddy Arlo asks Debra, "What will they do with my leg?" In the end we do not have to answer that question. Doctors opt instead to strip most of the skin off the thigh of the harvest leg and graft new skin from the other leg. He suffers terribly. Momma spends most nights sleeping on a cot in his hospital room. On a couple of nights, I convince her to sleep at my apartment. Giving her a break, I spend several hours with Daddy at the hospital. He is semiconscious, groaning and ducking his head as if dodging a pursuer. At one point he says aloud, "I never did anything bad enough to deserve this." My mind goes to the scene from Ghost when the wraiths come out of the sewer to drag the villain away. After an hour or more of him groaning and dodging, I tell him, "Daddy, you're kinda scaring me." He settles into a more peaceful rest.

In most of the 6 months since the bypass, Daddy is only out of the hospital for 2 weeks. His body is failing on many levels—dialysis for several weeks now, possibly weekly transfusions, and then the week before Christmas he suffers a mild stroke. After the stroke he tells our family physician, "Dr. Stewart, I can't do this anymore. I cannot live this way."

Dr. Stewart tells him, "Arlo, all you have to do is quit eating and drinking." Daddy does.

On Christmas Day, he is in and out of consciousness. When he comes around in the morning, I go to his bed and kiss his head. I am crying. He says to me, "I don't want to make you cry, sweetheart."

"Oh Daddy, you do what you need to do to take care of yourself. We will be okay."

Deb, Rick, and I linger most of the day. Dave, Russ, and Scott drift by. My kids are with their dad. Surprisingly, or not, they are mad at me for staying the day at the hospital and then driving back to Orem alone. Daddy dies on New Year's Eve, early in the morning. On the way to Gunnison for the viewing and the funeral, Trina is driving when we hit a deer, just north of Fayette. One of the legs flies across the windshield. Trina still thinks deer are the dumbest animals alive.

To the end of his days, I have a love/hate relationship with my stepdad over his abuse of my stepsister. For the most part I am the only person who keeps this issue conscious. In the end I am beyond proud of the way Daddy Arlo dies. Not many people have that kind of self-discipline. In the few weeks he is home from the hospital, he calls Penny, not identifying himself, and says only, "I am so sorry." He calls Ernie and tells him he is sorry, too—I am not sure what for—perhaps judging him harshly. My kids are mad that I do not include Ernie in all the family parts of Daddy's funeral. I ask them, "Exactly when is it that I get to be divorced?"

In addition to having lots of sex with Herb at his apartment, I also sleep a lot. Herb complains about me sleeping so much. I explain, "Because of my childhood, I have always been hyper-vigilant. For most of my life I have been sleep-deprived; much of it self-imposed. If I sleep easily with you, it is a sign that I trust you and feel safe here." He and I discuss in detail how a good healthy relationship can heal a lot of the damage from childhood sexual abuse. My Austrian therapist in California had told me that I still had more work to do on that. He never did specify what that additional work might be. Perhaps some of the undone work left me this vulnerable to an affair. In my MMPI class on use and interpretation of the Minnesota Multiphasic Personality Inventory, we discuss how school counselors usually score high on the psychopathic deviant scale, not pathologically high, but a definite peak, meaning they are generally not rule followers. Women who score high on the PD scale and high on the femininity scale are also more vulnerable to affairs. I have peaks on both.

Like many other times in my life, I happen on a song that captures perfectly the emotions of the moment. For the end of my marriage to Ernie the song is "I Can't Make You Love Me If You Don't" by Bonnie Raitt. I hear bits of the song all summer long, but always miss both the title and the artist. Ernie's father, my children's Papa, remarries after Shadow's death and lives near BYU. As I pull up to his new home, I hear the full song before I go to the door and pick up my final financial settlement check—one of Ernie's special touches is his use of a personal courier—someone always has to do his errands. Yeah, I realize that I am the one who had the affair, but I connect so strongly to the line about laying down my heart and feeling the power. The song reminds me of our first visit to the marriage counselor years before. We come home and I remember thinking we are going to make it. When we make love that night, it is likely the first time, maybe the only time, that I give myself wholly to him. As the marriage goes on and on, I find that I have to save more of myself, just to get by. More than once, in a meaner moment, I tell Ernie that I am sure he loves me as much as his puny heart will allow. Perhaps it's ennui that plagues me as much as depression.

The end of October I have my divorce hearing. I make Carrie Ann come with me. I am so afraid that the whole affair with Herb will be made public, and I will fall apart. Jackie, my Gunnison neighbor, tells me that under no circumstances should I go to divorce court alone. The day proceeds normally—no surprises or revelations. I do know that Ernie has gone to the Gunnison Telephone Company to get phone records from the last year. Herb's wife calls to ask him why our phone number in Gunnison was on her bill. Ernie also has Ox get a copy of my pay stub under the ruse of needing it for his landlord. Ernie wants to make sure he really has to pay the child support. I negotiate for a higher amount for alimony for a shorter term so I can get through graduate school. My strategy so far to deny, deny, deny seems to be working. I just have to keep up the front for two years until I finish my master's program. Fish on a hook.

5

WOODY AND ME

PART III

Herbert and I spend some time of each workday neck-ing in his office, especially after 5:00 pm when most of the other professors go home. Herb always keeps his door locked. Toward the end of the semester, the head of his department unlocks the door and enters unannounced, apparently checking on us. We are not disheveled, so we just wheel our chairs around to our respective desks and are engaged in working by the time he enters. One of his weirdest professor neighbors talks to me one day, saying something about my husband. I look at him quizzically and explain that I do not have a husband; I am divorced. For my birthday in October, Herb orders a jacket for me from Victoria's Secret. By Christmas he is receiving their mail-ers at his university mailbox. The mail is distributed by the department secretary. I tell Herb he better talk with the secretary, pleading with her to help him get rid of this nui-sance that someone else has obviously signed him up for. The catalogues continue to pour in. He orders a long red silk nightgown for me for Christmas. One day, while teas-ing him, I circle my sizes on a page of bras and panties.

~~

During my second semester in the school counseling program, I have two significant experiences in the group counseling class, which includes the students in the school counseling program cohort and the school psychologist cohort. The instructors, Mike and Randy, structure the course so that we spend the first 90 minutes of the night class learning and discussing group counseling theory, and the second 90 minutes we engage in group counseling. With a membership of more than thirty students, it takes some wrangling to manage the interactions. Early on in the course we are invited to join in a circle, take a piece of notebook paper, and, working on the paper behind our backs, tear out the shape of a horse. More than half of the students have shared their horses, laughing and joking about their efforts. I am holding back when Mike stands in front of me.

"You seem a bit reluctant to share," he observes.

"I am," I acknowledge.

"Do you know why?"

"I am just realizing that I do not like myself very much." I am tearing up.

"And have not for a long time?" he queries.

"Not for a long time." I cry silently.

During the following weeks, members of my cohort go out of their way to give me compliments, telling me how smart and competent I am. I agree with them. I do many things well, but that is a completely different issue from how much I actually like myself. I have much to think about.

The second incident occurs near the end of the semester. One night during our discussion just prior to the beginning

on the actual group counseling experiences, I ask a question—I am not sure what, and Randy responds,

"Dawn, you are the guiltiest, no, the second guiltiest
woman I know. I would like to run an experiment with you."
With my assent, he arranges the group members in a circle
and places me inside the circle. Then he tells the group,

"Dawn is going to go around the circle and each one of
you will give her something to carry."

According to the instructions I move from class
member to class member. Some give me smaller items,
others give me textbooks or loose-leaf binders. Generally, I
say thank you to the giver. I am more than halfway around
the circle, thinking about how I learned so much guilt from
my Momma when I realize that all of the items I am carrying, which by now fill my arms and are increasingly bur-
densome, are not, in fact my burdens. They are things that
belong to others. With this realization, I simply drop everything. I do not say anything. I return to my seat, leaving it
to the donors to retrieve their own items. Some of the class
members are mildly amused, a few are more than irritated.
I realize that guilt has provided me a lifelong framework on
which I have been able to hang many things.

~

Trina and CC fit in well at school; both find a group of
friends within a few weeks. They like the new ballet school,
but getting through my classes, through my campus employment, and then getting them to ballet is complicated. Just
before Christmas, I borrow $5,000 from Deb and use it to
buy Trina a little used Nissan Sentra, burgundy. Her part-
time job to pay for the car is driving herself and her sister
to and from school every weekday and to and from ballet

classes two or three times per week. She is a good driver and very reliable in this assignment. We even get her set up to carpool with two of CC's classmates in ballet. Their mother takes them to ballet, and Trina delivers them home. Our system works.

🖎

After the holiday break, I switch over to working in the office for students with disabilities. I administer tests such as the Woodcock-Johnson and meet with students to arrange for the supports and accommodations outlined by Dr. Roberts, my supervisor, in the student's psycho-educational evaluation. In late May, I get a call at my work office from the BYU Honor Code Office. They are expecting me at an appointment, meaning an interview, on Tuesday morning, which they already know will not conflict with my work schedule nor with my classes. They tell me the interview is part of a broader investigation. It is unnerving that they know so much about my schedule and are so imperious in their demands. I do not panic, but I am plenty worried. Herbert is disconcerted. When he was first hired at BYU, he was a bit of the golden child, the fair-haired boy. When he divorces his first wife, his brother-in-law, who is also in the education department tells him that since he is abdicating his role as a father, he will be happy to fill in for him. In reality, Herb is an exemplary divorced husband and father. When calculating child support, he divides his income by five and gives four-fifths of the money to his ex-wife for the care of his children, living on the other fifth. He is honestly never late with a child support payment. When each child turns eighteen, Herb's income goes up. His children are eligible for free tuition at BYU because of his continued employment.

I call Carrie Ann to talk about the pending interview with the Honor Code Office. She thinks they are after Herbert. She advises me to admit to nothing. We laugh about how both of us, when accused of something, tend to go way beyond mea culpa—you are right! It is all my fault. I did everything you say and more.

The interviewer, Brother Ogden, tells me they have had several calls about me. What, he wonders, is my relationship with Dr. Herbert Nielsen? I explain in the simplest terms possible. We meet when I am a student in his course. We stay in touch during my teaching internship because he provides me with more mentoring than I actually have from my student teaching supervisor, which is entirely true. When Herbert learns that I am getting a divorce and have been accepted into the School Counselor Education program, he offers me a graduate assistantship. After my divorce, when we decide to date, I seek another graduate assistantship. When did we start dating? Our first official date is in October, after my divorce hearing. We go to a Broadway musical at the Capital Theater. I actually see, and speak with, two women from Gunnison that night. When was my divorce final? November. According to the Honor code Office, we should have waited until after the divorce was final. I do not tell him that Herbert and I are planning to marry in August, nor that we are waiting until the end of the school year to tell my kids.

The Honor Code officer brings up another issue: A neighbor in my apartment complex saw Herbert and me leaving my apartment together one day last February. It was before seven in the morning. Explain that? I actually remember the day clearly. We had a light dusting of snow during the night, and when I answer the door, I notice that Herbert's are the only footsteps in the snow as he walks to my door, picking me up to drive me to school. My daughters are still at home—they have not yet left for school. I am in trouble because BYU students, regardless of their age—I am 45 years old—cannot have a member of the opposite sex in their living quarters before 7 a.m. nor after 1 p.m. I am so grateful that the neighbor had not noticed us on another day when we left later. My daughters had gone to school, and we just had sex on the floor of my living room. Herbert and I actually know exactly which neighbor calls. She lives kitty-corner across the parking lot. Herbert had been her student teaching supervisor, and he did not give her a good recommendation. There is more coming.

The interviewer asks me if I know anything about Victoria's Secret? I tell him that I know that Dr. Nielsen has received several monthly mailers from them, explaining that the photos of women in underwear were nearly pornographic. I report that I advise Dr. Nielsen to get help from the department secretary to stop the apparent subscription. The interviewer reports that one of the mailers was found in Herbert's desk with sizes circled on some of the items. Do I know anything about that? Over the weekend, in anticipation of the interview, I decide that I owe the BYU Honor Code Office exactly nothing. I am going to be asked about intimate details of my life by a person with whom I have no relationship. He is not my bishop. He is not my therapist. I find during the interview that rationale feels true. I cannot imagine making confessions to a total stranger. The interviewer requires that I meet with my ward bishop and have my Ecclesiastical Endorsement renewed within 2 weeks and have my bishop complete another confidential form for the Honor Code Office.

I call my bishop immediately to make the appointment. I know any delay will heighten the suspicions. I explain that I am in some trouble because Herbert and I started dating before my divorce was final. During my interview with the bishop, I explain my interview with the Honor Code office and cite my two specific violations, dating before my divorce is final and having a man in my apartment before 7 a.m. The bishop is very deliberate in going through the Ecclesiastical Endorsement form. For a while I almost think he is not going to sign it, eventually he does. I think he keeps the Honor Code form because he wants to talk with them before completing it. I flee his office with gratitude. If nothing else comes up, I am covered through the end of my program.

Things do not go so well for Herbert. Within a week he is summoned to the Smoot Building, the location of the BYU Administrative Offices, for what amounts to a tribunal, for lack of a better word. In attendance is the dean of his department, BYU legal counsel, and his ex-wife, Lana, and her friend, Sally. The two women present enough testimony about his failure to keep BYU standards by plying them with alcohol and engaging in premarital or extramarital sex that his employment is suspended on the spot. The dean of his department persuades the panel to keep Herbert on the payroll until the end of December when he will be eligible for his pension. This concession is granted. Herbert tells me that when he moves out of his house with Lana, she says to him, "I will destroy you." And she tries. Herbert is out of his BYU office within days. He gets into a graduate program for Education Administration. He has

enough experience and contacts in the school districts that
he has an administrator internship set up for the fall.

I am hired as one of two school counselor interns at
Provo High School, one of the best school counseling programs in the state, which makes it arguably one of the best
school counseling programs in the country. Herbert and I
move forward with our plans to marry in August. We qualify for a home loan before his job at BYU unravels. Construction on our tract home will be completed the first of
October, just before the loan approval runs out. Herbert
starts coming to church with me. One Sunday in mid-June
Herbert is not in attendance. The featured speaker is one of
my favorite men in the ward, one of two counselors for the
bishop. His subject is the "blackness of sin" or something
like that. He does use that exact phrase within the talk. His
talk is well-prepared and interesting. I am pretty sure that it
is aimed directly at me. As soon as I get home from church,
the bishop calls me to say that he wants me to come to his
office at 3:00. I recognize that this day has been set up as a
big manipulation for me. I tell myself that I am dealing with
rank amateurs. I have dealt with the world-class manipula-
tions of my sexual abusers. The interview with the bishop
is predictable. It does not in any way inspire me to confess
my sexual transgressions. My goal is to complete my school
counselor program, get a job, and support my children.

In July, the bishop calls me into his office again. The
bishop of Herbert's ex-wife has called him. They want to
advise me that Herbert is a predator and womanizer. I will
not find happiness with him. I tell the bishop I will consider
what he has said. I think about the warning on my walks
through the neighborhood over the next few days. While
I am out walking, I see a pickup truck with big mud flaps

adorned by those little metal women who look like play-boy bunnies. I have never seen Herbert treat any woman as an object. I think that Herbert's ex just wants revenge. I ignore the bishop's warning, feeling like he will do anything to manipulate me. I move forward with the plans for an early August wedding at Deb's country club.

Herbert and I do marry in August. My children sit on the front row and weep openly. After the ceremony they stand and retreat en mass down the center aisle. Debra meets them with her arms spread wide and tells them, "You do not have to be happy, but you do have to be nice." They come back and give us hugs along with the other guests. We move into our new house and work to make ends meet on two educator intern positions, each at half-salary, and student loans. As I near completion of my school counselor program in the spring, I have a conversation with CC. We are talking at the kitchen bar. I acknowledge that there have been lots of changes in her life over the past few years.

"If you ever need to talk, I am here to listen."

Looking me dead in the eye, she replies, "Why would I talk to you? I have friends."

I nearly fall off the bar stool laughing. "Well so much for my top-notch school counselor skills."

🪶

One Sunday Ernie arranges to meet Trina and CC early in the morning, eight or nine-ish, spending about half of the day together. When my daughters return home in the after-noon, they tell me that they accompanied Ernie and their other siblings to the office of an alleged counselor whom they call Byron. In the course of the conversation, they reveal that Byron tells them something like the following:

"Because of your mother's childhood sexual abuse, she was like a ticking timebomb. She exploded when she had the affair and left your father." It is hard for me to sort out which part of this story leaves me the most furious. I think I have to go with Byron, the alleged professional counselor, who has the hubris to analyze me without ever meeting me and then share that analysis in a professional setting with my children. I think I am next most angry that Ernie has the unmitigated gall to believe that the story of my sexual abuse is his to share with our children; I have discussed this, in a limited way, with some of our children, but not all of our children. Finally, I have full custody of Trina and CC. Ernie has liberal visitation rights. He does not have the right to haul our two minor children off the see a counselor without consulting me.

✒

At the end of May, the administration at Provo High School decides to combine the two school counseling intern positions into one full-time, full-pay position. Terry, the other intern school counselor, and I agree—we would both hire each other for the job. We both interview with the principal, two teachers and the chair of the school counseling department. The building principal, Dr. Patti Harrington, calls to offer me the full-time position; I am so grateful to have a job and so relieved to not have to go looking for employment. When I tell Trina and CC that the full-time job is mine, they jump up and down and scream with excitement. I think they are happier than I am. After all they have been through, they know that Mom can actually do this. She can take care of herself and take care of them.

✐

It is likely obvious to everyone that I should have chosen to attend a university other than BYU. I obviously was not capable and/or motivated to live by their strict code of conduct. I did consider going to the University of Utah to finish my bachelor's degree, but I would have had to move my three children to Salt Lake or leave them in Gunnison with Ernie—too much disruption for their lives. As it turns out my affair was far more disrupting, far more devastating than a potential move which I am not sure they would have agreed to anyway. Fish on a hook.

✐

After Herbert completes his Ed Admin program, he has nearly two dozen rejections before he hires on as the principal of a small alternative education high school. At last, he has a laboratory where he can test his theories. He self-publishes his text. He has a job he loves even more than being a professor.

Once Herbert and I have full-time jobs, I go to my bishop, Jack Christiansen, to begin the repentance process for my adulterous affair. There is nothing to do but tell him the full story, not the sexual details, but the timeline and full extent of our transgressions. There is a difference if it were a one or two-time offense as opposed to our weekly and, when we can get away with it, more frequent encounters. In order to complete the repentance process, I will have to attend a Bishop's Court, which means a meeting with me, the bishop, his two counselors, and the executive secretary. The thought of being alone in a room for hours with four powerful men—they all hold the LDS Priesthood, whereas women do not—fills me with terror. Perhaps this is one of the ways I have not recovered from the childhood sexual abuse. I am so distraught that Herbert talks with the bishop and the Stake President to get permission to sit in on the Bishop's Court with me. My Bishop's Court is held on a weeknight evening.

After I tell my story and answer any questions that they may have, Herbert and I sit in the waiting area outside the Bishops' Office while they debate my fate. The disciplinary measures can range from refraining from taking weekly sacrament, to probation, to disfellowship, to excommunication, which requires a rebaptism if the penitent soul wants to resume membership with the Saints. Herbert, as my co-conspirator, is also on trial. After more than an hour we are called back into the Court. Our discipline is disfellowship, with all of the restrictions of excommunication. We cannot take the weekly sacrament, nor offer any prayers at church, give any lessons, accept any speaking assignments or any church callings. After 6 months we meet again. The discipline of disfellowship and the restrictions are extended for another 6 months. After a year we are both restored to full membership and can participate in our ward activities. None of this process is reported to the membership at large, but everyone notices when a member does not take the sacrament. I have made my repentance and am at peace with the Lord. I confess to my stake president, who is also the superintendent of a local district, that I feel guilty about cheating my way into some excellent work opportunities. He tells me I will just have to pray for forgiveness.

Now that Herbert and I have full-time jobs he wants to replace my Nissan Maxima that has over 200,000 miles.

The cute little silver car goes with Ernie and I to California and back and then sees me through my bachelor's degree and graduate school. We are thinking Honda Accord, so we head over on a Saturday afternoon for a test drive. It is a good suburban mom car, not too exciting. In the used car section, they have an Acura Vigor, only 40,000 miles and the same price as the new Accord. The steering on the Accord is stiff but the ride is solid. The steering on the Vigor is tight; she has some go, a luxury sport sedan. I choose the Vigor. I am thrilled with my new used car, and now the Maxima is free for CC for school transport and modern, jazz, and some ballet dance classes at The Dance Club, a better fit for her than the more regimented ballet school. She is a new driver, but responsible.

The day before the Fourth of July weekend, CC wants to go to Gunnison with a girlfriend for the small-town parade, the fireworks, and the carnival at the city park, an annual fundraiser for the Lions Club. I am okay with that. Just hours before they are to leave, Trina says she is not going. CC wants to drive on her own. I express my concerns that she does not have enough experience for the 95-mile trip. She accuses me of trying, once again, to keep her from seeing her dad. By the time the two teens leave our house, I know she will be driving at least the last 40 miles on a two-lane road in the dark. Not surprisingly, they have an accident. About a mile north of the turn-off for the reservoir, CC pulls out to pass a car. When she sees an on-coming car, she overcorrects and loses control, the Maxima leaves the road on the opposite side of the highway, when the car hits the dirt shoulder it goes into a corkscrew roll, with two or three full twists and nose plants in a deep rut. Luckily, other cars stop to help, calling the ambulance and Ernie. I do not hear about the accident until nearly 10 p.m. I am so angry when Ernie tells me that he is not taking them to the hospital for exams—that the EMT checks are good enough. Of course, the car is totaled. I call the next morning, planning to drive down to pick up CC and her friend. She adamantly refuses—they are okay and she is staying until Sunday.

When CC finally makes it home, nearly 48 hours after the wreck, I quiz her carefully about what happened and how she feels. I express amazement that the two young women escaped unscathed. CC says,

"Momma, didn't I tell you that the entire time we were rolling and even when we came to a harsh stop, I felt like I was being held on someone's lap. I don't have any aches, no pains or bruises." Her friend has the same experience. I tell them both they were likely watched over by my father, Woody, and my stepfather, Arlo. They do not disagree. Woody may be the God of Cars.

With a houseful of kids, we often do hand-me-down cars as well as hand-me-down clothes. Luna has a nice full-time job and buys herself a used BMW, freeing up the 10-year-old Camry she has been driving. Dora drives one of Ernie's used cars and Ox drives the little Ford Ranger pickup. Trina gets the Camry, freeing up the burgundy Sentra for CC. She has the car for most of December. When she and couple of girlfriends want to go to a New Year's Eve Party a little over a mile away, I agree. It is nearing eleven when CC calls to tell me there has been an accident. They had changed their minds when they ran into some guy friends, not boyfriends, just guy friends. They decide to go up Provo Canyon instead and have a bonfire.

They scout their location while it is still light, then go down to the valley to buy firewood and hotdogs. They are good kids, no alcohol involved with this one. They head back up the mountain, cook their food and hang around the camp-fire until all the wood is burned up and the ashes are put out with snow. Heading down the mountain, CC lets Dan drive. He is the best driver in the bunch, so a good thing. The canyon is considerably colder. The roads have iced up. They hit a patch and slide into a tree, mashing up the front passenger side. They all have on seatbelts. No one is hurt. They have to walk nearly a mile to a house with a phone. She describes their location, but begs me not to come, one parent is already on the way. I go to the mountain anyway. I know the moment I see the car that the frame is bent and therefore totaled. One of the mothers says to me,

"I am just so grateful that no one was hurt."

"I am just so pissed that they were not where they were supposed to be, that I just put $900 into this car for a drive chain and an oil pan, and that it is now likely totaled." She has no response. My words are probably the reason CC did not want me to come up the canyon.

The next day I say to her, "This is second car you have totaled in 6 months: it is clear to me that God does not want you to drive."

"It is clear to me, too," she admits. I tell her that I will get her through the last half of her junior year, taking her where she needs to go when she needs to be there. "But you have to work with me. I still have a full-time job. Plan things out as much as possible." By the time she is a senior in high school we are spending 8 or 9 hours a week in the car together, to school, to her three or four times a week dance classes, and to her merchandising internship at the anchor store at the mall. Riding side by side every day, we are able to talk. For more than a decade, it will be easier for us to talk side by side than face to face. In the end, the car wrecks are a gift from the Universe.

&

In the meantime, Trina, the recipient of the Camry is living at home with us in Orem and planning to drive to the University of Utah to complete her degree. Herbert buys new tires for her car. Both CC and Trina wonder why Herbert would put new tires on a car he does not own? "So she can be safe," he tells them. After high school graduation, Trina, who originally had no real plans for college, gets one of two new scholarships from her ballet school to the new program at the local community college. It is enough to keep her in classes and completing her general ed requirements. Most of her friends are working, playing, and spending their money. This is the same choice she makes back in high school when she gives up cheerleading in tenth grade. At the time, before spring tryouts, she tells me, "I cannot do both cheerleading and ballet."

"So, what do you want to do?"

"I am sticking with ballet, but it will make a difference to all my friends."

"No?"

"Yes, it will."

"Are you sure?"

"On my worst day, I go to ballet, listen to the piano, dance, and everything gets better." She is right about the friends. They act like she betrays them, cutting her out of many social interactions. She gets the courage to move during her senior year.

She goes on to complete a BFA in ballet at the University of Utah, dancing some 30 hours per week. She is one of the few students in the program who works a part-time job to stay in school. After graduation she also completes training and licensing for massage therapy. And a Pilates certification. She tells me when it comes to exercising it is first, breathing; second, alignment; third strength and speed. I always have to remember to breathe.

☙

My first year as a school counselor is a huge learning curve. My second year I am still the junior counselor in the department. I am not the youngest, but I am the most recent hire. Everyone but me has an area of specialization or some expertise. Midyear we receive an application for the U.S. Army Planning for Life Awards. Bruce, the department chair, wonders if anyone wants to make the application. I volunteer, spending about 100 hours outside of my school days putting together the 3" binder-sized application. When I am done, I know all I have is a really good rough draft. I submit it to the state school counseling leader. She says it is one of her top five applications. The next year I spend another 100 hours outside of my contract time and come up with a solid application. This time we place second in the national competition. When I tell Bruce, our counseling department chair, this news, his only remark is, "Well I'd like to know who finished first." He doesn't thank me for the extra hours of effort. The following year I spend about another 40 hours outside of my contract hours upgrading the presentation and highlighting the program features that the judging panel thought were missing. Those elements were already in place, I just needed to emphasize them. This third year our application is recognized as one of two National Honorees in the U.S. Army Planning for Life Awards.

From a professional practice perspective, the actual work of analyzing a top-quality program serves me more than the award itself. I have not designed the program, but I am a strong contributor who makes a difference for students. I enjoy the all-expenses-paid trip to San Antonio, TX, to the American School Counseling Association National Conference and the friends and colleagues that I gain through that experience. I meet people who will become my professional learning community, influencing my professional practice for the next 2 decades. My second round of 15 minutes of fame is even better than the first. San Antonio is one of my favorite cities. Ernie and I stay there several times when we are taking our children to Corpus Christi to see their great grandma, Mamaw Boyd. For this new award at the conference, I have a room at the Hilton with a balcony overlooking the San Antonio River Walk. It is a bit of fantasy come true for me.

In August, after the summer recognition from the U.S. Army, I am back on contract and working at the high school, when I receive a call from the head of Student Services at the Utah State Office of Education. The woman who has been the specialist for secondary school counseling programs is taking a 1-year leave of absence. They invite me to take her place. I am speechless. Really, I do not know what to say. I am so silent that the caller, R. Lynn Jensen, suggests that I take the weekend to think about it. I agree to call him back on Monday. Of course, I want this opportunity, but as school counselors go, I am kind of a toddler with barely four years of experience. On Monday I call to accept the offer. The arrangement works like this: Technically, I stay employed by Provo School District. The State will "borrow" me for a year, paying the district for my salary. At the end of the year, I get to come back to a job that I love. Oh, and my salary for the year nearly doubles to the state rate.

I really like working at the state office of education. During my first 6 weeks, my most common response to technical assistance questions is, "I don't know, but I will find out." And I do, learning and working hard to do so, putting in 50 to 60 hours per week. I know I have 1 year to make myself indispensable. My youngest daughter has gone off to college, and I have the time and will to work hard. At the end of the year, the specialist who was on leave decides to go back to work in a school. They open the position for interviews. Having had a year of experience, I am chosen as the new full-time specialist for secondary school counseling for the entire state. Over the years, I have opportunities to participate with several national work groups: reviewing other applicants for the Planning for Life Awards, several national meetings on school counselor accountability, advising the development of a national model for school counseling programs. I make several presentations at the national level and many more at the state level. In 2009 I am recognized as the national school counseling director of the year. But my life will fall apart before that happens.

Herbert's new career progresses as well. He loves being an administrator for a large group of struggling teenagers. He works hard to create individualized learning programs and supports for each student. Herbert has always made friends with women more easily than he makes friends with men. He has two or three long-term male friends, but for the most part his day-to-day friends are women. He hires my two best friends to work at the school: Carrie Ann is a paraeducator who eventually becomes a special education teacher and Cassidy is the main office secretary. I am not concerned. Our marriage is solid, or so I think. We rarely have any disagreements. We work to make improvements on our house. Like Napoleon Dynamite says, "Girls like guys with skills." Herbert has skills, and I am a great assistant in putting in landscaping, building a deck, finishing the basement. For 18 months Herbert loses himself completely in creating a set of curricula for the core academic subjects with a format consistent with his instructional strategy. His detractors mock it as "the White Curriculum" because of the 3" binders in which it is bound. In frustration at his total submersion, I tell him he reminds me of Shel Silberstein's Jimmy Jet and His TV Set—only it's a computer.

🖋

Nine years into our marriage, Herbert begins having excruciating headaches. Thanksgiving weekend he develops a blood clot in his leg, requiring 2 weeks off work. Home rest does not improve the headaches, so he is given leave through the holidays. By January, his son-in-law, who works as an orderly at the regional hospital, has Herbert's MRI reviewed by one of the best neurosurgeons in the state. The diagnosis is hydrocephalus, which usually appears in men a decade older. He has surgery to put a shunt in his brain with a drain into his abdomen. After the usual recovery period, the pain and headaches persist. He stays on sick leave through the end of the year. In May the neurosurgeon decides to reconfigure the drain. After the surgery, I asked the doctor,

"Is he going to recover? 'Cause right now he is so not himself, and I cannot tell whether it is the pain, the meds, or maybe brain damage."

"And neither can I," he responds. "We just have to wait and see."

I try to breathe through the panic that is bearing down on me. By fall he improves but is not fully back to normal. The district removes him as principal at the alternative high school. They offer him the position of administrator for a new school for severe/profoundly disabled students. He dives into the work with gusto, working hard every week for the full week. On the weekends it is a different story. He often spends most of Saturday and Sunday in bed. If he goes out to do gardening on Saturday morning, he is most certainly in bed for the rest of the weekend. He no longer travels with me for the two national conferences I attend through my job every year. When Dora and her Swiss husband plan a trip to Switzerland with their two young children to visit her husband's family, Herbert suggests that I go with them. They welcome the extra help with the children. I love the personalized tour and intimate contact with the in-laws. Herbert sends me off with them for three weeks in Europe. I call from Paris, "I have seen the Seine. I can die happy."

Our marriage lurches along for another three years in the same rhythm. Herbert is less affectionate and much less sexually active, which he attributes to his health. During my school counseling program, I have many opportunities to take a variety of assessments. On a little instrument called the FIRO-B, I am identified as having a pathologically high need for affection. I find myself spending less and less time with Herbert. When we do spend time together, we usually watch a DVD, generally Broadway shows or hero films like Tombstone, Last of the Mohicans, Braveheart. One of the things Herbert likes about working with the alternative students and the special ed students is that he can frequently be a hero.

In January, realizing that I am spending less and less time with him, I make an offer:

"Hey, I am off work for President's Day. How about I come over to your office and help you tidy up. We can go to lunch."

"Oh, my office is already tidy enough," he responds.

I know instantly that this is not true. I spend enough time in his offices over the years to know that his office is never tidy. "It's almost like he doesn't want me around," I think to myself.

The next day Herbert says, "I know what you should do on President's Day. You should go spend the day with your grandson." That is a good option, even a preferred option from my perspective, but in my head, I am thinking, "Wow, he really does not want me around on Monday."

I find some time alone and call Carrie Ann. I retell these two conversations with Herbert, "I can't tell you why I think so, but I know the minute he says it that he is lying about his tidy office. What do you think I should do?"

"I think you should just drive down there on Monday and surprise him with lunch," she advises.

On Monday, Herbert thinks I will just be hanging out at home and taking my sewing machine in for some service. But I drive down to his office with sandwiches and dessert from one of our favorite eateries. When I get to the school, the parking lot is empty—no sign of his little silver truck, nor any other vehicles. I wait for about 10 minutes, then drive out to the street and back into the parking lot. I wait another 10 minutes and drive out to the street again, noting that there are only two cars parked at the curb. I write down both license plate numbers. I go back to the parking lot, positioning my car so that I can see him coming down the hill. After some 40 minutes of waiting, I see the truck. I am not wearing my glasses, and it is too far away for me to see if he is alone. At the entrance of the parking lot there are some large shrubs and trees that completely obscure approaching vehicles. He takes an inordinately long time to pass the greenery.

When he parks his car and gets out, he does not smile at me, which he usually does. I tell him I have only been waiting a few minutes and that I have lunch and dessert. He shakes the remaining ice in his fast-food drink cup—he has an endless appetite for fast food—and tells me has just had lunch, but we can have dessert. Before we eat, he needs to go down to the activity room at the end of the building furthest from the street. He points out a few things in the activity room to me, then goes over to the window and adjusts the blinds, opening and closing them several times. We also go by the sensory room, a 12×12 space with a padded floor and walls, and with light and sound controls outside the door. Every time I have been at his school, he takes me by the sensory room, carefully unlocking the door and relocking it after we step inside momentarily. He seems obsessed by the sensory room. I find all of this behavior mildly disturbing.

After my surprise visit to his school and his bizarre behavior, I start worrying that he is maybe having an affair. He talks a lot about the women he works with and some of the mothers of the students. Finally, I tell myself, "This is ridiculous. He is your friend. Just talk to him." On Sunday afternoon, we are sitting in the living room when I tell him what I have been worrying about for the past 2 weeks. The first words out of his mouth are, "Well, do you want a divorce?"

"Where did that come from?" I am stunned. "I thought we could always talk."

Over the next few weeks nothing gets any clearer. The day after Valentine's Day I find a receipt on the dresser from a florist for a $75 bouquet that was picked up on Valentine's Day. I did not get flowers for Valentine's Day. Not mentioning the receipt, I tell Herbert how disappointed I am about not getting flowers for Valentine's Day. He mumbles through an excuse—probably he did not feel well. I order my own bouquet of pale pink roses with white accents. Herbert is livid. At church on Sunday, I ask Cassidy if Herbert bought flowers for her on Valentine's Day. She does not say no, but she asks me why I am asking. I tell her about the receipt. I think of Cassidy because I know that both Herbert and I worry about her. Cassidy is going through a terrible divorce. I know that even though she no longer works for him, Herbert meets her for lunch every week to check in on her and cheer her up. But I also recall the time a year or so prior when I was heading out the door for a national conference and he asks me,

"Can I have Cassidy over for a sleepover?"

Flabbergasted, I flatly respond, "Herbert, that is not funny." I never joke about bad marriages or cheating behaviors.

For these first 2 months or so, I try desperately to save my marriage, reaching out, including, talking. At the end of March, I must go to a conference in Phoenix to make

a half-day presentation with a colleague. At the conference, I am sitting in a morning session in the same room
we will occupy after lunch. At the lunch break, I am so surprised to see my niece, daughter of my oldest stepsister,
walking up the aisle toward me. I have not seen her since
the funeral for her mother; my stepsister who shot herself
in the heart with a twenty-two pistol, nearly 20 years ago.
When Momma marries Daddy Arlo and we move to New
Mexico, this niece, one of the joys of my new life, is the
little 3-year-old who fits perfectly on my hip. I do not know
that my niece is a school counselor, and I do not know that
she lives in Arizona—too many moves and name changes
let me lose track of her. We go to lunch to catch up. The
connection we have always shared happens immediately. I
fill her in on all the details of my current situation.

My conversation with my niece gets me thinking. Children who come from abusive backgrounds have had so
many of their choices taken away that it is therapeutically
important to give them back those choices. I know from
many conversations that Herb has a history of serious abuse.

One night in Phoenix I kneel and pray for guidance in how
to proceed with Herbert. My answer is, "Let him go." I have
no idea what that might look like. I interpret this to mean give
him more choices. When I get home, I share my insights with
Herbert. He seems to understand. When I come home from
church on the following Sunday, he tells me,

"Cassidy says that Carrie Ann says that I am ripe for an
affair."

"Why would Cassidy tell you that?" I am incredulous,
both that the conversation happens and that he shares that
information with me. It becomes increasingly clear that
Herbert does not have good boundaries. He comes home

from school and tells me how the friend of one of his jani-
torial staff, a student from his days at the alternative high
school, has been talking with him about her surgery and
shows him the location of a scar by stretching her clothes
tightly across her stomach. Herbert tells me that he is
going to help her with some counseling. I remind him that
talking with younger women about their bodies is not an
appropriate topic for a boss. And I remind him that he is
not qualified for, nor licensed as, a counselor.

I recall a conversation that I had with Carrie Ann
nearly a year ago. At the time, Herbert tells me that one
of his previous employees, Lisa C., is trying to get her life
back together and he is willing to hire her back if she will
do some counseling with him. I remind him that he is
neither qualified for, nor licensed to be, a counselor, and
that it is unethical have a dual relationship with Lisa—he
cannot be her boss and her counselor at the same time.
When I relate this story to Carrie Ann one night after our
yoga class, she gets really angry and tells me about talking with Herbert about Lisa C. during her first round of
employment after she had worked at the alternative high
school for a year or so. Carrie goes to Herbert's office and
confronts him.

"Lisa C. is not doing her job and you know it. If it were
one of us you would be all over it. What's up with that? Are
you screwing her?"

Herbert denies any untoward engagement with Lisa.
I have not previously discussed with Herbert what Carrie
said about Lisa C., but I share the story with him now. He
claims he does not recall that conversation with Carrie
Ann. In fact, my conversations with Herbert have become
so confusing that I start keeping a notebook—a two column

steno pad with one column labeled "what Herbert says" and another column labeled "what I know to be true."

Herbert has always had a huge interest in astrology. He has consulted a professional astrologer for years. I have always had a fascination with metaphysics. Some of my first conversations with Herbert centered on what is real. I, myself, have been to see Peggy, his astrologer. The first time was just after I started graduate school. One of the things that Peggy tells me is that Venus is transiting my sun, an event that occurs only once every 80 years. It usually indicates finding the love of your life. She also notes that likely I meet Herbert earlier than my little Virgo nature would have liked. I have always presented myself to the world as a good girl. Herbert considers himself a top-grade amateur astrologer. He has dozens of books on the subject and a program on his computer that enables him to run a chart on anyone at any time. In the early years of our marriage, we are reading from one of the texts on an aspect in his chart. One of the observations states that "his need for a secret life will destroy him." Now, I look again for the quote, but I am unable to find it.

My yoga instructor gives me the name of a really good LDS astrologer. In regard to this seeming contradiction, my yogi tells me that at one point, Reed the astrologer, is investigated by his LDS Stake President, who, in conclusion, tells him to just keep doing what he is doing. One of the things Reed observes is that Pluto is in my twelfth house,

"Are you psychic?" he asks.

"If you had asked me that question before Christmas, I would have told you no, but now there are things that I just know about Herbert. Usually within a few days he brings me information to confirm what I thought I knew." My conversation with the astrologer is helpful.

I decide to see a counselor. I have an appointment within a week. The counselor, Rex, tells me that he cannot determine whether or not my husband is having an affair, but he can help me process what I am thinking and noticing. One of the big problems is that having had an affair with Herbert myself taints everything. Rex says to me, "One thing you might consider is getting tested for STDs. There are a lot of dangerous things out there and what does not kill you may make you wish you were dead." Rex and I decide that I will invite Herbert to our session next week. At the next session Herbert has an opportunity to explain what he thinks is going on. Rex observes,

"I do not know everything, but I can tell you that you [Herbert] are being awfully defensive. What she really needs is reassurance that you love her and are committed to her."

Rex reminds Herbert that his having had an affair with me taints everything because, "She knows how good you can lie." Herbert bristles obviously at this remark.

What I need is an opportunity to drop in on him at the school during the week just to see what is going on. I do that over the next several weeks, working in the classrooms volunteering with the care of the students. I work most often with Rachel, the mother of a severely disabled student that Herbert has talked about a lot. The first week, Rachel comments on my manicure—My nails are always done. My job is very public, and I dress for it. The second, week Rebecca has her nails done. The third week, Rachel wears a new top in bright turquoise, the same color as the jacket I wore the week before. I have no conclusions here—just noticing behavior.

On a Tuesday I am driving home from work. Carrie Ann calls to check on me. I tell her about seeing Rex and hanging out at the school. I tell her I have to ask her about something. I relate to her Herbert telling me that Cassidy says that she, Carrie, said that Herbert is ripe for an affair.

"Why would Cassidy tell him that?" Carrie is irritated.

"That was my question to him," I confess.

"You have to come see me before you go home," she says.

"Carrie, it is after seven, I have been avoiding going home. It will be eight by the time I get there."

"Nevertheless," she says, "You have to come see me before you go home. Promise?"

"I promise."

When I get to Carrie's house, she comes out so we can talk in my car. She tells me that when she was working with Herbert at the alternative high school, she could tell, almost to the day when I had confided to Herbert that Carrie and her husband were having some difficulties, especially related to sex.

"Herbert became more and more attentive, offering me counseling, trying to take me to lunch. He always wanted me to come over to your house to work on the Work Readiness Curriculum when you were out of town. One night we had worked on the curriculum at the school and it had gotten late. I gathered up my things to go. Herbert turns off the lights and then comes over to me and gives me a big hug. I push him away, asking 'What the hell do you think you are doing?'"

"I just wanted to show you how grateful I am for your help," he responds.

"Well, why did you have to turn out the lights?" she demands.

Herbert claims that he has no ill-intent. She tells me that she is so upset that when she arrives at her home she heads straight to the hot tub until her husband comes home. She tells her husband about the incident and then she says,

"Maybe I just misinterpreted it."

Her husband laughs, "Carrie, don't you know how men work? They will try something and then when it fails, they will claim innocence. I was hoping that with Herbert, age would do what religion could not."

Apparently, Carrie's husband always figured Herbert was a player. Carrie goes on to tell me that it was at this time that Herbert kept trying to get us all together for dinner and suggesting to Carrie things that she and I could do together. I tell her that he did the same thing to me to the extent that I said to him, "Herbert, Carrie is my friend. I can figure out how to work our relationship without interference from you."

Before I leave, Carrie says, "This information is yours to use as you need. Tell Herbert that I told you, don't tell him. Do with it what you will."

She continues, "Should I have told you about this when it happened?"

"No, I wouldn't have been ready to accept the information. You needed to wait until I could see it."

When I arrive home, I tell Herbert I am late because Carrie Ann and I were talking. That's all I say, but within the week he is livid when I refuse to have sex with him. "I told you I was going to take a break from anything that binds you to me."

"I have never done anything that even threatens our marriage," he declares.

"Well maybe you crossed the line once or twice," I rebut.

"Carrie Ann completely misinterpreted that hug," he is nearly shouting. I am surprised that he would bring this up.

I still have not mentioned any of the details of my recent conversation with Carrie Ann. I go downstairs to my little sewing room and start reading scriptures. He comes downstairs and glares down at me sitting on the floor. I realize how sanctimonious I might look. I close my scriptures and look up.

"Are you telling me that you will not have sex with me because of something you think I might have done?" he demands.

"Yes, that is what I am telling you." He storms off to bed.

I go to see Rex one more time. I update him with these most recent events. He says to me, "I cannot tell you whether or not your husband has been unfaithful. You do have some interesting incidents to think about. I do know that once you decide what you believe, you will know what to do."

Herbert develops neuropathy in his feet subsequent to the hydrocephalus. At night I massage his feet with Castor Oil—Balma de Christi—to help with the numbness and tingling. I continue this service even after I confront him about his potential involvement with another woman or other women. If I massage his feet after praying, Herbert claims that my hands are "so warm." As I work on his toes, he complains about unusual soreness in the fourth and fifth phalanges. I remind him that Louise Hay, in her book You Can Heal Your Life, associates the fourth digit with grief and relationships and the fifth digit with families and pretending.

"You are just making something out of nothing," he defends.

"I'm not the one with the sore toes," I note.

I do get checked for STDs. I tell my friend, Walstir, the physician who serves with me when I am president of the women's auxiliary in our ward what is going on. Without missing a beat, she says, "Leave him. Go now." I remind her that I have been divorced once, and that first divorce took me eleven years. I will need to take my time and be thoughtful. Walstir is a no-nonsense kind of woman. She grew up in Needles, the worst favella in Rio de Janeiro, Brazil. She went to medical school in Brazil, but she does her internship and residency in the U.S. She tells her Brazilian patients, "I don't do medicine in Portuguese." She also tells me, more than once, "People die. Everyone gets upset when I remind them of that, but it is a fact of life." She delivers all of her wisdom in a thick Brazilian accent.

🖋

After I get the results of my blood tests—all negative— I visit each of my children in person to tell them what is going on. I have to call Ox, who lives in San Diego. Trina tells me,

"I have been so mad at Herbert for the past year and a half."

"Why?" I question.

"He leaves you to go do everything on your own. You may as well be living alone."

CC and her husband tell me I can move into their two-bedroom apartment with them. They are living in Salt Lake City, mere blocks from my office. We make plans for me to move in the next weekend. The following Sunday afternoon, the last week of April, I load up my car with all of my shoes and clothes, my iron and ironing board, sheets, blankets, and my air bed with legs that I ordered out of the Sky Mall catalogue on a cross-country flight years earlier.

✒

Living in Salt Lake with CC and her husband and away from Herbert is a relief. I do not have to go home to the tension, my suspicions, and his denials. My children are kind and supportive, even though, for the most part, they think I might be a bit crazy. I travel north to Logan to visit Dora and her family for Mother's Day. I head out for their house on Friday evening, after work—their two children, ages 6 and 4, always beg me to come and stay "for days and days." They have purchased a beautiful 1910 bungalow that they are remodeling. I sleep on the futon in the living room with my granddaughter, who usually wakes me up at least once during the night when I sleep over. She leans up on one elbow as she says, "Grammie, you are making that noise again." She knows firsthand that I snore like a trooper.

On Saturday night we stay up late talking and laughing. Because of the remodeling project, the windows have no coverings. Sometime after 11 p.m. I look out into the dark—there are few streetlights in this little rural community—the hair on the back of my neck prickles, and somehow, I know that Herbert is out there. Around midnight we go to bed. The night passes uneventfully. In the morning we have breakfast and then my son-in-law prepares Mother's Day lunch for us. After lunch I pack up my things and take them out to my car. I notice that the rear passenger tire is flat. My son-in-law changes the tire for me, and I head to Costco to get the tire repaired. As the technician is preparing my bill, I ask, "Did I pick up a nail?"

"No," he hesitates, looking closely at me.

"What did you find?"

"Well, your valve stem was crimped in a kind of weird way."

"Could that have happened when I had those tires rotated this week?"

"No, no. Not likely," he replies.

            ⌁

This whole Herbert situation makes me feel like I am losing my mind. In fact, that is my particular heartbreak and his biggest betrayal—Herbert, who knows more than anyone how hard-won my sanity is, prefers to let me think I am crazy rather than be honest. This, in spite of my assurances early on that I could and would forgive him. He sits by me on the sofa in the living room one weekend afternoon before I move out. His blue eyes sparkling, he asks me,

"How can you be so forgiving?"

"It is different for men than for women," I tell him. "But I need you to talk to me about it."

Then the conversation turns, "But why does it always have to be your way? Can't we just let this go and not talk about it anymore?"

            ⌁

I am so much less effective at work. My colleague Tom, not knowing what is going on, but seeing that I am not working at my usual level, shows up in my office with an agenda and materials prepared for a meeting I have to run the next day. He repeats this behavior over the months from February through May. When I finally tell him what's up, he tears up and offers to cancel Herbert's presentation for the annual 2-day school-counselor conference he is planning for the second week of June. I tell him not worry about it. "I have become very adept at avoiding Herbert."

I call the best, toughest woman attorney in Utah County. It will take 6 weeks to get in to see her. I still want some hard evidence, so I try turning every rock. I call Rachel, the mother at Herbert's school, and make an appointment to talk with her in her home. When I tell her my concern, that Herbert might have been involved with her, she gets a brief, inappropriate smile on her face. I create my call list based on Herbert's patterns of behavior—excessive conversation about details of her life, perhaps an over-involvement in her affairs. I talk to the secretary at the school. Her car was one of the two cars parked at the curb on President's Day when I surprise Herbert at the school. Same behavior from Herbert with her—excessive conversation about the details of her life, perhaps an over involvement in her personal affairs. I talk to Myken, one of the teachers who was not a faithful Herbert fan, who only lasted 1 year at the school for disabled children. She notes that Herbert does keep a lot of women fans around him, but she saw nothing untoward, in spite of her differences with him.

I am presenting a day-long training for school counselors when I see Lucy, the mother-in-law of Lisa C., Herbert's former employee, in the audience. At the end of the day, she lingers a bit, so I go over to greet her. We chat for a few minutes. Lucy has always been friendly and sincere. I ask her if I could talk with her about a personal matter. I assure her that after I introduce the subject she may not want to continue and should feel free to walk away. My position at the state office of education gives me a lot of influence over school counselors, and I work diligently not to abuse it.

I start the conversation. "Lucy, I know that you and your husband were trying to help your son get full custody of his children after he divorced Lisa. I recall that Herbert was subpoenaed to testify at one hearing, but he never actually did appear in court."

She tells me that other circumstances came to bear and they did not have a hearing. "I know Herbert was quite concerned about having to testify. He was afraid he might not remember clearly after his hydrocephalus and the brain shunt surgery."

"Yes," I respond. "I know that he fretted about having to go to court for weeks."

"I am sorry that put pressure on him."

"Well, there may have been more to it. Herbert was extremely anxious about having to testify in court. Lucy, this is the point where you should feel free to end this conversation."

"Okay."

"Did you ever think that there might have been something going on between Herbert and your daughter-in-law, Lisa?"

"Dawn, it is so interesting that you would ask that. As you may have heard we had lots of concerns for our three granddaughters when they lived with their mother. They would often call me to say, 'Gram we are alone' or 'Gram, we don't have any food.' You know those little girls were just 8, 5, and 3. One night they called me. They were alone and it was late, after dark. I told them I would be right there. When I had them in the car, I asked, 'Where is your mommy?' The oldest says, 'She went to meet Dr. Nielsen. She said, "I have to do whatever it takes to save my job."'"

"Wow," was all I could say. I then share with Lucy my concerns about Herbert being involved with someone else and that I was just wondering if this was a pattern of behavior for him.

Lucy responds, "I always hoped there was nothing to it for your sake. I don't have any more than that. For us it was just one more concern for our little granddaughters."

I thank her for her time and for being so trusting with me.

I call Herbert's ex-wife, the mother of his children. "Janet, this is Dawn. You do not have to talk to me if you don't want to. I am just wondering did Herbert ever admit to you that he was having an affair?" I ask Janet this question because I know he was involved with another woman. I know her name. I know details.

"If you are asking me if I think he is having an affair on you, I will tell you that our circumstances were entirely different," she replies.

Actually, what I am asking is exactly whether or not Herbert could admit to her that he had an affair. Nevertheless, I reveal none of this by simply replying, "I understand. Well, did you file for divorce or did he."

"I filed for the divorce," she tells me.

I also know that after Lana went to BYU to destroy him, she filed for divorce.

More patterns of behavior. "My Lord," I think to myself, "How could I have been so gullible? God, how can he have been so manipulative?"

In preparation of seeing the tough woman attorney, I plan to go by the house in Orem to finish cataloguing the items we purchased during our twelve years together. Every major item I list on a post-it-note with the purchase price, and I line the notes up on the refrigerator door. One column for me. One column for Herbert. We agree on most everything. He is put off that I want the outdoor furniture. I open the garage door and point out to him the table saw, chop saw, nail gun and compressor that he is getting. Believe it or not, we have our most vigorous argument over the red-handled shovel. I am determined to have a new home with a garden. I will need the shovel. I concede completely to him the television and the Bose sound system. It is his only entertainment. We have a 403(b) in my name that we both contributed to. I want that $20,000.

On my way to Herbert's, Cassidy calls me, "Dawn, I think Herb is suicidal."

"What?" I am a bit incredulous.

"He says that he feels so bad, he just wants to end it all."

"Cassidy, are you still meeting Herbert for lunch every week?"

"Well, not every week," she replies.

"I need you to quit talking to him," I state.

"Why?" she wonders.

"I know you mean well, but you talking to him is not helping. I think he might be grooming you to be his next girlfriend."

"But we are just friends."

"It may be different for him." I tell her the story about him asking me if he could have her over for a sleepover. "Seriously, Cassidy. I am warning you. He may not be all that he seems."

When I get to Herbert's house, our house, he is getting ready to mow the lawn. I start the conversation, "Cassidy tells me that you told her you are suicidal."

Looking me directly in the eye, he says, "I did not tell Cassidy that." Then he gives me the weirdest smile as he places his garden hat on his head at a jaunty angle. Creeps me out completely.

When I see the lawyer, at the end of June, I am prepared with all these details of property and money distribution. We decide I will not ask for alimony, even though Herbert makes more money. He is ten years older than I. When he retires, he could come back at me for alimony. Nevertheless, when she asks if I am ready to move forward, I tell her I need some time to process.

🪶

The week after the Fourth of July, my little buddy Brian calls to invite me to lunch on Wednesday. He says he wants to see how I am doing. I tell Brian a bit about Herbert before I even talk with Tom at the state office. It is easier having a professional colleague to talk with that I did not have to see every day. Brian, who works for the student loan guaranty agency, is young enough to be my son, but we are good friends. Prior to Brian working at the Board of Regents, I always felt like the odd one out in my interactions there. Brian uses his position to include me in conversations and activities at the Board of Regents that have not previously included school counseling. Brian himself is a trained school counselor. At lunch, he asks,

"How's it going?"

"Well, Brian, you know my concerns about Herbert."

"Yes, how is that going?"

"I have to tell you I have turned every rock, and I still have no hard evidence."

"But?"

"In my heart of hearts, I believe that Herbert has been unfaithful to me in multiple ways with multiple women for nearly our entire marriage. I have no hard evidence." This is the first time I have said anything like this aloud. He expresses his sorrow and concern, and then we move on to other interests and other concerns.

☙

Later in the afternoon, I drive to Provo for an appointment with Jackie, my massage therapist. During the 40-minute drive to Utah County, I think about my conversation with Brian. It is true; I have no hard evidence. All I have are patterns of behavior, some weird conversations, and a gut instinct. Oh, and Herbert muttering, almost to himself, several times a week, "I'm a skunk; I'm a skunk." Thinking about the gut instinct, I see myself in a strong stance, feet shoulder-width apart, my elbows akimbo, my hands in Barbie posture near my hips with the thumbs facing out, framing my pelvic area. Is this my gut? Or is this my feminine core? Maybe Roseanne Barr is wrong. My uterus is a tracking device. Certainly, Rex, the counselor is right, "When you figure out what you believe, you will know what to do." After all the years of self-doubt, the years of feeling unworthy, the years of second guessing, I finally know who I believe. I believe me. I know what to do.

I have been going to Jackie for years. In fact, she works on Herbert for over a year, but he has not seen her in more than a year. Jackie and I share a lot. She knows my concerns about Herbert. I talk to her about my feeling psychic, telling her there have been times when I just knew things about Herb. Then a few days later, he reveals information that confirms my insight. I ask her,

"Jackie how is it for you being psychic?"

"Haven't I ever told you?"

"No."

"Oh, I see dead people," she admits. "And I talk to them."

"Oh, wow." I respond. Then Jackie tells me how she discovered her ability following the death of her husband's mother. I think about the conversations we have had about the comparative unhappiness of our marriages. Jackie continues, telling me that generally she does not like talking to dead people. For one thing it is exhausting and for another, it is often not good for people to talk with the deceased. At the end of her story Jackie turns to the corner and says something.

"What?" I ask wondering what she is doing.

She turns back to me and says, "Your father is here and would like to talk with you. Do you want to?"

"Well, sure," I sound a bit reluctant. We have talked enough about my growing up that I know she means Woody is here, not my stepfather, Arlo.

"He wants you to know that you are absolutely right about Herbert." She does not know what I admitted to Brian earlier in the day.

I am feeling a bit skeptical when she says, "He wants you to think of something white and fluffy." This seems ridiculous, white and fluffy," I think. Then "white and fluffy," and I remember. I tell her about the sleeping cat made of rabbit fur that my father, Woody, bought for Debra. I tell Jackie about making my mother get it down for me to "look at" and then I play with it until it falls apart.

My skepticism grows stronger. I am thinking that Jackie is also considering a divorce. Perhaps she would just as soon I get a divorce as she gets a divorce. I need a test to know if this is real. Then I just think of a question for which only my dad, Woody, would know the answer. I do not say it out loud. I just think of the question.

Jackie gives me the answer and then she says, "I have no idea what that means."

Holy shit, I know exactly what it means. She is almost certainly talking with my father.

"He wants you to know you have really good energy," she tells me.

"I do?"

"Yes, he really likes being around you. Even kisses you on the cheek."

"What?" I say, "How can that be?" I think.

"You feel it," she assures me. "That warm feeling on your cheek."

"It is true," I admit. "Almost every yoga session, after Sav asana, when I roll over on to my right side, I feel a warm spot on the cheekbone of my left cheek." I am still relishing this revelation when Jackie says,

"He says he has been busy doing his genealogy."

"Oh, so this is the year I get to find out who he is?" I am hopeful.

"No," she says. "You have to wait until after your mother dies." I am disappointed. Jackie speculates that Momma may be sitting on some information.

Then she continues, "He says that there is someone out there for you."

"Oh, Daddy, no. No thank you." I profess, "I am not very good at this."

"Nevertheless," she responds. "He is ready to pass the torch."

"Oh, someone to watch over me," I observe knowingly.

"No," she counters. "Someone to love you."

I am humbled.

That evening, when I tell my oldest daughter about my experience with Jackie and Woody, she says,

"Oh, yeah. Grandpa."

"What do you mean, 'Oh yeah. Grandpa'?"

"I used to talk to him all the time when I was little," she tells me.

"You never said anything?" I am incredulous, but I recall seeing her journal open with an entry that started "Dear Grandpa."

"When did you start?" I ask her.

"When we were living in the old house and Dora and I moved to the bedroom upstairs. I was really scared to be up there and far away from you and Dad. So, Grandpa showed up and would stay with us all night. He was there whenever I woke up in the dark."

This would have been about the same time that I had my conversation with Afton the babysitter about having friendly spirits in our old house.

"He was still around when we moved to the new house?"

"Yes."

"Do you still talk with him?" I query.

"No," she replies.

"What happened?"

"Oh, I got to be eleven and a half or twelve and I decided that it was kind of crazy to talk with your dead grandpa. So, I just stopped."

After weeks and months of second guessing, I know who I believe, and I know what to do. I call the tough woman attorney and tell her to file the divorce papers. I tell all my kids I am moving forward with the divorce. I tell my friends. The next week I feel so sad that the pain is nearly physical. No wonder I put off deciding for so long.

Having found my own way, the visit with Woody is a gift from the Universe.

Durward Young, left, and Woodrow Wilson Dean, age 16, right. June 1934

Ethel LaRue Yardley and her rescue deer.

Ethel LaRue Yardley in her mid-20's.

Woodrow Wilson Dean in his mid-20's.

Russell and Ethel Yardley, Yardley American Gothic I, mid-1930's;
Yardley American Gothic II, mid-1950's

Russell and Ethel Yardley, 40th Anniversary, February 1954

Margaret and "Charlie" Hall, aboard the paddle wheeler, SS President, 1942.

Woodrow, Margaret and "Charlie" Hall, Marion and Dean. Mount Vernon, Aug. 1932

ROLLA (BLACKIE) DEAN

ROLLA (BLACKIE) DEAN

St. Louis Post-Dispatch, July 15, 1937.

St. Louis Post-Dispatch, December 4. 1954

6

TURTLE IS MY TOTEM

I buy my first turtle from a vendor at Monument Valley High School when I am there on a school visit. It is after lunch, about two o'clock, the late afternoon sun not yet brightening the west-facing lobby with the grey and dark-sand-red floors. The Navajo man, thirty-something, has a small table covered with a dark cloth set off on the right side of the lobby, near the exit doors. My turtle is only an inch and a half long, carved of black stone; the turtle shell is inlaid with turquoise, with yellow, red, and black geometric shapes separated from the green, purple, and turquoise borders by a fine inlay of silver. It hangs on a black cord. It is not expensive. The vendor wraps it in single sheet of blue tissue, held tight with a piece of tape. As he hands it to me, he says,

"Turtle is a powerful totem—a wish for a long and happy life."

"I thought turtle meant the marriage of heaven and earth?" I query. This belief reflects my high hopes for my marriage to Herbert. I envisioned a strong, good man, well-grounded in the tenets of Mormonism.

"Same thing," the man tells me.

I thank him for my purchase and head out to the parking lot, eager to get on the road for the more than 6-hour
drive home. In time, I will come to understand that the
geometric shapes on the turtle's shell symbolize red mountain, blue mountain, yellow mountain, and black mountain.

Fast forward nine years. After my divorce from Herbert,
I live in the Sugar House section of Salt Lake City, a hip and
expensive area near Westminster College and the University of Utah. After eight years of *commuting—40* minutes
on a good day, 120 minutes on a bad day—I am now just 3
miles from my downtown office, buying myself an hour or
two every day. More thrilling than that—I qualify for my
own house loan. For the first time in my life, I am living on
my own, fully responsible for taking care of myself. Good
God, maybe I am not too late to join the Women's Movement. My little "early bungalow," built in 1906, is the perfect
girl house, 950 square feet upstairs and 450 square feet in
the shelf basement. Two bedrooms and plenty of storage.
With the help of Milan, a cost-plus-materials jack-of-all-
trades, I redo the bathroom leaving only the original oval
tub with its rounded enclosure. The bathroom floor slopes
2 inches in 6 feet. He levels the floor, installs new 1" hexa-
gon tiles in white with a black border and a new sink and
toilet. He fabricates a very cool shabby chic mantle for the
living room fireplace. We tear out the rickety bookcases
on either side. I move in as soon as the bathroom is func-
tional. I have lived with CC and her husband for nearly 6
months—long overstaying my welcome. They are kind and
gracious, but anxious to have their life back. Although I
close on the loan the 20th of September, I do not move in

until mid-December. The kitchen remodel will be complete by the first of the year—new white cabinets with textured glass door inserts in the upper cabinets, a wall of pantry cabinets 8 feet long, and, after twelve years of cooking on a $200 stove at the house I shared with Herbert, I have a ceramic cooktop with an oversize oven in the center island. Cooking is exciting again. I paint the walls any colors I choose. My white elephant for the office Christmas party is the wet paint rollers from my wall color choices—mostly Martha Stewart variations on beige—delivered in zip lock baggies.

Before the remodeling begins, I spend one lovely fall day in the basement with a pry bar, ripping out rickety wood storage shelves, figuratively ripping up Herbert, or at least ripping his heart out. I plan to settle in and take the winter to watch the snow, letting myself cry, letting myself grieve. My heart is completely broken. I read Ann-Marie McDonald's *Fall on Your Knees* when it first came out. Now I wonder how I, a seemingly strong and competent woman, can be taken completely to my knees? In the end, I never do have a really good cry over Herbert, much to my detriment. I do have plenty of time to perseverate.

~

It is winter three years later, after the death of Momma. Snow is falling; I call in sad to work. I am seeing my naturopath to get off Lexapro, the depression and anxiety medication I have relied on for ten years. The naturopath insists that I have psychological support, so I start with the community health counselor provided by my work for free. The counselor and I talk about Momma; we talk about Herbert. I realize that I am in deep grief. And I realize that I know this feeling from the months and years after I leave Herbert. I recognize that I have walked around in a state of unresolved grief for three years. It affects every aspect of my life. At work I am barely able to function for those first 6 months or so. My colleague Tom continues to cover for me even before he knows what is going on, producing meeting agendas and providing copies of materials to keep me going during public encounters.

During those years, one of my biggest challenges was just getting to work. In winter, I spent 45 minutes to an hour shoveling my walks and driveway after each snowstorm. When the weather warmed, I invariably wandered out to the garden in my pajamas and puttered in the yard. I was continually dragging into work after 9:00 am. Even our Monday morning nine o'clock staff meeting did not inspire me to arrive on time. Finally, Mary, my boss, pulls me aside to tell me she needs me to step up—I am section supervisor and need to set an example. Post-Herbert, during each subsequent annual performance review, I mention to Mary that I do not seem to be able to produce at the level I have been. For years she does not seem to notice what I am talking about. It is only after I have begun to recover, catching up mentally and physically, that she begins to think I am not doing my job. She never talks to me directly. I hear her assessment from others. I believe that she assumes my no longer attending church is the root cause. But that is a later story.

Before I finish with the community health counselor, he asks me why I finally left Herbert?

"He was making me crazy," I told him.

He gives a subdued chuckle and then says, "90% of the time when a wife tells me her husband is making her crazy, he is, in fact, having an affair."

*

I have a near miss with a bad man within a few weeks of closing on my house. I am in the yard working when an apparently pleasant man approaches and asks if I have any work for hire for him. I ask him how much he will charge to rip out the overgrown rosebushes along the very narrow walkway at the west of the house. We agree on a price, and he spends the afternoon on the arduous task. I pay him by check. When he departs, my new neighbor across the street comes by to tell me that this itinerant gardener has a reputation in the neighborhood for soliciting work and then following it up with a theft, often breaking and entering. I am sick with worry, asking myself repeatedly, "Who have I invited into my life?" After fussing about it overnight, I arise in the morning, well-before sunrise. I know what to do. I drive to my new home and give it a blessing in the manner of the Navajo. The sun on the brink of rising, I sprinkle cornmeal along the perimeter as I repeat a silent prayer, first to the East, then to the South, to the West and to the North, coming back to where I started. When I recount this experience to my friend and colleague, Lillian, who is half Navajo, she gets tears in her eyes.

"How did you know what to do?"

"It just came to me," I reply. After that experience I rarely worry about living alone or my personal safety. If a worry does crop up, I repeat the blessing, either outside, in reality, or in my mind, as if it were true. I will learn many things during my days on the Navajo Reservation.

*

My last July with Herbert, before I ever think of leaving him, I spend a week in Monument Valley, UT, the first of

what will become five annual stays on the Navajo Reservation. I work with a group of six state, district, and school-
level educators plus the art education program manager
at the Utah Arts Council to plan a Cultural Awareness
and Sensitivity Workshop for working school counselors,
hoping we can improve outcomes for our Native American students. Our first year, all of us, planners and participants, spend three days and two nights with a Native
family. Some participants have very traditional experiences
such as the woman who stays with a family who lives in a
Hogan, the traditional Navajo dwelling, with no running
water and relying on a generator for electricity. Others
have more contemporary experiences such as the participant who stays with a single mom who runs her own
little motel and attends Christian church on Sunday. Our
hosts are arranged by Lorissa, a business classes teacher
at the high school, who also works on her PhD at Northern Arizona University, making the nearly 3-hour journey,
one-way, at least once per week. Lorissa and other highly
educated Navajos work less for self-advancement and more
to make the modern world accessible for their people.

🖎

Growing up in Gunnison, Navajo people, Navajo families, are a common summer sight. They come to town as
itinerant work crews, primarily helping thin and harvest
the sugar beets and supporting the Gunnison Sugar Factory. After the Sugar Factory closes, the beets are shipped
to Moses Lake, Washington for processing. I am not sure
what the Navajos wore in the fields, but when I see them in
town the women are in traditional Navajo dress—velveteen
skirts gathered in three increasingly fuller tiers that end at

mid-calf and topped with a fitted velveteen blouse, generally in a matching color, long sleeves, an open johnny-collar that appears to be a pullover, a zipper under one sleeve to ease dressing. The skirts and tops, apparently washed often, develop a beautiful, crushed texture. The women wear their Native silver and turquoise jewelry with the colorful dresses of navy blue, pine green, or deep ruby red. The men wear crisp new jeans and fancy cowboy style shirts with snap closures, boots, and felt or straw cowboy hats. One time in the small grocery store in Centerfield, the daughter of the owners, a woman I went to high school with, pursues her out-of-control 3-year-old son up and down the aisles. In a futile attempt to slow him down, she yells, "Preston if you don't stop, I will give you to the Indians." A small dignified Navajo woman at the counter responds, "Uh, we don't want him." The grandmother of the errant child, who is working the cash register, chuckles with the Native grandma.

The summer I am 16, the Navajos do not come to help in the fields. We teenagers in town are pressed into service through announcements and calls from the LDS ward bishops. I spend a week working in the fields from 5 a.m. to 11 a.m. The actual activity, called "thinning beets," requires the use of a short-handled, specialized tool that clears a 3" space between the emerging beets, allowing them to grow to their fullest size. The short-handle hoe necessitates the worker bend forward at the waist progressing up each acre-long row. The work is back breaking and the pay miserable—75 cents for about 600 ft. Although many of our farmers, and thus the entire community, rely heavily on the Native labor, generally, we residents are not kind and gracious to these workers, these helpers. In the same way, we of the dominant White culture have never been kind and courteous to the millions of migrant workers who produce food across this country, working in orchards, fields, farms, and dairies.

≈

Now here on the Reservation, waiting outside Monument Valley High School, we participants in our first workshop speculate about how it might have been for the Native students who, as children, participate in the Indian Placement program, both through the LDS Church and through the Bureau of Indian Affairs. None of us have to worry about the potential abuse that so many of those young people suffered. They endured corporal punishment and emotional and other abuses for infractions such as speaking Navajo or otherwise honoring their culture and customs. Nevertheless, we are all nervous, wondering whether we will be liked or disliked, accepted or rejected. In order to ease the burden on our host families, each participant has a food box containing nonperishable basics: Blue Bird flour, coffee, sugar, oil, shortening, and Spam, and an individual supply of water in a two-and-a-half-gallon jug. We hope the supplies will ease our entry into their world. So, we sit on the warming sidewalk at the edge of the high school with our boxes, our fears, and our hopes that we will be enough.

≈

My host family is Frances and Stanley Holiday who live in a modern four-bedroom, two-bath house. Stanley, a medicine man—a traditional healer—performs his ceremonies in an Octagon, or modernized version of the Hogan. The traditional Hogan has been built with the same design since the 1400s. Every Hogan that I have seen has nine upright posts, symbolic of the 9 months of gestation with eight sides of nine horizontal logs that interlock without the use of nails. The roof is similarly octagonal, also interlocking with no use of nails, tapering to a one-foot-square opening at the top located over the central fire or stove. The wood used in the construction is traditionally cedar, giving the Hogan an aroma of earth and tree, dusty and subtle, a strong connection to the sacred land. The door always faces east with a male "ear" post on the left and a female ear post on the right so that everything said in the Hogan can be heard. The entire wooden structure is covered with an insulating, foot-plus-thick layer of red mud mixed with strips of bark, summer cooling facilitated by sprinkling the Hogan outside as well as the earthen floor and inside walls with water. When entering, inhabitants and guests move through the Hogan in a clockwise direction. The newer Octagons, like the one Stanley uses for ceremonies, have eight sides, and are made of wood and sheetrock with a tapering roof and opening for the fire or stove. When Frances picks me up, I am not sure whether I will be sleeping inside their home or outside on their property somewhere. I have my pack with tent, pad, and sleeping bag, just in case. Frances does invite me to sleep inside. I will be the first Belagana, the first White person, to sleep in their home, ever.

Frances and I chat a bit as we drive out to their house along several of the typical gravel roads that form the transportation system for the reservation. The roads are full of dusty potholes and dried-out mud puddles, interspersed with wash-boarding from the frequent travel. We pass a structure that I come to know as the Methodist Mission, the exterior a dark, mud-red stucco, deeper in tone than the surrounding hills. The home of Frances and Stanley is located about 15 miles northwest of the high school in a broad little valley, slick rock hills to the east and west. The south end of the valley is marked by Anvil Rock, high on a bluff above the gravel road. The Stanley home of white stucco with sky blue trim sits back from the gravel road about 400 feet. We turn into the drive marked by a metal gate with the initials SH in a circle in the center. A couple of wooden shed-like structures with sloping roofs and open on the south side, line the long drive. An outhouse sits off the road another 200 ft, equidistant to the house. The lower portions of the white stucco house are stained by the red dirt from the yard. One corner of the stucco needs repairing. A Kawasaki Mule is parked under the one large tree in the front. Frances' new cottonwood and sumac saplings grow at the back of the house, toward the west.

Inside the home, the gentle hum and cooled air from the AC is the first thing I notice, a rare and pleasurable sensation on the reservation. The large L-shaped living and dining area has blue and white vinyl floors, with horizontal wide-slat blinds at the window. A typical three-piece set of over-stuffed suburban type furniture, plaid in shades of tan and taupe, fill the room. The kitchen is to the right, at the back of the house, opposite the dining area with a Formica-topped table and unmatched wooden chairs. Further down the hall on the right are two bedrooms and a bathroom, which is painted a surprising bright green. This will be the girl's wing. Down the hall to the left are two more bedrooms and a bathroom used by Frances and Stanley and her nephew Randy, or so I assume. I never see this side of the house.

In addition to Randy, whom they raise from childhood, Frances and Stanley share their home with their daughter,

Vangie, and Vangie's children—Chandler, age 8, and Precious, age 5,—and their granddaughter, Kristin—Krissy, a beautiful young woman, a high school junior, who prefers life on the reservation with her grandparents to life in the city with her parents. All the inhabitants move generously to the side to make room for me—I have a bedroom to myself. During the next two days, Krissy and I will take the truck of her grandfather, Stanley—her chei, load up a 300-gallon tank, drive the half-hour back to town, fill the tank at the water station where we have to wait in line behind two or three other vehicles before it is our turn to fill our tank, which takes a good half hour. Then we drive back to their home to water the thirteen head of horses, the two cows, and the two-dozen or so sheep, and water the four cottonwood trees and the four sumacs that Frances is nurturing around the house. We unload the tank after every trip so that the truck is always ready to go for other activities and chores. Krissy and I will repeat this process four times during my two-and-a-half day stay, watering the animals twice per day and the trees twice per week. Krissy and I also do most of the feeding of the livestock, including bucking several bales of hay each day, giving Frances a break for a few days. Our recommended supply list includes a set of good leather work gloves for a reason.

My first night, Frances cooks fry bread with chicken drumsticks and white gravy for our supper. Afterward, Frances and Krissy take me to a Squaw Dance further north into the valley, near Locomotive Rock. They teach me the simple pause step. Our hands clasped in a figure eight, we move in a counterclockwise circle as the men chant in the drum circle. Our simple movements around the center fire are as meditative and soothing for me as a yoga session. We reluctantly leave at nearly midnight.

I am up with Krissy at 5:30 to tend the livestock. I notice one of the ewes has bailing twine caught in her hoof and around her leg. Later, I help Frances cut her loose, considerably easing the limp that has plagued the ewe, noting that next year I need to get a good pocketknife for my supply kit. After breakfast, Precious asks me to go hiking in the slick red rocks west of the house, killing time while she waits for her brother Chandler and her mother to return from Moab where Vangie has been in training for her job as a Head Start teacher. Early in our hike, I miscalculate the pitch of a large rock that is nearly the size of a house. Precious gets stuck on the steep slope. I have to scramble on my hands and knees to reach her and push on her butt until she reaches the top of the rock, losing my sneaker in the process. Note to self: Serous hikers wear shoes up to their ankles. The whole time I am struggling with Precious, I pray that I will not be responsible for injuring the child of my hosts on this little adventure. Once Precious is in a safe spot, I scramble back down the rock, still on hands and knees, retrieve my sneaker, and then scramble back up the rock to join Precious. After half an hour of strolling along the ridge, we find a safer way off the hills and back to the house.

Chandler brings Precious two cans of Play Dough, one blue and one yellow. I watch them make blue flowers with yellow spots and yellow flowers with blue spots. After a while, Precious has the dough mixed up into one big green ball. I show them how to pinch out a horse from a ball of clay. Precious and I make a horse family. Chandler takes my gemstone bead necklaces from my backpack, using them to make an onyx corral to keep out the horsenappers, a green bloodstone lake, a pile of opalite good feed, and a patch of rhodonite poisonous herbs. He uses a little plastic pirate figure for the horse napper. When he pushes the pirate off the counter I say, "Oooh, dead White guy!" That makes him really laugh. So, we play Dead White Guys instead of horse nappers, finding various means by which to do in the White guy.

During my time at the home of Frances and Stanley, two or three people come by each day to seek the healing knowledge and services of this medicine man. Some cash is exchanged, gifts are offered in honor of the anticipated blessing. Bartering is also involved. My second night at their home, Frances, with Stanley's permission, invites me to come to the Octagon with her for a ceremony that Stanley is performing. I understand this is a great honor. The patient seems a bit hesitant about my presence, but I make sure to keep my eyes averted, not looking at him as he strips naked and wraps himself in two clean sheets. This explains the stacks and stacks of clean flat sheets that Frances stores in the bedroom where I am sleeping. My four years of studying yoga helps me understand that I am watching a skilled energy worker. This work is very sacred to Natives and cannot be spoken about outside of the ceremonies. The family of the patient, grandparents and children, are all present. They seem relieved with the content of the ceremony, all of which is conducted in Navajo.

My last morning, Frances and I are up before six and out feeding and watering the horses before our tailgate conversation that I mentioned at Momma's funeral. Frances tells me how she came to know the Navajo emergence story, not from her mother or grandmother, as most Navajo women would have learned, but from her study and reading. During winter and summer, she and Stanley can talk about the songs and prayers designated for each season, piecing together the whole story. They are a remarkable couple. Stanley includes her in his work in a way that is not typical for a Native healer.

Frances is very kind to take time to teach me and talk with me about how things are done in the Navajo way. Later in the morning, Frances, Krissy, Vangie, Chandler, and Precious take me back to the high school. Only Rose, another participant, is there waiting for me and the others to return. I am surprised that Frances and her family linger. We all chat together for some time. Then Frances and I sit in the Hogan on the ceremony grounds at the high school to talk. She tells me when Stanley worked in the uranium mine, they lived in abandoned homes. Many times, more than one family lived in a Hogan or an abandoned home. If one family moved out, another might move in. We talk about how hard times make people stick together. When a few more participants return, Frances asks if we will all have lunch together. When I tell her yes, she is ready to leave. I realize she is still taking care of me.

In the afternoon, we share stories, processing our individual host-family experiences. One of the participants is very angry,

"Why did you not tell me how poor these people are?" she demands. She feels so guilty about eating their food and using their gas as they show her around the valley.

Lorissa, who is also our on-site coordinator, considers the question, and then asks her, "When you have guests in your home, do you like to share your favorite foods with them?"

"Yes," she responds.

"And do you like to drive them to see your favorite places and do your favorite things?"

"Yes," she repeats.

Lorissa always takes time in forming her questions and her responses. She tells us that when we ask her a question, or she needs to share some information with us, she always thinks about the question in English and then in Navajo and then she thinks about her answer in Navajo and then in English. Then she responds. She replies to our angry participant,

"Well, it is the same for the people of the Valley. They like to have visitors and share with them. The Navajo people, the Dine', have a different definition of poverty. For us, a person is not truly poor unless they have no family, they don't know how to work, and they don't have a place in the community."

Later I tell Lillian, "I want to be like Lorissa."

Lillian looks at me and replies, "I love you, but that will never happen."

At the high school, where we will be staying for the remainder of the week, we have three choices for accommodations: air-conditioned pre-built "portables," common on many public-school campuses, which are used by the VISTA workers for community activities; the traditional Hogan, built by the students, which overlooks the sandy amphitheater surrounded by a rock wall; or the sandy floor of the amphitheater itself. Participants settle into all three sites. Along with several others, I pitch my little two-person spring bar tent on the sand in the amphitheater, my door facing east, giving me a spectacular view of the traditional Monument Valley horizon, the Mittens, the buttes, the craggy skyline.

Settling back into my tent after my home stay with Frances, I notice that one pair of pajamas is missing, menswear styled, irregular pink and white stripes with a hint of green, short sleeves and white piping, one of my favorite sets of PJs ever. I sense that Krissy has taken them, but not for her personal use. I discuss the situation with Lillian. We think that Frances or Stanley needs them for a ceremony or a blessing for me. In my mind, it may be tied to a conversation I have with Frances in her truck our second afternoon together.

Frances asks, "Are you a church-going lady?"

"I am," I respond, explaining to her that my church activity has persisted through two marriages. She seems mildly surprised to learn that I am in a second marriage.

The response from Frances during our church conversation may have grown out of some hygiene issues I am having on the reservation. Frances and Stanley live in a modern home with full bathrooms, but prior to my home stay I am informed that generally the full use of the indoor bathroom is reserved for the elderly and the ill. Here, in the end of July heat, the average temperatures range from high 90s to well over 100, often the teens, sometimes the 120s. I avail myself those first two days of only the use of the basin, for what my Momma called a spit bath—a washcloth, soap, and warm water. I and all the other inhabitants of the house use the outhouse for toileting. I am only mildly alarmed that a Black Widow occupies a lower corner of the outhouse. According to Navajo tradition, this spider is a grandmother and cannot be disturbed. I hate spiders, but manage my fears, offering up a kind of prayer of respect. We all make room for one another.

Hygiene-wise, my huge complication is that I am suffering from bacterial vaginosis, the most troublesome symptom of which is a fishy odor from my vagina. I smell like tuna. Frances knows. Stanley knows. And the Rez dogs know. Although I am plagued with bacterial vaginosis for most of my marriage to Herbert, I do not think much of it, other than the discomfort, because I suffered from almost chronic vaginal yeast infections for most of my marriage to Ernie. Years later a new gynecologist says to me, "See! It's the dudes." Krissy tells me to feel free to use the shower that last day, which I decline. I can easily shower at the high school. I am not sure what Frances intends, but I know I trust her, so we will see what comes of the missing pajamas.

Nota bene: Frances and Stanley know at an Earth wisdom level, body wisdom level, what many women have suspected for years: If you smell like a tuna, your sexual partner is a rat. This long held suspicion is confirmed in a 2016 study of 3620 women ages 15 to 44, in twelve clinics which found:

A diagnosis of BV [bacterial vaginosis] was associated with reporting that one's partner possibly or definitely engaged in partner concurrency.

https://www.ncbi.nlm.nih.gov/pmc/articles/PMC5 429208/

The dudes were sleeping around. Herbert was sleeping around. The Rez dogs know it. Frances and Stanley want me to know it. Perhaps this is too much of a megillah, but I think not. The proof is in the pudding, so to speak.

During the rest of the week in Monument Valley, we spend our mornings with local educators and community leaders learning about the strategies that have helped students achieve. We have our sessions in the special ed classroom at the south wing of the high school in the morning and in the afternoon, we sit in the shade of the Hogan. The Hogan and amphitheater themselves are part of those efforts in improving student achievement; students use computers to figure the dimensions and proportions, detailing designs for the female Hogan, the traditional Octagon, and for the male Hogan, also very traditional and conspicuously evocative of a penis and testicles. The students participate in the construction, under the supervision of the elders from the valley. Clayton Long explains how students do better when they have time during their school day to study the Navajo language and culture. We travel to Kayenta to visit the tribal court and the mental health center as well as the Wednesday flea market. Lorissa shares a video she helps her students make called *Hear Our Voices*, which addresses the sacred nature of water and the threats to the existing water supplies of the Dine'.

We spend several afternoons with local artists and artisans learning about the artwork that is intrinsic to Navajo culture. Mary Holiday Black and her daughters and granddaughters teach us to make our own tiny Navajo baskets, telling us about gathering the reeds, stripping the bark, dying, drying, and then soaking the reeds, softening them as they weave the baskets. Mary Holiday Black has been declared a National Heritage Award Winner, a national treasure, by the National Endowment for the Arts for nearly singlehandedly preserving and expanding the skills for Navajo basket making. I purchase two of her traditional wedding baskets. Sandra Black teaches us to make bracelets using a loom and traditional beading, explaining how the colors of the beads reflect the four directions and the sacred mountains that appear in each of those directions: Mt. Hesperus to the East, Mt. Taylor to the South, San Francisco Peak to the West, and Mt. Blanca to the North. Sandra also has wares to sell. We buy up bracelets, hatbands, and necklaces.

On our last full day in the Valley, we all rise at 4 a.m. to arrive at the base of Mitchell Mesa before 5, while the moon still shines over the ragged landscape. We have received permission from the tribe to hike this iconic mesa, which rises 1500 feet above the Valley floor. We begin the hike in the dark, hoping to reach the top in time for sunrise, ambitious for the two-and-a-half miles ahead of us. The ragged, rock-strewn trail is a seriously degraded former service road for the uranium mine on the mesa that was abandoned in the 60s. The hike is vigorous, but worth every step. Once at the top, by mutual agreement, we each find a secluded spot for 30 minutes of quiet contemplation, overlooking the familiar landmarks—the Mittens, the Three Sisters, and the land itself, every square foot of which is sacred to the Native people. It is where they are born, where they bury the umbilicus of each child connecting them forever to the earth on which they walk. It is where they have their tribal and family ceremonies, clearing the sacred spaces by hand as they remove the tortuous tumbleweeds and other plants that impede the drum circles and the round dances. We take pictures of one another sitting at the edge of the mesa. My vertigo in full-force, I have to crawl to the edge on all fours for my photo. The descent to the bottom is nearly as challenging as the hike up. Once back in the Valley, we head to the Navajo Market, a loose collection of plywood shacks filled with artists, artisans, and Navajo treasures. Word of our workshop and our work has spread to the market, and we are surprised at the generosity of the vendors as we select our treasures.

Before we leave Monument Valley, we members of the workshop sponsor a dinner at the high school for our host families. We are thrilled to have the honor of serving them, the elders first, thanking them for our experiences. During our brief stay, word of our work and our goals have spread through the Valley. Before they leave the dinner, Frances, Vangie, and Krissy present me with a gift, a traditional Navajo bracelet crafted of silver and needlepoint coral, a beautiful sample of Navajo silversmithing, costing a dear penny for a family who works daily to get by.

The next morning before leaving Monument Valley we all gather for breakfast at Goulding's Stagecoach Dining Room. Most of us have one last round of fry bread, which has been a staple of our cooked meals during the week. Although some of the participants were heard to remark, "We can't eat like Dawn and Tom," a clear reference to our slimmer physiques and our fondness for mutton and fry bread. As we are leaving the restaurant, a pair of eagles soar out from the cliff above, circling over our head. As we drive up out of Monument Valley, up Forest Gump Hill, they seem to follow. We feel like it is a blessing.

Our second summer at Monument Valley is the summer after I move out of the house I share with Herbert. It is the last week of July, the July when I actually decide to divorce him. This second year, we leaders stay behind while the participants go on their home stays. On Monday morning, July 24th, we wake up at 4:20 a.m. so we can leave at 5:00 a.m. to arrive in Cain Valley, some 45 miles northeast of Monument Valley, at the home of Ben and Mary Stanley by 6 a.m. Jean, our art coordinator, stayed at the Stanley home our first year in the Valley. She tells us the pleasure she finds in waking each morning to the sound of Mary working her loom, the soft shoosh of the shuttle moving back and forth as Mary creates yet another rug masterpiece, the smell of Navajo tea wafting from the kettle. Ben, a former uranium miner, is recovering from a triple bypass. Ben and Mary move out of their original home in Cain Valley because of uranium contamination. Recent readings of ambient air in Cain Valley record levels of contamination that are still off the scale. The uranium mines on the reservation were operated by Vanadium Mining Company, VMC—weird connection: when Momma marries Arlo, the mining town we live in was Vanadium, NM. Ben and Mary work with the state agricultural college, Utah State University, on a project using plants to clean up the land, reading meters and making measurements three times daily. By the time we arrive at their home around six a.m., Ben has already taken his 2-mile walk, ankle weights still in place above his sneakers. Our service project today will be to dismantle a Hogan that is falling apart. Ben and Mary consider making repairs but decide it will be best to tear down the Hogan and rebuild.

Much to our surprise and concern, Ben climbs up onto the roof of the Hogan to begin the deconstruction. After a brief conversation about our concerns with Ben doing heavy work, I tell the others I will go up top to be his assistant. He will go more slowly if he works with me. Ben and I begin at the center vent above the stove, picking up one log at a time and tossing them to the ground below so that the six other workers can stack them in an orderly fashion. As the logs become longer, Ben and I each take an end to toss them below. We continually brush aside the dried mud and bark that has served as the insulating exterior, uncovering each new round of logs. Ben frequently warns me to watch my step, to not fall. We stop for a rest when we are down to two or three logs above door height. I sit at the edge of the opening while Ben converses with our friends below. The next thing I know I am in mid-air. I consciously think, "I am falling. I wonder how that will feel?" My shoulder hits first. I feel my head bounce twice. I hear Ben say, matter-of-factly, "Well, she fell."

As I regain consciousness, I hear the other participants talk about needing to get me up and out of the dirt. During our inspection of the Hogan, before we started working, we notice the evidence of deer mice. We all worry about Hanta virus. Lorissa reaches for my right hand to pull me up, groaning I offer her my left hand, rising to my knees and then to my feet. They lead me out into the sunlight. Someone brings a chair for me to sit in. I assure everyone that, "I am alright." By this I mean, "I am not dead." They discuss where to take me for medical help.

Once again, I assure them, "I am alright."

"You are the color of the grey dirt," Jean declares.

Cain Valley lies halfway between Mexican Hat and Monument Valley. Nevertheless, they decide I am going to the health center in Monument Valley, which is closer to

Kayenta, where there is more medical care, if I need it. Jean puts down the back seats of her Jeep Cherokee, making a place for me to lie. Beverly Benally, the Native mother of one of our counselor participants, sits beside me in the back of the jeep. Beverly, who has been estranged from her Native traditions, obtained permission to be an observer/ participant for the workshop, hoping to reconnect with her heritage. As Jean drives across the eternally bumpy road, I groan with each jostle. Beverly soothingly, gently squeezes my arms and legs, rhythmically moving from hand to shoulder, from ankle to thigh. She explains that she made the same ministration for her children when they were ill. I feel like she is holding me together. In my delirium, I ask Jean and Beverly over and over if anyone saw what happened. In my mind a bundle of energy hurls toward me as I am sitting on the roof of the Hogan, and then I am in the air falling. I see over and over in my brain three graphic images in nearly neon colors. Two of the images are simple, almost stick-figure-like landscapes. The third is much more complicated, intertwined cross-threads, not easily memorized. After these images have flashed through my consciousness several times, I tell myself, "These are important. I must remember them." At last, we reach the health center in Monument Valley. The bad news—they are closed for July 24th, Pioneer Day in Utah, commemorating the arrival of the Mormon Pioneers in the Salt Lake Valley. It is not a day for celebration among the Native Peoples any more than Columbus Day is a day for celebrating among Native Peoples. The arrival of the Whites was the beginning of the relentless decline of Native cultures and Native peoples. The good news—the road to Kayenta is paved and considerably smoother.

We arrive at the emergency room at the Health Center in Kayenta, AZ. They load me into a wheelchair and wheel me to an intake interview. I throw up during the conversation. Jean tells me the vomitus is "technicolor hurl." They wheel me out to the waiting room for a few minutes before taking me back to see the doctor. While I am waiting, an old Navajo woman in traditional dress, not velvet but a more practical cotton calico, and a scarf on her head enters the waiting area. I notice how flat her face is. She walks over to me, puts her face less than a foot from mine and looks me in the eye, cocking her head from side to side. To my surprise, I think to myself, "Holy shit. This woman is a witch." I promise you that I have never thought that about anyone in the literal sense. I know she is literally a witch, and she likely means me no good. I know from conversations with Lillian and conversations with some of my students at Provo High that the Black Arts are alive and functioning on the Navajo Reservation. I realize I am currently poorly defended, and I try to seal up my soul, my golden cradle, as we have practiced doing so many Saturday mornings in restorative yoga. I have the sense that she goes out into the hallway and puts a hook, for lack of a better descriptor, in my upper right shoulder blade. Then the nurse comes to take me back to a treatment room.

The attending nurse, a youngish Navajo woman, is aghast when I tell her I was working on top of a Hogan. She chides me, seriously explaining that no woman should be engaged in such work. The doctor comes in, notes that I am in considerable pain and offers me a shot of Tramadol, which I readily accept. The relief flows quickly through my veins. They order x-rays. The young Navajo technicians want me to raise my right arm. Not likely. I manage to move it forward and up a bit. The results show that I have at least a broken fourth rib, maybe more; a damaged shoulder, possibly rotator cuff; perhaps a broken collarbone; and a pulled ligament in my knee. Obviously, also a concussion. I will be released to go home with a supply of pain pills. While I am waiting in the pharmacy area, I meet a Navajo woman waiting on prescription eye drops for shingles. I tell her what happened and what the intake nurse said to me. She is an elementary school teacher, and she assures me that "women can do anything."

Jean, Beverly, and I have breakfast at a nearby café and then head back to Monument Valley. Apparently, I scared Jean to death with my repetitive questions on the way in. She has not had much experience with accident victims. Back at the high school, our co-workers are relieved to find that I really am okay. They wonder if someone needs to drive me back to Salt Lake, a more than 6-hour journey.

"Back to what?" I question. "My daughter's three-bedroom apartment where I can be all alone with my thoughts? Ruminating about my rat of a husband? No, thank you. I prefer to stay here." About this moment I realize if I stay, I will need help. Lots of help. Asking for and accepting help is a huge deal for me. I am accustomed to being the leader, the strong one, the caretaker. I get sincere and enthusiastic offers for assistance. They dive into moving my bed and belongings into the air-conditioned portables. Tom packs up my tent.

In the afternoon, Jean and I drive out to see Frances and Stanley. I have two bolts of navy-blue velveteen for Frances. Lillian has given me a pouch of Native tobacco for Stanley. When we arrive at the home of Frances and Stanley, I present the gifts to them. Then I explain what happened. And I ask Stanley for a ceremony.

"What kind of ceremony?" he asks.

"I have no idea," I confess. Admitting sheepishly, "You're the medicine man, I thought you would know."

I tell Stanley how this is the third time I have broken my collarbone. All three times occur around major incidents with my father, Woody—his death when I am three; my realization that he is never coming back when I am eight; and the recent visit confirming my suspicions about Herbert. Stanley says that he can get rid of this troublesome spirit. I explain that for the most part Woody has been a protector, a guardian angel, for me. I would like him to be around. I just do not want to keep getting hurt.

Stanley says, "Come back tomorrow night at 8:00. I will have a dream tonight, and I will know what to do."

I ask Frances if there are any special preparations I need to make. She tells me to wear a skirt and have my hair pinned up. Jean and I drive back to the high school. All of us decide to drive into Mexican Hat, pick up dinner and drive out to Muley Point to watch the thunderstorms dance across the Valley.

The next morning Tom, Janet, Lorissa, Allyn—another participant—and I drive out to Mystery Valley, deep in Monument Valley National Monument. When we are at these workshops we work hard not to act like tourists, but sometimes we slip away for an hour or two. We see the ruins and the wall of House of Hands, covered all over with handprints. We also see Lone Pine Arch and Half-Moon Arch. I see some German tourists climbing on a low wall of one of the ruins. I tell them, "Ne touchez pas. C'est tres, tres, vieux et c'est tres fragile." I do my best. Hoping that like most Europeans they understand several languages.

We spend the afternoon with all the participants back at the high school attending a lecture from Don Mose who started the traditional studies at the high school in 1994. We are meeting outside the Hogan. The metal archway above the path leading to the male and female Hogans has the Navajo words Naayeeji', or male "the Protecting Way" and Ho'zho'o'ji', or female "the Blessing Way." He teaches us the traditional Navajo greeting Ya'a t'e'e'h—hello, it is good, friendly, all is well and beautiful. Or "heaven it is to greet you."

After our dinner, Jean and I drive out to the Holiday's for the ceremony with Stanley. The thundershowers from the evening before take their toll on the roads. There are many puddles, and a few mild washouts with sand flowing across the gravel. Halfway to the Holiday house we come upon a mud puddle that covers the entire width of the road and is a good 30 feet long. After a minute of surveying the scene, I tell Jean to put the Cherokee in four-wheel drive. I show her a path to the left of the mud puddle that will take us up onto the sloping shoulder. I tell her to take it slow, about 20 mph, but steady and no matter what, do not slow down and certainly never stop—if she does, we will be on our side in the mud puddle. I do not need to be jostled again. Those days in Russ' '55 Chevy gave me some skills. Jean does a good, brave job with the tricky maneuver.

Arriving at the Holiday home, we go directly to the Octagon. Stanley carefully sets up his ceremonial pieces, tending the fire and the ashes. When he is ready, Frances asks me to repeat to Stanley my story about Herbert and my story about my fall through the roof of the Hogan. Stanley tells me that he briefly saw "a dark man. But he hid himself from me." Then Stanley asks me if I had a dark van. Ernie and I had a dark blue and tan Ford custom van. He says he senses a lot of conflict. Then he tells me he will give me a blessing so that the pain in my heart and the pain in my body will go away. Stanley also says, "The reason you wanted to come down for a ceremony earlier was to get away from all of the troubles that were depressing you." Was this a reference to the missing pajamas? Very likely, yes. As far as I know, this is my first ceremony, but Stanley sees it differently. And those PJs went somewhere.

Then Stanley spends nearly 45 minutes making a prayer in Navajo. Likely he repeated the same prayer four times, but not being a speaker of Navajo, I cannot be sure. After the prayer he offers me herb water to drink. He invites me to put some herbs on the fire and ashes, and to make my own prayer. Then he invites Jean to do the same. Jean tells me on our trip back to the high school that at the end of the ceremony, when she drank the herb water, she felt an excruciating pain hit her shoulder that travelled down her arm and out her fingers. When the ceremony is over, the heat of pain has left my body, and I feel at peace.

The next morning, we go to Kayenta to visit the Kayenta Mental Health Center, learning about the Western and traditional interventions that counselors use to help Native peoples. Because of the long and difficult history of the Native peoples, virtually all of them suffer at least from generational grief, compounded by massive misunderstanding of their issues and needs by the dominant culture. We go to the Wednesday Flea Market for lunch, steamed corn stew and blue corn mush for me. I buy a traditional skirt in ivory—I had to borrow a skirt from Janet for my ceremony with Stanley.

After lunch, we drive to Bear Mountain to the ceremonial grounds where Lillian participates in an annual Sun

Dance that the Navajo hold in collaboration with members of the Sioux Nation, where the Sun Dance originated. They honor as regular participants in the ceremony some survivors of the bombing at Hiroshima and their families. we gather near the juniper covered arbor, or as the Navajos call it, a circular "shade house." In a moment of time-warp weirdness, I can hear and feel the beating of the drums from the ceremony that took place here some 2 weeks ago. Not unlike many White people, Leona, one of the school counselors, keeps talking and talking, asking many questions. I am distracted and irritated. My time-warp connection fades away. The clear sound of the drums disappears. Lillian tells us how important participating in the Sun Dance ceremony has been to her. Then she invites us to each take a moment to pray.

Just as we are about to leave, I think, "I need to leave my symbols here." I find a stick and kneel in the dirt near one of the supports for the shade house, drawing the two more simple designs in the dirt. Lorissa comes close, looking over my shoulder as I draw, likely concerned about what I am leaving in this sacred place. I note with interest that I am content to wait until next year to ask Stanley about the images. I understand that not all of my questions need to be asked or answered. Ergo the difficulty with Leona asking incessant questions, not bad behavior, just typically White and maybe not appropriate for learning about another culture. In this immersion experience we learn to do better; to watch, to listen, to learn. Spoiler alert—I never do ask about or get information on what happened to my pajamas. Some questions don't need to be answered.

After leaving the ceremonial grounds, we drive on to First Mesa on the Hopi Nation, each of the other two drivers struggling to keep up with Lillian who is the champion Rez Driver, having spent most summers and many vacations with her grandmother who lives nearby. At First Mesa, we spend an hour at the visitor center with a docent who insists on no photos, no note taking, no recording, and no chewing gum. Afterward, we are free to wander the village, which dates back to 1690 when the Natives move from the valley floor to the mesas, in fear of attack from the Spanish invaders. The Hopi people here in First Mesa are friendly and welcoming, inviting us into their homes to see their crafts. Several of us buy hand-carved Kachinas— a small carving of a deified ancestral spirit revered by the Hopi and Pueblo Native Americans. We stop for supper in Keams Canyon and arrive back at the high school about 12:30 in the morning.

Thursday morning, we drive out to Cain Valley to see Ben and Mary to check on the final progress in dismantling the Hogan. When Ben sees me get out of the van, he flaps his arms like a bird, and we both giggle. Mary makes Navajo tacos for our lunch, fresh fry bread, beans, and seasoned meat, topped with lettuce and tomatoes. Mary is selling a small rug, 13x24 inches. I buy it for $85—likely half of what it is worth—a bargain and a good luck piece from my misadventure. We see Lorissa's grandmother, who is the only person who actually saw me fall. She was sitting on her front porch at the time. She says in Navajo that she can tell I will be well, that I will be okay. While we are out travelling in the Valley, the Kayenta Health Center calls the high school. The radiologist tells the secretary that I have three broken ribs—one under my arm, one high on my chest in front and one high on my back under the shoulder blade— the place where the witch put the hook—it will remain my most painful spot for weeks—the spot that makes me want to keep taking the opioid pain meds. Lucky for me that I choose to forgo the meds and instead focus on sealing up my body, healing my golden cradle that the witch pierced.

At the end of the week, we sponsor another potluck meal for the host families. I eat with Frances, Stanley, and Krissy. Stanley tells Rose, one of our participants, a bit of the Creation Story. Krissy says to me, "I love to hear Grandpa speak English." After dinner we have a concert by a Native entertainer, James Bilagody. Frances, Stanley, and Krissy laugh and laugh. As they are leaving, I give Stanley a carrot cake, one of his favorites, and shake his hand. He puts his left hand on my injured right shoulder, half hugging me and says, "You be good, okay?" Earlier in the evening he asks me if my mind is calmer? "Yes," I assure him, "calmer." Then he asks about my heart. I tell him it is open.

We help James Bilagody pack up his equipment, and he helps us practice our Ya'a t'e'e'h. He reminds us it is a blessing, not a question. In the morning before we leave, we have breakfast at Goulding's. As we leave, the eagles again come out to bid us farewell.

Once back in Salt Lake City, I follow-up with my orthopedist. He confirms the broken collarbone, which by now has a clear bruisey stripe about 2-inches wide from my collarbone down to my breast. The doctor remarks twice, a bit incredulously, that it is a miracle I am not paralyzed. "Usually if you fall backward more than four or five feet you are paralyzed." He continues, "I guess it is because you were doing a service project." He says that twice also. Mormons believe in service.

Actually, I think yoga saves my life. I tell others regularly that yoga saves my life twice, once figuratively and now, once literally. I begin studying yoga some four years prior to the current time, in September 2002, when Herbert develops the symptoms that lead to the hydrocephalus diagnosis and the placing of the shunt in his brain. I also just started a master's level program in education leadership and policy which will give me a license as a school administrator, a certification that my supervisors at work want me to have. So, I am working full-time, working on a second master's degree, and my husband is having brain issues. But two to three times per week I go to the yoga studio and for 90 minutes all I have to do is breathe and move. I could drop out of the master's program, but it was so much hard work and very competitive just to get accepted. When I explain my circumstances to my instructors, they all commit to work with me so I can stay in the program; I persist. For these two years, yoga is my salvation. With the fall through the roof of the Hogan, I am sure I survive because, through yoga, I surrender to the experience. Had I stiffened up or fought against what was happening, I feel certain I would have suffered the much more serious consequences that worried my orthopedist.

As part of my post falling care, I see Kristin, a yoga friend and my cranial sacral therapist. She soon has me working in my pain body, helping me regain my full range of motion. As we are working, she tells me my father, Woody, is with us, standing in the corner. She assures me that his presence is a blessing for us. She tells me he likes my energy. I feel the warm spot on my cheek.

Each year, after returning from the workshop in Monument Valley, we planners meet to debrief and begin plans for the next year. Prior to our first workshop, we meet with the participants orienting them to cultural differences and expected outcomes. The first year, we share with them several documents that are so old they were originally created on a typewriter and copied on a mimeograph. Nevertheless, they contain important information on words and customs that will be helpful to the participants. By the second year, we give them two books to read: *The Truth About Stories: A Native Narrative*, by Thomas King, and *We Can't Teach What We Don't Know: White Teachers, Multiracial Schools* by Gary Howard. King begins each of his five chapters with a variation on the cosmology reference to infinite regress, or turtles all the way down. The legend is that the world rests on the back of a large turtle, and that turtle rests on the back of an even larger turtle. I have a small carving representing turtles all the way down.

"Turtles all the way down" becomes a tag line for our workshops. We use it to explain any baffling situation or question. For Christmas one year, Tom, who is more inclined to celebrate Winter Solstice, finds seasonal cards with a row of watercolor turtles, each with a fir tree tied to their back. He distributes them happily.

In Chapter Two, King continues, "The truth about stories is that's all we are. 'You can't understand the world without telling a story,' the Anishinabe writer, Gerald Vizenor tells us. 'There isn't any center to the world but a story.'" So, for ourselves and for all the participants in our workshops, we have tried to change our narrative, about ourselves, about our students, and about what is possible.

Each year on the drive down to Monument Valley we stop at Ute Mesa and learn about traditions of the Ute Nation, stopping at the home of Wanda and Aldean Ketchum. Aldean, a White Mountain Ute, is a flute maker and performer who was featured in the opening ceremonies of the 2002 Winter Olympics in Salt Lake City. Wanda, a Navajo woman, is a skilled beading artist who shows off some of her many skills in the designs on the buckskin clothing Aldean wears for his performances. In recordings of the 2002 Olympics Opening Ceremonies, Aldean appears, wraith-like, at the top of the stadium, caught in a cold white light.

Wanda teaches us the Ute Bear Dance, the steps and formations, and how to use the shawls that she provides for us—a rectangle of polyester gabardine with fringe made of ribbon, a concession to modernity, much like the wood and sheetrock octagon compared to the traditional Hogan. The shawl colors are subdued, dark blue, dark green, and burgundy red, the fringe 6 inches long in harmonizing, brighter hues. Wanda explains that the bear is a symbol of strength for the Utes. She also explains that the bear is a bad omen for the Navajos. She tells us of the commitment she and Aldean have made to learning the many accommodations they allow in making their marriage, an alignment between traditional enemies, work. After the Bear Dance, we eat fry bread and beef stew. This version of stew more broth than the gravy that would be typical of dominant culture stew.

We are at Wanda and Aldean's, sitting in the protection of a bamboo grove they have cultivated to give shade to the south side of their house. There is also a tarp awning, making a kind of modernized shade house. This is our third year enjoying their easy graciousness. This is the first year

Wanda tells us how she watched her father drown in the nearby Green River. After his death she goes on "placement" with the Navajo Education program for the LDS Church. Her positive experience allows her to stay with her White family during the school year for eight years until she graduates from high school. Wanda tells us she lives in three worlds: Dine', Ute, and White; her beading symbol is the rose, representing both the many layers of her multiple lives and the Dine' ideal of Ho'zho'o'ji' which can also be interpreted as "Walking in the Beauty Way."

This third year is also the first time Aldean tells us of how he became a flute maker and artist. When he is 7 or 8, he finds a young hawk with an injured wing. As he cares for the injured creature, Aldean quickly learns the sound of the bird's chirp when he is hungry or thirsty. When the bird heals, Aldean releases him into the wild. The following summer his grandma wakes him one morning saying, "Someone is here to see you." Aldean goes outside expecting to see a person, instead, he sees the hawk on a nearby pole. The hawk calls to Aldean, and then flies up and joins a group of hawks circling in the sky above. It is that summer that Aldean goes to his grandfather, Billy, asking him to teach him the sounds of the birds and how to make the traditional flutes.

For five summer workshops our structure is basically the same. We leave Salt Lake City early on Saturday morning, stopping with the Ketchums at White Mountain Ute Mesa, for learning and sharing supper. Then on to Monument Valley, arriving at the school in the twilight, hastily unloading and setting up sleeping quarters. Mine, except for the days after the fall, are always in my little spring bar tent facing east and the rugged beauty of the Monument Valley skyline. On Sunday morning, from breakfast to around lunch time, the participants leave with their Native families for a two-night stay. While our participants are at their home stays, we leaders engage in various service activities. Those participants on home stays have no agenda other than to return to the high school about noon on Tuesday. Tuesday afternoon we debrief their experiences and prepare for our Wednesday in Kayenta, at the mental health center, learning about Traditional and Western healing, and at the Flea Market for lunch and brief shopping, then on to the Native Peace Court in the afternoon. Thursday and Friday, we spend with artists and a variety of teachers. Our third year we add in Kay, the counselor at Hopi High School. After our time at the visitor's center on First Mesa, we meet her at the home of her father, Rex Pooyouma, one of the Native code talkers who helped the Allies win the war in the Pacific. He tells us a few war stories and sings for us the song the other GIs make up for him, "Big Chief Pooyouma." All of us, including Rex, laugh and laugh. He is barely 5'2".

And then we watch the agile little 91-year-old balance on a chair as he stretches for boxes in the rafters of his home that is over 300 years old. Inside the boxes are sample ceremonial moccasins that he makes for supplemental income. They are red cowhide, the color of Herefords, ankle high with a fold-back collar and ties. The soles are thick white leather. He demonstrates how he soaks and molds the leather soles and hand stitches every pair. He traces the outline of our feet to custom fill our orders. We travel on to Kay's home, a red brick bungalow located in Keams Canyon where she is a school counselor at Hopi High School. Kay and her family provide us a traditional Hopi Feast—hominy stew, blue corn balls, mutton, and melon—and serve it to us on the floor of her living room. She explains that the newspaper "table" coverings laid on the carpet and the blanket "chairs" we sit on are typical for Hopi culture, teaching us the traditional "S" posture with our knees to the side. She speaks of how she uses the kachina, or spirit guide, of many students to help them through their high school education and preparation for the future.

Each year we are welcomed to the Monument Valley High School by the principal, Pat Seltzer. Pat tells us how she and her husband Jack came to Monument Valley to teach at the high school for a year or two. They stay more than 20 years, raising their two daughters in the small apartments available to the teachers. Pat loves her students and their families, working hard to help them access the world. She recently completed a survey in the community seeking to understand expectations for students. Generally, families are happy if students graduate high school, are employed year-round, and can live in the valley. Many students go on for more education. The biggest challenge is being able to live in the Valley. We meet three young men who grow up in a traditional Hogan with no running water and no electricity. All three have college degrees. One, a dental hygienist, tells us, "People will always have teeth, right?" Jack Seltzer, a science teacher, recently recognized as the Utah Teacher of the Year, helps his students create and maintain several gardens, including a peach orchard. He helps them cultivate willows for the basket makers. He helps them create and maintain a traditional medicine garden. And he helps them create and maintain a grandmas' dye garden for the rug makers. He also helps them care for and research drought resistant crops. They grow alfalfa for hay which they sell as a fund raiser for their projects. Several times each day during our stay, the high school intercom blares, "Jack Seltzer, Jack Seltzer, someone wants hay."

※

One evening during our third year, all participants are invited to the Octagon of Stanley Holiday. He tells us how he uses the traditional stories and teachings of the Navajo to heal those who seek his help, explaining how stories are to be told only during their proper season. Toward the end of our discussion, I have an opportunity to show Stanley the symbols that I saw over and over in my mind during my long and painful ride to the hospital in Kayenta. I tell him about leaving two of the symbols at the ceremonial circle on Bear Mountain. Stanley studies the images carefully. He tells me that I took the place of someone else in falling through the Hogan, and the witch I saw was travelling as a dog on the day I fell. Stanley then tells me how to heal the earth from my fall and to make my peace, which includes burying some dirt from the Hogan at my home in Sugar House and using water to seal the blessing. Luckily Lillian saves about a cup of that dirt for me from the previous year. When I ask her what I should do with the baggie of dirt, she tells me,

"Keep it until you know what should be done." Now I know.

※

Our fourth and fifth year we add in Canyon de Chelly and a tour with Alema Benally, a ranger with the National Park Service, who recounts the removal of many Navajos from Utah and New Mexico to Redondo Bosque in New

Mexico. She recounts the multiple forced marches of nearly 11,000 Natives and how only 4,000 survive to return alive to their homes some four years later. All Dine' suffer generational grief from this historical trauma.

Our fourth and fifth years we also meet Rex Harvey, a gifted traditional healer, who has served eight years in the U.S. Marines. The evening that Rex is coming to talk to us I feel his presence before I see him. Lillian would say our spirits bumped into each other. Walking along the sidewalk, I feel like I have been called to attention. I look up and see Rex across the parking lot of the high school. Average height, muscular build, dressed in jeans and a heavy white cotton shirt, his long hair in a traditional Navajo man bun, or Navajo woman bun—it is the same for both, hair pulled back into a vertical bun wrapped horizontally with white cotton yarn. Rex shares with us the Seven Spiritual Gifts to help us find our way in the world.

Rex Harvey notes, 7-28-2008

Gift 1) Dine'—the people themselves provide protection for the child

Gift 2) The clan or the family—the mother's clan provides love—the father's clan provides strength. Through love we learn the four cries: the child needs something; the child misses something or someone; the child is angry; or the cry of deep happiness. Through the father we learn strength of mind, body, soul, and spirit. The Maternal Grandmother teaches wisdom—learn to feed the spirit, take care of your physical body, learn your spiritual path.

The Paternal Grandfather teaches about happiness—accept every situation you are in—it is a teaching—there is a blessing behind it.

Gift 3) Language itself is a medicine—the sound of the language. White shell language is light. Turquoise language is water. Abalone shell language is air. And Black Obsidian language is earth or pollen. Words are a gift. Use Ya'a t'e'e'h in a way that constitutes you. The heat is healing me. Don't explain yourself all the time.

Gift 4) Your sacred footprint—acknowledge your spiritual side and rebalance—you should only have two shoes in your life. Always take your sacred moccasins. The first step is the thinking process. The second step is the planning process. The third step is your livelihood, where you are comfortable, safe, and secure. The fourth step is your spiritual values.

Gift 5) The Shadow which balances life—it energizes and will bring everything out.

Gift 6) Spiritual Values—sacred items such as a medicine bundle—-dirt and sand from the four sacred mountains, food, and water.

Gift 7) Spiritual Horse—each of us have 7 spiritual beings inside; mother, father, maternal grandfather, maternal grandmother, paternal grandfather, paternal grandmother, and self—the spirit horse is for spiritual transportation. Horse has a leader. He is curious about everything. If you want something good for you, you have to go get it. Horse can see all six dimensions. Horse teaches you discipline.

Rex tells us of a conversation with his young son as they are tending their horses.

"Whose horse is this?"

"My horse Daddy," his son replies.

"Who feeds this horse?"

"You do Daddy."

"Who waters this horse?"

"You do Daddy."

"Whose horse is this?" Rex asks us all. "Who feeds your spiritual horse? Who waters your spiritual horse? Who cares for your spiritual horse? It better be you."

His presentation continues. Horse helps us heal, helps us learn, helps us balance. We get bucked off and get back on. Life goes smoothly then out of the blue it goes badly. If you are going to have children, you need to understand life/death/rebirth. People who commit suicide appreciate death more than life.

Our last afternoon with Rex, he walks into the classroom and exclaims,

"What is this?"

We respond in our post-lunch drowsiness—our days are long and the nights seem short.

He continues, "Each of you has a spiritual flame at the top of your head. It should burn blue and bright. Yours are barely orange. We need to do something to wake you up." He gets us up, moving and talking. Rex tells us that his grandfather told him about the spirits in Monument Valley and how he is to be respectful in being there. Over the next few years, we see Rex as a presenter at several of our school counselor conferences. At one of the conferences, he tells us at the beginning of his presentation that as he travels through the mountain passes on his way from Monument

Valley to Salt Lake City, he sings ceremonial songs. He says, "You wouldn›t enter someone's house without first knocking on the door, right? Well, these passes are someone's house, and we need to let those who live there know that we are going through their house."

And then five years after we meet, Rex takes his own life. We are heartbroken. Perhaps, out of the blue something went badly. Perhaps, he appreciated death more than life. His teaching fits into the comprehensive theory of suicide developed by Thomas Joiner and explained in the May 23, 2013, issue of *Newsweek*. According to Joiner the trifecta for suicide risk is a thwarted sense of belongingness, a perceived burdensomeness, and a capability for suicide—as in "I am not afraid to die." This theory explains why our combat veterans are so vulnerable to suicide. Perhaps out of the blue something goes badly. Perhaps they appreciate death more than life.

During our first year with Rex, I learn from him the prayers to the seven directions which I incorporate into my morning yoga practice.

A prayer (or a breath/or both) to the East, the white shell and the people of the East.

A prayer to the South, the blue bead and the people of the South.

A prayer to the West, the yellow abalone shell and the people of the West

A prayer to the North, the jet-black obsidian and the people of the North.

A prayer to Mother Earth.

A prayer to Father Sky.

And a prayer for Dawn, may she walk in beauty.

Through this ritual, I learn my solid center. Sometimes my center is literally beside me—I am beside myself. I learn to look for what is out of balance—my time, my energy, my focus. What do I need to change? This is a way for me to honor Rex and all the other teachers who serve us. Like many before us who come to the Navajo reservation, we come hoping to help and leave vastly enriched.

My Māori friend Syd joins us the last two years. He has a PhD in community psychology. Syd is half-Caucasian and so also walks in two worlds. We ask him to use his professional knowledge and years of personal experience to give us an evaluation of our Cultural Awareness and Sensitivity Workshop.

Syd tells us that we have done a remarkable job creating an experiential cultural immersion. For our participants, we require them to write a 10-page final paper addressing questions from Gary Howard's *We Can't Teach What We Don't Know.* From the inception we have had an assumption of White privilege and White culpability. We ask ourselves and our participants about our biases, our history, our intentionality. Most of the participants come away with a positive experience and specific steps they can take to improve outcomes for our Native students. For the students themselves, each year we hear from the people in the Valley that if a family moves to Salt Lake City for work, they look for schools with a counselor who has participated in the workshops. Many of our participants hear experiences of our non-White students because of our time in the Valley.

🖋

I am thrilled when the Bears Ears Monument is created by President Barack Obama. For the first time in history, the tribes of the Navajo, Hopi, Zuni, Ute Mountain Ute, and Ute Indian Tribes come together to agree on the lands they want set aside. Our third year in Monument Valley for our service project we clear several acres of tumble-weeds, hoeing the weeds out by hand. Tom carries them to an ever-increasing pile at the edge of the clearing. We are advised rattlesnakes are in the area. It takes four of us most of the day to complete the work. When I ask Lillian why they do not just bring in a tractor, she explains that machinery degrades the sacred nature of the land, and this family is preparing for a ceremony. Imagine how these same Native people feel when the government rescinds the size of Bears Ears and shrinks the monument to accommodate mineral leases, extraction projects, and the use of heavy machinery everywhere.

We can have soaring discussions of the natural beauty, the pristine wilderness of Southeastern Utah and Northern Arizona, how protecting these public lands enriches us all. For me the issue is more elemental. The Native peoples of this area come together to ask that we set aside some of their traditional lands, to give more than respect, to revere their place and their traditions. After all the broken treaties, all the genocide, all the devastation of our Native peoples, of their tribes, could we not, just once, more than honor, perhaps revere their request? Could we at least protect the land that has always been theirs? Can we honor them as sovereign nations?

🖋

A couple of years before we have our first Monument Valley experience, on a Saturday morning in November, I sit around the large table, in the cool shadows of the conference room at the Utah Humanities offices, meeting with parent representatives from the five tribes in Utah—Shoshone,

Paiute, Ute, White Mountain Ute, and Navajo. I walk them through the document we use for on-site review of school counseling programs for incentive funding approval. As we go through the standards, such as School Counselor Training, Data and Program Effectiveness, Crisis Response, and Career Exploration, the parents wonder if we could make some specific accommodations for American Indian/ Alaska Native students consistent with the statewide AI/ AN Education Plan. Their requests are well within the scope of practice of the working school counselor. So, we incorporate into the program review standards indicators specific to American Indian/Alaska Native students. Do we know who those students are in our schools? Do we know their tribal affiliation? Do we understand sovereignty, cultural grief, social structure, and learning processes? I travel around the state holding focus groups for the new review document, which was originally just a yes/no checklist and is now a rubric identifying levels of implementation. I am invariably asked, "Why standards specific to this group?" and "Why can't we all just be Americans?" When Tom and I wait to present the finalized document to CMAC, the Community Minority Advisory Council for the Utah State Board of Education, the Specialist for Minority Affairs, a Latinx man who should have known better, pulls the two of us into the chair closet attached to the Board Room. Seriously, the chair closet for a dressing down by a peer. We have to duck through a half-size door. He tells us that we cannot proceed, that some of the other minority groups will wonder why this particular group. Tom and I tell the Minority Specialist, who does not have any supervisory authority over us and who is in a lateral position, that we are proceeding. We tell him we are not afraid to have those discussions. We get this much resistance for doing our jobs. They wonder, "Why standards for just this group?"

We respond, "Because they asked."

We get the CMAC approval.

The Navajo, the Hopi, the Zuni, the Ute Mountain Ute, and the Ute Indian Tribe come together to ask for 1.9 million acres. They get 1.35 million acres. It is their own land. Imagine the resistance.

I make my last trip to Moab for work on October 29, 2015. I near the junction between Highway 6 and I-70. The full moon peers over the eastern buttes just as the sun begins to sink below the western foothills. I have neither the equipment nor the skills to photograph this moment of pure magic. I pull over and get out of my car. As she emerges, the giant harvest moon looks rosy and nearly translucent against the purpling sky. The last glow of the sun lingers in the west. I am a lone traveler this evening, watching the earth and the sun in perfect balance, as they always are, blessing the Earth and her people, as they always do, here in my western sky.

7

TELL MY DAUGHTER

Back at home my world is changing. For my entire adult life, I have been a very active member of the Church of Jesus Christ of Latter-day Saints, the official name of the Mormon or LDS Church. For most of 50 years I have been engaged in teaching weekly classes in one of the LDS auxiliaries or providing leadership for one of the auxiliaries; Primary for children ages 3 through 11, Young Women for girls ages 12 to 18, and Relief Society for all women 18 and older. These are called auxiliary organizations for a good reason. While essential to the faith's mission of educating and training the members, they are outside of the LDS Priesthood that is the core of the organization. Women in the LDS Church are not ordained to the Priesthood, even though there is some evidence that Joseph Smith intended that women would eventually "enjoy this blessing." For four years I do teach Gospel Doctrine, a Sunday School class that includes male and female participants, but, otherwise, women do not instruct men. I have read multiple times the standard works, the Mormon canon, including the *King James Translation of the Bible* at least ten times cover to cover, maybe more, along with *The Doctrine and Covenants*, the *Pearl of Great Price*, and the *Book of Mormon*—that one more like twenty times. Although admonished to regularly read the scriptures, I feel safe in saying that most active Mormons do not read or know their scriptures. They rely instead on someone else feeding their spirit horse.

🖋

During the four years I teach Gospel Doctrine, I share the assignment with a male priesthood bearer, most of the years with Brian and a few short months with Brother Jones. We teach on alternate Sundays. Brian and I have an easy and respectful relationship. And then he gets another assignment. I am not many weeks into co-teaching with Brother Jones when I see him put a large manilla envelope in my mailbox in the afternoon following my morning lesson. Inside the envelope is a three-page typed critique of my lesson including several corrections on points of doctrine. I am livid. Within the hour I have returned the critique to the mailbox of Brother Jones with the following message scrawled on the back of his pages:

> Brother Jones,
> I have been called to teach Gospel Doctrine just as you have been called to teach Gospel Doctrine. I have a right to inspiration for teaching my classes, just as you have a right to inspiration for teaching your classes. You have not been called to be my supervisor, my mentor, nor my corrector. I am willing to grant you good intent this once. DO NOT EVER DO THIS TO ME AGAIN.
> Sister Nielsen

Brother Jones, no doubt, expects that I will bow to his greater authority and be ever so grateful for his help and guidance. I am not. Not many months after this incident, life with Herbert falls apart; I resign from my calling and move away.

🖋

For most of my adult life I have possessed a temple recommend, meaning I pay a 10% tithing and pass a yearly interview with my ecclesiastical leader. The first thing I let go of is paying tithing. Paying out more than $600 per month to the Church keeps my spending plan in continuous chaos. That's the way we talk about it—The Church in Utah means the LDS Church. Faithful Church members and leaders will tell you this is where I go wrong. LDS lore has it that as long as the person or the family pays a full tithe—10% of their income or increase—they will never have financial worries. To hear most members of the Church tell—it just happens.

The spring of 2007, prior to my tithing crisis, PBS airs a 4-hour documentary on The Mormons for the American Experience series. Many people at my work are upset. A woman co-worker declares, "They can't say that," in reference to statements about polygamy. I point out that they did say that. "Well, it isn't true," she declares. And then I walk her though how what they say is, in fact, true.

Most Mormons know the story of Mormonism, but they do not know the history of the Mormons. And often the story and the history do not match up. After the documentary airs, Dora calls me,

"Did you know about the rock in the hat?" she wonders.

"Yes, I know about the rock in the hat."

The Mormon story says that Joseph Smith translated the *Book of Mormon* from a set of Golden Plates, genuine gold plates, bound as a book, a very heavy book, delivered to him by the hand of the angel Moroni—the iconic figure with the trumpet that stands atop most every Mormon temple. The history is that Joseph, and his family, were active believers in a mysticism detailed by D. Michael Quinn in his book, *Early Mormonism and the Magic World View*. According to multiple sources, Joseph Smith uses a peep stone or a seer stone by placing it in a top hat, putting his eyes and face into the darkened space and dictating "translations" of the *Book of Mormon*. For the most part, Joseph speaks the translations through a blanket partition to a volunteer scribe, meaning that the scribe did not actually see Joseph making the translations. Likewise, no one ever physically saw the golden plates. Several witnesses saw the alleged plates under a cloth, claiming to have witnessed them with their spiritual eyes.

Dora continues her interrogation, "Did you know about the Mountain Meadow Massacre?"

"I did know about the Mountain Meadow Massacre," I tell her.

My former brother-in-law, a junior-high history teacher in Utah, had been raving about the travesty for years. In 1857, Mormons near Cedar City, UT, were skittish about a group of pioneers from Arkansas, the Baker-Fancher wagon train, who camped near their town for an extended period. On the morning of September 7, 1857, active Mormons met the Baker-Fancher pioneers in the meadow, and, as they walked alongside one another, the Mormons shot the intruders at point blank range, killing everyone except seventeen children younger than age 7 whom they took into their homes and raised. Some of the Mormons dressed as Native Americans and, for more than a century, unjustly blamed the slaughter on Native Americans in the area, members of the Paiute Nation. The bigger controversy than the massacre is whether or not Brigham Young knew about it or had ordered it. Until he was executed by a local firing squad, John D. Lee, the only local leader who stood trial and suffered punishment, claimed that Young knew.

Dora is aghast. She has been a sweet and faithful Mormon her entire life, my only child who serves an LDS mission. She is nearly 31. She and her husband, the French-Swiss guy with a degree in aeronautical engineering, begin to do research. Throughout my adult life, I have relied heavily on bibliotherapy to make changes, professional and psychological, through personal counseling and on my own. Dora and her husband start passing me books. My reading list includes the following:

An Insider's View of Mormon Origins by Grant Palmer

... By His Own Hand Upon Papyrus: A New Look at The Joseph Smith Papyrii by Charles M. Larson

No Man Knows My History by Fawn Brodie— Brodie, a history scholar at UCLA

Under the Banner of Heaven: A Story of Violent Faith by Jon Krakauer

Leaving the Saints by Ann Beck

Plus, several pamphlets on the connection between the Mormon temple ceremonies and the Masons

I share with them Quinn's book on *Early Mormonism and the Magic World View*. It is a tome, but nearly half is references. In my searching, I find Ken Wilbur's *The One, Two, Three of God*. I listen to the book on tape several times, even practicing his meditation on God in the first, second, and third person. Interestingly enough, *The Pearl of Great Price* begins with the book of Genesis written in the first person. Wilbur claims that he can tell you where God lives, depending on the type of God you believe in, declaring that most American Christians believe in a third-grade God, a dictatorial leader who dispenses rewards and punishments based on behavior.

Beck's book, *Leaving the Saints*, describes the pressures her father, the Mormon intellect Hugh Nibley, received from the leadership of the Mormon Church in making a rational case for "the text within a text" when the Joseph Smith Papyrii are discovered in the basement of the Metropolitan Museum in New York in 1947 and acquired by the LDS Church in 1966. The text within a text is Nibley's explanation of how the common funerary documents that comprise the Joseph Smith Papyrii could have been "translated" by Joseph Smith into the first-person version of Genesis and other apocryphal, biblical-type stories that comprise the *Pearl of Great Price*. The text by Larson further elaborates on this issue. My point here is not to provide a doctrine-by-doctrine refutation of Mormonism, but, rather, to provide some examples of how the story of Mormonism does not line up with the history of Mormonism and to understand my own thought processes. At the time, I wanted to make sure I left the Church for sound intellectual reasons, but perhaps it is, after all, a purely emotional decision. Maybe it is born out of pure lust. One of the behaviors that makes me ape-shit crazy is when someone declares that they know the motivations of another person. I think sometimes we do not even know our own motivations for ourselves. Talk about misalignment.

The text by Brodie provides additional examples of the misalignment between story and history, including the "extermination order" issued in Missouri by then Governor Boggs, that allows many Mormons to view themselves as the "most persecuted" group in history, including the Holocaust and the Spanish Inquisition. True enough, early Mormons, including Joseph Smith, suffered much persecution, hardship, and deprivation, but through a careful analysis of the historical documents owned by the Mormon Church itself, Brody illuminates how often the church members and Church leadership, in their righteous arrogance, threaten the existing locals that they will take over their lands, their politics, and drive the "gentiles" out. Gentiles, from the Mormon perspective, means non-Mormons, so called because the Mormons believe themselves to be literal descendants of the House of Israel, often through the tribes of Ephraim and Manasseh. Those early declarations are often followed by unexpected retribution. Well, unexpected by the self-righteous Mormons.

Dora and I talk often, comparing thoughts. My one recurring question is: "At what level do they—meaning the LDS leadership, the patriarchy, the priesthood—know that this stuff is not true?" This is a huge question. For most of my Church-going life I have been indoctrinated to "know that the Church is true." Indeed, for many years it was regularly stated across local, regional, and Church-wide pulpits that the LDS Church was the "only true and living church on the face of the earth." During my teenage years, I attended LDS Seminary during my regular school day. This is accomplished on a release time agreement with the local school district. The release time program, which allows participating students to leave their school and walk to an adjacent Mormon Seminary building, is part of every school district in Utah. It is one of the money-saving strategies that allows Utah to have the lowest per pupil expenditures in the nation. During my years in the LDS Seminary system, not only is the Mormon Church unquestionably true, but also the "Great Whore of the Earth," as described in the version of the *Book of Mormon* that I read growing up, is widely recognized as the Catholic Church. I do not know that the LDS leadership actually ever call-out the leadership of the Catholic Church as pretenders to the throne for world-wide leadership of Christianity, but in the trenches of Church membership that is the choice we are offered, fealty to the "true and living church" or fealty to the "great whore of the earth." Even though I live outside of Utah—my partial school year in New Mexico, four years in L.A. while Ernie attends UCLA Dental School, another 20 months in the Central Coast of California—I stick with fealty to the true and living church, The Church, for most of my adult life.

Through the years I have a few close friends who "leave the Church." For those who stay, the departing members are assumed to be leaving because of transgression, usually on the part of the departing, but also often because of the transgressions of a trusted person. For instance, I might have left the Church over Herbert. After all, how could a BYU professor have been unfaithful to me for most of our 12-year marriage? The answer is likely because he is a flawed human, just as so many of us are flawed humans. I might ask myself, prior to engaging in a relationship with him, how could a tenured BYU professor enter into an adulterous relationship with me? I think it is true love. I could ask myself, how could I, a true and faithful Mormon woman, engage in such an adulterous relationship? Perhaps I am hopelessly wicked. Perhaps this liaison suits some cosmopolitan version of myself—I have an affair because I am the type of woman who has an affair. It is more likely powerful psychological forces—his need to be a hero and my need to be loved. Two flawed humans on a collision course.

My friend and colleague, Hollie, tells me that when she leaves the Church, the hardest thing is taking off her temple garments, the oft-mentioned magic underwear that Mormons wear after they have been to the LDS temple to "take out their endowments." I don't know why we say "take out our endowments," I only know that is how we say it. Taking out your endowments means that the member attends a session at the Mormon Temple in which they make promises, or covenants, with Proxies of the Lord Jesus Christ and God, regarding church activity and commitments. After I cease paying tithing, it takes from August to December for me to get to the point of considering "taking off my garments," which just means no longer wearing them on a 24-hour basis. This single action is generally considered a sign of total apostasy. I take them off and leave them in a drawer for a few days. Winter is coming, and I miss the extra layer of clothing. I put them back on for a few days. I take them off again and take them to the basement for a few days. I bring them back upstairs and wear them for another day or two. The difficulty I am having is not just physical discomfort; it is deep psychological turmoil. I am wrestling with my eternal soul and the eternal consequences. Letting go of the Church feels like the Earth has tilted on its axis. My footing is no longer sure. I no longer know exactly how the world will turn out. I no longer know that if I just do A, and B, and C, then I will get my reward in heaven. Giving up that surety may be the scariest thing of all.

I know, from a practical standpoint, I will pay dearly for leaving the Church. In Utah, being a Mormon means you are automatically an insider, someone who is in the know, and, generally, someone who can be trusted implicitly. This implicit trust is one reason Utah has one of the highest rates of white-collar crime in the U.S. I saw an accounting professor from BYU make a PowerPoint presentation to explain this phenomenon: Mormons believe that God wants them to prosper, indeed, that the righteous do prosper—he had charts and data. Pat Bagley, a Mormon satirist and political cartoonist, has a cartoon that shows a young man standing in front of an LDS Church with a parking lot full of high-end cars. The sign in front of the church says, "Welcome to the Church of Jesus Christ of Very Successful Latter-day Saints." Because God wants us to prosper, we are gullible for any get rich scheme that will get us out of the darkness of poverty. Rumor has it that Ernie, my kid's father, invests $30,000 in a gold mine in Africa. He is surprised when it is nationalized.

Such belief in this kind of predestined prosperity has its origins with Joseph Smith himself. Fawn Brody notes of Joseph Smith in *No Man Knows My History* that: "[Smith] believed in the good life, with a moderate self-indulgence in food and drink, occasional sport and good entertainment. . . . And it is no accident that his theology in the end discarded all the traces of Calvinism and became an ingenious blend of supernaturalism and materialism, which promised in heaven a continuation of all earthly pleasures—work, wealth, sex, and power."

I will not pay so dearly for leaving the Church if I can be subtle. It is entirely possible to "pass" as Mormon. A person merely needs a rudimentary understanding of the jargon and the organization, along with the ability to nod and smile knowingly at the appropriate times. Unfortunately, I cannot be subtle. I rarely suffer in silence, and most everyone knows at least some of my anguish in wrestling with points of doctrine and realities of church function. At work I discuss my dilemmas in detail with Jeff the Elder and Jeff the Younger.

I make an appointment with my beloved former stake president. I ask him particularly to explain the practice of polygamy. Current LDS leadership will proclaim loudly that the "Church and its members no longer practice polygamy." However, it is still a doctrinal reality wherein current LDS practice allows that LDS men can, and often are, sealed to more than one woman, not simultaneously, unless there has been a divorce, but if a man is a widower he can be sealed to a second wife when his first wife dies and a third, if his second wife also dies, in effect practicing spiritual polygamy. It is common practice among the General Authorities of the Church to marry a spinster professor at BYU after the first wife dies. A woman who is a widow can marry again, even in the LDS temple, but that marriage is for "time only," so until death do us part. But the male members know, and expect, that in the next life they will be married for eternity to all three women, and possibly more, on the other side, if they are "true and faithful." Kind of the Mormon version of 22 virgins. Jack, my stake president, tells me that polygamy was essential to the early Mormon church, needed to build up the population so that the base of members could withstand the onslaught of trials and tribulations. And yet, I learn from the Brody text that all but one of Joseph Smith's plural wives were already married to other men—they had an available sperm donor. It is true that Brigham Young marries more than one of his twenty-seven wives as a means of offering her protection and livelihood, but the early practitioners of polygamy, including Joseph Smith and Brigham Young, kept secret for years their multiple wives from the original wives themselves and from the Mormon membership at large. Krakauer notes that Smith "did whatever was necessary, including bald-faced lying to conceal his polygamous behavior—not only from censorious non-Mormons but from all but a select few of his followers."

As I read *Under the Banner of Heaven*, I make a mental note that every active Mormon should be required to read at least one nonfiction book about Mormons written by a non-Mormon. Krakauer says things that take my breath away, like the bald-faced lying comment. Not because they are not true, but because we Mormons have a much more euphemistic way of talking about it. That includes the polygamy thing—we can put off thinking about it because that practice is for the next life. It is not a present reality for most active Mormons, especially women, in spite of the fact that polygamy is practiced faithfully among the Mormon fundamentalists.

David Leavitt, former Attorney General for the State of Utah and brother of former governor Mike Leavitt, notes, "That people in the state of Utah simply do not understand, and have not understood for fifty years, the devastating effect the practice of polygamy has on young girls." Such practitioners claim that the girls have a choice but being married before age 16, sometimes as young as 14, after years of isolation in their communities and years of indoctrination inside those communities, does not constitute much of a choice. When the authorities in Texas remove the children from the parents of the followers at the Yearning for Zion encampment in order to protect them, I agree completely because polygamy, as it is practiced among the Mormon fundamentalists, and as supported implicitly by modern Mormon theology, is inherently abusive. And that is one of my three big points of doctrinal issues with the Church.

My second big stumbling block comes from the stance of the Mormons on our LGBTQ brothers and sisters. Even when I was active and practicing Mormonism in all its details, I had a hard time with the Church's position on same sex attraction and action. One of my co-workers was in a rant about his lesbian sister and turned to me for support as he stated same-sex attraction was absolutely wrong.

"Oh, Murray, I have lived so much of my life without love that I have a hard time condemning anyone for taking love where they find it. Let us celebrate those among us who have love and happiness in this world."

As the world, and more particularly Utah, moves toward embracing marriage equality, the Mormon Church hardens its stand against gays and lesbians. On their website, The Human Rights Campaign provides the following information:

ON MARRIAGE EQUALITY

Same-sex marriages are not allowed in the LDS Church and sexual activity is grounds for being denied access to the temple, ordination, and other aspects of church membership. The church has a history of campaigning against marriage equality since the 1990s and the issue has become one of the church's foremost political concerns.

In November 2016, the LDS Church took formal steps to define marriage equality as a form of apostasy in its "Handbook of Instructions," a guide for Mormon leaders. The policy not only describes Mormons in same-sex couples as apostates of the faith, it also establishes disciplinary actions that Mormon leaders can take against same-sex couples, including excommunication. The new policy also took aim at the children of same-sex couples. It barred them from baptism and from joining the LDS Church unless they denounce their parents by the age of 18. This new policy, commonly referred to as the "November Policy," marks the first time a Christian church has enshrined a baptismal ban on children of same-sex couples. https://www.hrc.org/resources/stances-of-faiths-on-lgbt-issues-church-of-jesus-christ-of-latter-day-saint

I do not know what to say about this, other than noting the pain this stance has caused and continues to cause for many inside and outside of the Mormon Church. Interestingly, more than two years after the November Doctrine, a new revelation, from God, allows that acting on same sex attraction is no longer apostasy, but merely grievous sin, and the children of such liaisons can now be baptized and participate in Church. However, months after this "change of policy," the changes have not yet been incorporated into the written Church's Handbook of Instruction. My sister notes that this new revelation comes just before the spring semiannual conference of the Church and likely saves them from another round of protests and demonstrations. And another round of dismayed members leaving the Church wholesale as they complete paperwork in a park near the Mormon Conference Center in Downtown Salt Lake City.

My final point of doctrinal disagreement with the Church of Jesus Christ of Latter-day Saints is their racist views and practices, which have existed from the beginning and which persist into the present. It may be to my eternal shame and regret that I fail to fully recognize the pain-inflicting nature of this aspect until the summer of Covid-19, the summer of Black Lives Matter, the summer of George Floyd. Oh, sure, years ago I had a Native American friend with whom I used to laugh about whether or not she could become "white and delightsome," but I suspect it was funnier to me than it was to her. Even when I was a practicing Mormon, I did little to understand this racism and to actively disarm or change it. *The Book of Mormon*, as translated by Joseph Smith, provides the foundation for the Mormon Church. Beginning in about 600 B.C., the book follows one Lehi, his wife Sariah, and their children and descendants as they flee the wickedness of Jerusalem into the wilderness and eventually cross the ocean to the new world, allegedly becoming the ancestors of the American Indians, a supposition long since disproved through DNA and the oral traditions of the Native Americans themselves.

Early on in the *Book of Mormon*, Joseph Smith's translation declares:

And [God] had caused the cursing to come upon them, yea, even a sore cursing, because of their iniquity. For behold, they had hardened their hearts against him that they had become like unto flint; wherefore, as they were white, and exceedingly fair and delightsome, that they might not be enticing unto my people the Lord God did cause a skin of blackness to come upon them. And thus saith the Lord God: I will cause that they shall be loathsome unto my people, save they shall repent of their iniquities. And cursed shall be the seed of him that mixeth with their seed; for they shall be cursed even with the same cursing. And the Lord spake it, and it was done.

—2 Nephi, 5:21–23.

This harsh position appears on page 66 of a book that is 531 pages long. There are five such references in the *Book of Mormon*. This is the point at which I would insert a photo of a BLM protestor posted by Shaun King. The woman is blonde, a soccer mom or at least a comfortable suburbanite. She appears in a floppy hat, masked and holding a cardboard sign with simple printing, black and white lines side by side. It reads: "There were no White people in the Bible." At the bottom of the sign, in smaller letters, "Take all the time you need with that." Joseph Smith, like many of us in White supremacist Christianity, fails to consider that simple truth; all Bible stories are about the peoples of the Middle East, people of Color. But Smith certainly embraced the rule of hypodescent, defined by Caroline Randall Williams as "the social and legal practice of assigning a genetically mixed-race person to the race with less social power."

(https://www.nytimes.com/2020/06/26/opinion/confed-erate-monuments-racism.html). There is some evidence that Smith intended to be more embracing of the African Americans who joined the Mormon Church, going so far as to ordain to the Priesthood "some African Americans during the first two decades of the Church's existence." (https://www.churchofjesuschrist.org/study/manual/gospel-topics-essays/race-and-the-priesthood?lang=eng). Any vestige of that intent was erased by Brigham Young, who declared in a speech to the Utah Legislature on Jan. 23, 1852, "In as much as we believe in the Bible . . . we must believe in slavery. This colored race have [sic] been sub-jected to severe curses . . . which they have brought upon themselves. And until the curse is removed by him who placed it upon them, they must suffer the consequences." Brigham Young was off the hook for slavery and its conse-quences until God told him differently.

Echoes of Racism

According to Tasi Young, the Church further doubled down on [Brigham Young's] teachings through the Civil War and the modern civil rights movement (https://www.sltrib.com/opinion/commentary/2020/06/12/tasi-young-time-change/). In the summer of 2020, in a letter requesting the removal of names from buildings on the BYU campus, the BYU Black Student Union provides further examples of the overt racism through those years. George A Smith, Church President at the time, said in 1949 that "Negroes are not entitled to the full blessing of the Gospel," stat-ing further that interracial marriages were "most repug-nant." J. Reuben Clark, a member of the First Presidency of the Church, the three-man team that provides leadership of the modern Church, an ambassador to Mexico for the United States, and the man for whom the BYU School of Law is named, "strongly advocated for blood banks to segregate donations from Black and White people so they wouldn't be 'mixed.'" Harold B. Lee, another President of the Church, and the man for whom the main library at BYU is named, said that if his granddaughter "got engaged to a colored boy" while attending BYU, he would hold administrators accountable. And Ezra Taft Benson, yet another Church President, and a former Secretary of Agriculture for the United States, suggested that the civil rights movement for Blacks was itself a "communist deception." (https://www.sltrib.com/news/education/2020/07/18/byus-black-student-union/). Interesting that many among the far-right who oppose the social change promoted by the Black Lives Matter movement also suggest that it is a socialist plot, an attempt to destroy America as we know it. Most Mormons would exonerate the above-mentioned leaders and the above-mentioned declarations by noting that most of said leaders were not in the position of Church President, were not at the time the prophet, seer, and revelator.

So, after all of this resistance, finally, on June 9, 1978, the Mormon Church announces that, through a revelation from the Lord, the Mormon Church will extend Priesthood ordination and the temple endowment ordinances to Black members of the Church, having withheld from these Black members, for more than a century and a quarter, those very ordinances deemed essential for salvation and acceptance in the highest levels of the celestial kingdom. So, while the

Mormon Church puts considerable effort into missionary efforts worldwide to increase membership from the earliest days, here at home, hundreds of thousands of potential Black members are denied the temple blessings considered essential to the saving of their eternal souls. And each of the above-named past presidents of the Church are allegedly the mouthpiece of God on earth, each a "prophet, seer, and revelator."

In mid-June 2020, a petition started by members of the Church of Jesus Christ of Latter-day Saints and posted on Change.org states: "As members of the Church of Jesus Christ of Latter-day Saints we wish to join others in a heartfelt apology for the role that we have played in promoting racist ideologies and behaviors which have injured and burdened our brothers and sisters of African descent." The petition acknowledges the Church "has a long history of racist practices, teachings and doctrines, but we've taken steps to fix them, starting with ending the priesthood prohibition in June 1978." (https://www.change.org/p/russell-m-nelson-mormonsapologize). In 2019 the Church partnered with the NAACP to work together on self-reliance programs. In response to this partnership with NAACP, the Rev. Amos Brown, Chairman Emeritus of Religious Affairs for the organization, declares that "the Church's regret was demonstrated in its actions . . . An apology is implicit in 'Locking arms' with NAACP." (https://www.churchofjesuschrist.org/church/news/naacp-and-the-church-how-a-unique-partnership-is-blessing-gods-children?lang=eng). To me this feels something akin to saying, "The kindly old Christian is a slaveholder." I know from Shaun King and Ibram X. Kendi that kindly old Christians cannot also be slaveholders.

The Mormon Church has as its foundational document a book that declares a curse of a "skin of blackness" because of the wickedness of those thus cursed. The Church cannot embrace racist doctrine and then also declare themselves not racist. The Mormon Church is not racist in the same way it is not polygamous. It requires little digging to find the original doctrine in full sway for either issue. The huge problem for the Mormon Church is that eliminating the racist language from the *Book of Mormon* would mean eliminating or changing words of Joseph Smith, words that are allegedly the Word of God.

The Mormon Church has been recognized, more than once, as the cult of Joseph. As an illustration of this kind of adulation, I offer an experience from my days as a Gospel Doctrine teacher. Our local ward, generally comprised of more established and older families, welcomes in a new, young, shiny couple, recent graduates of BYU. In this Gospel Doctrine class, we are studying the *Doctrine and Covenants*, a collection of spiritual advice and doctrinal statements allegedly delivered from the mouth of the Lord Jesus Christ directly to the new Church President, Joseph Smith. During the discussion of said scriptures, the new young sister enthusiastically claims, "You can almost hear the voice of brother Joseph in the words." Not too gently, I chide the young woman, reminding her that, "The *Doctrine and Covenants* was dictated to Brother Joseph. If we hear a voice, it should be the voice of our Savior, Jesus Christ." This same cult of Joseph adulation leads to the creation of a genre of Mormon art in which both Jesus Christ, the plainest of men, and Joseph Smith, not notably handsome, are represented as light-haired, fair-skinned, Scandinavian Surfer Gods. Enough to make any woman agree to a polygamous marriage.

🪶

I am a 21-year-old mother of a 15-month-old child when Connie, my beautiful, smart, confident, and proud supervisor at the UCLA Placement and Career Planning Center asks me why Mormons have such a racist stance toward her and all other Black people. Connie, who looks so much like Barbara McNair, and I have talked about other deep topics during my months of employment. The Black Power movement is strong in L.A. and on the UCLA campus. During more than one lunch break, I walk west down Janss Steps, toward the Student Union, and stop at the grassy area north of the steps that provides a kind of impromptu amphitheater. I hear Angela Davis speak. I think I hear Huey Newton speak as the crowd and organizers pass the jar to "Free Bobby Seal." Or maybe the jar is to "Free Huey Newton and Free Bobby Seal" and the speaker is some other leader of the Black Panthers.

Before UCLA, I work for Pacific Telephone in the Axminster Hills office that serves Baldwin Hills, a comfortable community of primarily Black people. I know that Ike and Tina Turner and other successful Black entertainers live in the area. Judith, one of the members of my training cohort, and I trade stories about how I grew up in rural White Utah, and she grew up in Watts. She tells me how terrible it was to be afraid of her own people during the Watts riots. I confess my shame over my first encounter with a Black man in Salt Lake City when I am about 12. I use a terrible racial slur, not the n-word, when I see him. My cousin, a year older and way more sophisticated, tells me sternly to stop, reminding me that he is a person, too, and deserves respect. She is entirely correct. Our beloved

Grandpa Yardley, who is still alive at the time, would never have tolerated my behavior. Judith and our other colleague, Lori, who is as White and blonde as I, host my baby shower and are my first visitors when I bring that new baby home. Both sneak away from work for our visit, both supportive and compassionate friends for me.

This all goes to say that I had some awareness of and connection to Black people. Nevertheless, I stand there in the doorway of Connie's office and calmly explain to her my understanding of the position of the Mormon Church based on the curse of Ham theory. When I finish giving my best explanation, I ask,

"How does that sound?"

"It sounds like a lot of racist crap," she responded calmly.

And she was right. Could I have sounded any more like an ignorant, privileged White woman? After the June 1978 revelation from the Mormons regarding Blacks and the Priesthood, *Newsweek Magazine* runs an in-depth article on the history and implications of the change, not just in policy, the change in Doctrine with many quotes from members of the Church about this great new blessing. The article ends with an observation that while this may be a blessing for existing Black Mormons and potential Black Mormons it is an even greater blessing for the White Mormon members. And that is the truth. Eight years after my conversation with beautiful Connie, I am off the hook. Black people can enjoy "the full blessings" of Church membership. Of course, I note, especially as I moved out of Gunnison to live in more suburban and urban areas, as I encounter the relatively few Black people who live in Utah that they are exceptionally brave to live in this bigoted White state. In the early 2000s my son-in-law, the French-Swiss guy, has a friend from Europe attend BYU. Let's call this young man Magnus (say Mahg-Noose) the Magnificent. His father is a Scandinavian filmmaker and his mother half African. Magnus is a truly handsome man. Yet, in nearly two years at BYU he cannot not get a single White co-ed to attend so much as an ice-cream social with him. He eventually retreats to Europe where he is more widely accepted.

Dallin Oaks, a counselor in the current Mormon Church Presidency and next in line to be president, said in 2015 that the Church does not apologize for past misdeeds, but rather looks forward (https://archive.sltrib.com/article.php?id=2122123&itype=cmsid). Even so, the language in the text of the *Book of Mormon* remains the same. The practice of polygamy remains the same inside the Mormon Temple. And it is not until now, the summer of 2020, that I have paused to absorb in a significant way the hurt and damage that the Mormon Church, the Church of Jesus Christ of Latter-day Saints, has caused and continues to cause to Black people in general and Black Church members specifically. And, like the Mountain Meadow Massacre, the Church never apologizes for any of this. At the end of the day, the Mormon Church remains a misogynistic, homophobic, and racist institution.

I have many friends and family members who are active Mormons. Most of them are not misogynistic, homophobic, and racist. Most of them are good, kind, and well-intentioned. I leave it to them work out their own relationship with the institution that is the Church. I myself am an agnostic—I simply do not know. I hold a hope of Christ. How cool would it be if some really nice man somewhere could make every bad thing I ever did go away? No sarcasm.

⤳

Ox, who is not usually given to insecurity, says to me, "If I start going to Church again are you going to laugh at me?"

"Of course not."

"Why not?"

"If the Church helps you organize your life and make sense of the world, well, that is what religion is for. I support you in your choice."

I spend decades feeling pressure from the Church to call my children to repentance. That is not my job. My job is to love them. I do.

⤳

It has been nearly twelve years since I attended the Mormon Church regularly. It is interesting to note that in my first months and year of inactivity, I become what is known among the cynical as a project—meaning that many Mormons will be interested in you if they believe they may convert you to the true and living Church or otherwise save your soul. Often, anonymous gifts of bread and Sprite are left on my doorstep. In my time after leaving the church, I give myself permission to try things that I had missed in my twenties. I smoke pot. I sleep around. I am sure that most of my neighbors notice strange cars in my driveway overnight. I tell my Momma I am no longer attending Church.

"You were such a stalwart?" she notes incredulously. When she asks why or how, I talk with her about some of the books I am reading and my conversations with Dora.

Momma calls me a few days later to ask me to read an equal number of Church books. I assure her that in my 40 years as an adult member of the Church I have read many times more Church books.

Debra calls me. She is a bit miffed. "You only told Momma that you were not going to Church because you are afraid that she will die and know what you are up to." My sister is normally the most logical of people, but to this bit of illogic I respond,

"Deb, this from the woman who quit going to Church when you were 18?

"Well . . . ," she stalls.

"I told Mom myself because I do not want her to hear about it from someone else."

"Like who," she wonders.

"Like Russ, or snoopy old Connie."

We laugh.

"Anyway, think about it. When she dies, she will know even better why I am doing this. I guess I will ask Mom to come back from the next life and let me know if I am wrong." Momma never comes back.

🍃

In exploring other churches, I like the Buddhists best. But I like Sunday brunch and Sunday massages better. In the end I decide I am done with organized religion. In the end I decide I do not want a God who treats me like a third grader. I do believe that we each need a spiritual tradition or a spiritual connection. Early on, as I am sorting out these decisions, I reach out to Jackie, the massage therapist and my psychic connection to Woody. I call her late one afternoon. We have not talked for over a year.

"Jackie, this is Dawn."

"Dawn? Dawn, Dawn?" she asks.

"Yes," I assure her.

"Oh," she says matter-of-factly, "your father showed up in my car last week. Call me back in an hour. I will tell you all about it. I have to see this last client." And she hangs up, leaving me to consider the comings and goings of Woody and what he might say about the fate of my eternal soul. Finally, the hour passes. I call Jackie back. She does not start right in on the details of Woody's visit.

"What's going on?" she asks.

"I am thinking of leaving the Church."

"Oh," she says. "It's a vibration issue." Because of our many past conversations, I know she is referring to the writing of David R. Hawkins, MD, PhD, in his three books. She tells me I have evolved beyond the need for organized religion. We discuss this briefly. Dawkins is a strong believer in muscle testing and the veracity of his vibrational testing ability. The back cover of Dawkins' third volume, states, "On the referenced Scale of the Levels of Consciousness, which calibrates the levels of Truth from 1 to 1000, *Power versus Force* calibrates at 850, *The Eye of the I* at 980 and the final volume of this trilogy, *I*, calibrates at a conclusive 999.8." Dawkins himself is the tester of this Truth, a situation that I invariably find hilarious. It may be true—that he can test the truth of his own works, but I still find that hilarious.

Nevertheless, I can hardly wait to hear about Woody. I push the issue. "So, what happened with my dad?"

"Oh, he showed up in my car last week," She continues, "I was just driving along the street, and I became aware of a presence sitting beside me. 'Who are you? I asked.'"

"I'm Dawn's Dad," he replied

"Dawn?"

"Yes, Dawn," he affirms.

"Dawn, Dawn?" she questions.

"Yes."

"I do not even know where she is. I have not seen her in over a year," she tells him.

She says, "He filled my car with his laughter." She pauses, "And then he filled my car with his love."

She asks him, "Do you have a message for her?"

"Tell my daughter follow her heart," he says.

"That's it?" I ask.

"That's it," she confirms. Why can't these messages be more like the little instruction card for Cabbage Patch Dolls? You know, "Take me for walks in the sunshine and give me ice cream on Sundays." Something specific. I suppose it is not the nature of the experience. Perhaps I could muscle test the veracity. I am less sure of my skills in this area than Dawkins.

I ask Jackie, "When you see these people, do you see them see them?" She tells me it is more like an awareness. She tells me, "Your Dad is long in the face, tall and lean. He had on belt with a big silver buckle, a white t-shirt, and Levi's." When we cleaned out Mom's house, Deb and I found one photo of Woody balancing Deb on his hand so that she is blocking his face. He looks very 50s in his white t-shirt and Levi's, with a big belt buckle.

I guess I will have to make my own adult decision about the fate of my eternal soul.

&

I don't actually consider dating for the first year and a half after leaving Herbert. About a year in, I figure if my father, Woody, thinks there is someone out there for me, I better come up with some idea about whom I am looking for. Most of my positive requirements come from negative experiences with the opposite kind of man. I have a short list.

- A man of principle—this used to be a Man of God, but after I quit going to The Church, I had to figure out what that might actually mean.

- Man implies that he knows how to work, provide for a family, and manage his resources—too many Mormon men fall for the "God wants me to be rich scheme," promulgated by Joseph Smith, and get involved with all kinds of hair-brained financial endeavors. This behavior is endemic in Utah.

- A man who is kind, understanding of, and supportive to women and children—blessed or cursed by the Mormon patriarchy, many Mormon men have no idea how to have a healthy relationship—at least the ones I have met.

- A man who is curious about and interested in the world—after Ernie studied for his last national board exam in dental school, he slams the book closed and says, "I will never have to read a book again." I felt a bone-deep chill.

- Sense of humor—self-explanatory. Laugh or go crazy. In my DSM IV course in my school counseling program, the instructor was trying to teach us how to spin interactions with our clients in their language. He observed, "For Dawn, you will need to keep even the direst observations or information funny."

- Generally, content with and amused by life—I have listened to enough whining in my life.

- Makes love to me frequently and with passion—I add this after I sleep around a bit.

꙳

My first effort at dating has nothing to do with anything on this list. It is midsummer and I am driving home from a visit with Mom and John at the assisted living center. I decide to stop at Lowe's to see if they have any birch trees that I can plant along the west side of my girl house. In the garden center I encounter a rather mousy looking sales associate, who, in the course of our conversation, tells me he has a Harley and a master's degree in culinary arts. I find five river birch that may work. By the time we have loaded the trees into my car, a silver Acura TL S-type, which I love in a most unholy way, the sales associate, let's call him Jack, is flirting in the corniest of ways.

"Did it hurt when you fell?" he asks.

"When I fell?" I respond

"From heaven, 'cause you're an angel," he replies. I have been out of this game for so long, I actually find this flattering. With a laugh and a wave, I head home in the dark.

The next day I consult with Bonnie, a counseling colleague with a passion for landscape design. She has been helping me plan. Himalayan birch will be a much better choice for my project. So, I am back to Lowe's to return the river birch. Of course, I run into Jack. He asks if we can meet for lunch the next day. I figure I will at least get a Harley ride and a gourmet meal. I agree.

The next day, Tuesday, I agree to pick him up at his apartment, located in an old mansion near my girl house. He implies that he owns the apartments in the converted mansion. His little space is sunny and attractive. We are sitting on the tiny sofa, the love seat, when he begins kissing me. It has been so long since I have been kissed, and kissed passionately, that I am quickly caught up in the moment. Before I know it, my shirt is unbuttoned and he is in my bra, gushing about my beautiful breasts. Some sensibility returns and I start putting on the brakes. He claims he will suffer irreparable damage if we cannot continue. Good God, I am back in high school. I tell him I must go, and I drive to my house to collect myself before returning to work. Remember, I am still going to Church at this point— I am considering how I will have to confess this infraction to my bishop. I am at my house for fewer than 30 minutes when he calls to apologize, saying he will make amends by preparing a lunch for me. I ask if he needs to return to work. He says that he already called in sick. I give him my street address. What am I thinking?

I should not be surprised when he drives up in a beat-up, white Chevy minivan, no groceries in hand. We talk for a few minutes. I tell him I am hungry, and we need to go get some food. He offers to drive. The interior of the minivan is even worse than the exterior, ragged seats, the central cup holders covered in brown, sticky soda residue, and I note, without panicking, that there is a large coil of rope on the floor where the back seats have been removed. What am I thinking? I believe that he truly is harmless. He offers to introduce me to his adoptive family who own a small, local ice-cream plant with an on-site store and a connected pizzeria—this will do. He claims that he has a master's degree in culinary arts, and he is the creative master behind all of their flavors. When we arrive at the back door of the plant, we are in the bookkeeping and operations area. He introduces me to his mom and dad. After a short conversation, dad asks us if we want some ice cream. We select a flavor. He packs a pint for us, and then walks us to the cash register. This may not be the closest of relationships. Jack pulls out his wallet and comes up empty, looking to me. It is clear that I am paying for the ice cream and, ergo, paying for lunch.

A KFC is located just around the corner. We order lunch at the drive through and take it back to his apartment. He begs me to at least stay with him while we eat. We set our food down on the coffee table. Then he walks to the refrigerator, opens the freezer, and takes out a pint of vodka, hiding it behind his leg as he walks to the bathroom. When he returns the vodka to the freezer, it appears to be half empty. We eat our lunch, and he offers to take me home—recalling that we have been driving around in the minivan—I agree. I do not want to walk the few blocks to home. What am I thinking? It turns out the Harley has been replaced by a not unattractive, deep blue Honda Shadow. We climb on and are a half block into the drive when it occurs to me that he might actually be really drunk. At my house I invite him in, thinking he might sober up a bit before heading back home. We are sitting on opposite ends of my big cordovan red Pottery Barn sofa. I decide to tell him the story of Skeleton Woman, as told by Clarissa Pinkola Estes in Women Who Run with Wolves, one of my all-time favorite books. I am nearing the end of the story about Skeleton Woman. Jack is admiring my bare feet and then he begins sucking my toes, repeating more of his corniness from our first meeting. No one has ever sucked my toes. My first response is a deep sigh of eroticism. My second response is a gasp, and I pull my foot back, telling him to cut it out. I finish the story and move off the sofa.

He asks me to teach him yoga. I give him a demonstration of a sun salutation, which he also tries to make into an erotic encounter. I tell him it is way past time for him to go. He sits on a dining chair and pulls me onto his lap. By this time, I know I am stronger than he is. He tells me that he will buy a suit. That he will quit drinking. That he will go to church for me. I tell him that I am not interested in him, or anyone, who wants to change for me—with surprise, I realize this is true. I am done fixing men. I do not need anyone to change for me. I grab his arm and literally push him out the door. I hope the past hour has sobered him up, but I do not even watch as he rides away. After work the next day, I find a cheap silver ring and a note professing his undying love in my mailbox. I scrawl on the backside of the note that he is not to contact me in any way, no notes, no calls, no coming by my house. I drive it to his building and drop it in the mailbox. I call my nephew, a Salt Lake City police officer, to see if I need to worry. He does not think so, but I should check him out with mom and dad.

"Aunt Dawn, let me know if we need to go by his apartment or follow him around for a few days," he tells me.

On Thursday I go by the ice cream plant to see if mom and dad believe he is dangerous. I learn that they have befriended him, but that everything he ever told them is a lie. Culinary arts school happened in the U.S. Army, no disrespect to Army training programs, and not San Francisco. He is not now nor has he ever been their head creator of ice cream and flavors for their family business. He does not own the apartment building. And he is not heir to the family fortune, such as it is. He is, however, not likely dangerous. On Friday, after a morning meeting, I have lunch with a group of close counseling colleagues. They ask me how my new life is going. I regale them with my tale. By now we can all laugh uproariously. Lori, who is in a long-term, happy marriage, wants me to write up my cautionary tale for *More Magazine*. Holly, who is in her thirties and single, tells me that I will meet a much higher class of man at the grocery store than at the hardware store, assuring me that she speaks with the voice of experience. Rich, my age and in a long-term happy marriage, offers "an apology on behalf of all men." I buy two dating advice books and read several articles on-line. Bibliotherapy.

In the fall, Lillian lines me up on a blind date. I like this guy a lot. We meet at her house and talk for a while sitting in her family room. My date shares some personal experiences that seem like a Zen-based connection to the world and a tear slips down his cheek. I push aside my impulse to wipe it away. We go out for drinks, in this case carbonated, not alcoholic, beverages and then go for a walk along the river parkway. We happen on a family watching the Princess Bride on an outdoor screen. He has never seen the movie. We watch for a half an hour or so and then head back to the car. I say something that he interprets as racy, and he begins calling me Trixie. So, I call him Gator. We stay in contact. We talk on the telephone. He gives me a copy of Quinn's *Early Mormonism and the Magic World View*. I give him an audio copy of *The Four Agreements*.

"Don't you think that some Mormons actually believe the whole story?" I ask him on the telephone one night.

"I think some of them think it is a good yacht club," further clarifying that many members use association with the Church for social gain. I know that if I follow my current course and leave the Church that I will suffer socially and professionally.

We have one formal date. "You have great legs," he tells me as he guides me to the passenger side of his very nice Dodge truck.

With a groan, I confess, "I don't really like my legs."

"Thank you is the proper response," he chides me.

We have a lovely dinner at the top of the Joseph Smith Building in downtown Salt Lake. The Church has taken over the former Hotel Utah, using the lower floors for office space and providing on the top floors a very Mormon dining and reception center experience. I liked it better as the more pagan Hotel Utah.

One other weekend evening, he comes by my house, we talk and neck. He says, "Could I stay over and just sleep in your bed with you? No sex, just sleeping by your side."

By this time, I have figured out that he is pretty wounded as a result of a fairly abusive childhood. He may be even more damaged by his mother's refusal to recognize the beatings inflicted by his father, preferring to maintain the more acceptable Mormon myth of a loving and perfect family. I agree to let him sleep over. We sleep, talk, and laugh off and on during the entire night. In the morning he asks if I would like to go to breakfast. I suggest the little place on the corner a half block east of my house. We walk out on the porch, he looks up and down the street, and we walk to breakfast holding hands. Later, he tells me that it meant a great deal to him that I would just be open about being with him and not worry about all the prying neighbors who were likely watching our every move.

Gator's big conflict with finding a girlfriend is that he has two children who are just finishing college and launching their lives. He spends one or two nights of every week with them, enjoying these final months before they head out on their own. He has no time for a girlfriend. Nevertheless, he stays in contact through phone calls several times each week. In the middle of the week, he calls while I am driving on the freeway. In the course of our conversation, he mentions that he would like to go to a nice hotel and repeat the laying side by side and talking that occurred during our night together.

"You are asking a lot for someone who does not have time for a girlfriend," I tell him. He is taken aback.

The following Sunday he calls. The conversation veers toward how firmly he believes he does not have time for a girlfriend. I tell him if he were any kind of man, he would make a breakup, such as it is, face to face. He is at my house within an hour—not bad considering he lives 40 minutes up the freeway. He tells me this is it. I give him the wooden carving of a crow wearing a pair of red, high-top Converse that I bought for him on the Reservation. He is an accomplished wildlife photographer who gifted me with a beautifully framed landscape. He is less amused by the crow in sneakers than I am, and he does not want the photo back. I tell him to keep the audio book of *The Four Agreements*.

🖋

By December I decide definitely that I am leaving the Church, at least for now. On a Sunday I meet with my bishop to resign my position in the Primary Presidency, the children's program. I tell him, "I have too many questions right now."

"Lots of us have questions," he says reassuringly.

"Well, I want to be free to come to Church because I really want to be here," I counter.

He responds firmly, "I feel the spirit really strongly, and I am not going to let you get away with this." He all but shakes his finger at me.

My challenge is equally strong, "I feel the spirit too. I just have a different interpretation."

The spirit, when I feel it, is a sense of pervading love, so thick it is palpable. I first became aware of this feeling when standing in the doorway of my children's bedrooms at night, giving them a final check before going to sleep. At other times, I feel it most in association with Church experiences. In fact, I relate some of these strong spiritual experiences to Gator. "People in other churches have those same experiences," he tells me. Eventually, I come to associate this feeling with encounters with Woody. The kiss on the cheek.

~

For my birthday the previous year, Debra gives me one of those pseudo old-timey cards, hot pink background, a photo of a sophisticated grandma-type, with bubble hairdo, and a caption that reads, "Looking back, I should have slept around more." We laugh over the idea. I never get around to putting the card away or throwing it away, so it lies about for a year, maybe two, getting moved from place to place in the little shelf basement. Eventually I do decide I should sleep around. I pick my chiropractor, Fred, as a likely target. I know he finds me attractive. I make him an immodest proposal for Christmas. I tell my yogi and my cranial-sacral therapist that I have decided to have sex for the pure joy of having sex. After a lifetime of associating sex with guilt and pain, love and commitment, I try separating it out as its own end.

I also give myself permission to try other things that I missed growing up in the '60s. By New Year's Day, I have had illicit sex and smoked pot. The pot is good, but it burns kind of hot for me to really enjoy smoking it. The sex is good, but I soon discover that Fred's tastes run to the kinky. He does help me find another chiropractor, working to maintain a semblance of professional ethics between us. The sex is good, but I am clear that he is sleeping with other women. He has a vasectomy, which would not be necessary if it were just me. This is all to the good—I plan to use Fred to pass time while Gator gets his kids launched. No complications, right? Of course, Fred's pot use is concerning. If I get busted, I will lose my license, lose my job, and my photo will be on the front page of the B Section of the Utah newspapers because I am a state-level education leader. In the end, these real fears lead to some common-sense avoidance of pot on my part. I am livid one weekend when I discover Fred has a stash of pot in the nightstand on the opposite side of my bed from where I sleep. I remind him that if I get busted my life as I know it will be over. Just because I am paranoid does not mean they aren't out to get me, right?

Deb is appalled when I tell her about Fred's sexual practices. Early on he gives me a book to read, the premise of which is that pain is sexy. I assure him, that for me, pain is pain. Nevertheless, he frequently pulls out his literal bag of tricks, which he keeps carefully hidden under the floorboards of his study, seriously, from his two sons who are often around. Sex with Fred feels like a science experiment. How many variables to you need? For me, not many. For him, a lot. I am pretty sure I am not a prude. I do use a strap-on for him one night. Fred is surprised that I have an orgasm with him. I respond, "What is so surprising? The heat, the breathing, the movement, and the smells are all the same. I told you I like sex. I really, really, really, really, really like sex." Even so, within 3 months, I tell Fred, "If there is one thing that will break us up it is your kinky sex."

Nota bene: There may be a number of men who would like to be fucked. They just cannot figure out how that might be accomplished without sacrificing their self-concept or compromising their ideas of what is means to be a man. If you are in a position to help a guy out, or to help a woman out, for that matter, take a lesson from frugal Fred. I am thinking there may be a variety of tools. I am pretty sure that Freddie procures the low-end model, if you will. The one I use has no padding on my side of the apparatus. Only a thin piece of leatherette between the base and my mons pubis. These tools may be like bicycle seats. If you have a choice, get the 50-mile model, not the 3-miler.

✿

We have other issues. One Saturday, I am in my home office grading papers for the graduate-level course I teach during the summer. I see Fred in my driveway, looking through the dining room windows. He sees me at the computer and charges to the front door. When I open the door, he is livid.

"You were supposed to call me this morning," he accuses.

"Grading papers took longer than I planned," I explain.

"We have to communicate," he asserts. We walk to the nearby grocery while he continues his rant, talking about communication when all I want is to be left alone.

I am the Wife of Bath. My want is simple. In this relationship, as in all my relationships, I want the freedom to use my time as I choose. I am actually a good girlfriend, fun, available, and not needy. I must admit that I practice on Fred many of the strategies from *The Manual* by Steve Santagati, one of the best relationship books I have read, and I have read dozens. The book is written to help women survive relationships with bad boys. The strategies work. Smiley face. Fred and I do have fun together. He teaches me to drink wine and mixed drinks—gin and tonic is my fave. I meet many of his kinky sex friends. He thinks it is a big deal that he chooses to be exclusive with me—I did not ask. I host a party for his 60ᵗʰ birthday. CC and her husband help with the food prep. It is a smashing success. Fred and I cook together, and we have sleepovers. We help each other with yard work. I tell him how much I love sleeping out in the summer. He brings his old beat-up truck over to my house. We park it at the back of my driveway behind the gate, making the truck bed comfy with foam pads and blankets. We eat dinner outside, drink lots of wine, and laugh our way through a night under the stars. In the middle of the night, Fred helps me balance with my butt hanging over the side of the of the truck so I can pee in the dark. In the bright light of early morning, we have sex in the bed of the tuck. My neighbor, Frank, is already outside, smoking under his tree. Oh well. After that night, the old red truck is known as the Fuck Truck.

In the end, Fred and I last 18 months. In the summer of 2009, I am honored by the American School Counselor Association as the School Counseling Supervisor/Director of the Year. Before I leave for the conference, Fred tells me that I cannot afford to buy a new dress. More advice from the man known to all of his friends as frugal Fred. When we get to Dallas for the annual conference, several of my counseling colleagues and I go to a local mall. At Neiman-Marcus, I find a perfect Kay Unger dress on the sale rack. They do not accept my American Express card, so Lillian buys the dress for me. I buy the shoes and the jewelry. People tell me I look stunning when I receive the award.

In the first days of the conference, I attend a decision-making workshop presented by some of our elementary school counselors from Utah. As always, the elementary school counselors require audience participation. They want each of us to look at a real problem in our lives. They instruct us to fold a piece of paper into eight sections, making a storyboard. We consider a real-life problem by drawing or writing in the first seven panels. The eighth panel we leave blank until we take time to consult our wise people—which could be a trusted adult or our own internal guidance system. My storyboard, complete with stick figures, reads like this: 1) Fred and Dawn are friends. 2) They laugh and have fun. 3) They ride bikes and go walking. 4) They go to dinner and movies. 5) They go to concerts and plays. 6) Fred has a dark side [this stick figure has horns, a pointy beard, and a tail]. 7) What should Dawn do? Consistent with the instructions, I leave panel 8 blank. I fold up my little story board and put it away for a couple of days.

I attend other workshops and go to lunch and dinner with my friends and colleagues. Two nights after I create the storyboard and two nights before I will fly home, I take out take out my little paper to consider the question. The first thing that comes to my mind is advice from a beloved

Mormon bishop who told me, "Never, ever, ever argue with the Devil. You will lose. He is the father of all lies."

I am long past Mormonism, but, in my drawing, Fred looks like the devil. More and more lately he pretends to choke me while we are having sex. It is the gesture that pushes him to orgasm. I told him months and months ago his sexual tastes would be our undoing.

Fred meets me at the airport. It is near dinner time, and he has reservations for us. We have ordered drinks and an appetizer when he looks at me and asks, "What's different?"

I show him my story board with the last panel completed. It reads, "Run away. Run away." My stick figure is clearly fleeing.

"Whose idea is this?" he demands.

I tell him about the workshop and the advice to consult our wise people. "My wise people is me. I am my wise people."

"Your mind is made up?"

"My mind is made up."

We leave after the appetizers. Fred makes me buy back the road bike that he purchased for me but keeps in his garage. He tells Ox and his wife that he was planning to take me to Paris for my 60th birthday. All my kids kind of miss him, but they agree he is a son-of-a-bitch. It is just as well. He would have ruined Paris.

In the fall, I come home one evening to realize that Fred's anger is all around the outside of my house. I had been caring for Ox's two rescue border collies until they find a house. Those dogs destroy my back yard, running in constant circles, chewing on everything—my lovely little coral bark Japanese maple, all of my perennials, the strawberries, even the rosebushes are gnawed to the ground.

Frances' son, Emmanuel, has been staying with me for a few weeks while he completes some tests at the community college. Emmanuel responds to my complaining about my lost plants by noting, "Uh, maybe the dogs are vegetarian?"

On this particular day, I notice that the doghouse is gone. I call Ox. He reports that Fred came by with the Fuck Truck to help him move the doghouse to their new address.

I tell him, "I can feel Fred's anger all around the outside my house."

"He was pretty angry for some reason, pushing the trash barrels aside, and just generally crabby," he confirms.

Months later and even a year later, Fred calls just to chat. I know that he has a new girlfriend, Ox and his wife met her on their way to a party near where Fred and the GF were attending another party.

"Does she know you call me?"

"Well, no," he responds.

"I want you to stop. I do not want you carrying a torch for me."

🖎

I read articles about on-line dating. I put up profiles on Yahoo Personals, Match.com, and Chemistry.com. You get a qualitatively different man with each site—kind of like the difference between the hardware store and the grocery store. I learn how to meet and date safely. I learn that you can only learn so much about a person even in the most interesting of email exchanges. I had a wonderful discussion of books with a man who turned out to be best friends with one of my cousins during high school—a university professor with a really interesting area of specialization. Even so, in person, he was like a big mouthful of cotton—dry and unappealing.

✍

I try what I call on-line speed dating: In one day I meet
one guy for lunch, another guy for coffee, and another guy
for wine. While we are in line to order at the little French
bistro, the lunch guy says, "I have a place in Catalina. Will
you wear a bikini for me?"

"Maybe if I get to know you better," I reply. His profile
says that he is 60. My guess is closer to 70. When we are
saying goodbye in the parking lot, he actually invites me
home to his apartment to look at his etchings.

The coffee meet-up is an attractive, muscular Black man.
When he calls me months later to ask me out, I tell him I
am dating someone. He calls me Cracker. I don't think I am
a bigot, but I guess he did.

The wine date that evening is a contact in which every
e-mail includes three questions from the dude. He is retired
military and very methodical.

I meet another potential date in a park. He tells me he
is sure I am his future goddess. Another afternoon connection confesses that his profile says he is 50, but he is
really 60. His friends tell him not to admit to being 60. My
friend Cassidy offers better advice, "Would you rather be a
ho-hum 50-year-old or a smokin' hot 60-year-old?" After
his age confession, he tells me that he has recently moved
from the East Coast and does not have a driver's license.
He wonders if I would like to drive him south to see the
National Parks? Probably not.

On the other hand, I meet some really amazing men
on-line. I have a day-long ride on a Harley with a man who
has a heart replacement at age 29 and goes on to earn a
PhD while he is a single dad. His young wife leaves him and

the kid when his heart goes out. Irony, huh? We have sex at the top of a mountain, pulling ourselves together just in time for a minivan pulling in to the picnic grounds. I meet a very cool retired math teacher who has also been a single dad. He is widower of 18 months who says he wants to accompany me to a conference on the East Coast. He backs out. I meet an interesting and handsome Jewish architect who cooks a pork chop dinner for me. I meet an intriguing geriatric counselor with a wonderful voice who is also a widower. He needs to move a bit more slowly and, like the architect, is taken aback by my intention to date more than one man at a time. I don't have sex with more than one man at a time, but I do date more than one man at a time.

※

I meet the guy who I think will be my one and only one-night stand, Zac, on Chemistry.com. We do have some chemistry that carries on out to the long-since emptied parking lot where we make out like crazy. His car has magically reclining seats. The passion continues on to my house when I invite him to "Come home and finish what you started." We date for the next couple of months, cooking and eating together, drinking two bottles of wine on most nights—a carry-over from our first date. His face is a bit ferret-like, but he has a beautiful body with beautiful skin. The sex is fabulous. He travels to Texas to finalize his divorce. He tells me that he is staying at the home of his former mistress. I am not fazed by him sleeping with another woman. As luck would have it his niece is in one of my graduate classes. I mention I am dating Zac; Her mother, a well-known educator, is the sister of Zac's ex. The niece tells me that he has never been faithful to any woman ever. Then I catch him in a lie. Two weeks in a row he explains that he is not available on Saturday because he needs to accompany his ex-wife to a wedding reception for the child of some close friends. In my best revenge-of-the-women move, I use him for sex when he comes to pick me up on Friday, and then I confront him about the lie. I tell him, "If you needed a night off, you could just say so. Don't make up a cockamamie story about going to the same wedding two weekends in a row."

"Aw, c'mon baby. I'm sorry. Let's go to my brother's like we planned." I ask him to listen to a Willie Nelson song I have recently discovered "If I Were the Man That You Wanted, I Would Not Be the Man That I Am."

"I deserve more than being remembered in a Willie Nelson song," he protests.

I assure him that being remembered by Willie is way more than he deserves. I break it off clean, quick, and final—just like *The Manual* advises. I am beyond proud of myself. I am finally capable of trusting my inner guidance systems. With Herbert, I realize that after years of self-doubt and not trusting myself, along with his willingness to let me question my own sanity, the person that I believe is me. With Fred, I find that when I consult my wise people, my wise people is me. And now with Zac, I know exactly when to say when. When is now.

❧

One Wednesday, when Zac and I were deep into our routine of two bottles of wine most nights, I am driving home, completely exhausted at five o'clock in the evening. I plan to go home, make scrambled eggs, and fall into bed. I am 5 minutes into my 15-minute drive, when Dora calls me.

"Mom, Jared's wife, Nanette, has a genealogy question. He sent me a message on Facebook."

"I know. I heard her voice-mail last night. I will call her Saturday," I assure her.

"He says she found your half-sister."

"What?" I am sleepy and incredulous.

"She found your half-sister. She wants you to call her."

I call my niece Nanette before I even make the scrambled eggs. The story is this: She is waaaay Mormon and preparing a lesson for the adult women on doing genealogy, and suddenly she thinks she ought to do some genealogy. She is a young mother with five children under the age of 8. When would she have time? Still, she gets on Ancestry. com to see what she can find. All of my siblings, including her husband Jared's father, are apprised of the Woody/Don situation and my lack of success in unraveling that story. To her surprise she finds a four-year-old email on Ancestry.com from a woman who is looking for one Woodrow Wilson Dean. Using her internet sleuthing skills, Nanette has the woman on the phone within 24 hours. She is fairly certain she is my half-sister. Within the hour I am on the phone with Judy, who might indeed be my half-sister. We talk at length. I tell her about the driver's license in the name of Woodrow Wilson Dean and the two social security cards in both names. She speculates that my father might have stolen her father's identity. We both fleetingly worry that my father killed her father and stole his identity. Through the years as I search Woody's genealogy and come up against one dead end after another, I jokingly assert that my missing father was a Mafia hit man.

I know that Woody, her dad, works as a chauffeur and that she and her sister were on a Pet Milk calendar distributed in southern California when they were very young. Both pieces of information I gather from stories told to my Momma. But that is information that could have been shared from one man to another. We wonder how we can solve this mystery. She asks if I have any photos of the man I know as Don Stevenson. She tells me that when her parents divorce in California, her mother and grandmother cut Woody's face out of every photo. She has only the memories of a 6-year-old when her beloved father disappears.

I find my blurry photo of Don Stevenson sitting on the back of the bear that he shot back in his days with the Yardley family. I take it to the best photo lab in the city to see if they can improve it. I send the only somewhat improved photo along to Judy and follow up with a phone call. She tells me how grief-stricken she has been since learning that her father died so many years ago. She had accepted that he was likely no longer living, but she did not know he was long dead before she was even old enough to know how to begin looking for him. The blurry photo is inconclusive for her. I only know it is Don/Woody because Momma tells me it is so.

I am surprised to learn that neither Momma nor Debra has any interest in meeting Judy or knowing the rest of the story. I call Judy on Thanksgiving and Christmas—trying to stay in touch and getting to know her better. In January, when I register for the ASCA Conference that will be in Boston in late June, I call Judy, and we make tentative agreements to meet at the conference. She leaves Southern California when her husband, Barry, retires as a schoolteacher. They move to western Massachusetts to a city highly recommended as a good place to live. And the place has cows. Judy loves cows. Barry is teaching again, but when he finally retires, they hope to settle in Cape Cod.

Judy and I talk off and on over the months. We discuss getting a DNA test of some kind. We move forward with our
plans to meet in Boston.

≈

Post Zac, I do some serious dietary modifications and
up my exercise program to lose the 15 pounds that I gain
since starting to drink wine, especially the two bottles of
wine per night with Zac. I talk with my Naturopath about
my inordinately high capacity for alcohol.

"Well, how much can you drink in one sitting?" he queries.

"A couple of gin and tonic before dinner. A couple of
glasses of wine with dinner," I reply.

"And still stand?"

"Yes, still stand, and walk reasonably well," I assure him."

"What is your genetic heritage?"

"My mother is mostly English. My father, as far as I
know, is mostly Irish."

"Often the Irish have a large capacity for alcohol con-
sumption. It can be a set up for alcoholism." Then he warns
me about the dangers of binge drinking and how hard it is
on my body.

When I talk about this conversation with Ox, he tells
me about his experience when he is a student at Snow
College. He is driving around one weekend day, when the
small-town police officer pulls him over for a minor driving
infraction. As he rolls down the window to greet the officer,
the officer declares, "You reek of beer."

"I have been drinking beer," Ox freely admits.

"Get out of the car for a field sobriety test," the officer
orders. When Ox performs all the required moves without
error, the officer again notes, "You reek of beer."

"I have been drinking beer," Ox assures him.

The officer administers a breathalyzer. Ox blows zero. The breathalyzer may have a little malfunction in his favor. Au contraire, mon frere; the officer administers three breathalyzer tests. Ox blows triple zero three times.

"You reek of beer," the officer declares in exasperation.

"I have been drinking beer," Ox says yet again.

"Well, I can't arrest you," the officer admits, giving him a warning for failure to signal and sending him on his way.

I have seen a couple of my daughters with a hangover, wrapped in a blanket and barely able to move the next day. I honestly have never had a hangover. A few years in the future, my girlfriend from Tennessee will come to Utah for our annual experience at the Sundance Film Festival. We usually see ten to twelve screenings during our four or five days together. One year, we go to dinner with my husband, Robert, where we share two bottles of red wine. When we get home, Robert talks us into tequila shots. She and I make it through three; I think he hits four, maybe five. It is well past midnight when we go to bed. In the morning, I have to work for half a day.

Nicole remarks, "Wow, it has been a long time since I woke up drunk."

"Oh," I respond dully. "Is that what this is?" That day is really my only bad post-drinking day ever. Nevertheless, I have to learn to moderate and modify my innate behaviors toward alcohol. By the time I meet Robert, I pretty much know that after two glasses of wine, I am ready for sex.

Post-Zac, post-Match, post-Chemistry, and post-Yahoo Personals, I finally knuckle under and pay for eHarmony. Once again, I find a different quality of man. I have e-mail exchanges with several, meet a few, date a couple of times.

There are some for whom I have more interest than they have for me. There are some who have more interest for me than I have for them. When I meet Robert, I have read *Act Like a Lady, Think Like a Man: What Men Really Think About Love, Relationships, Intimacy and Commitment* by Steve Harvey. His premise is close to Steve Santagati—women have to stay on their toes to stay ahead of the men who will take advantage of them. According to Harvey, women can tell if a man really cares for them when he will provide for her, even a sack of groceries; when he will protect her, walking on the street side of the sidewalk or offering her an arm; and when he will proclaim that she is with him, even introducing her as his girlfriend. In return men need to have time, loyalty, and the cookie, but they have to earn that expectation. Steve illustrates, explaining that in his first real job he had to wait 90 days to get full benefits. He advises taking the possibility of sex off the table in any new relationship until you have dated or hung out or linked up for 90 days. I am not sure he says so, but my observation is that this guideline tends to separate the men from the boys. Any guy worth his salt and who is actually interested in you will hang around. Even Santagati says that he never has sex on the first date, and he will wait for 6 months, even a year, to have sex, if the woman interests him, although he is less rule-bound on the preliminary time frame. Santagati's other big advice: catch him with your body but keep him with your mind. Bibliotherapy.

🖋

Robert shows up on eHarmony in late November, one of several possible matches for the week. The premise of the eHarmony site is that both parties complete a lengthy initial process, including a psychological profile, then their algorithm presents some potential matches each week with whom you can engage in a series of getting-to-know-you activities. I review the new batch of candidates with Lillian. In his profile photo, Robert wears jeans, a denim jacket, and Dr. Martens, nonchalantly squatting beside a big black Mustang. Lillian, looking over the lineup, taps the photo of Robert with her long nails, and says, "Oooh, good nookie!"

On-line dating is kind of like a second job, requiring regular attention on a weekly or twice weekly basis. I usually put in a couple of hours midweek and several more on the weekend. I don't mind completing the interactive, "getting to know you" games that are part of eHarmony. Robert tells me that he is not interested in the games. He just wants to get to know me. He suggests we meet midweek for dinner. I suggest we meet for burgers. He tells me, "Instead of burgers, I suggest seafood. Instead of paper napkins and paper plates, I suggest china and table linens." Hard to resist. He offers to pick me up anywhere in a clearly marked company vehicle. That I firmly resist. I agree to meet on Wednesday, after my nail appointment, warning him, "Josie is a talker. I will try to keep her focused on the business at hand."

The afternoon before our first meet up at Oyster Bar, we get a snowstorm. Robert texts me to use the valet. He will pay. Josie does talk, and I am late. In addition, I am unfamiliar with this location in Cottonwood. I can see the restaurant in the distance through the snow and the windshield wiper blades. Nevertheless, I keep missing the turn that will get me to the parking lot. By the time I get inside the restaurant door, I am nearly a half-hour late. He is standing in the lobby about to leave. I apologize profusely, and we sit down to seafood, wine, and table linens. He is an electrician by training who works as the chief estimator for a large commercial electrical contractor in the state. He can read plans and figure estimates that are in the millions of dollars, tens of millions of dollars, hundreds of millions of dollars. I know from his profile that he grew up in the East, Pennsylvania to be exact. He is a Vietnam veteran with a bronze star and a gold palm from the Republic of Vietnam. When I tell him my background, he observes, "Oh, you are highly educated."

"I am," I assure him. "I am highly educated. I have a bachelor's degree in English teaching and have completed two master's programs, one in school counseling and one in school administration."

"Whoa, I am not so educated." He is almost apologetic.

"Oh, really?" I say, "Let's look closely at this. Is it true that you were in the U.S. Army?"

"Yes."

"And did you learn stuff?"

"Yes."

"And did you go to war?

"Yes."

"And did you learn stuff?"

"Yes."

"Then, did you become an electrician?"

"Yes."

"And that apprenticeship took 5 years?"

"Yes."

"And as part of that apprenticeship did you take some college classes?"

"Yes."

"So, in all of that training did you learn stuff?" I ask him.
"Yeah, I learned stuff."

"Well, that is all I did. I learned stuff. You had about 7 or 8 years of highly specialized training, and you learned stuff. And I had about 8 years of highly specialized training, and I learned stuff. It looks like we are about even."

As the evening progresses, I observe that at work he is known as Bob. I ask him what he wants me to call him? "Call me Robert. It's more intimate," he responds. I am pretty sure he will call again.

Midweek I get an email at work. "Wanna get a beer?" Robert asks. We agree to meet at a low-key local sports bar near my house. By our third date I tell him about the 90 day "no cookie" rule. He assures me that is no problem. On our fourth or fifth date we are on my big velvet sofa making out like mad. Rather abruptly he disengages. He tells me, "I need to go. I told you I would wait. I want you to trust me. I have to go." It is one of the nicest things any man has ever said to me. Hmmm, I trust myself, and I am learning some new skills.

Robert and I fall quickly into an easy alliance. Beer and casual suppers on Thursday, more formal dates on one weekend night. He even gives me a friendly Christmas present. When his kids come to town for an after Christmas visit, I meet up with them for pizza at a popular spot near the university. We share the 36" custom pie. Robert is tall and lean, 6'2" and 183 lbs. His twin boys are taller, 6'3" and 6'5" and leaner—they are still in high school. The taller one plays football, the older, by minutes, digs cars. Both have full heads of hair, one muddy blond and the other one dark and almost curly. Robert is full-on balding which I do not mind, thanks to my beloved Grandpa Yardley. His daughter is tall, lean, and pretty with a full smile. She covers her naturally blonde hair with dark color. The hungry boys finish every slice of the giant pizza. The rest of Christmas break Robert devotes to the brief time he has with his kids who live in Washington state. For New Year's Eve, he and I go to one of the local ski resorts for dinner and to see The Torchlight Parade.

For Valentine's Day, a weekday, he sends me some pretty dang fabulous flowers at my work—the women ooh and aah. My friends, Jeff the Elder and Jeff the Younger, think he is pretty whipped. I assure them he is the least PW man I know. When Robert picks me up for our week-end date, he notices his flowers on the dining table and then he notices another smaller bunch of flowers that Zac had dropped by on V-day, hoping for the happy ending he did not get. Robert and I go to dinner and a movie and then return home. His goodnight kiss is much more ardent, and it soon becomes apparent that I will need to be a real stickler if we are to make it to 90 days. Well, we have made it 80 days, so we both get a happy ending. A couple of happy endings, as a matter of fact. By March, he is talk-ing about me accompanying him to Pennsylvania for his semiannual visit to his parents. Then he rescinds the par-ent's visit invite, muttering something about maybe being premature. In the end, I go with him, mostly because he has gotten used to not being alone. Truth be told, I am not sure exactly how he feels about me. During our five days in PA, we take a day trip to New Hope, an artsy little town on the Delaware. For me it feels much like Park City. It is a beautiful spring day, not quite warm, but pleasant. We stop for an afternoon drink at a little sidewalk café. We get into a conversation about the nature of our relationship and where this might go. He still seems noncommittal. I know he is very self-protected, having met me following a real heartbreak. I am a bit cautious, not wanting to be the consolation prize. I do admit to him, "I am not in love with you yet. It could happen, but I am okay to go slow." I also confess that I am used to men being a lot more effusive with me—more like his parents who are willing to gush about my cute clothes, my cute shoes, and my overall cuteness. Then, being the man with more common sense than any man I have known, he guides me into a conversation about my two husbands who were more than willing to declare their love for me, then follow up with behavior that was definitely not loving. He says that if he falls in love with me, I will know it by his actions.

On the way back to his parents', we stop at a little out of the way winery, arriving at Mom and Dad's just in time for Friday night happy hour with the next-door neighbors, Hugh and Sue. Earlier in the day, in a phone call from New Hope, Robert also invites his friends to happy hour. They bring their daughter. We stay an hour or so and then all five of us leave to meet Joey Z at the West Easton Firehouse, a kind of country club for blue collar workers, linoleum floors, grey Formica tables, and red Naugahyde chairs reminiscent of a 50s kitchen. I am introduced to punch cards and steamers which sell for about four bucks a dozen. They are delicious.

When we get back to Mom and Dad's a little after eleven, they are waiting up for us, dressed in their jammies and bathrobes. They need to have a talk with the son they call Bobby. Dad leads off,

"You put your mother in a really tough spot tonight."

"What did I do?" Robert is puzzled.

"You invited guests to happy hour that we were not expecting. Your mother almost ran out of food," Dad responds firmly.

"I didn't know they were bringing their daughter," Robert defends.

"Even so," chides Dad.

"I really am sorry," Robert tells them, but the truth is that we are both more than slightly amused. Robert tells me that his parents are kind of like Ozzie and Harriet Nelson or June and Ward Cleaver and this is definitely a "Leave It to Beaver" moment. Then Dad tops off the moment by turning to me and inquiring, "What was your favorite part of your day, sweetheart?" They knew we had spent the day in New Hope.

Without mentioning the details of our conversation, I cite the time Robert and I spent talking at the sidewalk café.

"Ask me. Ask me," Robert interjects.

"What?" his dad responds.

"This," declares Robert. "This is my favorite part of this day," he tells them in his teasing manner. And we all laugh, knowing that there are no hard feelings.

✍

At the end of May, I have to go to Portland for a week of work meetings on a project we share between several state agencies. Robert and I talk nightly by phone. I tell him about the fun we have at an adults' night at OMSI, the Oregon Museum of Science and Industry. My favorite activity is launching water rockets. Robert visited OMSI several times with his children when they lived in Portland. We make plans for him to pick me up at the airport when I return to SLC on Friday evening. Not surprisingly, our Friday afternoon conference session is laid back and a bit slow. I cope by sending Robert a text:

"The afternoon session is slow and boring. I am getting through it by having a sexual fantasy about you."

I have his attention. He asks for details. I provide them. By the time I leave for the airport, we are both anticipating getting back together before the night is over. Imagine my disappointment when my flight is cancelled. I will be spending the night at a hotel near the airport. I text Robert—we are both so bummed. On my walk from the airport to the hotel, I stop at the convenience store where I buy two single serving bottles of wine as a consolation. For the rest of the weekend, I will have my friend from North Dakota staying at my house. She is coming to town to spend time with her son who is in the middle of treatment for a rather advanced case of testicular cancer which he ignored out of sheer terror, not having a parent close by in whom he could confide.

My North Dakota friend and I share small plates, drink wine, and have a wonderful time catching up. When I relate to her the details of my missed Friday night rendezvous, she insists I drive to Robert's and make it up to him. By the time I get to his condo, he is finished with his bachelor dinner of potato chips and beer and very surprised to see me. We go upstairs. I give him a very happy ending. He tells me, "Tomorrow night is all about you, sweetheart."

When I get back to Sugar House, Dory wants to know how things turned out. I share with her the "tomorrow night is all about you, sweetheart." She determines that she will move to a hotel in the morning. I am relieved that I get to follow through with my romantic plans. By morning I realize I cannot, must not, betray my friend in this way. It is too late. She has made reservations at a nearby hotel. I believe this is my most callow moment. We are still friends, but only through her capacity for forgiveness.

As luck would have it, "tomorrow night is all about you, sweetheart" does not turn out so well. Robert arrives to find me dressed in blue jeans and a lacy lingerie top. I have freshened up the small plates from the night before and have added a couple of candles. My kitchen looks and feels like a total seduction scene. Within less than a minute, Robert is visibly agitated. After 10 more minutes he says,

"I don't feel well. If you don't mind, I need to leave."

"Actually, I mind very much," I respond.

He leaves anyway, literally bolting out of my house. I feel so hurt and betrayed that I go into my study and create profiles on two new dating sites. On Monday, I am supposed to go with him on a 4-hour ride with the Mustang Club. I am in agony. The sad truth is that I have no idea whether he even likes me or not. The thought of sitting beside him for four hours is more than I can bear. I send a text—a very cowardly way to break a date—telling him that I am feeling very unsettled and need to spend my day in the garden. The rhythm of our dating days is broken. I do not hear from him for weeks.

In the interim, I meet the widower math teacher. He wants to go to Boston with me for the school counselor conference. We date heavily for three weeks then he sends me an e-mail. He tells me that perhaps things are moving too fast. He tells me that perhaps he feels like he is being unfaithful to his dead wife—she has been gone for 18 months or more. I should tell him that perhaps he did not think this through thoroughly. It is just as well that I get to Boston alone. My plans to meet my half-sister, Judy, have come to fruition. We meet for dinner, and we enjoy it so much, we also meet for breakfast the next morning. We talk about our mutual and separate histories. We make tentative plans for her to come West. She wants to visit a high school friend and see her father's grave.

*

I keep dating over the summer. I send Robert an e-mail on his birthday. He tells me that perhaps he realizes with regret the path he chose. I assure him we can remain friends, but I am not sure I am interested in dating him, perhaps for the present. Paul McCartney comes to town on tour. I am heartbroken that I cannot go, even if it would be alone. As it turns out, I am so ill with a summer cold by the night of the concert, I could not physically have made it to the venue. By the time we head to another annual workshop in Monument Valley, I have seen a doctor for a second time, worrying that I have pneumonia. They take x-rays and give me an antibiotic pack. Two days into our workshop, the doctor's office calls to tell me that I do indeed have pneumonia. I must go home to rest immediately. Perhaps I will follow the doctor's orders next year.

*

In mid-August I send Robert an e-mail. "Wanna get a beer?"

"Why would you wanna get a beer with a jerk like me?" he replies.

"You are not a jerk. You are just dazed and confused." I tell him. We make plans to meet on Thursday, like we used to do. Thursday night we meet at the usual sports bar. Once again, we fall into easy conversation. Three beers in, Robert brings up what is really on his mind.

"I have to confess. I left your house in the midst of an anxiety attack. I am so ashamed and embarrassed I can barely talk about it. What red-blooded American would not have jumped at that scenario? Instead, I leave in a panic."

I am not unmoved by this confession. However, I am determined to keep him hanging in the wind a bit longer. "I will be happy to date you again. But I am also going to date other men. I am not leaving all my eggs in one basket."

We make a date for the weekend. After a morning and an afternoon of three-par golf, he suggests that we stay together for dinner. I decline, telling him I have a dinner date with someone else. Nevertheless, by Labor Day, we are in an up-scale hotel in Park City for the long weekend. We start out Friday night with strawberries, champagne, and sex, followed by a nice open-air concert with a local band. Back in the Valley, I keep Robert and a couple of other men on a string for most of the fall. As I hoped, the plan keeps me from feeling too vulnerable and keeps him from being disengaged.

After our dates Robert rarely stays all night. He usually does his walk of shame around 1:00 a.m. Part of the issue is I still snore like a trooper. One night in early November Robert is still in my bed when I have a dream. More than a dream. My father, Woody, is in the room near me. I reach out to touch him, but he stands back. I start to cry. By this time, I am on my feet, thrilled to be so close to the man I have missed for so long. I think to myself, so this is how big my dad is. This is how much space he takes up. I do not see his face clearly. Then he looks at Robert sleeping and smiles. He looks and me and smiles. Then he starts to walk away and turns back to smile again. As Jackie said, he is ready to pass the baton.

By late November, I have decided I am not interested in dating other men, at least until Robert figures out and declares what his intentions are. By Christmas Eve he tells me that he did not renew his subscription to e-Harmony. I tell him that I took down all my profiles more than six weeks ago. "Touché!" he exclaims. He asks, in a very round-about way, if I would be interested in living with him. I am interested. And I am neither eager nor interested to consider anything more permanent. Robert thinks we need to start spending weekends together, adding, "You know I am in love with you."

"Really?" I respond more than a little surprised.

"Of course. I thought you could tell," he assures me.

"How would I know?"

"I hold your hand when we are walking," he declares, "and, I introduced you to my kids."

It is true. I have known his kids for almost a year. After meeting his kids when they were in town for the holidays a year ago, I meet them again during this holiday visit. After we go to Pennsylvania that first spring, I accompany him to the Seattle area for the high school graduation of his twin sons. After this, our second set of holidays, we begin spending time with his daughter as she looks for a starter home. Her price range means that she will live on the west side of town. We are out on a Saturday and have looked at a couple of properties for his daughter when we drive up onto the west bench of Salt Lake City. As we go up the hill, I feel my heart open up and some 10 blocks further on I notice a sign for an open house. We stop in. The agent tells us that he wants to show us a spec house further west. We agree to a showing. Although it is a tract home, it has some nice amenities: tile floors, granite countertops, two-tone paint—the walls a dusky Tuscan yellow that I have been using in all of my houses since 1975.

As we are leaving, Robert says, "I can even see that red velvet sofa of yours in the living room." More technically, it is the Pottery Barn cordovan red velvet sofa.

"You hate that sofa?"

"Yeah, but I can still picture it in this house." Within the week he has made an offer on the house, 10k below the asking price. They counteroffer but agree to pay the closing costs. He is approved for a second mortgage. All of this takes place within weeks of when Momma dies. The house is way west and our view of the west hills is unobstructed. I am very clear that the setting reminds me of Gunnison and the years with Momma in the pink house.

I tell my kids Robert and I are moving in together. CC asks me, "You're not going for LaRue's record then?" I tell her not immediately.

A few days later, Luna asks, "Mama, what do you love most about Robert?"

I know this answer, "He is Mr. Good, Right, and True. In any situation he will do the stand-up thing. He has more common sense than anyone I have known." She nods, as I add, "And he is enough of a bad boy to keep me interested." We both laugh.

❧

By June we are settled into the house. His big leather bachelor furniture fills the family room. My velvet sofa and chair and the black distressed sideboard fill the living room. He also hates the distressed sideboard. "I am willing to get rid of many things for you, eventually, but the sideboard stays, regardless." My walnut colonial chest on chest and iron bed, with all my Paris wall art go in the guest bedroom. I have the third bedroom for the study—the three-car garage has two bays devoted to his 2006 Black Mustang GT and his electric blue 1967 Cobra kit car, tubular frame and a 427 engine, as close to the original as a reproduction can be. I ask him months ago what kind of mileage he gets off these guy cars? "I don't care," he responds nonchalantly. My midsize Japanese sedan gets the third bay. I tell him, "There is so much testosterone in that garage that I practically get a sex change every time I walk through." The master bedroom is filled with the furniture from his condo guest room. I think it is called "Caribou Creek" or "Wild Yukon." It begs for dead animal decor. He had better furniture in his master bedroom, however, it was exactly like the master bedroom furniture that Herbert and I bought. It feels like a bad omen. I insist we get rid of it.

By summer, we have settled into our living arrangement. In the middle of June, I return about 10 p.m. on Wednesday evening from teaching a class in a school counselor education program. Our annual school counselor's conference starts the next day. I am presenting three back-to-back sessions on school counseling and the use of data. I am buzzing around getting my materials together. I start upstairs to the bedrooms, suddenly remembering one more thing, I spin around, and, thinking I am on the bottom stair, I step off. I am on the second stair. Completely out of balance, I fly forward. The ball of my foot hits the tile floor, stops, and my body continues the forward momentum. There is a loud snap and a thud as I hit the floor at the far wall of the front entry way. Robert and his son who is staying with us went to bed some 30 minutes prior, but the commotion brings them immediately downstairs.

"What happened?" Robert is alarmed.

The pain in my foot and lower leg so overwhelming that I cannot speak for several more breaths. I explain the fall.

"What do you need?"

"Please bring me an ice-pack from the freezer, a dish-towel and one of those stronger codeine tablets in the cabinet." I can stand and even walk gingerly. We make it upstairs. I take the pain killer with some milk and a cracker or two and secure the soft ice pack to my foot with the dishtowel. Some 20 minutes later, I am sitting up in bed, crying because it hurts so badly.

"I am thinking since we are already awake, we should go to the emergency room," Robert offers.

I reluctantly agree, thinking I do not want to be a bother. Again, I can walk gingerly to the car.

The x-rays confirm a broken right foot, a Lisfranc fracture, the kind of injury common when riders fell from horses and the foot stayed stuck in the stirrup. Without an adequate repair, I will have a life-long limp, but the surgery will have to be delayed until the considerable swelling subsides. I am sent home with crutches and more pain pills. In the morning, Robert drives me to pick up the keynote speaker for the conference at her hotel, and he delivers both of us to the hosting high school. He carries my presentation materials inside. My presentations today are with all the secondary school counselors in the state, many of whom are hoppin' mad over the requirements I have made for them to provide data regarding their effective interventions with students. I have had many of these conversations over the past 2 years, and I feel confident that I can still converse through a bit of a drug haze. I make it through the day. My dear friend and colleague, Rose, offers to drive me home. Once again, I am going to need some help getting through this.

I see the surgeon on Monday. Lucky for me, he actually repairs more than a 100 Lisfranc injuries each year. He asks,

"Which was worse, the broken bone or the ligaments?"

"I think the ligaments. It hurt so much I could barely speak. I felt like I kinda folded my foot in half—the toes coming up over the arch."

"That is exactly what happened," he says. Yowzers. We schedule the surgery for the end of the month. He tells me I can drive short distances to work. No cross-state trips. I just need to drape my injured foot over the console so it is out of the way and use my left foot for brakes and gas. "But take some time to practice in a parking lot and neighborhood streets before you head out on the highway." Surprisingly, I master left-foot driving rather easily.

The morning of my foot surgery, Robert drops me off at the surgery center. He does expect me to be pretty self-sufficient. CC will pick me up just before noon. A round of anesthesia, an hour or so and five screws later, I am good to go—no weightbearing for 6 weeks. The nurse tells CC to take me home, give me a light lunch—mizithra pasta is her plan—and two oxycontin. I hear the nurse, two oxycontin. We go back to CC's house. Lunch is delicious, I take my meds and with the crutches I make it on my own to her bedroom to lie down. I wake up about 3:30 p.m. needing to pee. I make it to the apartment-size bathroom, that also has a potty chair for her toddler and a bunched-up rug. I lose my balance, and, trying not to put any weight on my injured foot, I fall like a log against the bathtub. It knocks the air out of me. My daughter, who has been changing a diaper, enters in a fright.

"Momma, do we need to call an ambulance?"

"No, I just knocked the air out of me. Give me a minute." Then I put my arms behind me and in a triceps pushup, I raise myself onto the bathtub and then stand up. I use the toilet and make my way back to the bedroom to lie down again. I dose some, but an hour or so later, I ask CC to check my back because it really hurts. She cannot even see a mark.

Robert picks me up just before 5. As we head home, I groan with every bump, telling him what happened and suggesting we should stop by Instacare.

"What about just going to the ER at the hospital?"

"No, no, no, the co-pay is $100. At Instacare it is only $35."

At Instacare, I explain my fall to the attending physician, and he sends me off to x-ray. This time I am in a wheelchair. Some minutes later he comes in, looks at Robert, and says,

"Well, I have good news and bad news."

Robert is hopeful, "What is the bad news?"

"She has six broken ribs, three of them in two places, and a punctured lung."

"Well, what is the good news?"

"The ambulance is on the way."

"I can drive her."

"No. You can't. We have to keep her under medical care."

At the hospital they wheel my stretcher right into a Level 2 trauma suite. The colors are bright and sunny, yellow paint on the walls. The doctors, nurses, and staff in grey, navy, and yellow scrubs. The three-person team of doctors includes the brother of the orthopedist who repaired my foot this morning. They tell me they will be inserting a chest tube. They leave the female physician to drape me up for the procedure. She carefully leaves my right breast fully exposed to the entire surgery room and the wide-open hall beyond. Robert is nowhere in sight. The woman physician explains that she will medicate me prior to placing the chest tube, inserting the syringe into the IV port that is already in place. In mere seconds after the medication, I report, "Oh wow, the entire room just went pixilated. Which is not an entirely unpleasant experience."

Then I notice over in the left-hand corner of the surgery suite a long, grey hallway with someone waiting, clearly a construction in my mind. "You're kidding?" I offer, whether aloud or in my mind, I am not sure.

"I have to choose?" I am a bit incredulous.

"You have to choose," someone, whoever I am conversing with, responds.

"Well, I am staying here where it is a lot more fun."

The voice continues, with a warning, "It will be long and grey and filled with pain." I thought they were talking about the hallway. Then, what seems like mere seconds later, I open my eyes, and there is Robert right in front of me. He sticks around to get me settled into my room and then heads off to bed.

Well after nine o'clock my kids show up in my room.

"You didn't need to come," I assure them.

"Yes, we did," they say almost in unison.

Ox and his wife think someone needs to be sued.

Luna points out that everything that is wrong can be fixed. And then she fixes me with a pointed stare, "Do you think you could have waited just a minute for some help?"

CC is hurt. She feels like Robert blames her when he calls to tell her about the trauma. I am pretty heavily medicated, and I mostly just want to go to sleep. This is Thursday night.

The next two days are a nightmare. They get me up several times a day to walk the hallway with a walker. I cannot put weight on the broken foot so, using a walker, I move my full body weight with my upper torso and the broken ribs. I cry a lot. Saturday, the brother of the orthopedist comes in and removes the chest tube with one quick jerk, saying, "I think you can go home tomorrow."

I start to cry, asking him, "Home to what? I can barely feed myself. I cannot even go to the bathroom on my own. I live in a two-story house. The pain is not under control. The nausea is not under control. And I cannot tell if the nausea is from the pain or the meds." Agreeing to change the nausea med, he offers,

"How about we keep you until Tuesday?"

On Sunday, I call Deb. "I need you to help me find a rehab center that will take my insurance for ten days."

"You can stay here," she says.

"You hate house guests?" I am unsure.

"You can stay here," she assures me.

I am at Deb's for ten days. She feeds me and keeps me on my meds, including the twice daily injections of anticoagulants. I have the pain under control. During the day I need nothing. About 4 p.m. I take one pain pill and another at 8:30 or 9:00 when I am going to bed. She gets me into and out of the shower. The physical therapist comes my third day. The simple exercises are beyond uncomfortable. I hear some patients call PT physical torture, but I always feel better the next day. I am off work for more than a month.

🖋

Robert's dark-haired twin son joins the Marines during the last half of his senior year of high school. The day before my foot surgery and the near-fatal fall, he heads off for boot-camp. For weeks Robert anxiously waits for a letter. Our new home has no landscaping. After I return home from my stay at Debra's, we often sit outside in the afternoon, enjoying the shade of our three-car garage, joking about how trashy we are as we sit there in our folding camp chairs. Often, we are waiting for our late afternoon mail delivery. The Marine has been at boot camp for over a month, and Robert anxiously awaits any word. This particular afternoon, a letter finally arrives. Robert comes down the hill from the mail-box, waving the letter in his hand. He is nearly dancing in the street. Once back in his red folding chair, he opens the letter, reading aloud, tearing up over the reports of the highs and lows of boot camp. After he finishes reading the letter, he looks at me, his eyes still moist with tears.

"I love you, baby," I say softly.

He looks at me with an expression close to panic and replies, "And I am awfully fond of you, too."

Trying to keep my expression unchanged, I look at him and think, Holy shit. What have I done? What was I thinking, giving up my independent lifestyle, to live here, completely dependent on someone I may not even know? Holy shit.

Later in the week I send Robert an e-mail while he is still at work, suggesting that we might want to see a counselor to talk about the nature of our relationship. His response is something akin to, "Are you fucking nuts? I am not going to a counselor with you nor with anyone else."

I persist, "Nevertheless, it is a fair question for me to ask you how you feel about me. I really am not interested in having a long-term relationship with someone who refuses to be emotionally involved with me." We do not continue the discussion when he returns home that evening.

On the weekend, we are sitting in our family room on his big dark leather bachelor furniture. He is on the sofa, and I am lying on the loveseat with my injured foot elevated, as usual. He looks distraught. I ask him if he is okay?

"I am just so twisted up I can barely sit still."

"Oh baby, I am sorry you are so twisted up with me."

He looks perplexed. "Why would I be twisted up with you?" he asks. "You are the solid center of my life."

I am stunned. I respond, "I thought you were upset that I suggested going for counseling."

"I am not going for counseling," he states flatly.

"I get that, but asking you how you feel about me is still a fair question."

"You are the solid center or my life," he repeats, "the part that helps me get through every other thing." Then he explains his worries are for his twin sons getting their lives launched and for his daughter who is struggling with a difficult job and an unsatisfactory relationship. I listen to his woes contentedly, knowing that I am good for at least 6 months in the "how do you feel about me" department.

꧁

I return to work part-time about the middle of August. My good friend, Jenny, has just retired. She drives me to work for a month. Robert picks me up at night. In mid-September, Robert and I are watching the evening news when he mentions the clutter, meaning some papers on the dining table and a few items that need to be taken upstairs. I use a knee scooter inside the house, one upstairs and one downstairs. I move up and down the stairs on my bum. I am still on crutches getting into and out of the house, dragging my knee scooter into and out of the car. I respond,

"Really? 'Cause my foot hurts all day long, every day. I can hardly wait to get home and put it up at night." By mid-September I am back at work full-time and am able to drive myself to work, but handicapped parking does not mean that getting into and out of any handicap accessible building will be easy or convenient, only possible. Opening doors that swing toward me is damn near impossible. So is trying to get to meetings with anything other than my crutches and my purse.

By the end of September, I drive to Sanpete County for meetings with schools and counselors. In midafternoon, I stop at the cemetery to visit Momma's grave for the first time since her funeral. When I see the headstone with her name on the right and Woody/Don on the left, I realize that he was the person waiting for me in the long, grey hallway at the trauma suite. I believe he would not have let me leave this life. I get out my phone and play for Momma Bette Midler singing "Shiver Me Timbers," the concert version where she says she believes that the words are really about just trying to get someplace, "just trying to get outta here." In December, I have surgery to remove the screws. I have been faithful in attending physical therapy, and I try to approximate a normal pace. I am reminded of Momma training herself to walk again by hanging on the hallway handrails and persisting until she can make it all the way through the halls of Apple Tree. It will be February before I feel like I will actually recover fully. The voice in the trauma suite was right. It has been long and grey and full of pain.

~

    Robert and I decide to go to Sedona for Martin Luther King weekend. I have just been released from my walking boot. He books a bed and breakfast, which turns out to be so disappointing that he moves us over to the Hilton. They give us a two-bedroom casita if we promise to attend a 1-hour sales-pitch, which we do, landing a week in Hawaii the following year. We have a wonderful time eating at the local restaurants, attending a lecture on locating the famous Sedona vortexes, taking a shuttle wine tour, and drifting through the many art galleries. I am enchanted by the striking white bark of the Arizona sycamore trees that grow on every street and in every open area. Tall and wraith-like, I call them ghost trees. Robert says to me,

    "We could be happy here. I could walk along the streets like a normal person, and you could float along the sidewalks three or four feet off the ground."

    We do check out some of the local real estate. We will have to do some serious searching if we are to find anything in our price range.

    On our way home, we are nearly to the Arizona-Utah border when I get a call from my sister, Judy. "I just spoke with a woman who says her grandmother raised our father, Woody."

    This grandmother was Woody's older sister. Her granddaughter, a woman named Joan, who calls Judy, is potentially our first cousin, once removed. Joan tells Judy that our dad's mother, our grandmother Bertha, dies on Christmas Day, just after Woody turns 11. No wonder Momma never meets his family. Judy assures me that Joan is very nice. I will call her when we get home.

Apropos of nothing, Robert, driving my car, speeds up Highway 89, from Sedona to Salt Lake City, only two lanes here in lower central Utah, when a local constable pulls him over; he is going 90 in a 65. The ticket will cost him $394.

8

TIME TRAVEL

When Robert and I get back to Salt Lake City, there is an email from Judy that includes all of Joan's contact details. She lives near St. Louis. I call Joan—she is nice. She confirms the information provided to me by the Social Security Administration: My father's parents are Bertha Snyder and Harry Dean. Then she adds more facts. Harry and Bertha have seven children, Nell Margaret—Joan's grandmother, Ethel, Rolla Spencer, Sara, Rosie (died as an infant), Mary Jane, and Woodrow. One detail stands out: As far as I know Woody never mentions to Momma that he has a sister named Ethel, even though Momma's full name is Ethel LaRue, and Grandma Yardley's given name is Ethel May. Joan assures me that the older sister, Ethel, was "a wild one" and older brother, Rolla, was a "maniac." I do not question her meaning.

Judy and I start e-mailing more frequently. I am burning to know for sure that the Deans of St. Louis are my father's family. In my files a find a copy of the 1930 Census that lists Woodrow Wilson Dean living in the household of Charles Hall, Joan's grandfather. The record shows Woody with the correct birthdate, but this person was born in

Missouri, rather than Alabama as the California driver's
license indicates. I print a copy of this census record in
March or April of 2003, shortly after the release of all the
1930 Census data, and more than 9 years prior to my contact with Joan. I pencil a note in the margin "He lives with
sister and brother-in-law." Before we find Joan, Judy and I
discuss having a DNA test to confirm our siblingship, but
we never pursue it. We have so many questions about our
father and his family. Judy was old enough to remember
some of the St. Louis family. I barely have memories of my
father, and Momma had no knowledge of my father's family
at all. I tell Judy I will do some research on the details of
DNA testing.

✑

I call my nephew, the genetic researcher. "Hey Wade,
this is Aunt Dawn. Where are you? Can you talk?"

"Hey Aunt Dawn, I'm in Italy. I can talk." He is in Italy
on business for his employer, a research company working
on a complex diagnostic tool. I explain to him my recent
discoveries.

"How do I find out for sure if Judy is my sister."

"Oh, Aunt Dawn, genetics can be tricky. Paternity is
easy. It's a $100 test and the answer is yes or no. Siblingship
is much more complicated. All you will get is a probability,
and it is much more expensive."

"Well, what kind of probability are we looking for? And
how expensive?"

"You want something upward of 70 or 80%. And it will
be a thousand dollars, maybe fifteen hundred." We catch up
on his family, and I thank him for his insights. He tells me
I can call any time.

I begin searching the internet. I find a site that is running The March Family Special for a siblingship test. The new sale price is $450 dollars. I call Judy. She is interested but cannot afford to split the cost. No problem. I just received my income tax refund—you guessed it—$450. I order the kits for each of us. We have them within a week. We talk on the phone on the day we send off the swabs. Results should be back in five business days. We agree that I will call her when the results are in, before I look at them.

I am at work on Thursday morning, the first week of April, when the e-mail with the results attached hits my inbox. I call Judy. I open the report, scanning the document, reading aloud, "DNA Report, Alleged Sibling One, Alleged Sibling Two, we each have test numbers, a list of some 18 'locus' numbers with corresponding Allele sizes for each of us alleged siblings." Ah-ha, a text box at the bottom, "DNA testing was done to determine siblingship of the alleged siblings. Based on testing results obtained from DNA loci listed, the probability of half-siblingship is ninety-nine percent. The likelihood that they share a common biological parent is 143 to 1." Wahoo! I am in the family. After decades of knowing almost nothing about my father, I now have a solid connection to him, to his family, to half of my history. I'm on to the discovery.

Judy and I share the results with Joan and with another cousin, Nancy, the daughter of Woody's sister, Mary Jane, who was 15 when her mother, Grandma Bertha Dean, dies on Christmas Day. Mary Jane also moves in with the oldest sister, Margaret Nell. Joan e-mails photos. One is Woody, age 15, and his friend, Durward, holding their violins after the Spring Recital. Durward wears a three-piece, modern looking, light-colored suit. Woody is in a dark waistcoat,

light pants, a white shirt, and striped tie. His face, his face—
is the same shape as mine. It is the very image I see every
morning in the mirror when I pin my hair back to wash.
Judy has a photo of herself at age 16 also looking very much
like our father at age 15. My father is a handsome man. Joan
sends photos of Woody the first summer with the Halls,
after his mother's death. Woody, Marion, and her brother
Dean hold puppies in the shade of a large tree. I note with
pleasure that Woody, Debra, and I share the same luxurious lashes—lashes I see on a couple of my grandsons. Wish
I had Woody's obviously thick hair.

Judy, Joan, Nancy, and I continue to email back and
forth over the weeks, trying to make sense of the time lapse
between the last contact Woody has with the St. Louis
family in late 1946 and his appearance at JC Penny's in the
spring of 1948. And why in the 4 years he was with Momma
he never reaches out to the St. Louis family? Near the end
of April, Joan sends us an email with an attachment, a
hand-written letter from her mother, my cousin Marion:

From: Joan
Sent: Tuesday, April 03, 2012 10:33 PM (Eastern
Time)
To: Dawn; Judy
Cc: Debra
Subject: Letter from my Mother

Hi Cousins,
I have attached a letter my mother wrote to you. We
have always given her a hard time about her hand-
writing, so she decided it was best to print this on
notebook paper with "lines." Perhaps we have kidded

her too much! She is left-handed and reading the grocery list was an opportunity for us to interpret some very strange items. J

Love, Joan

The handwritten letter with carefully printed words betrays her 89 years:

Dear Judith and Dawn,

I am your cousin, Marion Hall Brewster, niece of Woodrow Wilson Dean. The last time I saw you, Judith, you were a little baby, about to move to California, so I was doubly delighted with the picture of yourself and family.

The last time that I saw Woodrow was in the summer of 1944, in San Francisco. He was working for Kaiser Shipyards, making aircraft carriers to be used in the South Pacific against Japan. Somehow, he got a pass and security clearance for me to tour several ships. I saw planes landing and taking off decks. I had to wear a hard hat and was quite thrilled by seeing all this.

Woodrow and I always got along very well. We had a wonderful week visiting with each other and touring the San Francisco area.

I thought you both would like to know about his growing-up years. Woodrow, at age 11, and his sister, Mary Jane, 15 years of age, were left orphans when their mother died. Their father was already gone. Their mother died on Christmas Day in 1928. Their house was next to our house, and they were staying with us when their mother was in the hospital. Her death was a terrible blow but thank heaven our house was already like another home to them. Woodrow and my brother, your cousin Dean Charles Hall, shared a room and Mary Jane and I shared a room. I was a few months from my fifth birthday when Grandmother died. My mother, Nell Dean Hall, was the oldest child in their family, and she and my daddy easily obtained guardianship of W. and MJ. We were now, as all the neighborhood people called us, "the Hall kids."

Life proceeded smoothly. The boys wanted violin lessons, and I was already taking piano lessons. Mary Jane liked music but had no desire to play an instrument. She was content to listen to us make music.

We played outside a lot and loved to climb the big maple trees in our yard. I would go up quickly, but sometimes I became a little frightened when coming down, and Woodrow was always right there to help me.

The boys joined Boy Scouts—they really enjoyed scouting, especially the camping. Woodrow worked hard on merit badges and became an Eagle Scout. Next, he worked on a lifesaver certificate and obtained it. The Scouts tapped him for a camp counselor, and he spent several summers at camp.

We were Episcopalians and Woodrow joined the church basketball team. He was a busy person, always doing something and was very popular in high school.

My mother started a series of 5 o'clock Sunday Suppers, and we could each invite a guest to have baked beans, hot dogs, and hamburgers. After supper we headed for the basement and some wild games of ping-pong!

When Woodrow introduced me to people, they would invariably say, "oh, is this your little sister?" And he would always say, "Yes, sorta," and everyone would laugh. Woodrow and Mary Jane never used "aunt" and "uncle," except on gifts. We all felt that the "little sister, sort of" described our relationship.

We are all so glad that we have found you—or is it you found us!

Marion

Joan tells us that the St. Louis family is so concerned about Woody's state of despondency following his divorce from Judy's mother after the birth of their second daughter in April 1943 that the family sends Marion to California to check on him. Marion shares three photos of Woody at the house in Richmond, CA, where he rents a room. She notes that in each successive photo Woody moves off the porch, drawing nearer to her as she takes his photographs. Judy believes her parents divorced in early 1944. After Marion's visit, Woody then follows Judy, her baby sister, Nancy, and their mother to Southern California.

While we wait for the DNA results, Judy sends an email, sharing memories of her father:

From: Judith
Sent: Saturday, March 31, 2012 9:21 AM (Eastern Time)
To: Joan
Cc: Stevenson, Dawn; Debra
Subject: Re: Hello

Good Morning Cousins,

From my memories I believe I was about five when I last saw my daddy. He picked me up for a visit in a convertible and bought me a beautiful little "party dress." We also got ice cream cones. That memory was reinforced by my aunt Jannie who was the wife of my mother's eldest brother, Jim. She and their first child lived with us for a while during WWII. She said my grandmother was very angry that he hadn't bought me something more practical. My aunt told me that she found him to be a very handsome, sweet man! I also heard from my mother's first cousin that he saw him in 1945 or 1946 and that he had "peppered" him with questions about me. I actually believe that he, Don Code, said that meeting was in St. Louis, but I could be mistaken. My mother had also mentioned that he was driving a taxicab in Long Beach in 1945 or 46 and the Calif. Driver's license that Dawn has with his name on it indicates that it was a chauffeur's license.

Dawn and I have submitted swabs for a DNA test to prove or disprove our "sisterly" connection. We are very excited!

We are having Easter with our daughter Wendy and extended family.

Love to all,

Judy

I share some memories of Momma, noting that she was a quick wit and liked to make us laugh. I ask Judy a question about Woody's wit and humor, she responds:

From: Judith
Sent: Tuesday, April 03, 2012 10:33 PM (Eastern
Time)
To: Stevenson, Dawn
Cc: Joan; Debra
Subject: Re: Hello

I heard little about him [Woody] or his wit but do
know that my beloved Uncle Eddie really liked him
and he [Eddie] was my "hero" as I was growing.
Uncle Eddie was my mom's brother and as he did
not marry until I was about 12, he was my special
father figure and the godfather of my first son. In
fact, his wife, my aunt Shirley, mentioned that he
thought Mom should have stayed married to Woody
because he thought she would have had a happier
life! My personal opinion is that my grandmother,
when she came to live with us after the death of her
youngest son, poisoned Mom's mind because Daddy
was not in the service and her two surviving sons
were. I loved my Nana, but she never approved of
any of her children's spouses. Ironically both of my
uncles were married for life to their wives! Mother
on the other hand blew through four marriages and
assorted boyfriends. . . . very hard on me and I suspect that my sister's distrust of men is a result of
those failures.
     Judy

In Southern California, Judy tells us they settle into a
duplex at 9508 So. Manhattan Place, Los Angeles. They
have two bedrooms, one bathroom, and a kitchen with a

breakfast nook where they eat all their meals. The little duplex houses, at various times, Judy and Nancy, their mother, their grandmother, and their maternal great grandmother, who dies there. They have blackout curtains that they close at sundown and a big radio in the living room where they listen to FDR and war news. Judy lives there when she starts kindergarten. I wonder if this is the duplex Woody references when he tells Momma that he left his ex-wife with a duplex for her child support. Not true—he left them with nothing. Without explanation, Woody disappears. Before the end of fall, 1946, he is gone from her life.

✒

The first Saturday of May, Robert and I have been working in the yard. During the warm months, we often work ourselves into oblivion in the garden, but it is early in the season, so tonight, we are not too tired. I get out my computer to check on e-mails from the cousins. I find the following:

> From: Nancy
> Sent: Saturday, May 05, 2012 3:19 PM
> To: Stevenson, Dawn; Joan; John; Judy
> Subject: Cousins. . . sit down and hold on to your seats.
>
> Hi to all of you. I have some news that I wanted to give you when we met sometime, but I prayed about it and thought if I told you now, you might be able to investigate further.
>   First, I have an address for Woodrow Wilson Dean, where Mom thought he worked, I don't know where she got this info, but she never found him.

George W. Cadwallader Ins. Bonds and Finance
105 W. Ninth
Fine Long Beach, California.

When I told my brother, Don Prack, about this and Uncle Woody's new identity, He said, "I knew it!!!" He said he always thought Rolla Spencer Dean had something to do with his [Woody's] disappearance. Rolla was an older brother, born 4/26/1905 in Granite City, Ill. Rolla was a hit man for Buster Wortman. (You can look him up under Gangsters in St. Louis or East St. Louis, Ill. Rolla, AKA Blackie Dean the Dynamite Man) When [my brother] Don lived in St. Louis and tried to get into the union in concrete business, they wouldn't let him in as he was related to Blackie. He didn't even know Rolla or never met him and Don never told my mom as it would have embarrassed or hurt her. So, Don and family just moved to Florida as there were no unions here. I only met Rolla once as Aunt Ethel had a little corner store in St. Louis and she had to go into hospital for surgery, so my mom said she would run the store for her. I went with her to help. That was the first time I met Aunt Ethel. One day a big black car pulls up and a man that looked like a gangster (black overcoat with collar up and a hat on) got out and came in. He looked at me as I was doing the magazine rack and said "where's Ethel?" I said in the hospital, but that my mom was in the back room, he went back to the storage room, spoke to my mom for a minute or two and left. We never saw him again. It was scary to me as a teenager. Then Mom explained who he was!

When Uncle Woody left us and disappeared, there was an investigation going on of Buster Wortman. Uncle Woody at that time was working for Southwestern Bell Telephone (only phone co. around at that time). Uncle Woody was a line man climbing poles, and he was as straight as an arrow. So, Don and I think he must have gone into a Witness Protection Program. We have no proof, but it makes sense as how could he have completely changed his ID? I wonder, if that were the case, since he died in 52, if any information could be accessed through the FBI or CIA.

Rolla married Catherine Moriarty, she had a son Billy Wolf, then she and Rolla had a daughter [name withheld]. Mary-Jane kept up with her as she lived in Orlando, FL. I think she was in the service, Navy or Coast Guard. Haven't found any addresses as Mom's house was in the No Name storm in 1993, 5 foot of water in her house and we lost a lot of her paperwork.

Sometime in the 50s Catherine shot and killed Rolla as she said he was supposed to be out of town but came home in the night and she thought someone was breaking in. She was never arrested or charged. (Everyone was probably glad Rolla was gone!) I don't know anything about Catherine or Billy after that.

Well, I think that's all. I certainly dumped a lot on all of you, but I'm not getting any younger so thought you all should know.

I love you all,

Nancy

Psalm 46:10. . . Be still, and know that I am God. . .

Robert and I whoop and holler and nearly laugh ourselves silly. Before I have even read the "Cousins sit down"
email, Joan sends us her response:

From: Joan
Sent: Saturday, May 05, 2012 4:48 PM
To: Nancy; Stevenson, Dawn; Judith; Hall, John
Subject: RE: Cousins . . . sit down and hold on to
your seats.

Judy and Dawn, I did warn you there was another side
to the family! I have quite a few articles on Rolla. He
was indeed a very colorful and bad person. Mother
never met him. He was convicted of robbery (and I
believe Ethel's husband was in prison, too) and sent
to prison but a group of politicians requested Rolla
be pardoned so he was released early. Obviously,
he had connections. He was married to a woman
named Ethel Vollmer around this time, but I don't
know what happened to the relationship.

I have articles about his death. It was determined that it was self-defense. Since his sister Ethel
remained in touch with Catherine, I assume there
were no hard feelings. . . geez Louise. According
to the articles, in December 1954 the couple had a
disagreement at the Wortman's bar over Rolla and
another woman. The articles say he took her home,
went back to the bar, returned later, and beat her. She
picked up a gun and killed him. Strangely enough
Rolla, Catherine, and Ethel are all buried together

in the same family plot along with Rolla and Catherine's first child who died as an infant.

Nancy, I also thought about the connection to Rolla, but then thought the idea of a problem on the gambling ship made sense. The federal protection program did not start until the 1970s but I guess it could have been a state program of some kind. I thought he might have witnessed something on that ship and then literally ran for his life. It does sound reasonable that someone may have helped him with a new identity since he had a new social security number too.

Does Don remember anything else? Does he know anything about Harry Dean, your Grandfather? He was a bit colorful, too. Grandmother stated that he was dead on Bertha's death certificate, but I get the feeling from something I heard that he might not have been. HOWEVER, Bertha seems to have been a well-bred, well-educated lady! See, we do have a good side.

Love to all,

Joan

Sat 5/5/2012 5:04 pm, "Stevenson, Dawn" wrote:

BTW, my mom said many times that she thought Don/Woody was a well-educated and well-bred man. She wondered what he saw in a shy country girl like herself. Mom was a bit shy and tended to keep to herself, but with her friends and family she was great fun. I think that Woody probably appreciated that she was somewhat reserved with strangers. Dawn

Sat 5/5/2012 10:50 pm from Judy

Well, my Dears this only adds to the intrigue! Have I told you about my aunt Daisy?? Better known as "The Whirling Dervish"! I came home from school one day to find her whirling around our living room (she and my Uncle Joe Code) had come to visit my grandmother, who lived with us. When she saw me, she stopped in her tracks. . . Pointed at me and announced "I see you with many children, not all your own!" Since I was only about 15 at the time, I remember being shocked and embarrassed and speechless! I have learned since then to "roll with the punches" (surprises in life). I suspect that Dawn and I are not going to be that surprised at anything we learn and that it will all eventually help us to get a better look at the "big picture" that was our Dad. I relish each revelation!
Love you all,
Judy

So, here is my full-blood Uncle, a big-time mobster, only one generation removed from my current life. And according to Cousin Marion, my dad, Woody, sounds like the original Boy Scout. I e-mail all the cousins, telling them I could never have made up a better story. I think we girls should adopt Moll names. I am going for Sunny. Judy says she is happy to be known as Red. Nancy will adopt a childhood nickname, Nina-gets. And Joan will be known as Bones.

Through our e-mails we begin making plans for a family reunion. Nancy, Nina-gets, has a class reunion in St. Louis in September on a weekend that works for all of us. I have to talk a bit to get Debra to agree to attend. She finally agrees. As the summer progresses, I become increasingly worried about Deb retreating further "into her cave"—that is how she describes her tendency to withdraw from society and isolate herself in her home, reading, generally murder mysteries, late into the night, drinking wine and spirits to keep herself company. I talk to my niece, Chrissy, the school counselor in Arizona. We make loose plans to do an intervention. I go so far as to call Deb's counselor, John. I share my concerns and talk about my hope for an intervention. I acknowledge that she will be really angry with me. John agrees that she will be angry. He asks why I want to do this. "She is my sister, and she is killing herself. I would like her to live. I can take the anger." Chrissy makes plans to come to Utah the first weekend of August. We all plan to stay at Deb's house for a girls' weekend. We have fun cooking, watching movies, and drinking wine together. On Sunday morning right after breakfast, I broach the topic of my concern. Debra is livid, beyond livid, especially when I tell her I have been so worried that I even talk with John. She tells me that, as always, I have over-stepped my bounds. That she cannot believe anyone would ever believe I was qualified to be a counselor to anyone. That I couldn't possibly have any training or experience to know what I am doing. Before Sunday morning, Chrissy expresses her misgivings about our loose plan. In retrospect, perhaps I should not have blustered forward. Deb is so angry she tells me to get out of her house. I grab my things and head for the door. Then she says she will drive me home. I persist, telling her I will call Robert to come get me. She backs off, now insisting that she will drive me back to my house, which is near the airport, before she drops off Chrissy.

Over time, Debra will reveal that she actually calls John because she is so upset with me. In a string of irate phone conversations, she tells me that she spends five sessions with him. This can only be good. Deb was her most fun, most well-balanced and happy self when she was seeing John regularly during her separation and eventual divorce. Of course, she also tells me that John says I only did what I did to embarrass her. I am not sure that is exactly what John says, but I am sure that is what Deb believes. I hold out hope that she will get over her anger enough to make the trip to St Louis for our Dean family reunion. Before my ill-advised or ill-fated intervention, we picked out the flight time together, so I know she knows the schedule for all of us: Debra, Robert, and me. The morning of our flight, I keep hoping to see her at the airport, but Debra does not show.

Robert and I fly into St. Louis and rent a big old Chrysler 300. We drive to our hotel in Chesterfield where Cousin Nancy is staying, not many miles to Joan's home. My sister Judy and her son, Ken, are staying at a hotel much closer to Joan and her husband, Ken. I feel a slight twinge of jealousy—I want to be in with the family at the same level as Judy—even if that means being in a closer hotel. As if our family were not confusing enough, we tend to use the same given names over and over, much like my brothers David and David, and my sisters-in-law, Julie and Julie, we also have our Ken the uncle and Ken the son/nephew. Before this is over, we will have another Kenneth, in addition to my son-in-law, Kenny, and two Todds and a couple of Gavins. Robert and I will meet Cousin Nancy the following morning, after her reunion activities, but for this afternoon and evening we are going to Joan's.

Joan and Ken have a comfortable suburban, two-story house in a graceful, shaded St. Louis suburb. The double doors reveal an open entry with stairs to the second floor, the hardwood treads and entry floor finished in a lustrous warm oak, pale colored walls, oak door casings and window trim, warm wood balusters and handrail. The formal dining room on the left is filled with a gleaming wood table, chairs, and hutch. On the right is the pale colored living room, light carpet with the white sofa and big bay window. This room is also open to the back of the house with more windows and plenty of light and sunshine—my kind of house. When we arrive at Joan and Ken's, her mother, Marion, and her sister Anne, are waiting to greet us, as are my half-sister Judy and her son, Ken. Judy is still pretty, even in her late sixties, her hair still strawberry-blonde. Her son Ken is handsome and solid, maybe Glen Campbell graying. I have seen the wedding photo of Joan and her second husband, Ken. They are a good real-life, 60ish Barbie and Ken. She is blonde, genuinely willowy, with the kind of long slim bones I have always admired and really good blonde hair. We look enough alike that we could be sisters. Ken is equally good looking, thick gray, Ken-style hair with a well-trimmed Van Dyke beard and mustache. Sister Anne also pretty and sophisticated in a high school English teacher way.

After introductions are made, I sit on the sofa, next to Marion who is a small, bird-like woman, with a mass of thick white hair. She is old enough to be my aunt, but is actually my cousin, the only person I will ever meet who grew up with my father. Marion turns to me and announces,

"I am a feminist, you know?"

"You are?" I query.

"Well, I had to be," she proclaims. "My brother Dean was a male chauvinist pig."

I am going to like this woman. She goes on to tell me how she was born frail, a child who was not expected to live past 4 or 5, and yet she persisted. She went on to get a degree in piano performance from the University of Michigan, loving her time in Michigan so much that now she and her daughter Anne, who never marries, spend August on Mackinac Island, far from the heat of a St. Louis summer. Their annual getaway suits Anne's romantic and literacy disposition.

We spend the afternoon talking in groups small and large. Marion talks of Woody and Mary Jane coming to live in their home and retelling how the four of them—Mary Jane, Woody, Dean, and Marion—become known as the Hall children. Marion tells of the summer that her brother, Dean, and Woody think they find the easy solution to their lawn mowing assignment. They go up the street and borrow a half dozen goats from a neighbor, carefully staking them out in the yard. Their only error: failure to account for the clean sheets hanging on the clothesline. The goats, munching on the sheets along with munching on the sweet grass, damage the sheets beyond salvation, much to the consternation of Mother Nell, who prefers Margaret, and her husband, and much to the dismay of the boys who add the cost of replacing the sheets to their summer responsibilities. After I share the story about Jerry and the goodbye letter, Judy's son Ken refers to Jerry as the Wichita Lineman. Yes, I recall that Nancy mentioned in the "cousins sit down" email that our father, Woody, worked in Missouri as a lineman. Surprisingly, or not, our conversations carry on long past the dinner Joan has prepared ahead of time: baked chicken, green salad, and twice-baked potato casserole, a kind of upscale version of Mormon Funeral Potatoes. In my cookbook I call them Joan's St. Louis Potato Casserole. Reluctantly, we head back to our hotel well-past 10.

The next morning, Robert and I meet Cousin Nancy in the hotel lobby, following her instructions to "look for the shortest woman around." She is short, about 4'8". I am 10 inches taller than she, and Robert has a good 18 inches on her. Nancy is jovial and roundy with a head full of curly warm brown hair. After the reunion activities of the night before, she is ready to join our Dean Family Reunion.

Nancy brings along a packet of photographs of Woody and his family. Our favorite is an 8x10 black and white of Woody in a dark suit, with a tie and pocket square. We call this one Debonair Woody. Judy notes that the photo cannot show it, but our father's hair is an amazing dark auburn. With a frisson of recognition, I know the exact color of his hair, not from any lost childhood memory but from other incidents in my life. As a ninth grader at Gunnison High, I remark to some of my girlfriends, "Doesn't Dick James have the most beautiful hair?" They look at me like I am speaking another language. Dick James wears his thick, dark auburn hair back in a full and carefully controlled pompadour when all the rage is for boys to have Beatle Bangs. Nevertheless, I clearly have an emotional response to his hair during hall passing. Dick is in eleventh grade, good looking and tall, well over 6 feet, freckled, soft spoken and shy. He would likely be mortified that a little ninth grader has a crush on his hair. Over the years, I occasionally see a man, most often a younger man, with thick, dark auburn hair that makes me catch my breath—just for a moment. I know the color of my father's hair.

We are not long into our morning conversations before we realize that Judy, Joan, and I have broadly differing views from Cousin Nancy. We are White, college-educated, and suburban. She is a Southern Evangelical, the disparity increasingly evident in our brief conversations about same sex attraction and abortion. We are on opposite sides of the room on those issues. When Nancy tells us life begins at conception—her pastor said so—I am mean enough that I challenge her to send me the scriptural reference. I believe I have read the *King James Translation of the Bible* enough to know that such a reference does not exist. Nevertheless, we put aside our differences for the sake of family and head out to a local restaurant for lunch.

After lunch, Joan has designed a tour of St Louis and surrounding areas so Judy and I can visit the houses where Woody grew up. Our first stop on Clayton Avenue is now part of a golf course in Forest Park. Then it is on to see the grandparent's home site, then two homes in Bridgeton, on to St. John's and the red brick house with the second-floor veranda where Marion tells us the family ate on warm summer evenings. This is the home of the sheet-nibbling goats. The conversation also reveals that Marion sleeps in the bedroom nearest the veranda to keep Woody and her older brother Dean from sneaking off in the night. So maybe Woody was a little more rebellious than your typical Boy Scout. We visit the site of the home where Judy's mother grew up. Judy tells of the tragic death of her mother's youngest brother. In a freak accident the 11-year-old falls backwards off the porch railing into the cement stairwell to the basement. His neck is broken, and they move him twice without medical aid. Later that night, young Richard Allen has a seizure which severs his spinal column, and he dies. And finally, the house where Woody and Jane make their first home. Somewhere along the tour, Nancy reveals her fondness for her Uncle Woody, who bought her a Jenny Lind twin bed and a treasured doll. Nancy is so heartbroken when Woody apparently abandons them, she tosses the beloved doll into the hole in the backyard as fill for a soon-to-be-built swimming pool.

After the house tour Joan presents each of us with a little photo album of the home sites, and where possible, photos of the occupants at the time. During the tour we also stop briefly at the high school where Woody graduated, learning the story of how he broke his back when playing basketball with the Episcopalians. The Hall parents have to borrow money for the required surgery. The injury renders him forever 4F for the military draft. So, Woody never is in any kind of military service, one more piece of misinformation, another lie. We go on to see the community pool. Earlier in the morning, we see a photo of the lifeguards lined up. Woody wears impossibly nerdy swim trunks complete with a belt, but knowing Woody, they were likely very stylish. After finishing our tour, we drive to a traditional Italian restaurant on College Hill. Joan notes that this is a landmark St. Louis eatery. After dinner we head off for our separate lodging, agreeing to meet one last time for Sunday Brunch. This entire St. Louis trip is one of the most satisfying experiences of my life. For the first time, I know where and how my father grew up. I know people who loved him and cared for him. Marion tells me that after Woody disappears, they never stop looking for him, checking phone books in every new town or city, hoping to see once again the tall, handsome man with the amazing dark auburn hair.

Before we leave St. Louis, Joan presents us with a piece of needlework from Grandma Bertha, a nosegay that was part of a larger project, a bedspread of embroidered muslin for Marion's girlhood bedroom. The quality of her lazy daisy stitches, to say nothing of the amazing display of French Knots, evidence her skill as a needleworker, supporting the claims of Marion and Joan that Grandma B was a woman of refinement who, in her youth, studies Latin, and who occasionally works outside her home as a cook.

✍

Twice in my life I take a deep dive into newspapers. First, when Ernie and I buy the Star Theatre in Gunnison. The second deep dive into newspapers comes in learning the stories of Woody and Uncle Blackie. When Robert and I meet my Dean family in St. Louis I see many of the newspaper articles that Joan has collected on Uncle Blackie. I plan to fly to Florida to see her at the new retirement address. The two of us will pore over the articles, putting them into a story for Blackie. But we have a pandemic. I think I will have to put my plan on hold until we can travel again. Then I find Newspapers.com. For a minimal fee, I buy access to over 400 newspapers. I begin searching for Rolla Spencer (Blackie) Dean in and around St. Louis from 1920 through 1955. After I look for articles on Uncle Blackie, I start looking for articles on Woodrow Wilson Dean. Inevitably questions arise or I get curious about one detail or another. I do more searches. In the end I read more than a thousand news articles from across the United States. I save nearly 400 articles to my Ancestry tree.

I immerse myself in reading and writing, thinking more about past times and distant places than our current reality.

In the words of Jerry Garcia, "What a long, strange trip it's been." My dining table frequently bears stacks of diaries, journals, letters, and printed articles, post-it notes everywhere. The sensation amplifies with the bizarre time in which we are living—the year of COVID—the isolation, the loneliness. Until now, this story has been memories and personal accounts. Now the source material shifts, these news articles a much less personal means to tell a very personal story.

🖋

As if our lives are not complicated enough, Ernie and I decide to buy the local movie house, the Star Theatre. Ernie is looking for a tax write-off, back in the days when he still thinks he can spend his way out of taxes. We want a place for our kids, ages 14, 11, 9, 7, and 3, to work. And we love movies. When I was a kid, on most Friday nights Momma gives me a quarter, and I meet my friends at the movies. Twenty cents for a ticket and a nickel for a candy bar, Baby Ruth, Butterfinger, Three Musketeers, Milky way. One of my favorite movies ever—which was way too old for me—is *Lonely Are the Brave* with Kirk Douglas. I think I watch it alone—maybe my friend Jackie, the horse girl, saw it with me. I always hope for a horse named Brandy.

I learn how to book movies and make box office reports. The kids help in the cleanup for the Thursday-Friday-Saturday showings. When the film is appropriate, they often run the concession. Everything is priced in increments of a quarter, which they learn to add quickly in their heads and count out change. We keep the tickets, the ticket reports, and the money from concession sales in popcorn bags in the bottom drawer of the study. Our kids soon learn that they can tap this ready cash supply. They sneak off once or twice a week to the video game machines around town, or, as Ox did, buy a $10 or $20 bag of candy and stash it in a culvert. This is the house of the dentist. We do not eat candy. At about the same time that we purchase the theatre, the first video store opens in town, making a significant impact on movie attendance. I book the first R-rated movies ever to be shown in Gunnison, starting with *Body Heat*. I sit on the back row with all the kids when we watch *E.T.*, which we cannot book until nearly a year after release—we are a small potatoes operation. My youngest, CC, cries so much in the final scenes that her t-shirt is soaked. One year we run two movies a week, Monday-Tuesday-Wednesday and Thursday-Friday-Saturday. I see 104 films that year. If you can stand a second or third viewing, it is a good film.

The theatre is a beauty of a building. Built in 1912 by Sims Duggins, a leader in getting electricity to Gunnison, in part to run the movie theatre. Two or three years after opening, Duggins adds a stage to accommodate itinerate vaudeville shows. The story has it there was once a dancing elephant up there. The basic structure is brick and a bas-relief façade with swags and medallions. Originally two winged victories stood on supports under the twin archways. There is a full apartment with two bedrooms above the theatre. It would make a fabulous bordello. I think if we can get this building on the historic registry, we can get some money for a complete restoration. I look into the process and make initial contacts. One requirement is a comprehensive review of the local newspaper for any mention of the building or associated activities. I start a deep dive into the *Gunnison Valley News*. I do not read every article, but I review every weekly paper from 1910 to 1987, over 4000 four to six-page publications. For many years the issues are ten pages, including national news, state news, comics, and crossword puzzles. I scan every issue and read at least an article or two. I work on Thursdays for two years, stopping often to read items of interest, including Grandma Yardley's gardening column in 1952 and 1953. I read updates on the war efforts for WWI and WWII, the rationing and subsequent effects, the local Red Cross units meeting to roll bandages, to make first-aid kits and to knit socks. All the little towns in Gunnison Valley—Centerfield, Mayfield, Fayette, and Axtell—have their own weekly social column where a good time was had by all.

We have the final review for approval for historic status with the state architect after we are living in the Central Coast of California. We fly home for the meeting at the Star Theatre. He tells us the building has nearly perfect acoustics. We have several classical guitar concerts on that stage courtesy of our friend Tim, my best friend from junior high, and his association with the Utah Classical Guitar Society. During his day job, Tim is a farmer and sheep rancher. It takes a toll on his hands and fingers. The architect also tells us that if the theater and the building next door, which housed the original J.C. Penny's, were in Salt Lake City, they would be the perfect venue for Repertory Dance Theater. His wife is a dancer and RDT is looking for a new home. Historic status is granted. We eventually sell the theater, but not before I completely piss Ernie off by telling him I am going back to college and no longer working the theatre.

🖋

One of my favorite stories ever about our small-town newspaper comes from my brother Big Dave, a Marine in Vietnam, right after the Tet Offensive. Momma sends him a box every month or so. She puts in cans of peaches along with the cookies and any other small items he has requested, everything packed in back issues of the *Gunnison Valley News*. Not surprisingly, Dave is the most country kid in his unit. With the first box, the city boys, especially the Black men, laugh uproariously over the small-town doings. Then Dave gets another box. After mail-call, the men sit in a casual circle, there in the jungle, passing around another can of peaches, each man fishing out a slice or two with his ka-bar. One of them says, "Hey, Bird, did your Momma send any newspapers in this pack?" Another one says, "We should read some." And another, "Yeah, I wonder what Lester Hansen is up to this week?" A moment of normal life there in the jungle.

When I am in elementary school, junior high, and high school the *Gunnison Valley News* offices, meaning a desk piled high with business materials and the print room with the big press, are in the basement of the bank building. I am sure I made more than one field trip to see the printing operation, Wes Cherry, the owner and publisher, looming large in his big, rubberized apron and giant gloves used in the actual printing process. In high school I remember talking with Wes about ads and articles on our school activities for the *News*. I smell the ink; I hear the sound of the press. By the time I am researching the Star Theatre, the printing has been outsourced, the bank remodeled, and the News Office moved to one of two small offices that are part of the Star Theatre building, the other small office occupied by the barber shop.

As early as summer 1944, after Marion's visit with him in San Francisco, Woody leaves the Kaiser shipyards in the San Francisco Bay area for Southern California. Cousin Nancy says her mother believes Woody works for George W. Cadwallader Ins. Bonds and Finance, 105 West Ninth, Fine Long Beach, California. Cadwallader's business address often appears in newspaper advertisements as "105 West Ninth at Pine—likely the source of the confusion for "Fine Long Beach." Woody's California Chauffer's License lists his address as 103 West 9th St., Long Beach, perhaps next door, a servant's quarters or a duplex.

Of Woody's alleged employer we know that in the 1920 Census, George W. Cadwallader is 24, divorced, a swim instructor, and living at the YMCA with several dozen other young men. Not a terrible position for a young man before the beginning of the Great Depression. By the 1930 Census, George W. Cadwallader is married to Isabelle Elizabeth, age 31, and living in the home of his in-laws, Mr. and Mrs. Russell Sage in Long Beach. Cadwallader's occupation is listed as insurance sales. His wife's family are apparently well-connected in Southern California. The lead story of the Society column of the *Wilmington [CA] Daily Press Journal*, on July 21, 1936, reads: MESDAMES BOND AND CADWALLADER FETE BRIDE-TO-BE. The event is held at the home of Mrs. Cadwallader's parents in Long Beach. The Cadwalladers will accompany the bride to her approaching wedding in Sacramento.

Cadwallader has come up in the world. Being featured in the local Society pages will be a thing, for George himself, but more often for Mrs. Cadwallader. The Society column of the *Long Beach Independent*, on April 30, 1944, under the heading "Gay Activities at Long Beach Social Centers," reports the Cadwalladers at dinner and dancing in the Riviera Room at the Villa Riviera.

On June 23, 1944, the *Long Beach Independent Journal*, again on the Society page, reports, Mrs. Cadwallader participating with the UCLA Women's Club at an event to honor two young women, one a high school graduate, the other a junior college graduate. The refreshment table features blue and gold flowers. True Bruins here.

And finally, one more item on Mme. Cadwallader from The Society column of the *Long Beach Independent* on July 24, 1944, reports an event for Alpha Gamma Delta Sorority.

In the meantime, I search for George S. Neely, II, the name on the little brown notebook with the seal of the Connecticut Mutual Life Insurance Company in which Woody keeps his addresses. The *Long Beach Independent*, not on the Society page, on September 20, 1944, reveals that George Neely was jailed for carrying a concealed weapon, a zip to be specific, given to him by an aircraft worker. Neely did not know it was illegal to carry it. The article also mentions that Neely was recently acquitted in a charge of contributing to the delinquency of a minor—Miss Ann May Huffman, 16 years old, missing from her home for several months.

Wahoo! George S. Neely, II, is our kind of guy. This incident likely occurs in a window of possibility for Woody's arrival in Southern California, and the elements are familiar. Woody was an aircraft worker—perhaps one of his compadres helped connect him to Neely, or he knew Neely directly from the Kaiser Shipyards. And of course, there is the illegal firearm—a zip gun was a homemade weapon. It is likely naive to think that Woody has been completely untouched by his family background. And then there is the insurance connection, both to Cadwallader, as well as Neely, and add to all that the $50K insurance policy Woody buys years later for Momma and all of us, perhaps in anticipation of his eventual demise. Perhaps I am adding two and two to make eighty-four.

Long after Woody disappears from southern California, Mr. and Mrs. G. W. Cadwallader continue their lives as usual. The *Long Beach Independent*, under a column titled, "We, The Women" on Oct 22, 1948, reports the Cadwalladers and others anticipating a state convention of bridge players.

≈

Joan reports that her Uncle Dean, older brother of Marion, Joan's mother, and my cousin, had an on-going struggle with his wife, Shirley, who was forever bringing up theories about what happened to Woody or suggesting they renew efforts to find him. Invariably, Uncle Dean tells Aunt Shirley to give it a rest, to let it go. Joan remains convinced that if there is anyone in the family with whom Woody would share his secrets, it would be his nephew Dean Hall with whom he grew up. Woody is four years older than Dean Hall, but Woody regards him as a brother. And Dean is apparently worthy of such trust. The scene in *Game of Thrones* in which they discuss Jon Snow's parentage comes to mind. Someone declares, "It's a secret!" to which Varys, the eunuch replies something like, "Nonsense, when five people know, it is information." Dean's son John is the source of the speculation that Woody also works on the gambling ship that briefly anchors off the coast of Long Beach, an idea that he somehow gleans from his father. Uncle Dean, Cousin Dean, knew how to keep a secret. He knew enough to not go snooping around in ways that would lead to others knowing Woody's secret.

Even before the prospect of a gambling ship, there are gangster related troubles in Long Beach, CA. The *Long Beach Independent*, September 23, 1945, reports that "shocking developments are tumbling out of the Mullen murder . . . Witnesses have been intimidated or assaulted. A woman witness has been badly beaten by thugs. Spano, once a suspect, now a prosecution witness." This crime story is the biggest ever in the history of Long Beach. The article asserts, "Hoodlums are finding Long Beach a haven is no longer a matter of conjecture." No familiar names and faces here in Long Beach, but the details match much of the happenings in St. Louis. The trial does not turn out so well. An editorial in the *Long Beach Independent* of February 8, 1946, laments the failure calling it a "sickening spectacle" that features a "parade of convicted jailbirds, racketeers, and a confessed murderer as witnesses" for both the prosecution and the defense. One defendant has an alibi that he was running a crap game miles away. The writer, Lawrence A. Collins, editor and publisher, wonders, "Who protects or allows these rackets in the county?" Collins responds to his own question, "The answer is that our law enforcement agencies are responsible. There were not many 'big shot' operators called as witnesses, but the scores of small racketeers were evidence that large operators collect from small fry."

Into this atmosphere Tony Cornero Stralla announces in the *Long Beach Independent*, April 23, 1946, his plans for gambling in Southern California. Cornero, a former "admiral" of a gambling operation off the coast of Santa Monica that shut down in 1940, plans to open a "deluxe, new gambling" ship by the second week of June, spending a half million dollars to refit the old Navy ship.

Cornero's plans are not without controversy in and of themselves; nevertheless, he proceeds. The *Long Beach Independent*, May 31, 1946, reiterates: The gambling ship will open June 17. Patrons will be ferried by water taxi to the ship anchored 6 or 7 miles offshore. Tony reports that his dispute with the AFL Sailor's Union of the Pacific over the hiring of a union crew has been settled.

Nevertheless, efforts are afoot to stop the gambling ship. The *Long Beach Independent*, June 18, 1946, reports that Long Beach Chief of Police Alvin P. Slaight has sent City Prosecutor Albert C. S. Ramsey a request for him to cite "various city ordinances covering the operation of water taxis to and from" gambling ships. Slaight also seeks information on "a restraining order issued before the war which is said to have restrained the department from interfering with the operations of water taxis engaged in such operations."

Water taxis will become a huge issue for Cornero and his gambling syndicate. Within days, the *Independent* on June 23, 1946, reports, that the city of Long Beach, according to C.S. Ramsey, has drawn up an "air-tight city ordinance to prohibit water taxis from carrying passengers to gambling barges." They have been "studying the law and we believe our proposed ordinance will effectively block operation of water taxis from this city."

Opposition to the gambling ship extends to the state level. On July 26, 1946, the *Independent* reports Governor Earl Warren declares the state has "'ample power' in existing state laws and statutes to prevent the operation of gambling ships off the California Coast." Warren responds to a telegram from

Fred N. Howser, district attorney for Los Angeles County, and candidate for Attorney General. Howser wanted the special session of the legislature to make further rulings to ensure the prevention of the gambling ship, but the telegram arrives after the session had adjourned.

Cornero's troubles are not yet over. On Sunday, August 1, 1946, the *Independent* provides an update: "The United States' Marshal's Office last night took charge of Cornero's nearly completed gambling ship, the Lux, and placed a keeper aboard the floating casino as the result of a libel filed in federal court yesterday." Four of the ship repair contractors engaged in the "remodel" claim that Cornero's business agent refuses to make payment of $12,828 for labor and materials supplied to the ship between July 20 and July 30. The contractors stop work on Tuesday. "All of the libellants are members of the All-In-One Marine Service." Not one to waste an opportunity to make a statement, Cornero tells the reporter that "a permanent injunction served by District Attorney Fred N. Howser to restrain him from operating a gambling boat in California [was] 'just a worthless scrap of paper.'" Cornero clarifies himself, "That's because I don't have a dime's worth of interest in the boat." The reporter notes, wryly, "Furthermore, when the time comes for Tony's boat, or rather the boat Tony doesn't have a dime's interest in, to operate, he let it be known he will do some serving of papers himself upon public officials."

The article goes on to report Tony saying that the boat will, "sail the day after I serve some papers on Chief of Police Slaight and others." The papers to which Cornero refers are those identified in an item on June 18th that allegedly provides Cornero a restraining order against attempts to stop water taxis from ferrying gamblers to the

Lux. The report states that signs for the water taxis have been installed and a two-story building that will serve as a waiting area for patrons has been completed. The water taxis will be operated by, or at least the operation will be "fronted" by, George Garvin who, in 1934, obtained the original permanent injunction against Long Beach and the City of Los Angeles. The article provides details about the gambling ship, a 90' bar in the gaming area, the smaller bar in the café, the décor, and the impending installation of the gaming machines. The last line is an observation by Cornero regarding his improvement costs. Original estimates were $200,000 but the actual bill is nearing $600,000 because "workers took their time," Cornero says.

By August 7, 1946, the *Monrovia News-Post* reports thousands at the gambling ship. "Cornero's over-touted gambling ship Bunker Hill [the legal name for the Lux] struck a mine—a gold mine—on its opening night as thousands of dime and dollar players almost fought each other at the Long Beach dock for a turn at off-shore gambling." Water taxis flowed in a steady stream across the choppy seas, carrying 60 persons each to the neon-lighted vessel. Trade did not dwindle through the night prompting Cornero's aides to state they would "keep the ship open 24 hours a day 'if the customers keep coming.'"

Also, on board are plainclothes men from the district attorney's and sheriff's offices who make no attempt to stop the gambling operations. Earlier the Assistant District Attorney says, "Twenty-four hours operation should give us all the evidence we need."

The opening of the gambling ship does not mean that all issues have been resolved. An editorial in the *Long Beach Independent*, on the same day, laments:

Cornero Opens at Sea

As the swanky gambling ship Lux opened its docks to gambling mobs of suckers many good people called us asking what can be done. Our answer is we don't know what can be done about Cornero because of the legal questions involved. Senator Knowland tried hard to get the senate to take action but senators dodged the issue.

We agree with all the people who have called us that something should be done. It is a definite challenge to the community and to the nation. It is not so much that gambling will go on, but this community will be the nesting place of all the dregs of society that are drawn to wherever it flourishes.

It is hard, however, for us to get excited over this gambling ship which will be several miles out at sea. We understand that there will be 150 slot machines on the ship. There are ten or twenty times as many slot machines in the county operating illegally that could be stopped in one night.

Our law enforcement officials, meaning, sheriff, district attorney and police departments have been quite vocal in what they would do if Cornero opened. One would think the thought of gambling had shocked their sensibilities. We hardly accept their protestations as being sincere because if they are sincere why do they not clean up their own back yard before weeping over garbage that litters up a yard miles away.

It may seem strange to say so, but it seems to us Cornero is the most honest of the lot. He openly says what he intends doing and there is no law to stop him. While politicians make headlines promising things they probably cannot do, or maybe things they have no intention of doing, Cornero openly starts to operate.

We respect, may we say, his guts. It is hard to respect law enforcement officials who allow more gambling in the county than will be done on Cornero's ship. We despise all the vice and sordidness that surrounds his operation, but we will not join a hypocritical crusade against the gambling ship until we see some honest action close to home. When thousands of slot machines are banned in the county, we will get excited over those on Cornero's ship.

It is doubtful that Cornero is paying off any one for protection. He is standing strictly on the legal point that the state of California, the county of Los Angeles, and the city of Long Beach have no jurisdiction over operations outside the three-mile limit. He has expensive lawyers, but he is smart to realize he would be wasting money to pay state or local officials for protection.

This is not true of gambling in the county. Slot machines, pin ball payoff, bookies and other gambling cannot operate in the county without protection of law enforcement officials. These facts are so apparent we ask these officials to clean up their own yards first. Then they will sound more convincing when they talk about Cornero. —L.A.C.

Entertainment for the patrons on the LUX is short-lived. On August 9, 1946, the *Pomona Progress-Bulletin* reports a thousand patrons marooned on the gambling ship. "'Admiral' Tony is arrested on August 8th, "just 48 hours after his financially fabulous opening," and his fleet of water taxis are impounded. Then, in an effort to rescue the stranded gamblers, the authorities offer immunity to the taxi crews, but Cornero refuses, telling them, "You impounded the boats. You get them off." Meanwhile, "A player aboard the Lux reported to *United Press* by radio phone that gambling went on 'as usual' thru-out the night, with players laughing off the idea of being marooned." Subsequently, the police recruit a small fleet of other boats to remove the 800 gamblers and some of the crew left on the floating casino. The last rescue boat leaves at 1:30 a.m. The only remaining question is whether or not the gambling ship can continue to operate during the inevitable court fight coming Tony's way. The county also expected "Stralla to try to get a writ preventing authorities from interfering with water tax operation pending a court decision."

On August 10, 1946 the *News-Pilot* in nearby San Pedro runs photos of Cornero and a group of passengers on the Lux, the caption underneath: "As Tony Cornero (left) operator of the offshore gambling ship Bunker Hill walks from a jail elevator in Los Angeles after release on bail many patrons of his floating casino (right) waited yesterday on the boat's landing platform for one of five water taxis to take them ashore." About 150 persons remained on board the Lux, most of them crew members. I search the faces of the patrons and staff in the blurry newspaper photo looking for Woody. I got nothing.

On August 14, 1946, the *Long Beach Independent* headlines yet another obstacle for Cornero and the gambling ship. The Railway Commission will assume jurisdiction and any future water taxi operation will be placed under the railway commission and supervised as any other public utility.

Then Cornero's trouble hits even closer. The August 18, 1946, *Long Beach Independent* provides an update of weekend action in Tony's world: "While legal difficulties continued to keep 'Admiral' Tony Cornero's gambling ship Lux patronless, one of his aides, 'rugged little' Jimmy Utley, fought for his life last night in a Los Angeles hospital." Cornero's aide, Jimmy Utley, was brutally beaten on Friday night. "While Betty Hutton, Dorothy Lamour, Loretta Young, Cary Grant, Robert Young and a score of other picture greats were held at bay by an armed thug, a companion struck Utley more than a dozen times across the head with a blackjack." Remaining true to the "code of the underworld," Utley tells police, "I didn't see who did it. If you arrest them, I won't prosecute." Utley's skull is fractured. He has a concussion and a broken wrist. Because Utley "had the bingo concession" on the Lux the police are unclear whether the beating is an attempt by an out-of-town gang to "muscle in" on the eventual resumption of gambling operations, or whether it is part of a bookie feud "among big time operators" in Beverly Hills. The report concludes that Cornero, unsuccessful in finding other locations from which to operate in Southern California, is working "below the border at Tijuana and Ensenada" to find a place for the "$1,000,000 floating casino."

The *Long Beach Independent*, August 22, 1946, updates us on the gambling ship: Deputy County Counsel, S.V.O. Pritchard alleges that Cornero "entered into a criminal conspiracy to transport patrons to the ship for gambling purposes" as proven by $18,000 transferred "from Cornero by devious means." Cornero, though not on trial himself, stands at the back of the court during the morning session, and is "seated inside the railing during the afternoon session."

The article continues with details of the testimony of a special agent for Bank of America who tells that $378,407.93 was transferred from the account of "Seven Seas Steamship and Trading Co, A. C. Stralla, President, to the account of steamship Lux and owners, A.C. Cornero, agent." And then covers the testimony of Chief Quartermaster Glen H. Wright, commander of the Coast Guard Cutter who had "shot the position" of the Lux, declaring it in compliance with the 3-mile limit. Wright was then subjected to a "bitter cross-examination." The article sums up the day: "At the end of the time, it is not clear in the average spectator's mind whether the Lux had been three miles from the entrance of the harbor or had been within the continental limits." The attorney for the defense argues continually that "inasmuch as the boat was outside the continental 3-mile line, it would have been impossible for criminal conspiracy to have occurred."

Interestingly, Woody tells Momma that he serves in the Coast Guard during World War II, not the Marines as reported in several of the news articles about his death. When Cousin Joan first tells me that Woody works at the Kaiser Shipyard in San Francisco, I assume that Woody's inspiration for the Coast Guard story comes from there. Now, in researching the gambling ship I wonder if Woody becomes familiar with the operations of the Coast Guard when he lives near the Port of Long Beach. Is it the port where he learns to back braid the ropes, as sailors do, for our swings in front of the San Pitch Inn?

The State of California issues the Chauffer's License for Woodrow Wilson Dean on October 9, 1946, showing the address adjacent to Cadwallader's Insurance Agency. So Woody is in Long Beach for most, if not all, of the gambling ship kerfuffle and is also still associated with Cadwallader. And Dean Hall, Woody's nephew believes he is working on the gambling ship.

≈

When Ernie is in dental school at UCLA, his best friend from high school, Dan, lives in Torrance, located toward the south of the L.A. Basin, between UCLA and Long Beach. For a couple of years, Dan owns a beautiful little vintage 23-foot sloop, all white with dark stained trim. A half dozen times, or so, we go with Dan and his wife, Jeanette, and their 3-year-old son and our baby girl to go sailing around the Long Beach Harbor. One chill morning, we go sailing in the fog, carefully zigging between the huge ships at anchor in the port. We never leave the breakwater, so the trips are always smooth and soothing. With berths below deck, we can even put the baby to sleep and enjoy several hours of grown-up time.

Ernie also has a couple of friends in his UCLA class who are sailors. Pete H. and Fred K. invite us twice to go sailing with them. Like Dan, the boat they use, which belongs to Fred's family, anchors at San Pedro, so we again go sailing around the Long Beach Harbor. Fred's boat is a 30-foot trimaran. Fred, a great storyteller, shares tales from the summer that he, his dad, and his brother sail the trimaran to Hawaii and back. And he tells of their heartbreak on another day, when the boat goes over offshore near Redondo Beach. They quickly remove the sails to save the day, to save the boat, swimming the sails to shore and leaving them on the beach, and swimming back out to right the boat. When they return to the beach the sails are gone—a loss of thousands of dollars.

During most of these sailing adventures the song in my head is "Brandy." It likely reveals my level of unhappiness that at least once on every sail in the harbor, I wonder if I could find a good sailor and run off to sea. Years later, we are in our Ford custom van, driving south on the 405 Freeway, when we hear "Sailing" by Christopher Cross for the first time. The Friday afternoon traffic is at a crawl here, just north of LAX. With all the windows open, I can feel the texture of the air, a moisture and weight that we never get in our high mountain desert. This close to the water I can smell the sea. Driving right next to us, in the lane on our right, is a light butter yellow Rolls Royce. The minute I hear the first few bars of "Sailing," I am in that exact spot on the 405, the window open, the ocean air, right by the yellow Rolls Royce.

Our Ford van is a real beauty: Navy blue with sand-colored accents, four sand leather captain's chairs with navy and sand houndstooth inserts. A leather bench seat in the back. Just right for the seven of us to travel to California or to Texas. We luck into it on a used car lot in south Provo. They put it out that morning. Only 6,000 miles, and we save $8 or $10,000. The salesman tells us that it belongs to Jimmy Osmond, but he sells it quickly because his parents, George and Olive, are coming back in town. He trades it for a much more conservative Volkswagen. We know this is true. When we cannot figure out how to lay down the back bench, Ernie calls Jimmie Osmond's manager, and he tells him how to remove the headrests, so the bench will lay out flat.

Richard Bach once wrote something like: Sailing distorts time. Flying distorts space. Searching through these news articles and trying to sort out the story of Woody feels like both. At moments, time and space seem to disappear. We have a photo of Woody on the beach, near the Hotel Laguna, the most accessible beach in his life. He is smiling, fit and handsome as ever. An ocean breeze lifts a lock of his hair. Perched effortlessly on his shoulders is a pretty woman. He stands with arms akimbo, looking out to sea. I think my father is happy this day.

Small wonder, then, that whenever I visit Momma's grave, I always play Bette Midler singing "Shiver Me Timbers," live concert version. "Blue water, she's my daughter. I skip like a stone."

⚘

Tony soon gets his day in court. Much to the consternation of Judge Fred Miller, the trial goes on for three days. On August 28, 1946, the *Long Beach Independent* reports that for the second day county officials plod through a hearing "where George Garvin, Water taxi operator, seeks to have the county release 11 impounded boats and to restrain officials from interfering with their operation to the gambling barge Lux." S.V.O. Pritchard goes so far as to cite a case in which garbage from "the city of New York, dumped 21 miles at sea, floats onto the shores of New Jersey." Pritchard declares outright, "Garbage from Tony Cornero's boat floats up on the shore of California, brother." Then Pritchard lays out the financial scheme:

> Cornero transferred $18,000 from his Seven Seas Trading and Shipping Co, to the account of the steamship Lux, Tony Cornero, agent, then to the account of Frank A. Gruber, one of Cornero's

associates, thence to the account of Ernest Judd and finally to Garvin. Pritchard called on R. E. Dickenson, local bank manager. Pritchard contends that Garvin entered into a conspiracy with Cornero and others to circumvent a permanent injunction which forbids Cornero to conduct a gambling ship in California waters.

As Cornero continues to press his case, neon lights on the million-dollar boat, the "most expensive luxurious floating casino ever constructed," continue to shine across the water, easily visible from Long Beach. With a note of melancholy or maybe irony, the article concludes: "But within the ship and in the large gambling room the roulette wheels were covered, the slot machines silent, the 90-foot bar deserted and nary a pair of dice clattered across the many crap tables."

Day three, August 29, 1946: The skipper of the Lux testifies that even when officials shut down Cornero's operation and impound the water taxis, the boat "was anchored well beyond the three-mile limit." Captain Robert C. Burdett testifies that he makes "numerous calculations" and determines that the location of the boat was between three and one-half to three and two-tenths miles outside the 3-mile limit. Noting that "A nautical mile is one third longer than a land mile."

On cross-examination, Burdett states he was hired by Cornero and accepted orders "from Cornero as the legal agent for the Seven Seas Steamship and Trading Company." Then Judd testifies that he borrows $35,000 from Cornero "so I would have him on a hook so that he would favor my water taxi company." Then after borrowing the money and arranging to buy water taxis, he is advised by his doctor that he must "take it easy if I want to live." So, Judd transfers his interests in the water taxis to George Garvin and later loans Garvin $20,000, stating "he and Garvin previously had agreed that if the Lux did not operate the docks, [the] water taxis would be used for sport fishing."

The article concludes with a mention that Dr. Arthur Braden, chairman of the Los Angeles County Committee for Church and Community Operation wanted the ship closed. "We consider the opening of a gambling ship off the coast of California a serious, tragic, and unfortunate event." Do three adjectives make it worse?

Garvin prevails and the *Long Beach Independent*, September 1, 1946, relates that "Admiral Tony, who reopened the becalmed vessel at noon yesterday was an interested 'observer,' emphasizing that he had nothing to do with the water taxi business." Nevertheless, Tony pushes back his signature hat, "when Chief of Police Alvin F. Slight and City Prosecutor Albert C.S. Ramsey arrived." Tony declares he is glad to see the officers "however, there was no denying the suave former coal heaver was disconcerted as his eyes passed along the line of waiting patrons standing back to stomach for some 500 feet. His attorney immediately took over the situation." Charles Stratton, from the district attorney's office, said even though he is present he is leaving all decisions to Long Beach officials, "But local police had full support of his office." Stratton wants another 48 hours "to accumulate evidence for a court of equity."

At the landing for the water taxis two signs are posted:

Water taxis leaving this dock operate only in foreign commerce and operate under and comply with laws of the United States of America. The owners, operators, captains, stewards, and crew of the water taxis do not solicit anyone to visit any particular destination.

A federal statute makes illegal for anyone, including local authorities, to board all water taxis, against the master's wishes, and all the water taxis carry masters.

The jury is convinced. The *Long Beach Independent*, September 20, 1946, reports that two of the water taxi operators are freed after the 11-member jury deliberates for 3 minutes. "The two water taxi men, brothers Harmie L. and Maxie C. Adkinson, skipper and deckhand on one of the water taxis servicing the Lux, testify that they were merely deckhands and had received their jobs through their union hall hiring." Both brothers claim that they ask all patrons their desired destination and simply take them there. City Prosecutor C.S. Ramsey has not yet decided whether to prosecute another sixty-three water taxi and shoreside employees facing similar charges.

The United States Marshals Office takes custody of the Lux where it anchors a mile off the coast at Rainbow pier, posting a notice of the seizure on the side of the ship. Cornero and his attorneys say he will fight the seizure "to the utmost." Reportedly, Gov. Earl Warren had direct orders from President Truman to seize the ship. "Deputy Marshalls were authorized by federal court order today to remove 50,000 silver dollars and 300 cases of liquor from the seized gambling ship Lux to safekeeping ashore." The federal suit, alleging that the Lux had "violated its license to engage in coastwise trading by remaining at anchor" outside the 3-mile limit. "The suit seeks forfeiture of the Bunker Hill—legal name for the Lux—to the government on grounds that it was used for gambling purposes, although licensed only for coastal trade."

The *Long Beach Independent*, October 2, 1946, reports that all financial records as well as the names of some "stockholders" in the gambling ship Lux have been subpoenaed and will be delivered to a grand jury who will decide whether or not Tony failed to meet the requirements of his license when he anchored his gambling ship off shore from Long Beach.

All of this attention on Admiral Tony and his gambling ship has ramifications across the Long Beach Area and Los Angeles County. The *Long Beach Independent*, September 1, 1946, reports:

Nonexistent' Gambling

Shuts Down Here

Bookmakers, card rooms and all other forms of gambling have been shut down tight in Long Beach and the surrounding section of the county since last Thursday.

Police conducted a close search for a half dozen slot machines, the only things reported still operating, but met with little success for the machines have been running for a few days in various restaurants, garages and other places of business and then disappearing.

The shutdown in town was so tight that one place, whose owners always have enjoyed immunity from arrest, closed down two poker tables and a pangini game.

Tills took away an estimated profit of at least $250 a day from one operator. Those who shut down reported only that "orders came down for us to shut down tight—so we have."

Horse players, who have been placing their bets with local bookies or bookies located nearby in Los Angeles County, either were telephoning their bets to bookmakers in Seal Beach or other sections of Orange County or being forced to bank or buy groceries with their pay checks.

How long the shutdown would be enforced was problematical. The local and county enforcement officials always have maintained that gambling has not existed within their jurisdiction.

Therefore, since gambling never existed, they could not tell how long the gambling, which never existed, would be closed.

However, the places in which gambling has been conducted, in the city and county, and the persons who conducted the gambling, still are here. The buildings haven't been rented, and the professional gamblers haven't left the city.

So, it is assumed by one and all who are interested, that the gambling games soon will be operating again. Both in the city and the county.

The *Long Beach Independent,* November 24, 1946, runs an update: Admiral Tony Cornero has one move left to save his million-dollar gambling ship from Federal agents. He must, within five days, "establish sufficient grounds to file an appeal." According to Tony's own statement, the barge "made a neat profit of $173,000 in the first three days of operation." Judge O'Connor has already ruled that seizure of the gambling boat is legal and "should be forfeited to the federal government because it lacked motive power, and it was, in fact, a gambling barge rather than a coastwise trading vessel." O'Connor also ruled that no law was violated in painting the name Lux on the boat because the hull and boat number still displayed the legal name, Bunker Hill. "Not settled by the judge was who owns the $40,000 in silver dollars which was seized when the boat was taken and is now claimed by Cornero as his personal property." Also, the federal grand jury investigation into "Cornero's methods of financing and equipping the barge for gambling" has not been settled.

Late in 1946, Long Beach and the surrounding Los Angeles County could be tough and treacherous places. In January 1947, the brutal and much publicized murder of Elizabeth Short, who became known as the Black Dahlia occurs. She and her murder become famous as a symbol of the newly crime-ridden Los Angeles at its worst, a dangerous place, especially for women. The Los Angeles Times reports that customers at a drug store in Long Beach dub Elizabeth Short the "Black Dahlia" as a joke in reference to the film noir murder mystery, The Blue Dahlia, which was released 9 months prior to her murder. Some joke.

Two newspapers advertisements appearing in 1952 in the *Long Beach Independent* Press-Telegram give me the creeps. The first appears on August 24, 1952, the other on December 14, 1952. The text of both ads reads the same: "It may sound like 'old stuff' to you—'take it easy; speed kills.' But don't let your . . . weekend be the death of you and your family. Start for your destination early; slow down after dark. Make sure your brakes, headlights and windshield wipers are in good working condition. Be careful about passing. Use your hand signals. Above all stay on your guard every minute you're behind the wheel." The ads are sponsored by the Long Beach Insurance Agents, including George W. Cadwallader.

A further search reveals that I am making much ado about nothing. The "Bring 'Em Back Alive" admonition appears word for word in the *Corsicana Daily Sun* of Corsicana, Texas on January 31, 1952, and again in *The Mercury* of Pottstown, Pennsylvania on May 12, 1952. Both of these versions are accompanied with a gruesome photo of a male victim behind the wheel of a smashed-up car. The photo may be the reason the campaign was not widely adopted.

🪶

Momma and Woody have high hopes for their life together. My breath catches a bit when I see their names side by side, echoing my birth name. The Salt Lake City based *Deseret News* on April 30, 1950, headlines "Highway Inn Reopening Is Announced." A brief article follows:

MT. PLEASANT The San Pitch Inn, located on the Fairview-Mt. Pleasant Highway and formerly operated by Hershel Jensen, has been reopened by Don and LaRue Stevenson. Plans are under way for expanding equipment so that chicken and steak dinners can be served, Mr. Stevenson said. Plans also call for a summer garden in the front-yard for out-of-door dining in the summer and the installation of a children's playground. Stevenson is a native of

St. Louis, Mo. Mrs. Stevenson is the former LaRue
Yardley of Gunnison.

I have an old business envelope with a return
address that reflects the dream of Momma and
Woody:

> The San Pitch Inn
> Sportsmen's Headquarters
> P. O. Box 476
> Mt. Pleasant, Utah

San Pitch, the name of a Ute Chief, is used on the mountains north of Gunnison, the mostly dry river that originates
in those mountains that passes through Gunnison, and on
an aspiring roadside café at the west side of U.S. Highway
91. Chief San Pitch is the origin for Sanpete County. Maybe
the business plan for the San Pitch Inn has not solidified—
family dinners, sportsmen's headquarters. Perhaps in those
days they work together. I am just 6 months old. Woody
and my brother Russ will put up the back-braided swings.
Momma says Woody is a good cook. They customize the
sauce on the hamburgers: Miracle Whip diluted with a bit
of condensed milk. But we have Russ's recollection that
the roadside café was more of a honky-tonk, and Momma
sings, with a lilt and a laugh, "Hey Good Lookin'" for all of
her life. She obviously loves it.

≈

Cousin Joan, the mainstay for genealogical research for
our family, is a super sleuth with uncanny internet skills,
at least for our generation. She can find out anything. Joan
helps all of us unite. Before I send her copies of the names

and addresses in Woody's little brown notebook, Joan finds a very brief newspaper article about the "car wreck that killed my dad," which is how I have thought about the event for most of my life. I maintain naivete and a tone of victimization in that wording. My whole life, I think Woody falls asleep and has a head-on with a lumber truck. Now I am astounded to learn that it is a three-car crash. The June 27, 1952, issue of the *Mt. Pleasant Pyramid* reports, "Don Stevenson, 34, proprietor of the [San Pitch] Inn north of Mt. Pleasant, and the father of four small children, met death in a three-automobile pile-up on Highway 89 . . . " However, in twelve different news reports of the accident, there are three differing versions of how the three-car pile-up occurred. The variations follow:

The *Mt. Pleasant Pyramid*, June 27, 1952: Officers who investigated said the collision occurred when a southbound car operated by Mr. Stevenson came over a rise on the highway and struck an auto head-on driven by Mr. Percy Hemming, 60, of Boulder, CO. Another car driven by Mr. Raymond Rish, 34, Joliette, IL, and with his wife and two children as passengers was involved in the smashup, but escaped injury. . . . Mr. Stevenson was returning home from Clear Creek, where he had put in a long shift for a drilling company. It is presumed he fell asleep at the time of the accident.

The *Ogden Standard Examiner*, June 23, 1952: Trooper Thomas Barrett said cars driven by Stevenson and Hemming collided head-on when Stevenson pulled out to pass the Rish car.

The *Salt Lake Tribune*, June 23, 1952, provides a bit more detail: Officers said the collision occurred when a southbound car operated by Mr. Stevenson, travelling in the wrong lane, came over a rise in the highway and struck an auto driven by Mr. Hemming head-on. Mr. Hemming attempted to turn to the right to avoid the collision.

The *Provo Daily Herald*, June 23, 1952, introduces a bit of conflict: Investigating officers said witnesses told them Stevenson's' car crossed the center line without apparent reason and crashed into the opposite-bound Hemming machine. They believed Stevenson dozed at the wheel. The crash occurred a few miles from Birdseye on U.S. 189 between here and Sanpete County. Both Stevenson and Hemmings were alone in their cars . . . A family in a third car that rammed the Hemmings machine all escaped injury. Driver was Raymond F. Rish, 34, of Joliet, Ill, who was accompanied by his wife and two children. State Troopers Thomas Barrett and LaMar Horrocks investigated.

The *Salt Lake Tribune*, June 25, 1952, confirms: State Troopers Thomas Barrett and Lamar Horrocks said the Hemmings and the Stevenson car collided head-on. The Hemmings machine was also struck from the rear by a car driven by Raymond F. Rish, 34, Jolliet Ill. No one else was hurt in the pileup.

The *Provo Daily Herald* June 24, 1952, mentions: Don M. Stevenson, 30, of Mt. Pleasant driver of the car into which Hemming's car crashed, died instantly. Then a third car ploughed into the wreckage.

Salt Lake Telegram, June 24, 1952, noted as (Special) reiterates: The Hemmings machine was struck from the rear by a car driven by Raymond Rish, 34, Joliet, Ill. No one else was hurt.

So, to state the obvious, the Joliet car cannot have been travelling south and was passed by Woody and then also travelling north and rammed the Hemmings' auto. This is not Schrodinger's cat. Unless the Joliet auto, having forced the Stevenson auto into the Hemmings auto, then passes the initial impact, turns around and rams the Hemmings auto from the rear to make sure both drivers are dead. Judy, Joan, and I wonder if Woody were driven out of his lane by the car from Illinois, perhaps retaliation from Uncle Blackie and his cronies. Perhaps something did happen on the gambling ship. But we are thrown off that theory by the passengers in that third car, the wife and two children. Nevertheless, three different accounts of the accident seem highly suspect.

Our suspicions are amplified by a conversation I have with my Momma and a subsequent conversation with Jackie, the psychic massage therapist. Sometime during fall of 2010, before Momma dies, we are walking the halls at Apple Tree. She is talking about Woody when she tells me, "You know I told him to wait until morning to come home, to not drive after the long day of work, but he set out anyway. And then, when I went to his cabin after your father died to clean out his things, I found all of those documents laid out like he wanted to be sure I found everything. I worried that maybe he had committed suicide because we were so poor, and there was that insurance money." The documents she refers to are the two Social Security cards, the CA driver's license, and the little notebooks, one black, one brown.

Some weeks later I stop by Jackie's office at the end of the day. Because she is my psychic connection, I want her to determine whether or not Robert is the guy my dad was talking about when she confirmed my suspicions about Herbert. I ask Jackie,

"So, the guy you saw 'out there for me' is his name Robert?"

"You know that's not how I work," she responds. I am deflated.

"But I will tell you the guy you are looking for has your dad's smile," she reassures me.

I pause for a moment to consider that smile, then I start, "Oh, did I tell you that my mom was afraid my dad committed . . ."

"Shush," she tells me. "He says to tell you shush." And then she says, "I have never had one of them tell me 'shush.'"

⟜

When Luna and are driving to St. George, the time we nearly run out of gas and I tell her Woody is the God of Cars, I also tell her that I think the mob has Woody killed.

Luna reports that Woody acknowledges, "I am the God of Cars." Then Woody tells her, "No, it was my time. It was just my time."

But then there was the $50,000 life insurance policy, so he must have worried about something.

⟜

In the spring and summer, before our family reunion in St. Louis, I submit to the National Archives two FOIA requests for information on Woody, Blackie, and Buster Wortman. I come up with nothing. During those months Joan tracks down one of the names in the little brown notebook with Woody's addresses. The man is a former Navy pilot who was stationed in San Francisco. We speak with his son who tells us his father remembers those flying days, those adventures, like they were yesterday, but his current memory is not sharp. I send the son photos of Woody. He shows them to his father. We speak on the phone. His dad has no recollection of that face. I contact the Long Beach Historical Society. They have nothing I do not already know. The Federal Witness Protection program did not start until 1970. California had an early protection program, but when I contact the California Witness Relocation and Assistance Program, I find they have no access to historical documents. When my aunties are still alive, I take photos of Woody to the Yardley Family Reunion, neither Aunt Beth nor Aunt Althea remember that face. We pay a price for locking up our memories. In the end I have nothing.

Right or wrong, my mind goes back to my time on the Reservation in Monument Valley and the lessons I learned. I think of my friends Stanley, the Navajo healer, and his amazing wife and helpmeet, Frances, my teacher. Once again, I consider that not every question needs to be answered. We have found our family and Woody has, perhaps, come home. I have so much more than nothing.

9

UNCLE BLACKIE

Shortly after Nancy's "cousins . . . sit down and hold on" message, Joan starts sending newspaper clippings about Uncle Blackie. The first one she sends is from the *Joplin Globe*, Dec. 4, 1954: The headline blares EX-CONVICT SHOT TO DEATH BY WIFE, declaring in the first sentence that Blackie's wife, Catherine, is charged with murder—contrary to Nancy's Hold on To Your Seats message. Blackie is described as an ex-con with more than 240 arrests who serves 6 years in the Missouri Prison. Officers report Catherine shoots Blackie after they quarreled and he beat her. Catherine says, "I went to our bedroom, got his revolver out of a dresser and started back to the kitchen. We met at opposite ends of the hallway. I pointed the revolver and pulled the trigger." The story concludes with details about Blackie's involvement with the Steamfitters and the AFL Teamsters Unions.

The scene, as described above, reads like the script of a gangster movie. It is the script of a gangster movie. Among us—Judy, Joan, Nancy, and me—only Nancy ever saw Rolla. Even Joan's mother never met her Uncle Blackie. And here he is bigger than life.

How will we figure out the story of my uncle Blackie, who we will soon learn is a hitman, and my father Woody, the Boy Scout? And contrary to Marion's letter, their father, Grandpa Harry, also likely mob-involved, is still around, at least at the time of Grandma Bertha's death. We have far fewer details of Uncle Blackie's growing up years, but with his arrest record, which is actually in excess of 240 times, a number reported years in advance of his death, newspapers of the day document much of his life.

We know from the 1910 U.S. Census that Harry Dean and Bertha Snyder Dean are living in St. Louis with Nellie (who eventually drops Nell, preferring to be known as Margaret), Ethel, Rolla, and Sarah. By the 1920 U.S. Census, Harry and Bertha have a change of address, but are still living in St. Louis with all of their surviving children: (Nell) Margaret, Ethel, Rolla, Sarah, Mary Jane, and Woody. Rolla is age 13 and Woody is two and a half. Within the decade, Harry will have disappeared from the family; Rolla will be working his way toward prison; and Bertha will be dead. Truth be told, family stories have it that Harry is not around all that much even as the family grows, generally appearing to father yet another child. During Woody's childhood, Bertha, when employed outside of her home, often works as a cook for two wealthy families in St. Louis. And, although Marion claims in her letter that Grandpa Harry was "gone" by the time Bertha dies, Marion tells my cousin Joan, her daughter, that once a stranger with dark hair and startling blue eyes shows up at her teller window at the bank. Without a word he tosses a passbook at her, finishes his business, and then stands at the wall across the lobby and stares at her. Joan cannot confirm, but she suspects the passbook had the name of Harry Dean. So, Woody gets his dark Auburn hair from Grandma Bertha, and likely Uncle Blackie gets his dark hair from Grandpa Harry.

We already know that Blackie serves 6 years in the Missouri penitentiary, is arrested more than 240 times in his life, and dies a few months short of his 50th birthday. Blackie's first arrest is at age 16. So, on average, he is arrested nine or ten times per year for most of his life, other than the nearly 7 years in prison. And that prison stint happened early in his hoodlum career.

We get our first real glimpse of Uncle Blackie in action in the *St. Louis Post-Dispatch* on Sept 20, 1926, which reports, in details both thrilling and alarming, a story guaranteed to sell newspapers. The headline reads: BYSTANDER KILLED IN FIGHT OF POLICE WITH HOLDUP MEN. Two officers on patrol happen on a small crowd clustered on the street. A Black teenage boy tells them a robbery is in progress at the ice cream store. The officers turn into the alley and face a coupe speeding toward them, "Three men inside and one hanging on the running board." Just when they think there will be a mash-up, the coupe turns down a side alley with the man on the running board firing five shots; the officer returns three. Then both cars are out onto St. Louis streets about 5:00 p.m. on a Saturday evening, careening through traffic with another broad turn that brings them up on the curb near a pool hall. The man on the running board fires another five or six shots, a bullet from the bandits strikes a 16-year-old Black youth standing near the doorway of the pool hall. The police gain on the vehicle and the officer with the gun, who holds his fire in traffic, reports they are close enough that he "recognized the man on the running board as Duncan, and I saw Dean inside turning to look back." A few more reckless maneuvers and the stolen car driven by the robbers wrecks into an oncoming car and the police vehicle sideswipes a "touring car loaded with [a Black family]," including a 12-year-old who is seriously injured. The chase continues on foot. Officer Tabb captures Blackie. Officer Gahn pursues Duncan into the arms of two other officers who have arrived to assist. And two more officers capture Arger Michaelo. One of the robbers gets away.

The officers take Dean and Duncan back to the Grafeman-McIntosh Ice Cream Company, where they are positively identified as two of the robbers. They find a sawed off-shotgun and two revolvers in the stolen and wrecked coupe. Although both Duncan and Dean are positively identified, neither will answer questions. Surprisingly, or not, Blackie is out on $10,000 bail for four previous charges. The judge "sets aside bonds of $5500 each" which would have both Blackie and Duncan at liberty, again. The next day the fourth of the young robbers is arrested at the courthouse, where he has appeared on another charge.

The 16-year-old, Sanford Brown, dies immediately by a single bullet to the chest near his heart. The other young man, James Robertson, age 12, suffers a skull fracture. The robbery netted $120.00 from a delivery driver and some cash from the drawer.

This news article starts in the inside column on page three, so not a lead story, of the *St. Louis Post-Dispatch*. It has no by-line. We do not know who provides the skillful detail of the gun chase or notes the two tragedies involving the Black adolescents. We do know that one of the lead reporters at the *St. Louis Post-Dispatch* was Paul Y. Anderson who started at the paper in 1914. His stories were published by the *Post-Dispatch* for the next 23 years. Subsequent to his reporting on the 1917 Race Riots in East St.

Louis, Anderson testifies for a U.S. Congressional Committee, earning him national recognition and high praise from the Committee who note that Anderson "reported what he saw without fear of consequences, defied the indignant officials who he charged with criminal neglect of duty; ran the daily risk of assassination, and rendered invaluable public service by his exposures." In 1923 Anderson initiates a national campaign to free political prisoners jailed in the U.S. during WW I. "Anderson led the field work. When he was through firing, the political prisoners were out of jail, and the first national crusade of the *Post-Dispatch* had become a triumph." In 1925, Anderson covers the Scopes Monkey Trial in Tennessee. Then his early work on the Tea Pot Dome scandal in the *Post-Dispatch* leads to the eventual jailing of oil magnate Harry Sinclair and Secretary of the Interior Albert Fall. Anderson's effort to reopen the Tea Pot Dome investigation earns him the Pulitzer Prize in 1929. Toward the end of Anderson's career, Heywood Broun, founder of the American Newspaper Guild, said of Paul Y. Anderson, "Taken in his entirety, he stands up as a man deserving of love and homage from every working newspaperman and woman in the United States." So, whether or not Anderson writes about the activities of Uncle Blackie, he contributes to a reputation for high-quality journalism at the *Post-Dispatch*.

Cousin Joan provides an earlier news article from the *Post-Dispatch* that sets the stage for Blackie's decades-long running battle with law enforcement in the St. Louis area. The article, dated March 19, 1926—my Momma has just turned 3—tells of a court appearance during which Joseph McDowell, age 20, alleges officers beat him to force a confession. He provides x-rays of his fractured jaw as proof.

McDowell, Blackie Dean, age 18, and James Duncan, age 23, have been arrested together as robbery suspects. The judge declares, "This is not the first time a man has convinced me that police have mistreated him, and if the statements can be proven, I personally will provide the money to prosecute the guilty persons. There is no earthly reason why a man should be mistreated by police." Neither Dean nor Duncan testify at the hearing.

So, by late adolescence, Blackie, only 18 or 19, is a known associate of several men on the wrong side of the law. Police officers easily recognize him. By the time he robs the Ice Cream company, he is already out of jail on a $10,000 bond for four other robberies. When presented with yet another bail request, the judge finally keeps Blackie locked up. This money could not have come from his family—at least his mother, a mostly single mom who works off and on as a cook. So even though he is still a teen, Blackie is important enough, or valued enough, that someone backs him with big chunks of bail money. Attempting to give Blackie some redemption, I ask Joan if he turns to a life of crime to support his mother and younger siblings—not likely. He is not even living at home at the time. And then there is poor James Duncan who claims, regarding a prior robbery at the printing company, he was forced to drive four youthful robbers from the scene where two policemen were murdered. And yet, Duncan was himself heavily involved in the ice cream robbery. If you are going to be a liar, Jimmy Duncan, be a good one.

🖋

Uncle Blackie goes to the Missouri Penitentiary for the robbery at the Ice Cream Company. We see no other news about him until August 5, 1934, when the *Post-Dispatch* story headlines: WARRANT AGAINST MAN CAUGHT IN AUTO CHASE, and a leader, "'Blackie' Dean Accused of Driving Car with Altered License Plates." The car chase runs 5 miles and ends when Blackie crashes into a pole. A second man jumps out and runs, the police shooting at the escapee. The license plates on the car when they stop it have been altered by cutting and soldering together two sets of plates. A set of genuine plates, issued to Dean, are also found in the car. This article reports that "'Blackie' Dean serves 10 years in the Missouri Penitentiary for high-way robbery and was released in 1932." The Ice Cream Robbery occurred in 1926. Prison records show that Blackie was received at the Missouri Penitentiary January 28, 1927 and was discharged on June 4, 1932. He serves less than 6 years, max, but is given credit for time served as he waits in jail. And contrary to the article, his sentence was for 7 years, of which he served more than 6. Nevertheless, multiple future reports will state that he was sentenced for 10 years.

An article in the *Post-Dispatch* on September 1, 1936, provides some follow up on Blackie's time served and his subsequent status in relation to the law: This time Blackie is the victim, or at least, suffers the most. The article opens with, "Rolla ("Blackie") Dean, a former convict frequently questioned by police in their investigation of numerous bombings in the city was shot and wounded seriously before nine o'clock last night in a hall of the University Apartments." The shooter, John E. Shipp, former convict and stepfather of Blackie's current love interest recounts that Blackie had beaten him the night before over his "alleged lack of interest" in his stepdaughter, Mrs. Bernice Douglas and her 16-year-old daughter, who live in the Shipp apartment. Shipp, also an ex-con, tells police, "He beat me and threatened me Sunday night. When I saw him in the hall, I was afraid. I took out my revolver and fired one shot at him." Bernice describes the altercation of Sunday night as a "family quarrel." She accompanies Blackie to the hospital, telling police that when Blackie recovers, she plans to marry him. His wound is serious, the bullet cannot be removed without a blood transfusion.

The article also reports that Governor Park restores Blackie's citizenship on March 29, 1935, subsequent to his prison sentence. The article goes on to name all 30 of the signers and their affiliations. The list takes up two long paragraphs, and among other names we find at the top Robert E. Hannegan, Chairman of the Democratic City Committee, who later serves as the U.S. Commissioner of Internal Revenue from October 1943 to January 1944. Hannegan also serves as chairman of the Democratic National Committee from 1944 to 1947 and United States Postmaster General from 1945 to 1947. Further down the list is Deputy Constable Thomas Callanan, who, as luck would have it, is the younger brother of Larry Callanan, who will in time be identified as Uncle Blackie's real boss. Eventually the two brothers will partner in a prosecutable crime. These revelations on the signers look like the work of Paul Y. Anderson—at least it is his style. We are interested to know the motivations of the signers of Blackie's petition for restoration of citizenship. No answers are forthcoming.

Near the end of the article the reporter reveals:

Dean has been picked up more 100 times for investigation and a year ago was one of three men shown to newspaper reporters at police headquarters by

Maj. Albert Bond Lambert, Vice-President of Police Commissioners, as "the men responsible for most of the bombings in St. Louis." Dean, however, was never convicted on such charges.

Just to sum up here, Blackie is out of prison in June 1932. This is now September 1936 and a year ago Blackie had been picked up more than 100 times—in three years—so every ten days. By comparison, the back half of Blackie's career is much slower. The reporter notes that Blackie is never convicted on such charges, but he or she does not ask how Uncle Blackie gets away with this? The backing of thirty St. Louisans with some power and position may imbue him with more impunity than being twenty.

Alfred Bond Lambert in this article is also the head of household for whom Grandma Bertha is employed as a cook. She and Mrs. Lambert, Myrtle, become fast enough friends that Joan's Grandma, my aunt Margaret, reports that Myrtle Lambert often visits Bertha at her home adjacent to Margaret's, arriving in her chauffeured limousine. We wonder if Major Alfred Lambert, as President of the Police Commissioners, recognizes Blackie, the well-known bomber, as the son of Bertha Dean, the family cook? Uncle Blackie has been in the Missouri Penn for nearly 2 years when Grandma Bertha dies in December of 1928, the same year Lambert sells Lambert Fields, which will become St. Louis-Lambert International Airport, back to the City of St. Louis. Whether or not Major Alfred Bond Lambert recognizes Blackie as the son of the family cook some 7 years after her death likely depends on whether the Major and Mrs. Lambert were the kind of married couple who talk about everything or the kind of married couple who talk about nothing.

Nota Bene: Interesting, the son of Maj. Lambert and Myrtle is frequently identified as Don L. Lambert. His full name is Donaldson Liscombe Lambert. We always wonder how Woody comes up with his alias.

⚓

Bernice, true to her word, marries Blackie, who was likely right about the "disinterested attitude" of her mother. Evidence of the lack of interest can be seen when Bernice's mother Daisy gave permission for Bernice Pauline to marry at age 15. A year later, Bernice gives birth to a daughter whom she names Daisy Eileen, after Grandma Daisy, and who now appears in this story of the hallway shooting as a 16-year-old. Being shot in the hallway foreshadows Blackie's eventual end. The "Convict Shot" article includes a photo of Bernice who looks surprisingly similar to Ox's first wife, exceptionally pretty, her face innocent and open, wide-eyes, pretty mouth.

Prior to his involvement with Bernice, prior to his prison sentence, Blackie marries Ethel Volmar. He is 20 years old, but lies on his marriage license application, stating that he is 23 years old—he has to be 21 to marry in Missouri. For whatever reasons, Ethel, age 22 at the time of their marriage, remains married to Blackie throughout his prison sentence, and then public notices of the *St. Louis Post-Dispatch* on January 17, 1936, under Divorces Granted, list "Rolla from Ethel Dean." So, three and a half years after prison, Blackie leaves Ethel again. And he is free for Bernice in September of that same year.

Blackie does not stay out of the newspaper for long. An October 19, 1936, short news story on page 22 of the *St. Louis Star and Times* begins: DYNAMITE TRAIL

POINTS TOWARD 'BLACKIE' DEAN and the leader, "Purchaser tells police explosives were bought and hidden for former convict." The story reports that Blackie has been questioned in several recent bombings. As part of those investigations, police recover eight sticks of dynamite and 125 percussion caps. And Blackie has another nickname, "Blackie the Dynamite Man." He also establishes a pattern with the police that looks something like catch and release.

By 1937 Blackie becomes part of a larger story. The *St. Louis Post-Dispatch*, July 15, 1937, runs a half-page article on page six. The headline and lead read: "SIX QUESTIONED ON RACKETS AND MURDER OF DUNN. Police try to link killing of gambling hall bouncer with his activities in union circles."

Another lead over the three columns on the right declares, "Questioned About Labor Racketeering," followed by six photos of apparently known hoodlums, including "Bab" Moran, Sylvester Baldwin, Joseph Costello, Lyle Shaw, Harvey Beavers, and the last photo on the lower row, Rolla (Blackie) Dean. He is an attractive man, not as handsome as my father, his brother, Woody, but this may be a mugshot—no one looks good in that light. Rolla has a head full of thick, dark hair. I am guessing it is black. According to the *Rolla [MO] Daily Mail*, July 29, 2015, the early settlers of Rolla, MO., "selected 'Rolla' for the name, which as the story goes, was a worthless hunting dog." I doubt Grandma Bertha, or was it Grandpa Harry, knew this brief history when it came to naming their son, but the origin does not bode well.

Of the men in the photos, the July 1937 article tells us that all are questioned in the death of "Pudgie" Dunn, a twice-convicted murderer and husky bouncer at the largest gaming establishment in East St. Louis. Dunn is gunned down at 3:50 in the morning by a shotgun blast as he returns to the front door of his apartment building. The article states, "All of the prisoners denied knowledge of the murder and declared they could throw no light on the case. Mrs. [Lucille] Dunn, who was also required to testify, 'became hysterical before the hearing and was a nervous witness.'" Probably Lucille was scared witless at being in the same hearing with six hoodlums, at least one of whom likely pulled the trigger on her husband. Mrs. Dunn claims in the days preceding his death, she hears nothing from her husband about potential threats. She states that upon hearing the gun blast, she goes to the entrance of the apartment building and finds her husband lying in a pool of his own blood. Dunn arrives at the hospital barely alive. He does not identify his killer, neither to his wife nor to the attending officers. Another resident of the apartment building, who also hears the gun blast, reports the sound of someone fleeing down the alley.

The murder investigation is part of a broader investigation of the infiltration of local unions by known mobsters. The specific allegations against the six men are listed including:

> Harvey Beavers and Rolla (Blackie) Dean, former convicts, who police said tried to get jobs with the Gasoline Workers' Union.
> The investigators, who began with the theory that "muscle" methods in a labor racket were responsible for the murder, were inclined to minimize the labor angle, although continuing their investigation

along that line. Also, they were delving into Dunn's activities in gambling circles on the East Side and were not overlooking revenge as a possible motive.

The article concludes that the inquest yields no useful information for the investigation. Other interesting facts are mentioned. "[The] Ringside" establishment at 313 Missouri avenue, half a block from the East St. Louis police station, was bombed last March. Subsequently a Venice gambling place was bombed, with indication of a reprisal. There has been no further trouble and persons familiar with the situation asserted that a truce had been arranged." Publicity around the efforts of gangsters and ex-convicts trying to muscle into the unions for bartenders, waiters, and miscellaneous hotel workers has spurred the unions to clean house and expel some of the above-named men from their ranks. The bomb blasts and Blackie "The Dynamite Man" mentioned in the same article is concerning, an observation not made by the reporter here. At least as concerning is the exercise of mob muscle on a union for the miscellaneous hotel workers, 3,000 strong, primarily Black workers, trying to find some strength through unity, also not mentioned specifically in the article.

The mobs infiltrating the local unions get the attention of the editorial staff at the *Post-Dispatch*. An opinion piece, again with no byline, in the *St. Louis Post Dispatch* the next day, July 16, 1937, emphasizes the need to clean up and clean out labor unions. The piece, titled DOWN WITH THE LABOR RACKETEER! declares that "Labor unions, like Caesar's wife, must be above suspicion. When they begin admitting known criminals to their ranks and into union offices, they damage the whole labor movement.

With gangsters in executive and organizing position, gangster methods come into use." The opinion article cites the
investigation of the murder of John J. (Pudgie) Dunn as
ample evidence of the need for a clean-up. The piece also
lists all of the usual suspects identified by the photos in the
news article the day before, including Blackie, along with
their union and non-union violations, noting that Pudgie
Dunn himself has union cards in his pockets at the time of
his death. The article declares that "rooting out the gangsters and keeping them out will mean the virtual end of
bombing, window-smashing and assaults in labor disputes."

Before the year is out, a lesser, but equally damning
charge and consequence appears in a minor article in the
St. Louis Post Dispatch on December 30, 1937: A charge of
vagrancy against Rolla (Blackie) Dean was dismissed yesterday . . . at Bellville, after Dean promised to leave St. Clair
County and remain away for at least a year." Belleville, IL,
and St. Clair County are just across the Mississippi River
from St. Louis. Blackie has become persona non grata in
his own community. Well-known and not welcome. Maybe
he will make a New Year's Resolution, but probably not.

Nearly a year passes and then on November 21, 1938,
a long article in the *St. Louis Post Dispatch* headlined:
"BAKER FAILS TO IDENTIFY EX-CON" discusses an
investigation of attempted murder of Lee Baker, a Black
man and a witness in a bombing charge, who was in pro-
tective custody when three men find his hiding place, pull
him into an auto, then try to murder him. Much discussion
is devoted to uncovering by whom and by what means the
secure location of Mr. Lee is revealed. Several of Blackie's
known associates, including Bab Moran, are arrested for
questioning. According to the story "Also arrested today

was Rolla (Blackie) Dean, bomber and former convict. Dean, hobbling on crutches and bedridden much of the time in recent months, was released almost immediately." Neither Joan nor I can find any additional information on the nature nor the reality of Blackie's incapacitation. It may be: if you live by the sword, you die by the sword. Or if you are going to be a liar, be a good one. I suspect that Blackie's injuries were legit and most of those involved, on both sides of the law, had some idea of the origin.

A related article on the same page in the November 21, 1938, *Post-Dispatch* declares: STARK DECLARES WAR ON ORGANIZED CRIME IN MISSOURI. Stark's big question, featured in one of the leads, "Many criminals are known but seemingly can't be convicted. Why?" The article details the heads of several agencies whom Stark will enlist "to make war on all of this, a war of extermination on known murderers, gunmen, gangsters and all their combinations and machinations."

Governor Stark serves only one term from 1937 to 1941. Stark's family owns Stark Nursery, the oldest nursery in America and, at one time, the largest nursery in the world. Stark himself graduates from the Naval Academy and serves in WWI, so, he has the makings of a good leader, but may, in the end, fall short of the mark.

*

Stark's declaration in 1938 to "exterminate murderers and gangsters and all their combinations," echoes through the Mormon sound chamber that still exists inside my brain. Mormons originally settled in Jackson County, MO, believing it to be the location of the Garden of Eden and the site on which the Second Coming of Jesus Christ will occur.

The Mormons are driven from Jackson County, but "given their own county [Caldwell]" in 1833. However, increasing numbers of Mormon converts from the United Kingdom and the eastern U.S. led to the expansion of the Mormon settlers into surrounding counties. One huge issue for the Missourians is the increased number of Mormon voters and their influence on local and state elections. In response to increasing harassment, and often violence against the Mormon settlers, a speech by Sidney Rigdon, well-recognized mouthpiece of the Mormon Prophet Joseph Smith, does nothing to calm the waters. In his speech in the public square at Far West, MO, on July 4, 1838, Rigdon declares:

> We take God and all the holy angels to witness this day, that we warn all men in the name of Jesus Christ, to come on us no more forever. For from this hour, we will bear it no more, our rights shall no more be trampled on with impunity. The man or the set of men, who attempts it, does it at the expense of their lives. And that mob that comes on us to disturb us; it shall be between us and them a war of extermination; for we will follow them till the last drop of their blood is spilled, or else they will have to exterminate us: for we will carry the seat of war to their own houses, and their own families, and one party or the other shall be utterly destroyed.—Remember it then all MEN.

By fall of 1838 tensions between the Missourians and the Mormon Saints has reached a climax. On October 27, 1838, Governor Lilburn Boggs sends a dispatch to General John B. Clark of the state militia advising that he has received information of the most appalling character, which entirely changes the face of things, and places the Mormons in the attitude of an open and avowed defiance of the laws, and of having made war upon the people of this state. Your orders are, therefore, to hasten your operation with all possible speed. The Mormons must be treated as enemies, and must be exterminated or driven from the state if necessary, for the public peace—their outrages are beyond all description.

The Mormon War follows the Boggs Extermination Order, Executive Order No. 44, leading many Mormons to declare themselves the most persecuted people on the face of the earth. By the end of 1838, the Mormons are driven from Missouri, and settle across the river in a swampy area that becomes known as Nauvoo, IL. We'll see how Governor Stark fares in his war of extermination against the gangsters in Missouri.

🍃

On December 13, 1939, a year after Stark's extermination declaration, a letter to the editor of the *St. Louis Post-Dispatch*, notes that a previous letter, "goes a little too far in giving the Governor the credit for eliminating Pendergastism [in Kansas City]." The Dec. 1939 letter further notes that "while Gov. Stark must have known how corrupt that [Kansas City] ring was, he used this as a steppingstone for higher honors." Thanks to Pendergast, Kansas City is also known as the Crime Center of the Midwest. And perhaps an easier target for Stark's extermination orders.

"Forget Paris"

An article in the *Omaha World-Herald* begins, "If you want to see some sin, forget about Paris and go to Kansas City." During the 1920s, when this statement earns Kansas City the epithet "the Paris of the Plains," it was the most rebellious spot in the United States. Prohibition runs from January 1920 to December 1933. In Kansas City, Tom Pendergast, more commonly known as T.J. or Boss Pendergast and his corrupt police force known as the Pendergast Machine, run the city from the mid-1920s through late 1939. During that time "alcohol flowed freely and not a single citizen was convicted of manufacturing, transporting, selling or possessing booze during the 13-year period when alcohol was banned nationwide . . . At the height of Kansas City's heyday in the 1930s, there were more than 100 jazz clubs hosting performances and jam sessions that would launch the careers of musicians such as Count Basie and Charlie Parker." A quick look at Wikipedia also reveals: "Pendergast himself only briefly held elected office as an alderman, but in his capacity as Chairman of the Jackson County Democratic Party, he was able to use his large network of family and friends to help elect politicians (through voter fraud in some cases) and hand out government contracts and patronage jobs. He becomes wealthy in the process, although his addiction to gambling, especially horse racing, later leads to a large accumulation of personal debts. In 1939, he is convicted of income tax evasion and serves 15 months in a federal prison. The Pendergast organization helps launch the political career of Harry S. Truman, a fact that causes Truman's enemies to dub him 'The Senator from Pendergast.'"

On December 31, 1939, the *St. Louis Post-Dispatch* notes that, "The suit which Gov. Lloyd Stark last May directed Attorney-General McKittrick to file against United Service Car Co. of St Louis and associated interests for maximum liability estimated at $1,848,250 for alleged violations of the state insurance laws, is still pending without action." The following article incudes allegations from all parties involved against all other parties of failure to perform: investigators, McKittrick, and Stark.

On April 3, 1940, the *Post-Dispatch* reprints an editorial from the *Chicago Daily Tribune* supporting the *Post-Dispatch* in a contempt of court suit because of a comment made regarding a judge's disposition of a criminal case. The reprint states outright, "The Tribune has long admired the valiant fight of the *Post-Dispatch* against the alliance of crime and politics in St. Louis and Missouri."

Certainly, Governor Stark recognizes the challenges. Or maybe he recognizes the importance of appearing to take a stand against the kind of lawlessness described in the article of November 1938 headlined "Baker Fails to Identify Ex-Con." In said article, three associates of Lee Baker, the "[Black] Witness," state that Baker tells them if he cooperates with the St. Louis Police, they promise to hire him as a detective.

On May 19, 1940, the *Post-Dispatch* announces, "Gov. Lloyd Stark, one of the major figures in the Kansas City clean-up of crime and political corruption opened his campaign for the Democratic nomination for United States [Senator]." Stark is a fierce competitor with Harry Truman for the U.S. Senate as well as Maurice Mulligan who "contributed greatly" to the end of Pendergast.

The conflicts in the three-way race are further clarified in an editorial in the *Post-Dispatch* on July 28, 1940, which asks, "What if the race between the Governor, who led the fight on Pendergast, and former District Attorney [Mulligan], who prosecuted the unconscionable spoilsman, would open the way for Senator Truman's nomination? Are the Democrats ready for that? Are they ready to put back on their ticket the man who Boss Pendergast literally lifted into the Senate?"

The problems with the laws in Missouri regarding criminal activity are further explained in an editorial in the *Post-Dispatch* on Sept. 26, 1940, AN OVERDUE REFORM, cites two of "the worst features of the criminal code." One is mandatory severance by means of which criminal defendants, even though jointly indicted, can be separately tried. Another is a needed change in procedure that will allow a judge to grant or refuse bail to "persons convicted of a felony who have previously been convicted of a felony . . . The present bail laws are so framed as to give the professional criminal a right to freedom on bond so he can go out and commit further crime in order to pay his lawyers."

So, now we understand how it is that Blackie was out on bail for four other felonies, when he is captured following the robbery and running gun chase at the Ice Cream Company. And although Blackie is arrested literally hundreds of times, the ice cream robbery is the only offense that results in a prison sentence or significant jail time. We wonder why?

Continuing the misadventures of Uncle Blackie, a brief article on Page 4 of the *St. Louis Post-Dispatch*, January 9, 1939, describes a particularly unlucky night. The article actually only references Blackie as part of a larger group. It may mean that my uncle's presence is not the most scandalous part of the story, especially as he is referred to as

Rolla Dean, rather than Blackie. Apparently, Justice W.E. Cedarberg dies at the wheel of a heart attack when he is pressed into service to drive five St. Louis residents from his home on U.S. Highway 61 back to St. Louis. Cedarberg has Rolla Dean and two women, all intoxicated, in the back seat of his car. The arresting officer transports the other two drunk men. "Not far from Farmington, Cedarburg suffered a heart attack, and the automobile ran into a telephone pole. No one was injured." We wonder what was happening in that back seat? Just asking.

Joan and I are fairly certain that there are eventual repercussions for Blackie. We notice that Bernice is not one of the two drunk women with Blackie and Cedarberg. No doubt Bernice also notices that only Blackie rides with two drunk women in the car with Cedarberg. According to Joan, Grandmother Margaret often claims that her father, Harry Dean, was a womanizer and all-around ne'er do well. It appears that bad-apple Blackie does not fall far from that tree. By October 1940, Blackie and Bernice are divorced. Bernice eventually marries for a third time. She dies in Corpus Christi, TX, in 1997. Had I known about her during the 1980s when Ernie and the kids and I were visiting Texas, I might have been able to meet her. Who knows?

In the meantime, we see little news in the papers about Blackie. I find two articles in the *Tampa Bay Times* from March 1944 promoting a wrestling match with Blackie Dean, the "behemoth" from St. Louis. Can Blackie be pursuing another line of work? I check with Joan. According to Blackie's prison record he is 5'9" and weighs 150 pounds, so not a behemoth—more of a little scrapper. This information surprises me. Woody's California driver's license shows he is 6 feet tall and 180 pounds. I assume that Blackie was more of a big boy, part of what makes him believe he is even more invincible than a teenager or a typical twenty-something.

Later that same year, Blackie makes the newspaper with another car incident, this from the *St. Louis Post-Dispatch*, December 31, 1944, just in time for the New Year. Blackie appears at City Hospital with "severe lacerations and bruises on his head." Blackie claims he loses control of his car, runs over a curb, through a wooden fence and hits a tree. "Police thought from his appearance he had been beaten in a brawl." The article also mentions that Blackie is "employed by Lee Turner, pin ball machine distributor and associate of Ted Cronin, boss of the AFL Service Car Driver's Union." It is likely no coincidence that Blackie is connected to the AFL Service Car Driver's Union that was the alleged target of Stark's 1939 suit. People in trouble often know other people in trouble. And then we hear nothing of Blackie for nearly 2 years. It appears his activities have become less public. Or maybe they move to another locale.

~

Out West, June 22, 1952, has rolled around and the news of the death of one Don Stevenson, eventually to be recognized as Woodrow Wilson Dean, hits the newspapers and circulates in the small towns of Central Utah. The event shows on the timeline for his brother, Rolla Spencer Dean, aka Blackie the Dynamite Man. However, in the Dean family of St. Louis, in my sister Judy's life, the event is unknown and unremarked.

~

Back in St. Louis, more than 2 years pass before Blackie's name appears again in the newspaper. The March 23, 1947,

St. Louis Post-Dispatch leader declares "Judges Looking Into Appointment of Mrs. Rolla Dean," with a second line claiming "Husband Arrested 244 Times." The issue at hand is the appointment of Mrs. Rolla Dean as a deputy of Sheriff John Dougherty. Mrs. Dean is hired under the name of Mrs. Catherine Moriarity Martin, claiming she is single, but she is married to Blackie at the time. Catherine is appointed in October 1945 and remains a courtroom deputy at $165.00 per month until November 1947 when she leaves to go to the hospital following a farewell party in her honor. In the interim, Catherine gives birth to a daughter on November 23, 1946, Mary Joan Dean, who dies on December 7, 1946. Catherine declines to give the *Post-Dispatch* the date of her marriage to Blackie. The article includes a detail seemingly unrelated to the business at hand but interesting in our search of the story of Uncle Blackie, "Mrs. Dean was divorced on July 30, 1945, from William L. Martin. They had one son over whom a fight for custody is being waged." Billy is about 11 years old at this time. Sheriff Dougherty is under heavy investigation, but he and his attorney deny reports that he is resigning. Mention is also made that Dougherty faces charges in circuit court for leaving the scene of an accident when his car crashes into a taxicab, injuring the driver and the passenger. More impunity.

Emphasizing one point from the article: In the history of the St. Louis Record room from 1917 to March 1947 Blackie has 244 arrests, and this is seven and a half years prior to his impending death in December 1954. Let us redo the math here. Blackie is arrested for the first time when he is 16 years old, so 1921. He spends nearly 7 years in the Missouri Penn. So, in 23 years he is arrested 244 times, more than ten times per year, or nearly every month. The article notes that Blackie's arrest record "has seldom been equaled and never excelled in the annals of the St. Louis Police Department." This article provides just an inkling of how deeply embedded into St. Louis crime and politics that Blackie has become.

≈

No other news of Blackie emerges until November 27, 1951, the *Post-Dispatch* has a short article detailing the kind of violence Blackie dispenses: "Morris Wildman, an automobile mechanic, . . . was shot twice and seriously wounded in a tavern fight last Saturday night, [and] has identified a photograph of Rolla (Blackie) Dean, a former convict, as the likeness of his assailant." Wildman says he was shot in a dispute. He cannot or will not explain the dispute, but he says the shooter remarks, "You think you are tough, do you?" Then he draws a pistol and shoots Wildman in the abdomen and right side and flees.

≈

We wonder if Blackie ever feels the need to get out of town. We do not see him in the news for nearly another year. We keep thinking that the long arm of the law will eventually catch up with him, but Blackie seems to always slip away. And yet he is ever present. Our next sighting of the ubiquitous Blackie is November 18, 1952. According to the *Post-Dispatch* he is once again part of a bigger story. John Randazzo, a hauling contractor, is beaten, but whether by J. Vitale, restaurant owner, or with brass knuckles by a detective sergeant, is under dispute.

And, Blackie, as usual, is in the thick of it, and this trouble is not going away soon. On November 21, 1952, the *St.*

Louis Globe-Democrat runs this story on page one: "Hood-lum John Vitale refused to testify yesterday and last night before a Circuit Court grand jury." Vitale also refused to sign a waiver of immunity which would have meant "that any testimony he might have given could not be used in returning any possible indictment against him."

Two columns of the three-column story include photos of John Vitale, Louis (Red) Smith, Joseph Costello, Vernon Blair, and Rolla (Blackie) Dean. Photo credit is given to *Post-Dispatch.* The story lays out the charges and cross charges: Randazzo and cab driver Vernon Blair allege that Sgt. Dougherty administers the beating. Dougherty and his partner, Detective Mundt, deny Randazzo's allegation. And then reporter Woods introduces one additional element: Reidy, in his unauthorized investigation outside of normal police procedure, also discusses the case with Joseph Mathews, a former policeman and a political crony of Reidy. Mathews is no friend of Doherty's. Mathews has moved on and is now an investigator for the office of Prosecuting Attorney William Geekie. No conclusions are drawn, but many questions are raised, including the last line of the story, "And last, but not least, why do policemen, of whatever rank, frequent a hangout for the city's gangsters?"

Next, Blackie makes the front page. The photo, actually larger than the smaller article, relates to a more ordinary happening, dated February 19, 1953. The caption under the *St. Louis Globe-Democrat* photo reads: "Sheriff Tozer Got His Man." The sheriff was out to serve a summons which Blackie had successfully evaded for 8 months. He delivers the papers to Blackie, seated behind the wheel of his car and photographed through the windshield. The served papers identify that "Dean was named in a $7,500 damage suit filed last June . . . in an accident at Natural Bridge and Clarence avenues involving Dean's car." Police have been watching Blackie's house and notify the sheriff that they have pulled him over.

Likely no coincidence that the sheriff, the reporter, and the photographer happen to be at the same spot at the same time. One wonders what happens in the disposition of all these charges and allegations against Uncle Blackie and so many other gangsters and hoodlums. Ironically, in this photo, and most of the other photos of Blackie, he has kind of a baby-face coupled with a deer in the headlights look.

Within days another big story breaks. Page one, upper right corner, February 22, 1953, The *St. Louis Post-Dispatch* reports: LARRY CALLANAN REPORTED GETTING $125,000 A YEAR OF STEAMFITTER'S 'EXPENSE' LUG. Callanan gets half of the dollar per day assessment for each union member that creates a fund of $250,000 annually. He is not required to make an accounting.

The Callanan article clarifies several details in the life of Uncle Blackie. First, Blackie and Callanan were confined in the Missouri Penitentiary for nearly identical periods of time from 1927 to 1932. Second, contrary to Cousin Nancy's assertion that Blackie worked for Buster Wortman, this article makes it clear that Blackie is in the employ of Larry Callanan, Boss of the Steamfitters' Local 562. We also see in the article references to two previously known associates of Blackie, Babs Moran and Harry Beavers, who was also in the Missouri Penitentiary for murder at the time of the incarceration of Callanan and Blackie.

A follow-up article three days later, Feb 26, 1953, in the *Post-Dispatch*, describes Buster Wortman's connection to Callanan and Blackie: "Frank (Buster) Wortman, East side gang leader and Chicago Capone syndicate representative, carries a card in the Steamfitter's Union. Wortman has not worked at that trade since World War II when he and Callanan were employed at the same defense construction job." Wortman is not the only surprise cardholder in the Union. "The ease with which men with prison records can become union members is in decided contrast to the difficulties experienced by ordinary apprentices in attaining credentials entitling them to the $23-a-day pay of a working steamfitter." A Grand Jury calls for the investigation seeking appearances from the following:

Lawrence (Mad Dog) McBride, ex-convict, who was charged with participation in an industrial bombing in Cuba, MD.

Arthur J. Berne, convicted burglar

Raymond (Cutie) Fishell, ex-convict and former associate of the late "Dinty" Colbeck murdered gang leader.

Rolla (Blackie) Dean, ex-convict, and

Harvey Beavers, who served a term in the Missouri Penitentiary for murder.

The article goes on to name fifteen other felons and ex-convicts working for the union. And while the 20 men are pulled off jobs to delay the serving of subpoenas, Callanan himself is out of town and cannot be summoned to appear before the Grand Jury.

Not surprisingly, or maybe at long last, counter measures are taken against Callanan, Blackie and all. The March 19, 1953, *Post-Dispatch* reports that "drastic measures to rid the AFL Teamsters Union of gangsters who have infiltrated several St. Louis locals were voted last night . . . The stewards . . . authorized Harold Gibbons, secretary treasurer of the union, to call a strike at every warehouse in the city if any employer negotiates with any person other than an accredited union officer." Gangsters, who have not even bothered to obtain union cards, have used threats of force to interfere with union negotiations several times in the past 2 years, also demanding fees from employers to influence union labor agreements. The allegations get specific:

> Three St. Louis district gangsters previously identified with efforts to infiltrate the labor movement are among those who have interfered with the teamsters, the informant said. They were named as Frank (Buster) Wortman, reputed East Side agent for the Chicago Capone syndicate; Rolla (Blackie) Dean and William (Bozo) Remphry, all former convicts. Circuit Attorney Edward L. Dowd revealed recently that both Wortman and Dean also have cards in AFL Steamfitter's Union 562. Dean was questioned by police in 1937 about efforts to get into the AFL Gasoline & Service Employees Union, and both Dean and Remphry formerly were bodyguards employed by the AFL Service Car Driver's Union.

Ten days later, the March 29, 1953, *Post-Dispatch* reports a change of status for Blackie and Bozo. Both of them have been dropped from the council payroll. "The purported duties of Dean and Remphry in the council, central body of 13 Teamsters' locals, was not learned." Interestingly, the national Teamster's Union sends Jimmy Hoffa for the cleanup of the local union.

As if the Callanans were not having trouble enough, the *Post-Dispatch* on October 3, 1953, headlines, "Callanans Questioned In Murder Of Hale; Head of Steamfitters, Ex-Sheriff Deny Any Knowledge of Killing of Former Unionist." The Callanan brothers are questioned by police, as are "George Seaton, business agent for the local, and John F. Burke, secretary-treasurer." Police announce they are looking for Blackie Dean and Harry Beavers, Jr. who have been Callanan's bodyguards.

Harry Hale, who has been a director of the Pipefitter's Welfare Educational Fund and who helps set up the union financial records, "was shot down with a 12-gauge shotgun in the open doorway of the garage at the rear of his home." The assailant flees in an automobile, but a neighbor gives the police the license of the escape vehicle, which turns out to be a combination of two existing license numbers. The news article does not comment that a soldered license plate and the shotgun are two of Blackie's calling cards. The investigating authorities want to know if the murder of Hale, originally named Harry Huffendick, a three-time former convict, "is connected with the bombings last February of the Steamfitter's offices. . . and outside the home of former Sheriff Thomas V. Callanan." They are also concerned with a bomb placed outside the Steamfitters' headquarters the previous week. The bomb, fuse unlit, includes a note advising Lawrence Callanan to leave town.

Hale's wife, Alpha, sleeping on the rear porch, wakes at 12:35 a.m. when "her husband opened the garage door and turned on a light preparatory to putting his machine away." A loud blast sends her to the garage where she finds her husband seriously injured. Neighbors call the police. "Hale was still breathing when police reached the scene, but was unconscious and died on the way to City Hospital."

> Mrs. Hale said her husband went out Friday night for the first time in about two weeks; he suffered from a serious stomach ailment and spent most of his time at home. He said he was going to buy a new hat. The hat . . . was found in his automobile parked in the alley. . . . In checking Hale's movements Friday, police learned that he went into the King-del [Toggery] Shop with another man, described as being 5 feet 8 inches tall, stockily built and of Greek or Italian descent. The man bought a hat and paid for Hale's also. After leaving the store Hale visited a tavern nearby; police were informed. Detective Chief Chapman, learning of this development, commented, 'That's probably where the kiss of death was put on him.'"

Police speculate that a killer was sent to Hale's home when he is seen out and about. Hale, who was a business agent before his appointment as the original director of the welfare fund, "reportedly was ousted several years ago following a disagreement with Lawrence Callanan." He has not been able to work because of his health, so his wife went to work in a manufacturing plant. "Ill-feeling between Hale and the Callanans increased when Mrs. Hale took an active role in the political campaign against the Callanan faction last year." After the campaign, Hale says he receives a phone call informing him Callanan is out to get him. Nevertheless, Hale appears twice before the circuit court grand jury investigating the bombings aimed at Callanan. Of the threat from Callanan, Hale comments, "He isn't trying very hard, because he knows where I can be found, and hasn't shown up." Alma Hale "said she was unaware of [Hale's] criminal background until he was questioned in the bombings." The Hales have two young children.

Then, as if Blackie's life is unraveling, the November 24, 1953, *Post-Dispatch* reports that a shotgun is fired at the home of Blackie and Catherine shortly after midnight, shattering two windows. Later, at 2:30 a.m. a bar stool is hurled through the glass of the front door. The incident is not reported to the police.

Blackie and the Steamfitters' have garnered national attention. A syndicated column from Victor Riesel appears in newspapers from Pennsylvania to California. This is one of three articles I take to the Yardley Reunion the summer before meeting Woody's family in St. Louis. My nephews, the genetic researcher and the computer programmer note, "Wow, Aunt Dawn, you cannot make up stuff this good." The *Oakland Tribune* features the following on a page titled LABOR COMMENT:

Oakland Tribune, Friday, Dec. 18, 1953

Crime Syndicate Fights Back in Union Probes
By VICTOR RIESEL NEW YORK,

Dec. 18. Was I writing this one for the movies, all the major studios, pooling all their Jim Cagney's, Edward G Robinsons and George Rafts, could not cast it as it rolls in real life on the dark streets of our big cities?

The mob is fighting back. Fenced in by at least three Federal Grand Juries, one state investigation, one county probe, one congressional search and heavy pressure on goon hunts in four other states, the crime syndicate which has made some unions part of their racket, is slugging back.

On the New York waterfront, big black cars glide up to the AFL men, slug them and leave them fractured in the gutter. Nine of these men are now in the hospital.

In a recent garbage strike, a knife and blackjack squad in a fast car swooped down on other workers.

UNION AGENT SLAIN

There have been more battles, but the most significant violence came with the 12-gauge shotgun blast which sent Harry G. Hale, a former St Louis Steamfitters Union Local 562 business agent, right out of this world, along with the knowledge he had of the union's welfare fund of which he was once director.

Brother Hale departed suddenly this society while standing in the doorway of his St. Louis garage a few weeks ago. And the police for some reason began searching for an old Capone hand by the name of Rollo "Blackie" Dean who was on the local's payroll for a while with little to do but draw his check. Rollo apparently drew enough to get himself a new home. But some mean fellow blasted it full of shotgun holes shortly after Hale's death. This thing could get real rough after a while and the Federals want to take a good look at it all, including the welfare fund, which is causing such commotion.

So, two Grand Juries are being impaneled there for action this week. More, indictments safely can be predicted. At the same time the St. Louis civic leaders are trying to get the FBI and Treasury probers and accountants to go across the river into southern Illinois, where shooting is expected especially in and around the unions which control atomic energy installation labor.

CHICAGO HOT SPOT

There is more pressure on the government for an examination of Chicago and you can count on some of the House Labor Committee Congressmen to get up and shout for it immediately after Congress reconvenes unless the political pressure is too great A House Labor sub-committee, incidentally, will soon head for Minneapolis under the chairmanship of Rep. Wint Smith (R., Kan.), a man who just doesn't like to get pushed around.

Meanwhile, out Detroit way, a Wayne County labor rackets Grand Jury has been extended for six months. And the U.S. Attorney there, Fred W. Kaess, is just about ready to summon witnesses before a Federal Grand Jury in Detroit. Most of these hearings will pivot upon the vast welfare funds which bring some union officials terrifically profitable commissions from controlled agencies which, in turn, place them with the major companies. So lush a touch has this become that some of the most powerful operators in the rackets have told their people to forget the petty stuff, keep their unions clean, but get the welfare fund business.

Some of them certainly succeeded, and many an honest union chief has angrily pointed out that this is made easy because of the difficulty unions have in placing their insurance directly with the insurance companies. Apparently, they all must place their business through agents. Of course, it should be pointed out here that there are scores of clean insurance agents but there are those who aren't. They have been kicking back literally millions of dollars to those who control the unions under suspicion.

HEARINGS SLATED

Most of this will be spotlighted by special New York State investigators who will hold hearings before and after Christmas. It is reported that some of these funds have "lost" as much as 40 cents on the dollar. It should also be pointed out that AFL President George Meany, undoubtedly wearied and harassed by the exposures of a network he inherited, will continue to move although he already has spent much of the past year fighting a many-fronted war on the interlocking crowd. Some of us asked Meany the other day just what he would do. He looked squarely at us and said, "We can match their muscle with muscle and. we'll take a good look at those welfare funds as soon as anything is exposed." It's a tough fight for a man who's been president of a 10,000,000-member, outfit less than a year.

Although these details are revealed nearly 7 years after Woody disappears from Southern California, there is a potential connection to Cadwallader, Insurance, Bonds and Finance. And, to Woody.

Following only days after the national column, the *St. Louis Post-Dispatch* on December 21, 1953, on page one, summarizes much of the recent union related violence: four bombings in a year that involve labor bosses or "men associated with labor in the Democratic party here" may result from an issue about which candidate to support for governor in the 1952 state primary. The article recognizes that the racketeering investigations underway in eastern Missouri and eastern and southern Illinois have been "touched off by a series of stories in the *Post-Dispatch* in 1951, telling of shakedowns and other abuses in the labor field." The article goes on to summarize 15 recent incidents of related violence.

In any of the reported incidents, perhaps all of the incidents save shooting out his own windows, Uncle Blackie could be, likely is, a suspect—Blackie, the Dynamite Man, who has been wielding a shotgun since he was age 19. The strong potential connection is summarized in a brief article on January 5, 1954, in the *Edwardsville [Illinois] Intelligencer*: "Underworld insurrection growing out of recent bombings in this area was reported to have been connected to the murder of John (Buddy) Lugar. Police disclose that hoodlums blamed Lugar for the bombing of a St. Clair County tavern and shotgun blasts at the home of Blackie Dean. "Lugar had been shot to death on a rural road in Illinois within hours of two men inquiring about him at several bars. In summary, the article says, "Dean, sought by police both here [in Illinois] and in St. Louis, was reported to have had an interest in the bombed liquor establishment, The Sunny Hill Tavern . . . [the] next day two windows in Dean's home were shattered by shotgun pellets."

Other articles appearing near the same date, provide additional details, some trivial: Lugar was not likely a target of robbery. He was wearing two watches, a ring, a diamond stickpin and carried $173 in cash. Lugar was wearing a "dapper" blue double-breasted suit, with a white shirt and a brown hat with four bullet holes. At Lugar's apartment they find another forty equally dapper suits, twelve hats, and more than a dozen pairs of shoes. And details, not so trivial, revealed on page 3 by the *St. Louis Post-Dispatch* on January 3, 1954:

> Long known as a hoodlum, Lugar, 53 years old, had been arrested here more than 200 times. He was sentenced to 15 years in Des Moines, IA, in 1932 for possession of burglar tools in an attempt to break into the Capital City Bank. However, he was paroled after serving less than four years following intercession on his behalf by several public officials, including John W. Joynt, then a circuit judge in St. Louis and now a practicing attorney here. Another who interceded for Lugar with the Iowa parole board was John F. Dougherty, then a justice of the peace in St. Louis and later Sheriff. Another arrest of Lugar was in connection with the $1,000,000 Grand National Bank Robbery on May 25, 1930, in St. Louis, but the grand jury returned a no-true bill after investigating the case. Lugar was picked up after his uncle, Harry Farrar, had told detectives his nephew was one of the robbers. However, Farrar refused to testify against Lugar.

Perhaps the million-dollar heist explains Lugar's penchant for fancy clothes and fine jewelry. This same article reports that Lugar has a fondness for gifting lady friends with large diamond rings. But the most telling detail of this article may be the information about one John F. Dougherty interceding on behalf of Lugar with the Iowa parole board. This would likely be the same John Dougherty, who, in March 1947, hires Blackie's wife Catherine.

When Lugar is murdered, Uncle Blackie is still being sought in connection with the death of Harry Hale on

October 2, 1953. Then on February 10, 1954, this short item appears on page 3 of the *St. Louis Post-Dispatch*:

Rolla (Blackie) Dean, ex-convict associate of the Wortman gang who was picked up Monday night in East St. Louis for questioning in the New Year's Day murder of John (Buddy) Lugar, was released yesterday after questioning by police. Dean denied any knowledge of the shooting. Charges of carrying a concealed weapon were placed against Dean after a loaded automatic pistol was found in his belt as he drove up to the Paddock Bar, . . . Operated by Frank (Buster) Wortman. The concealed weapon charge is set for a hearing next Monday.

Before we know it, the year is nearly over. It is December 4, 1954—Blackie is dead. Headlines about his death appear in Florida, Illinois, Kansas City, St. Louis, and other cities in Missouri.

On December 5, 1954, the news articles continue in Indiana, Sedalia, and St. Joseph, Missouri. Page one of the *St. Louis Post-Dispatch*, along with some of the other items, provide us with details. Catherine's own words:

"My husband came in after 8 o›clock, and the fight started again," Mrs. Dean told officers. "He hit me on the head, and body with his fists. I went to our bedroom, got his .38-caliber revolver from a closet and started toward the kitchen, where he had gone for a drink of water."

"We met at opposite ends of the hallway. I pointed the revolver and pulled the trigger. I did it for the children."

Mrs. Dean said she had never had a pistol in her hands before, "and if there had been a safety on it, I wouldn't have been able to shoot it." "I shot him, and it's over," she said. "I just wanted to stop him. When you live with someone like Black, you don't open your mouth."

Further details reveal that although the argument happens on Friday night, the police are not advised until Saturday morning at 9:00 am when they get a phone call from Catherine's 18-year-old son, William Martin, Jr. When they police arrive, they find Blackie on a bed, dressed only in his underwear and shoes. He had been shot five times in the chest and arms. The Belleville sheriffs take Mrs. Dean, dressed in "an expensive gray suit and fur jacket" to a state's attorney's office to make a statement. We also learn that "Mrs. Dean is the former Catherine Moriarty, and is the daughter of a retired policeman, Martin Moriarty. Her brother, Cpl. Martin Moriarty Jr., Lucas Avenue District, and Chief of Detectives James Chapman went to Belleville yesterday to talk with Mrs. Dean, at the request of Belleville police." Joan says the names for Catherine's father and brother may be off. James Moriarity is Catherine's father. The most telling detail of Catherine's account is "When you live with a man like Black, you don't open your mouth." She calls him Black; she knows he is tough, even at home.

On December 5, 1954, from the *St. Louis Globe-Democrat*, page 2: A photo of the Dean home just outside of

Belleville, the house a style that we recognize today as mid-century modern. Imagine the brick in that typical dark rose color. The front porch and entry door are covered by an extension of the low-pitched roof. Imagine the kitchen with smooth blonde cabinets and modern appliances, perhaps even a dishwasher. The aluminum slat awnings on the three front windows are each adorned with a large, cursive "D." The caption under the photo reads, "THIS IS THE HOME at 7109 Northern Ave., just outside Belleville, Ill., where Rolla "Blackie" Dean was shot and killed yesterday by his wife Catherine." Below the photo of the house are Blackie and Catherine. The photo of Blackie comes from the "Sheriff Tozer Got His Man," item from February 19, 1953, Blackie seen through the car windshield, behind the wheel. The accompanying photo of Catherine shows her eyes downcast, perhaps wearing the expensive suit and fur jacket. The caption under these photos read, "ROLLA 'BLACKIE' DEAN, left, notorious hoodlum and former convict, was shot and killed yesterday at his home near Belleville by his wife, Catherine, right, shown here at the Belleville Jail, where she was released after posting $5000 bond."

Catherine buries Blackie in a family plot in Belleville next to their infant daughter, Mary Joan, who died in 1946, only 2 weeks old. Catherine, and perhaps her brother Martin, the policeman, bury their mother in the same plot in 1956 and their father in 1959.

Catherine is charged in the death of Blackie. First, the coroner rules Blackie's death a homicide and Catherine, charged with murder, is held overnight on December 11, 1954. On December 20, 1954, a Belleville Grand Jury indicts Catherine on a charge of manslaughter. On December 28,

1954, Catherine pleads innocent. In June 1955, a court in Belleville finds Catherine shooting Blackie justified, done in self-defense.

Catherine and her former husband, the father of her son, Billy, remarry. They remain married until her death in 1980, an also apparently tumultuous relationship. On November 26, 1963, *The St. Louis Post-Dispatch* reports that after a night of drinking, Catherine returns to the apartment that she shares with William L. Martin and her now 13-year-old daughter. She goes to the kitchen and retrieves two paring knives. She puts one knife in the hand of the sleeping Martin, and with the other knife, she stabs him in the back. In the ensuing knife scuffle, she is cut on her hip. William declines to press charges. A follow-up article on November 28, 1963, says that after her release, Assistant District Attorney Curtis Crawford has Catherine rearrested after he learns that "she has been taking psychiatric treatment." Whether Catherine has a history of mental illness, or this is a result of her life with Blackie, we have no definite answers.

I know in one DNA analysis for a health condition I was told that I am a carrier of one of the MTHFR genes "associated with certain types of mental illness," not specified. We have some history of mental illness in my family. That Catherine was attracted to Blackie may be explained by the observation of my instructor for a master's level seminar on substance abuse. He reports that one of his clients, who has been clean for a year, finally travels out of town and stops at a mall in a city he has never visited. Within 5 minutes, the client reports that he is approached by a complete stranger who wants to know, "Hey man, you wanna score?" Utterly baffled, the now clean client wants to know how this happens? The instructor explains, "Shit radar." Carrie Ann tells me she once saw an old film clip of Carl Jung. In a flickering, grainy image, Jung says something like, "You walk into a room, and someone immediately catches your eye. Run. Run like hell. They are exactly what you don't need." Shit radar.

Catherine is buried in the family plot with Blackie, their infant daughter, and both of Catherine's parents. We think this may have been the choice of their surviving daughter, who is still alive. Thanks to super sleuth Joan, we know where the daughter of Blackie and Catherine lives. By way of the internet, we have seen her home with the white-picket fence. Joan writes to her after we start putting the family together. She receives no response. I write again a few years later. No response. We conclude that she has no interest in family engagement. Out of respect to these apparent wishes, we exclude her name here. In other times, under other circumstances, Judy and I, Joan, Nancy, and Blackie's daughter, along with all our other siblings and cousins might have all grown up together. Perhaps Blackie's daughter may have helped us unravel some of the mystery around Woody, his disappearance from the St. Louis family, and his reappearance in Utah with a new name.

10

SETTLING IN

Robert flinches noticeably when I tell him, "I'm a world class liar." Not a favorable confession from your spouse, right? Think about it. I was not even 3 years old when my father dies in a car accident. Everyone assumes I will be okay, enough so that I do not even attend the funeral. And, as an inherently happy and patient child, I am okay, but just barely. In a family photo of the entire Yardley clan, thirty-four of us—Grandma and Grandpa, all the aunts, uncles and cousins, everyone except my younger brother, Nick, and other youngest cousins, Elaine, Diane, Coleen, Jerilyn, and Kevin, all not yet born, I sit cross-legged at the lower left, on the floor next to my cousin, NaDene, looking as far away as a 5-year-old can look in a group of relatives. My shoes are cast off to the side. In elementary classrooms, I daydream endlessly, my brain drifting outside the classroom more often than it is inside the classroom. A contributing factor to my distraction: we never discuss my father's death nor any of the emotional repercussions. Momma has no words for grief. She is emotionally tidy—keeping most feelings locked away. Then of course there is the childhood sexual abuse; I am not the first young person to guard such abuse as my darkest of secrets. My way of compensating is to be as okay as possible. As normal as possible. I do my normal dance. In the end, my ability to do so saves my life, but I do have to uncover the wounds, pull off the scabs, and cleanup the psychological detritus. By the time I arrive at the door of the BYU Honor Code Office, lying about having an affair with a professor is a fairly emotion-free decision. I tell them I am okay—I am. I tell them everything is fine— It is. I do my normal dance. I stay in school. I finish my program. My daughters dance in the kitchen when I get my first full-time professional job. I survive. My children survive. Not that this justifies everything or anything—it's just how it works.

Most of us don't need anyone to tell us when we mess up. We know when we have screwed the pooch, or, in this case, the professor, without anyone pointing out the error of our ways. We are our own worst critics. I have spent hours, maybe even days and weeks in self-castigation. I have an entire list of my character flaws. When I went to Church, I spent hours, maybe even days and weeks in repentance trying to get past my evil ways. In the end, I prefer Occam's Razor, the simplest explanation is likely the most plausible; I have a survival skill. It does not have broad applicability.

Now, in the days of #metoo, I could make a case that I was taken advantage of by my older, considerably more powerful university professor. A clear case of quid pro quo. Of course, I would also have to acknowledge my own collusion in my own abuse. A not unusual consequence of childhood abuse. And, not to worry over much about the doubling up of ownership pronouns—Shakespeare uses as many as four possessives at a time.

In October, after the summer of the Broken Foot, The Pneumo-Thorax and The Long Grey Hallway, I go with Luna to Clearwater, FL, for my birthday weekend. She uses air miles for the airfare and more points for the Hilton. We walk onto the white sand beaches daily and spend hours drinking and talking, waiting for the flash of green as the sun sets in the Gulf Ocean. We buy beach sweaters at the surfer shop. Robert calls to wish me a Happy Birthday, telling me,

"I picked up something I think you will like." Luna predicts something spectacular.

When I get home, Robert takes me to dinner and presents me with a diamond tennis bracelet while we are having pre-dinner drinks in the bar. The man has class.

The following October, after our trip to St. Louis to meet the Dean Family, Robert takes me back to the same restaurant for my birthday dinner. We sit in one of the smaller rooms on the second floor when he gives me a large card in a pink envelope.

I note, "This card is kind of mushy for you, baby."

He smiles and shrugs. Then he clears his throat, squares his shoulders, and sings—a Capella, perfectly pitched, in the middle of the restaurant—"I Love How You Love Me." He follows with a knee on the floor and a flourish of a truly spectacular diamond ring. The man has style and class. We do not set a date.

A year later, on Tuesday morning before Halloween, we are up at 5:30 a.m., as usual, starting our day. No lights. There in the dark, at the foot of our bed, he says,

"I think we should get married on New Year's Eve." Having married the mother of his children on Valentine's Day, he is going big here.

"We can make that work," I assure him.

"But do we have to get married at the Courthouse?" he wonders.

"I think I can put together a party," I reassure him.

I begin immediately to make plans. It has been 15 months since my botched attempt to intervene with Debra and alcohol. She has not yet spoken to me. Nevertheless, I send her a text asking if she will be my Matron of Honor when I marry Robert. She responds,

"Dawn, I am happy to stand up for you and Robert, but if you expect me to run your errands and do your work—that's not me."

She conveys the same message to Luna, who laughs and then responds, "Oh Aunt Deb, my mom can plan a wedding. She just feels really bad that she does not have a relationship with you." Her message is perfect.

Robert and I marry at five o'clock on New Year's Eve at the Grand America, the only five-star hotel in Salt Lake City. Debra stands up for us. One of Robert's twins, the Marine, is our best man in his dress blues. The other twin is deployed in Afghanistan. We save an empty chair for him. All of my children attend with all of their children. Robert's daughter and her new beau are there. His stepdaughter and her husband cannot make it down from Seattle. Robert's nephew from PA is there with his girlfriend. Cousin Joan and her Ken come from St. Louis. Sister Judy cannot make it. Jenny, my oldest friend from Gunnison and her new husband, also Ken, are there. Carrie Ann and her husband are there. Cassidy is out of town. Most of my book group with most of their spouses are there. My surviving brothers and their spouses all come. I tell my siblings I realize that Daddy Arlo died on New Year's Eve, that Momma died on

New Year's Eve. Robert and I are making a newer, happier memory. I do not need to be a world class liar with Robert.

A few weeks after the wedding my five-year-old grand-daughter talks about it. "Grammie, I saw Robert stomp on that cup."

"What else did you see?"

"I saw your red shoes."

"What did you like best?"

"The cake was delicious." A Martha Stewart design. Three simple layers of chocolate cake, filled with chocolate mousse, covered with white ganache, topped with a short champagne glass over-flowing with multi-color fondant confetti. After Robert and I have a slice, we feed the grand-kids first.

🪶

Robert retires on April 15, 2016. On April 20th we leave for a 32-day, 7,500-mile trip across the country. Deb says she would have to kill someone if she were to share a car for a month. Not us—we like each other. Our first stop is Fort Collins, CO to see Bobby. His parents were best friends with Robert's parents. They have known each other since kindergarten. Now, the relationship is Christmas cards. Next stop is Salina Kansas. I want to see the Tall Grass Prairie National Monument, the last stand of contiguous prairie against parcels of farmland. Not much to see this early in spring, not even a buffalo, just buffalo chips, but I am happy knowing it is there. We stop in St. Louis for a long weekend with Cousin Joan and Ken. Then, we are off to Nashville for a couple of nights with Nicole, my partner in crime for the Sundance Film Festival—she and I have the same taste in films and in men. Nicole, meeting Robert within weeks of my meeting him, pronounces him a keeper. He happily sends us off to watch indie films and drink wine during our Sundance rendezvous. In Nashville, we visit the Parthenon replica and the Andrew Jackson homestead. We eat hot barbeque. We sample flights of whiskey.

By now we have settled into our travel routine—whether cross country or abroad. We rely on our lodging for a lite breakfast—coffee and something. For lunch in the car, we have nuts, celery or carrots, cheese and crackers. Then we feel like we deserve a nice dinner. Neither of us have an appetite for fast food. On this trip we also include in our daily routine making up limericks. One or the other of us spots a sign or a building that provides inspiration. Sometimes we work on them together. They are usually raunchy and are hilarious to us. Sometimes we take all day to finish a rhyme.

After Nashville, we plan to see the Rock 'n' Roll Hall of fame, but when we are with Bobby in Ft. Collins, he hooks us up with his brother Billie who owns a thousand-acre horse farm in Lexington. Billie's avocation is horse breeding, 200 horses, 40 colts this year. We visit for several hours with Billy, his young wife, and their new twins. They have added on 4000 square feet for the nursery wing. Then we head to Columbus, OH. We make the Rock 'n' Roll Hall of Fame a day later than planned. We admire the displays and enjoy a 1-hour recorded Springsteen concert. I could wander for another day or two, getting lost on the endless connections of music, artists, and key influences, but the next morning we leave for Niagara Falls. We have a corner room at the Hilton on the Canadian side overlooking American Falls. We ride Queen of the Mists and take the tour behind the falls. We barely miss getting tickets for a Paul Anka concert. In the morning I get up early for a walk around the parkway. The daffodils are in full bloom along the river. Travelling south through New York, I am surprised that spring has not appeared in the countryside. Everything is grey and brown. We plan to stay in Easton with Robert's parents for five nights. They are not doing as well as we assumed. We cancel plans for Baltimore, where we hoped for a night with his nephew, the one who came to our wedding. We will skip Great Smoky Mountains National Park.

Robert's Mom has a strong and vibrant personality. During our weekly phone conversations, she covers her diminishing abilities. I am so surprised that she cannot remember whether or not she ate breakfast an hour after eating. We find several caches of medications not taken. We talk with brother Rich. He knows several women who will contract to come to the house two or three times per day to see that meals are prepared or purchased, and meds are taken. The women will help with light housework. We make several pleas for Bob and Ruth to accept this arrangement. Robert replaces the side-by-side furnace and AC thermostats with a single programmable unit. Mom has been running the furnace and AC simultaneously. His Dad, Big Bob, has macular degeneration and cannot see to make corrections. We figure out how to repair the plaster and get a locked cage to prevent further temperature adjustments.

Robert and I take a 2-day side trip to Cape Cod to see my sister Judy and her husband, Barry. They live there year-round. Judy loves it. Barry says they may have been overly swayed by their summer visits. It is cold, but the Atlantic is beautiful. We have a full-lobster dinner. The next day we drive along the shoreline to Provincetown for a browse through boutiques and galleries, and, of course, lobster rolls. It is good to see my sister in her own home.

We return to Pennsylvania for two more nights with Bob and Ruth and then drive on to Colonial Williamsburg. We are on the road two hours when Big Bob calls to say that the mailman found his cousin Donald hanging in the basement. We know that Donald recently institutionalizes his wife Kate for Alzheimer's, signing away everything but his car and his house. He makes sure that Kate is taken care of and then decides it is all too much. He leaves a note in his mailbox. The mailman finds him dead. Donald is the cousin who helped Robert get into the electrician's union. "Do we need to go back?" I query. He ponders a moment, "No, let's not. Dad is not even going to tell Mom. It will only confuse her. We would confuse her more." The price of aging in America.

Colonial Williamsburg is interesting and fun. We participate in the evening pirate trial by candlelight and the ghost story tour the next night—also by candlelight. We make sure to see the twice daily fife and drum parade. We buy a blue Chinese vase for our bedroom. And we are off to Statesville, NC to see Robert's friend and colleague Glen and his wife, Suzie. Robert and Glen have been working on electrical bidding projects cross-country for more than a decade. They previously worked together for 10 years in another company in Utah. We check in to our hotel, and we meet for dinner. Glen and Suzie are both very funny. We have Mexican food. We drink margaritas, and we laugh for hours. For most of our hotel nights we use Hilton points. In 32 days, we only pay for four room nights. This is not one of them. We leave in the morning for Lady's Island, SC, near Beaufort.

Mike and Jeannine welcome us to their SC home. Mike and Robert worked together until Mike's retirement 4 years earlier. We visit local fish markets. We walk along the coast in Beaufort. We drive past the Marine base at Perris Island. Mike and Jeannine have a beautiful fishing boat which we sail around the intercoastal waters, rich breeding grounds for abundant marine life. We happen on a pod of baby dolphins and their mothers at feeding time around five p.m. We watch for most of an hour until they disappear. Jeannine is a good cook, and we have lovely lunches at home. When my Momma dies on the morning of New Year's Eve six years prior, we had plans to have dinner at the home of Mike and Jeannine. There was nothing more to be done for Momma, so Robert and I do go to Mike and Jeannine's where we comfortably share my story of Momma's dying.

After South Carolina, we drive to Savannah, GA. During the open-air trolley ride Robert says, "Believe it or not, I could see us living here." We walk along the river where we see a large sailboat. A posted sign gives details of the boat's proportions, including a 30-foot mast, a declaration that the crew will not reveal the owner, and a plea to not bother the crew who have work to do. Robert takes off across the street without me. Hurrying to catch up, I trip on a railroad track, sprawling on the asphalt. I gather myself, and bark at Robert about leaving me behind. I understand that Donald is on his mind, but I still need him to mind me, too. We only stay the day, then we drive to Atlanta where we find too much city for Robert.

The next morning, we are off to Huntsville, AL where we will meet the parents of Laura, one of my colleagues at work. Her dad, John is a semiretired dentist, his wife Rosemary a long-retired Pan Am flight attendant. She tells

Robert about the many flights she made returning soldiers to the U.S. from Vietnam. In the backyard, under a layer of leaves and a tarp, John and Rosemary have the smallish sailboat that they used in a trip around the world in their early days. We walk to the Baptist Church for lunch. John takes us on personalized tour of the church. The chapel feels very Mormon. I stand at the podium, feeling like I am about to give another talk in another Church meeting. John takes us on a larger personalized tour of Redstone. We see the massive Saturn 5 rockets. A lifelong resident of Huntsville, he has many insider anecdotes to share. For dinner we go to Walton's Family Restaurant. They have Jell-O salads on the menu just like Momma used to make. I order the cranberry-apple version.

In Memphis, we walk along Beale Street, but skip Graceland. In Arkansas, 5 miles off the freeway, we find a winery established by Swiss monks a century ago. The organic rosemary chicken is delicious. We race on to Oklahoma City, timing it between tornado watches. Driving is an amazing way to see the changing landscape of the country. We notice the regional shifts in topography and plant life. For our entire trip, Robert does all of the driving except for two hours our first day on our way to Fort Collins. For the first three mornings, I ask if he wants me to drive. He always says no.

"This is a point of honor for you?" I ask.

"Yes," he responds.

Our last stop is Santa Fe, NM. We have timed our trip for the Friday night restaurant tour with the Santa Fe School of Cooking. Our tour guide, Lois, an Indigenous woman, is a successful food photographer in L.A. when one of her elders asks her if that is her highest calling. Within 6 weeks she moves to Santa Fe to study Indigenous cuisine. Gaining some experience, she has an opportunity to make a presentation at a national food event where four or five old White men tell her 1) there is no such thing as Indigenous cuisine and 2) if there were such a thing, she is not qualified to talk about it. Lois goes to the University of New Mexico and designs her own PhD program, a combination of geography, sociology, agriculture, psychology (why does grandma's apple pie taste better than anyone's) and food science. Lois tells us of the eight magic foods that were unknown around the world until Columbus and others make contact with the new world: beans, corn, squash, tomatoes, potatoes, chile, cacao, and vanilla. So, no potatoes for the Irish, no tomatoes for Italians, no chile for Thai food. You get the picture. The restaurant tour is worth every minute. We stay in the Drury, with Santa Fe Spirits Bar on the roof, the best place in town to see a western sunset. Plus, the Drury has a good ghost story. Robert takes me to see the Loretto Chapel. While he claims to care nothing for religion, he loves the story of the spiral staircase and its mystical builder. We plan to stay in Moab the next night but decide to drive straight through to home.

❧

In December, I am invited to participate in a panel discussion at an international conference on school counseling in Verona, Italy. We have to pay our own way, but part of the trip can be a write-off. We can pull the money from my 401K. We make plans. The direct flight from Salt Lake City to Paris is almost magical. We board at 5:00 p.m., have dinner and a drink or two, then read and sleep. In the morning we wake up in Paris, eleven o'clock local time.

We stay in Rue Cler, walking distance to the Eiffel Tower. I practice my French on Duolingo; I am fifty-percent fluent. Enough to keep us out of trouble. Two taxi drivers tell me I have good French. We eat two nights at the Café Bosquet. On the second night I forget my purse. Our wait person, a woman, chases after us, finding us next door in Le Pharmacie, teasing me about the return of my bag. We laugh and kiss both cheeks. She says, "I love you guys." A little French goes a long way.

We take a day tour to Normandy, leaving at 7:07 a.m. from the Gare Sainte-Lazare. In Carentan, we meet our tour guide, Francis, a native of Normandy. He knows that Robert's father landed second wave at Normandy Beach with the First Infantry Division, the Big Red One. Our first stop is the little church at Ango-ville-au-Plain which served as a hospital for casualties on both sides, changing hands several times during the battle. The young American medics caring for the casualties had 2 weeks and 3 weeks of training, respectively. The benches of the church are still blood-stained. We see Sainte-Mere-Eglise, the village memorialized in the Longest Day. As we drive through the Normandy countryside, Francis tells how the Nazis dug trenches inland from the sea, flooding the farmland as a deterrent to an attack from the land. He points out to us all the gardens and farms that have incorporated the metal mesh from the landing strips built by the allies in mere days—fences, gates, trellises. We see Point du Hoc, the highest point between Utah Beach to the west and Normandy Beach to the east, attacked by the United States Army Ranger Assault Group. Only half of the initial force made it from the beach to the base of the cliff. With a force of 500 men, 77 were killed and 152 were wounded.

We continue our drive up the beaches with aging bunkers and aging bomb holes. Francis, 40-something, has done his research. He parks and then walks us to draw #3 Red Dog, where the Big Red One comes ashore. We call Robert's father. We mostly hold it together. Robert tells him, "We are in the exact spot where you landed." We take photos of the beach and the water's edge, more than two football fields away. We take photos of the distant points of the arc of the beach where massive machine guns spray the incoming soldiers. We take a photo of the relative safety of the inlet and the draw. Robert collects a small container of sand. Big Bob tells me some years earlier, "The water was already red with blood when we step off our landing craft." Our guide, Francis, tells us that if we dig in the sand or turn over a large rock, we may still find blood stains.

On to the cemetery. I hear from others it will be a moving experience. It is. Big Bob gives us the names of two friends who die at Normandy. Our guide Francis cannot find them among the buried dead. Families had the option to repatriate their loved ones home. The rows of marble crosses and Jewish stars are tragically beautiful. We call Bob again from the tile mural that depicts movements of all the troops. We see on the map where he fought inland to Caumont and then south to St. Lo, battling hedge row by hedge row, 6 weeks of fighting to arrive at St. Lo on July 18, 1944. Big Bob eventually walks most of the way north to Le Havre where the troops board ships for home. On his way to Le Havre, a staff sergeant asks to review Bob's Service Card. He says to him, in the presence of the NCOs, "Do not let any of these guys push you around. You have done more than any of them." Neither Robert nor his father can speak on that phone call across the sea, across the years. We simply weep.

We hear from our guide, Francis, and others, of the enduring gratitude of the people of France. Back in Rue Cler, I buy a pair of Mephisto sneakers, mentioning to the shop owner our trip to Normandy. We tell him of Big Bob's contribution. He is a bit younger than we—so, a post-war baby. He says, "For your family, this was a great sacrifice. For us, it was our country. We thank you." The train tickets, the tour guide, and our day entirely worth the time and money.

In Paris, we drink champagne at the top of the Eiffel Tower. At the Louvre we see the Mona Lisa where an Asian chic with a selfie-stick takes at least two dozen selfies with Mona in the background. I have loved Monet for years and l'Orangerie does not disappoint. But now I put the Musee d'Orsay at the top of my list. At the d'Orsay I am in the Central Hall, the large clock on my left, a row of sculptures lined up on the descending levels in front of me. On my far right is a larger-than-life size statue of Eve After the Fall, her entire being agonizing over the apple. At the end of the row, on my far left, is Woman Bitten by a Snake, breasts fully exposed, arms flung wide allegedly in agony, but it may be ecstasy. For sure, I am going with Bitten by a Snake. Over my right shoulder, in a small anteroom, hangs Cabanel's Birth of Venus, painted 16 years after the Clesinger snake bite sculpture, perhaps inspired by the agony or the ecstasy. These contrasting representations begin my casual study of how women are portrayed in art through the ages.

We fly to Venice, soon realizing the error of our ways in bringing big American suitcases. We drag them over cobblestones and bricks. We lug them up and down bridges with stairs. Robert is not a fan of Venice. It is cold and stinky. I know we will never be back, so we take the long Gondola tour. I ask Marino, our Gondolier, whether or not he likes his job. "This is my city, and I have a job," he says with a wry smile. We see St. Mark's Square and the Guggenheim Museum with an exhibit by Tancredi, not males, not females, just dots and breathtaking. Then we catch a train to Verona. We bought tickets for the express, but we get on the regionale—stopping at every town. Each train station is covered with an impressive display of graffiti.

In Verona, Robert has a cold and hides in our studio on Via Venti Settembre for the two days I am at the conference, drinking the Italian version of Theraflu. Our first night we go to Café Carducci, recommended by my friend Jay, one of the conference organizers. The Café, booked for the evening, sets up a little table to the side, and we have one of our favorite meals ever, cheese and salami sampler, pumpkin risotto, tagliatelle, and Fantasy of Naples dessert. Navigating Verona is easy. We turn left out of our flat, cross the bridge over the Adige, through the old part of town. At the plaza, before the fortress, turn left past the upscale shops to another plaza, around the marble sidewalks and a slight left to the University, location of the conference. We attend the closing celebration for the conference that highlights several nice school counseling programs reaching out to under-served youth. School counselors making a difference around the world. The elegant evening includes a twelve-course dinner that begins at 9 p.m. and wraps up shortly after midnight, with the chef giving a demo of the dessert. Walking 25,000 steps per day we see St. Anastasia church, several Christmas markets, Castel Vecchio, and the pink marble Arena. At the Castel, climbing up the ramparts, I realize with some surprise I am not the agile girl on the tack shed at Uncle Tom's farm, nor the maybe overly confident housewife who stands on the roof of the first floor to wash windows on the second floor. We walk through the old part of town, on our way back to Via Venti Settembre, a gun shop on the right catches our eye. We stop for a look when a very tall man in a track suit in a particular shade of blue passes behind us. He is talking loudly, but all we hear him say is, "Hard fucking man."

"What was that?" I ask Robert.

"I have no idea, but he has me by 70 pounds, so I'm not asking." Robert says the tall stranger was following us and talking for a short time. I notice this man, in the particular shade of blue, early in the day, near the upscale shops as we walk to the Castel. He is smiling at us, standing head and shoulders above the crowd, so much so, that I think he is on scaffolding. At the advice of my daughter and the French-Swiss guy we have been careful not to draw attention to ourselves as Americans. For the most part we pass as German—until we speak. Not sure what this encounter means, we lay low in our apartment the next day. Happy for the rest and the discovery of a laundromat down the street in the opposite direction from the bridge. When we return to Café Carducci on our last evening, the staff greets us like we are long lost family, clasping our hands and kissing our cheeks.

We catch a train to Florence where we stay in the Airbnb of Lucia, my friend Jay's Italian teacher. We walk to Piazalle Michelangelo the first afternoon. Lucia's apartment is a few blocks from the Arno. She walks us to the restaurant of some friends, Sweet Fish, where I have the best fried potatoes I have ever eaten—lots of umami going on. We cross the bridge into old Florence. We see the Duomo at night with a crescent moon above. Lucia gives us directions to another restaurant of friends—Italian fusion. For dessert we have deconstructed carrot cake with cream cheese ice cream prepared by the Japanese pastry chef. Globalization. One way or another, we get lost going to The Academia to see the statue of David, so we see only the outdoor replica, with a chorus of three dozen velvet-suited Santas singing in the background—a fusion experience in itself. At the Uffizi we see Botticelli's Venus—the one thing I wanted to see when we planned our trip to Italy. Around the velvet rope, fathers instruct their pre-pubescent sons about the meaning of the painting. Oh, to be a fly on the shoulder in one of those discussions. We have coffee and dulci on the terrace at Uffizi.

Lucia drives us an hour into the Tuscan countryside to the Nipozanni Winery, part of Frescobaldi. Her friend, Stephania, gives us tour of the winery and the estate. We see the family chapel damaged during World War II. The vineyards have been in the family since the 1300s. We see the family wine cellar, including bottles of 500-year-old wine. As each child is born, they are given wine from the best recent vintage, 500 bottles to male children, 200 bottles to the female children. We can tell who the drinkers are. We have the executive lunch cooked just for us and served in the family dining room next to the kitchen. In the family room we see snapshots of family members with Queen Elizabeth along with four large pieces of priceless art. We ship a case of wine to ourselves c/o my daughter in Washington state. Liquor laws in Utah do not allow direct wine purchases. The winery posts ads for an electrician— Robert protests that he knows neither the language nor the regulations. I think it looks like a golden opportunity.

We take a cooking class with Lucia's friend, Laura, hand rolling our orecchiette pasta with artichokes, salad of oranges and fennel, and an olive oil cake. She is so relieved that we do not insist on making Tiramisu. We see Hotel Luchessi. With a word or two at the reception desk, Lucia gets us access to the roof. E. M. Forrester wrote *Room with a View* at Hotel Luchessi. *Room with a View* was filmed at Hotel Luchessi. As an English major, I nearly weep with joy. I have Robert's cold. Two evenings in a row we stop at the bar at Luchessi. I ask for hot tea, with lemon, honey, and whiskey. The second night the bar tender asks if it is a family recipe. I tell him it is my recipe for how to burn out a cold, especially if I can climb under a pile of quilts and sweat the night away. This cold lingers for weeks.

We catch our final train to Rome. The suitcase error comes fully home. We do not realize we have reserved seats on Coach 7. We enter on Coach 4. Our suitcases are so big we cannot even roll them down the aisle. We are blocking everyone. Robert tries to carry the suitcases over his head, in absolute frustration he moves us backwards to the empty area at the front of the car. The train begins to move before we notice Car 3 is the bar car. We seek refuge. Robert is beside himself. I order drinks, and strike up a conversation with the bartender, explaining the humor of our faux pas, or whatever is the Italian equivalent—maybe passo falso? With a gesture of absolute kindness, the bartender moves us to a table with room for the giant suitcases, making us comfortable for the next hour or so until we arrive in Rome.

Our first night in Rome we set out to explore the area around Piazza Navona and the Pantheon. I book us into a boutique hotel so off the beaten path that cars cannot drive there. We have to drag our big suitcases over a half block of cobblestones. Our room is lovely with a black and white tile floor, an optical illusion of steps and ledges, our window overlooking backyard gardens across the wide cobblestone walk. After our exploratory outing, we are ready to go back to the hotel, but we are a bit unsure. Robert looks at me and plaintively laments, "It is dark. We are lost, and we do not know the language." We use the Sesame Street solution and backtrack by landmarks for the few blocks we traveled. Being lost will be a theme for us in Rome. At least three times we stand on the street with a map that we turn in circles. Every time a citizen of Rome, generally in our age range, asks where we want to go. Then they communicate to us how to make our way. A little English, a little Italian, a lot of kindness. St. Peter's is closed for a special ceremony, but we the see the square, the Sistine Chapel, and the Vatican Museum. The day is glorious. We wear only our sweaters. In the Vatican Museum, I find a ceiling panel of God, seated on a throne, horn-like lightning bolts at each corner of his forehead, attended by unwinged seraphim. My Momma always tells me that Mormons have horns.

In our trek through Paris and Italy, we find that we are only good for half a day of museum viewing, then we are in sensory overload. How much beauty can one absorb? In Rome, Robert has our Pakistani hotel clerk in stitches with his imitations of Hercules and his declaration that he has seen enough marble penises and marble breasts for a lifetime. In every city, we love sitting near the plaza in an open-air café, watching people, talking about our day.

We see the Senate, Palatine Hill, and the Coliseum. Our tour guide, a genuine Italian broad who lives a decade or two in Hawaii, tells us how the Coliseum originally had a silk covering of the entire open ceiling area. The aristocrats sit on the lower levels, the hoi polloi on the upper levels. Even the prostitutes and their aristocrat patrons are accommodated on the upper levels. The red brick Senate building is still sturdy, all the corners square. We see where the usurpers try to burn the body of Caesar. Et tu, Brute? We see the Spanish Steps and Tivoli Fountain, even in December packed with tourists. The further south we go the more we see Carboneri and Soldati armed with automatic weapons. In Rome, a city saturated with history, the world changes. We find Mimi e Coco, a *Vinoteca* near our hotel. We meet the women owners who explain Mimi e Coco means the shirt and the ass. One of the patrons tells us it is good luck to share a bottle of wine with a citizen of Rome. We trade bottles and *saluti* one another. After three weeks, we fly from Rome to Amsterdam, and Amsterdam to Salt Lake City.

Back in Salt Lake City I have a hunch about the tall man in the particular shade of blue. I find the professional basketball team in Verona wears that blue color with yellow. I check the roster. I find the face. I send him a Facebook friend request. He accepts just in time for me to see his Fuck Boys Christmas video. He is twenty-one and harmless, but he does have Robert by 70 pounds and 45 years. We are still FB friends, kinda, meaning I can look him up and see what he is doing. He has changed teams.

✒

When Big Bob gets the little package of photos and sand from Omaha Beach, he calls Robert, telling him he cries like a baby. Robert offered to take his parents, or even just Big Bob, to the 60th and 75th anniversary celebrations for D-Day. Big Bob declined. Macular degeneration leaves him legally blind since his late seventies. He thinks he will not be able to see. He tells Robert he should have gone. Mom Ruthie agrees; they should have gone.

On Veteran's Day we get one war story from Big Bob. Sometime during the 6 weeks battling inland from Omaha Beach to Caumont and south to St. Lo, a French officer joins his unit. Most of the men believe he is a spy, a member of the Resistance. The French officer choses Bob, who is a BAR man—Browning Automatic Rifle expert—to go on a midnight walk to gather information. They cross a bridge over a small pond when gun fire erupts. Bob realizes they are behind enemy lines. The officer tells Bob to wait there in the dark until the gun fires dies down and get back to his unit on his own. Bob dodges enemy fire, crosses the pond in the water, carrying his BAR over his head. He makes it back to his unit just as the sky begins to lighten. They never see the French officer again. During one of our Pennsylvania visits, Bob mentions to me that making progress hedge row by hedge row included some fierce fighting. Like many WWII veterans, like many other veterans, Big Bob keeps most of his stories to himself.

🖋

Post-retirement Robert consults 20, sometimes 30 hours per week for his former employer. I get a 1- or 2-day-a-week job at Chico's at City Creek. I like getting dressed up and going downtown again, and I have a new group of friends. Ty, my boss, and his husband, Chad, are my favorites. In the course of our work conversations, I reveal that I sewed all of my daughters' wedding dresses. They want to see photos. I show them the silk satin dress for Luna with the leg o' lamb sleeves and the Alençon lace. Then I show them her second dress: silk double crepe, with a high band collar, mesh yoke, and long fitted column, a Vera Wang pattern. I make covered buttons with loops all the way up the back of the yoke.

The dress for Dora when she marries the French-Swiss guy is silk linen, scoop neck, short sleeves, self-piping at the neck and raised waistline. I embroider the bodice with silk ribbon and seed pearls, a spaced cross-stitch pattern she saw in a bridal magazine. The A-line skirt with slight elongation in the back is hemmed with horse-hair braid. The dress flows beautifully when she walks across the grass at the reception center. Trina marries a fireman in an Empress Josephine style dress made of embroidered silk organza—the same fabric seen on Galadriel in Lord of the Rings. I clip back the beading along every seam and then stitch all of the beads back in place. I make silk charmeuse piping for the wide scoop neckline, the cap sleeves, and the high empire waist. The Vogue pattern has no train; she wants one. I give it my best shot. The photographer shows how well it drapes. The beautiful dress fits her ballerina body perfectly. CC gets an ivory silk dress with side ruching and a full skirt, trimmed with shadow embroidery lace from Australia. She does not actually get to wear it. Her fiancé is from Ukraine and out of status when his work is visited by labor inspectors who record his social security number. They marry two days later at the courthouse. She wears white pants with a white top and a pastel blue spring coat. They use the reception money for his green card. Completing our international family, Ox marries a woman from Brazil. No wedding dress for her at the courthouse in San Diego.

I appear in several of the wedding photos. One or more of my work friends remarks, "You look so different." To which I reply, "Well, I'm happier and I like myself better." Our teammate Judy, a retired surgical nurse, and the most new-age among us notes, "Oh, just that—You're happier and you like yourself better?" I nod and smile.

I am happier and I do like myself better. I am lucky to have Momma's pretty skin and the sage advice of a daughter who is a master esthetician. But I also have a face-lift 6 weeks before Robert and I marry. I sold my house in Sugar House and have some extra cash. My big concerns are the skin under my eyes and the skin on my neck. Robert's enthusiasm is nearly insulting, nevertheless, I charge ahead.

The same day surgery is performed at the doctor's office. I have been careful to select a surgeon whose expertise I have triangulated. He is respected by his peers, by local estheticians, and by his patients. After surgery my head is bundled up with inches of bandages. I sleep sitting up for 2 nights. I return to the plastic surgeon's office for the bandage removal 48 hours later. His assistant and his esthetician are my country-girl homies. One grew up in Circleville, near the spot where Robert gets the speeding ticket, the other is from Ephraim in Sanpete County, home of Snow College. They are so excited for me to see the result. "Don't you look fantastic?" they ask. I take one look in the mirror and think "Silence of the Lambs." Seriously that is the first thing I think, "Silence of the Lambs." I see the stitches all around my face and around my ears—completely creepy. Plus, the stitches give me fits. Whatever my body is supposed to have to dissolve stitches is missing. The doctor and his nurses have to pick out every one of the hundreds of stitches over the course of three or four visits. How many people have trouble with stitches? Ten percent. I ask them how many people have this much trouble? Maybe two percent. I may be a little late in thinking that it is kind of weird to cut off my face and sew it back on. But the result is very nice—old friends think I just look well-rested as opposed to eternally surprised.

It has been 8 years now since the facelift. The results are supposed to be good for 5. I still look different than I appeared in all those wedding photos. I am still happier. I still like myself better. And I am in a marriage where I am truly loved, treasured even.

In a novel I can no longer find, the dying sea captain writes to his lover, "Susannah, you were the greatest gift that was ever made to me. May you be loved. May you be cherished in your heart, and in your mind and in your bed." I am.

🖋

Robert's mother has a heart attack 6 weeks shy of her 96th birthday and survives. His father, who just turned 95, calls. He wants us to come to Pennsylvania to help move them into assisted living. We have been talking to them for several years about moving into a care facility. They have been adamant in their refusal. The first summer we talk to them, their rejection of the idea and the conversations are so strident that I say to Robert,

"I don't mean this as harsh, but your mom and dad have no real respect for you and your brother, Rich."

"Yeah, I know. They are always right. They know every-thing," he replies.

I finally feel like I understand Robert's parents when I see the movie Brooklyn. The heroine, having established a life in the U.S., goes back to Ireland for a visit. Most of the adults she encounters act like she could not possibly know her own mind or have any ideas different from their expec-tations. Robert's parents are deeply entrenched in this old school, old world thinking. The older generation entirely in charge in their world. Robert tells me for years he came west because he had the original helicopter mother. I have seen Big Bob chew out this 65-year-old son, even after all these years, for not taking the Post Office job he arranged. Robert's declaration, "I didn't want to be a postman," still falls on deaf ears.

Robert's brother Rich, 9 years younger, not a 60s rebel, not a Vietnam vet with his fill of following orders, knuckles under to his parents. He takes the job at the Post Office. A year in, he stops by to tell his mom, who is sunning in the backyard with Mary Lou, that he doesn't think the job is for him. Mom stands up, getting in his face, "Do not do anything to embarrass us." Rich is in love with Mary Lou's daughter, Sue. He stands down for 30 years, telling us he hates every day of work at the Post Office.

Running is Rich's salvation. He is a marathon man. He qualifies twice for the Boston Marathon, finishing in the top 200 at both events. His reputation established, he tests running shoes for magazines and shoe companies. He always has two or three pairs he is trying at a time. After he retires, he becomes a courier for the large hospital system in the Lehigh Valley, a job he loves. He makes friends all along his route, including a couple of doctors whom he teaches to run and train.

*

We are in Pennsylvania less than 48 hours after Mom's heart attack. For the first time in their lives, Dad gives Robert and Rich the blue plastic file box containing all of his financial information. Mom and Dad have done a good job of putting away money here and there. By our calculations, with his Post-Office pension, social security, plus these investments, they have enough to keep them in assisted living for 15 years. We move fast. Sister-in-law, Shelly, scouted around. She has two possible facilities, one near their home of 50 years, and the other 5 miles from Rich and Shelley's house. We go with the one near Rich and Shelley. We finalize plans in one afternoon.

We determine that we will empty the house entirely, in case, in a month or two, Mom and Dad decide they want to go home. We determine what furniture will fit into the one-bedroom suite they will have at the senior living center. Full-size sofa, no. His and hers easy chairs, yes. Kitchen table and chairs, yes. Rock maple dining table, chairs, and hutch will go to a co-worker of Shelly's. The beds cannot go, but one dresser and nightstand will work. Mom will be in rehab for ten days. We call the airlines to extend our return tickets for another week

We text the grandkids: who wants what? Lists are made and items set aside. We call a local bric-a-brac dealer who identifies the items she can sell. We honestly measure the arrangement of the wall hangings that will work in the new place, so they will seem exactly like home. We move Dad, Big Bob, into the new digs three days prior to Mom being discharged. Before Big Bob's move, I sort through every item of clothes to see what he wants to keep and what can go. He has lost so much weight that his Dockers look like a skirt gathered around his waist. We buy four new pants and shirts for him. A new set of underwear and socks—a challenge for a size 13 shoe. We make our best guess for Mom. She has most of her everyday clothes with her at the rehab center. She wants her stacks and stacks of panties, but we collude with the staff at rehab and the assisted living center to tell her that Depends will be the undies of choice from now on. Shelly has Mom's jewelry box. Grueling details.

I order a new 3.5 ft white Christmas tree for their coffee table. Amazon will deliver tomorrow.

After Bob moves out of the house, we are literally on the street giving away household items. A set of dishes to the Latinx family across the street. They also take all the extra bedding and towels. We luck into a youth worker who takes all the pots, pans, and kitchen items for her kids aging out of foster care who are trying to furnish their own apartments. I absent mindedly drop a 3" beer opener that looks like a penis and testicles into my purse. Imagine explaining that to TSA? Another neighbor takes the mattresses and box springs. We are in our last afternoon before moving Mom into the center. There is a pile of odds and ends, and an ancient oak side-board that has been abused as a work bench in the garage. One call to 1-800-Got-Junk, and we are finished.

When Mom sees the new apartment, she declares it looks just like home. There is a little side table with the cuckoo clock and the wooden scene lamp as well as her rocking chair. Big Bob wonders, "Can we really afford this?" We assure him, "You are good for 15 years." We have another day and a half to get them finally settled in before we fly out.

We will be back in March to ready the house for sale and to pick up the items the kids want: Grandma's Bavarian china for a daughter, antique tools for one son, monogrammed glassware for another. Robert wants the intricately carved antique cherry chair with the mother of pearl inlay. With her permission, I get Ruthie's wedding dress, rayon—all the silk used up in the war—leg of lamb sleeves, wasp waist, flowing skirt with a train. A cascade of trapunto hearts falling from the netting yoke. Stunning.

Before the return to Pennsylvania, the first week of March, I get a text from CC. She wonders if Mary Jane is my half-sister.

"Mary Jane is Woody's sister, so she is my aunt"

"Oh, and your dad was Woodrow Wilson Dean, right? I have someone on 23 and Me reaching out. We are 2nd cousins. Just trying to make connections. His name is Kent S., sound familiar?"

"No, the only one of Mary Jane's kids I know is her daughter, Nancy. See if he knows her?"

"Will do. Woody's parents were Harry Dean and Bertha Snyder, correct?"

"Yes, this guy knows his (poop emoji)"

"No, this is me on Ancestry. Just wanted to make sure I knew what I was talking about."

I explain that I am getting my nails done. Texting is a challenge at the moment.

"So, this guy is telling me his grandmother's maiden name was Ethel Dean. Do you know who she was?"

Holy Cow. Have we found grandkids from Woody's sister Ethel? I ask her, "Do you know how old this guy is?"

"No. but I did FB stalk him. I think he lives in Elmhurst, IL."

I respond, "LOL I am reading this while walking and almost fell on my face."

"That's why they say multitasking is impossible. I'm doing something else, too."

I call CC after my nail appointment. I want her to ask Cousin Kent if he knows about Uncle Blackie. I will check with Joan. Also, I remind her of our trip to Pennsylvania in a week or so. Ask him if we can meet?

The next day I text CC again, "Any more messages from Cousin Kent?"

She checks in on 23 and Me, "Oh darn. No word yet. I may have scared him off."

In the meantime I call Joan. She tells me that Aunt Ethel, who we will now call Bad Ethel, has two little girls, ages 3 and 5, or maybe 4 and 6, whom she sells to a wealthy family in St. Louis in the early 1930s. Joanie texts back:

"Did you say Kent S? If so, he is on our ancestry sites as a DNA match."

"CC says his name is Kent S."

Joan texts, "Hmm. I'll do some snooping." A few minutes later she sends another message, "'One of the little girls had a son, K.T.S., born 1954. I do not see any other Kent in the obit. Think this is him?

I tell her, "My insight with Ethel is that maybe she let her little girls go to save them from the family business?"

Joan, ever the realist, says, "Heck, no. My grandparents were raising them. She showed up one day to get them and immediately sold them for big bucks to a very wealthy Jewish couple. I suspect Blackie knew them."

Once again, I am taken aback, "Holy crap—well so much for good intentions. How do you know all these stories?"

Joan says she learns most of this insider info from listening to her mother and grandmother talk. Little pitchers have big ears and all that. Then Joan tells me more details about Bad Ethel and the two little girls. Her Mom [my cousin Marion] knew the little girls because they lived together.

"After Bad Ethel shows up and takes them, my grandparents were really upset. That is when they no longer had anything to do with Ethel. The girls show up in Mom's dance class one afternoon. My grandfather spoke with their new 'dad,' and he confirmed the story." The girls were never in the dance school again. Joan reports that she has some contact with another of Bad Ethel's grandsons. He tells her that they lived a very good life.

Joan continues, "The little girls, once grown, even meet Ethel, but do not like her. The nephew met her, too. He says they all thought she was very mean."

I message back, "Wow, Bad Ethel is right. Those little girls were lucky to be away from her. Cousin Kent did tell CC that he remembered someone from the family visiting with them when he was young. He was not sure who it was."

Joan continues, "Bad Ethel moved to AL at some point, living with a guy for years. Ethel also stayed in touch with Blackie's widow, but neither knew anything about her children. Geez Louise."

I respond, "We are lucky to have been raised away from all that. Sheesh. Ethel, Blackie, and Catherine are all buried together, right? What a drama. We want this screenplay written by Diablo Cody, the woman who wrote Juno."

Robert and I are on the road in our F-150 pickup—white, of course, like every other F-150. Driving or riding in that truck is like being in a high-profile Lincoln—big and comfortable. We get a message from CC which is a screen shot from Cousin Kent:

"She can call me or text me at XXX-XXX-XXXX when she gets closer to the St. Louis area. I contacted my cousin through FB messenger about this, but have not heard back yet. She lives in ID and sometimes drives cross country."

Cousin Kent and I make plans to meet at Panera Bread, originally known as St. Louis Bread Co. He will text directions for a location near the freeway.

〰

We meet Cousin Kent and his wife, Chrystal, at St. Louis Bread, er Panera. First thing, I tell them I am a liberal. He is a liberal, too. Second thing, I tell them I am no longer a practicing Mormon. Cousin Kent, who prefers his middle name, Teddy, short for Theodore, so Cousin Teddy tells me that during college he was active on the campus interfaith council. He goes on to say that usually only the Jewish community, represented by him, the Mormons, and the Reformed LDS show up for meetings. "And the LDS and the RLDS will not even look at each other."

They bring photo albums. We see them in their wedding clothes, the white yarmulke brings to mind the Mormon temple clothes. They have three kids and four grandkids. We talk about our families. I tell them about finding my half-sister Judy and cousin Joan. They explain that they had a relationship with Bad Ethel. They know nothing about Uncle Blackie. We spend nearly 90 minutes. Robert is anxious to get back on the road.

I text Joan. "We had a great time with Cousin Kent, who prefers his middle name, so Cousin Teddy. He and his wife Chrystal were HS sweethearts. We saw photos of their wedding. He is an IT guy—CC FB stalked the wrong guy. They knew nothing of Ethel's family. The story they know is that she fell on hard times and had to give up her children. His mom is still alive and living in Boise with Teddy's sister." I have this detail wrong. It is Dan's mother who is alive and living in Boise. I send Joanie a photo of Robert and me with Teddy and Chrystal at Panera.

She responds the next morning, "Top o' the mornin'! Just saw the photo this a.m. Thank you! Not seeing any resemblance, lol. Maybe he really is adopted!! [emoji]"

I tell her, "It totally cracks me up that we have Jewish cousins. But he said his mother used to say, 'My Irish eyes are telling me that isn't true.'"

Joanie, writes, "Seriously? I'm wondering if Bad Ethel or Mary Jane told her that?"

🖎

The thought of Jewish cousins, while incongruous with my growing up, turns out to be not such a distant possibility. During my early years in Gunnison, I hear vague references to Clarion and the Jewish settlement 5 miles southwest of town. Follow the Farmer's Freeway west past the sloughs and the horseshoe where we ice skate in winter, round the curve to the south and there is Clarion, a Jewish settlement in Sanpete County. If I were still living in Gunnison, I would know that three interpretive panels about Clarion, UT, were installed on Main Street in 2016.

I only see Carrie Ann, who grew up in Manti, about once a year now. When I tell her I have Jewish cousins, she giggles and then she says,

"I always wanted someone I could wish Happy Hannukah." And sure enough, she sends me a Hannukah message.

When I talk with my last, best Gunnison friend, Suzie, we laugh when I tell her I have Jewish cousins. We do not talk of Clarion, but she says something on the order of, "Oh goody. You have a whole new line of food and new holidays to explore." She is right.

Cousin Teddy's wife has been a great connection. I know from our Panera meeting and from her posts on Facebook that she, Teddy, and their children are observant Jews. Whenever I have a question about her celebrations and her practices, I email or DM her, and she gives me all the information I am seeking. I am hoping for a family recipe for challah.

🖋

On Memorial Day Robert and I sit outside in the shade of our upper patio. We move into this new house 8 years prior, and, as one of our best investments, we hire a land-scape designer. We have an upper and lower patio, a rock retaining wall, and two sets of stone slab steps in the back-yard. We have a flagstone seating area with another rock wall and slab steps at the front door. We hope to complete the entire plan for the project over 5 to 6 years. We take 7. Before the end of that first summer, we plant thirteen large caliper trees, maple, birch, Bloodgood Japanese maple, Brandywine Crab, and Fuji Cherry. All are now mature. Robert and my oldest grandson build garden boxes by the garden shed. Robert and I install a continuous fountain, a large lotus-looking urn. My yoga frogs bask in the sun and splash in the water at the base. Tree pose, frog pose, rock the baby, and Ekapadarajakapatasana.

Not surprisingly Robert is troubled this day. His par-ents' lives and living conditions are drastically reduced from their Ozzie and Harriet existence. His father, 6'4" and always strong is less strong—not the 20-year-old that went ashore at Omaha Beach. One of Robert's twin sons, the Marine, left the first of May for a 6-month tour in the Middle East. His other twin son leaves in August for a

second Army tour to the Middle East, a training mission
to Jordan. Robert, as usual, keeps his troubles to himself.
I sit in witness of his concerns. Likely, for the first time in
my life, I sit still for the entire day. We drink beer. We eat
nachos. We snack on veggies. We move in and out of the
shade as the sun moves. After dark we sit by the fire pit,
alternately talking and silently meditating as we watch the
flames. The heat column ruffles the leaves of the nearby
birches. This is the summer I learn to sit still. We entertain
less. We sit in the backyard more. I have many days to practice sitting still.

In addition to being friends on Facebook with Cousin
Teddy's wife Chrystal, I am friends with Cousin Dan and
his sisters, Sarah and Leah. I recently told Chrystal I was
working on our family story. I had some questions for her.
Was Grandmama, aka Bad Ethel, always part of Teddy's
life? Was it an open adoption? Or did they wait until they
were on their own to connect with their birth mother? She
DMs me:

> When Teddy was in college his mom put an ad in the
> paper and Hilda Peck saw it and contacted Grand-
> mama to respond to the ad and contacted Teddy's
> mom and [her sister]. J. (Teddy's mom) had to do
> this for work to get her birth certificate and that's
> where she saw her birth Mother's name. Hilda was
> the one who arranged for the adoption long ago. It
> was not an open adoption. [The little girls] were at
> the Missouri Children's Home in Florissant, MO a
> couple of years before they got adopted.

So, the adoptive family goes to great lengths to protect Bad Ethel's two little girls. They change their birth names. They keep them from situations which may have been embarrassing such as running into Marion at the dance school. They even construct a really believable back story about the adoption. They protect them from the hard life of Blackie and Ethel, and yet make it so that Grandmama can have a place with them. And, as Cousin Dan says, "they had a really good life."

Half-sister Judy, Cousin Joan, and I are simply amazed that Ethel, Blackie and Catherine, their infant daughter, and Catherine's parents are all buried in the same plot. We shake our heads in collective wonder. So, no hard feelings, okay? Turtles all the way down.

🖋

I make challah the afternoon before Thanksgiving. Making the dough is easy; braiding together the strands will take a bit more practice. Robert and I each enjoy two slices of the warm bread. I gain three pounds overnight—a testimony of how little tolerance my body has for wheat. Dang! Bread is my favorite food in the whole wide world.

POSTSCRIPT

Ernie dies of Covid on Sunday morning, December 6, 2020. His death is brutal for him and for our children. He had been transferred from the Gunnison Hospital to the regional medical center on the preceding Wednesday. On the Thursday prior to his death, he had a CT Scan revealing metastasized colon cancer on his liver. He had never had a colonoscopy—surprising for someone in the healthcare industry, or not; Ernie never was a planner.

Robert sees this impending tragedy before I do. On hearing that Ernie has been transferred to the regional medical center Robert looks at me and says, "This is going to be rough, baby. You need to let yourself cry." As each medical complication is revealed to them, our kids call me two or three times every day to process. I cry rivers of tears along with them. Late Friday afternoon, our children have one hour to decide how much to intervene. Three of them want to let him go. Two of them want to keep him alive at any cost. That night they restart his heart twice and transfuse the six units of blood he lost through his GI tract overnight. On Sunday morning, with Trina and her husband, in full PPE, present, they unplug him. He is gone in 20 minutes.

Days before his death, hours really, Luna requests on her FB page that friends and family post memories of Ernie. I have to give my children something real. I stay up late writing and make this post on Dec. 5 at 12:15 am.:

> "Ernest, my first husband and the father of my five children, is in the ICU at UVRMC, likely dying of COVID-19. He has multiple risk factors—76, overweight, diabetic. He had a knee replacement the first week of October, from which he has not fully recovered. Yesterday evening, our children had to make some really difficult decisions really fast about how much to intervene. Please have your Advance Directives in place.
>
> Ernie and I have been divorced for 28 years. Our kids asked for memories of their father. I make this post for them.
>
> In high school, Ernie and his life-long best friend Dan Eldon Brough performed numerous slapstick sketches, often including piano and bass fiddle. Ernie and Danny loved to make music and loved to make people laugh. The home of Dan and his wife, Jeanette, was our favorite vacation destination. At first, many days spent in the sand and waves—Hermosa Beach between Avenue I and J. And later, many hours spent in the pool at their house at the top of the Palos Verdes Peninsula with the awesome view of LA. Jeanette's Mom and Dad, Joyce and Elmer, and her brother and sisters were, still are, our California family.

In 1967–68 Ernie became part of "Eight Penny Suitcase," arguably the best band on the BYU Campus that year, rockin' the house with "La Bamba" and "Gimme Some Lovin.'" Ernie was on keyboards and vocals. Sam Kershaw, who also became a life-long friend, was lead guitar and lead vocals. Ralph Geddes was the drummer. And the completely cool George Spilsbury was on the bass guitar and vocals. Sam, Ernie, and all of them insisted on a clear sound and strong rhythm. No muddy music from this group.

In Gunnison, Ernie had bands with his brother, Randy Larson, and brothers-in-law, Nick Anderson and Ron Marshall, my life-long friend, Tim Christenson, and LouDonn Petersen and others, in various configurations. They played gigs from Ephraim to Cedar City, anything from the bar to the Elks' Lodge to weddings and reunions. They practiced in our basement. Have amp, will travel.

At home, Ernie had a reel-to-reel TEAC recorder on which he could lay down multiple tracks of sound and music, tinkering endlessly. I heard from Sam's wife, Nan, today. When Sam died in Oct 2006, she found multiple CDs that Ernie made of these tracks—marked Ernie's Songs and Sam's Songs and multiple dates.

In the family room, Ernie had a great sound system and great speakers for The Mamas & the Papas—"California Dreaming"—Fleetwood Mac, *Deep Breakfast*, Toto—*Africa*, The Alan Parsons Project, and the Charlie Daniels Band.

One of our daughters once snagged a loose $20 from her Dad to make an unauthorized purchase of

a cassette tape—Sic Sic Sputnick. Her father oblig-
ingly recorded Willie Nelson over the tape for her.
He thought it was hilarious.

When we bought the Star Theatre in Gunnison
in 1981, he installed a Dolby sound system. He loved
movies, and he wanted them to sound good. During
one early showing, Ernie, as the projectionist, tried
to turn down the sound on the F word, but turned it
up instead. Also hilarious.

Ernie could be a good cook, making delicious
Tex-Mex food—his mother's heritage, and a respect-
able barbeque, courtesy of his Texas grandpa. But
he was also known for making his kids Nightmare
Hash for breakfast—anything in the fridge was fair
game, spaghetti, corn-meal mush, anything. If he
could fry it, they could eat it. Ask them!

Ernie loved music. He loved to perform. He loved to
make people laugh."

In June 2021, Luna, Dora, Trina, and CC are beside
themselves when they read Chapter 4. Woody and Me,
Part II. They find my assessments of their father entirely
too harsh. I have softened some of my judgments for their
sakes. Ernie wanted to be an actor or a musician. I have
said for years that the worst thing I can say about Ernie was
that he was the unhappiest person I know, and he took that
unhappiness out on those closest to him. Perhaps the greatest source of Ernie's unhappiness was this unfulfilled desire
to pursue a career in entertainment. His parents could not
support such an impractical choice. And neither could he.

BIBLIOGRAPHY

Beck, Martha. *Leaving the Saints: How I Lost the Mormons and Found My Faith*. New York: Crown, 2006

Broderick, Carlfred B. *It Came Out of the Blue, Like a Scheduled Airline: Guarding Against Adultery and Weathering Tribulation*. Covenant Recordings Inc., 1983.

Brodie, Fawn M. *No Man Knows My History: The Life of Joseph Smith*. New York: First Vintage Books Ed., 1995.

Harvey, Steve. *Act Like a Lady Think Like a Man: What Men Really Think About Love, Relationships, Intimacy and Commitment*. New York: Harper-Collins, 2009.

Hawkins, David R. *Power vs Force: The Hidden Determinants of Human Behavior*. Carlsbad: Hay House, 1995.

Hawkins, David R. *The Eye of I: From Which Nothing Is Hidden*. Sedona: Veritas, 2001.

Hawkins, David R. *I: Reality and Subjectivity*. Sedona: Veritas, 2003.

Howard, Gary R. *We Can't Teach What We Don't Know: White Teachers, Multiracial Schools* 2nd ed. New York: Teachers College Press, 2006.

King, Thomas. *The Truth About Stories: A Native Narrative*. Minneapolis, University of Minnesota Press, 2003.

Krakauer, Jon. *Under the Banner of Heaven: A Story of Violent Faith.* New York: Doubleday, 2004

Larson, Charles M. *By His Own Hand on Papyrus: A New Look at the Joseph Smith Papyrii.* Cedar Springs: The Institute of Religious Research, 1992.

Palmer, Grant. *An Insider's View of the Origins of Mormonism.* Salt Lake City: Signature Books, 2002.

Pinkola Estes, Clarissa. *Women Who Run with the Wolves: Myths and Stories of the Wild Woman Archetype.* New York: Ballantine Books, 1992.

Powell, John. *Why Am I Afraid to Tell You Who I Am.* Niles: Argus Communications, 1969.

Quinn, D. Michael. *Early Mormonism and the Magic World View.* Salt Lake City: Signature Books, 1998.

Ruiz, Don Miguel. *The Four Agreements: A Practical Guide to Personal Freedom.* San Rafael: Amber-Allen Publishing, 2018.

Santagati, Steve with Arianne Cohen. *The Manual: A True Bad Boy Explains How Men Think, Date and Mate—and What Women Can Do to Come Out on Top.* New York: Crown Publishers, 2007

Wilbur, Ken. *The One, Two, Three of God.* Louisville, CO: Sounds True, 2007.

ABOUT THE AUTHOR

Dawn survives a turbulent childhood, marries young, and returns to college as a nontraditional student with five children living at home. She becomes the valedictorian of her local junior college. She eventually completes a B.A. in English Teaching. She also earns an M.S. in Educational Psychology, School Counseling and completes another master's program in Education Leadership and Policy.

In her professional career, Dawn wins two national awards: The US Army Planning for Life Award in 1998 for exemplary school counseling programs, and the American School Counselor Association School Counseling Program Coordinator/Supervisor of the year in 2009.

She authors the 2008 Utah Model for School Counseling Programs and is the editor for the 2012 manual *Strategies and Resources: Dropout Prevention in Utah*. She has written agency code and legislation, as well as articles in school counseling magazines and peer-reviewed journals, and multiple implementation guides, promotional materials, and reports for the legislature. As a founding member of the International Society for Policy Research and Evaluation in School-Based Counseling, she and one of her graduate students write "Chapter Two, What Government

Policy-Makers Need to Know" for the publication *International Handbook for Policy Research on School-Based Counseling.*

Dawn teaches in the school counselor education program at Utah State University for six years and at University of Phoenix for fifteen years. At UPhx, she teaches graduate level Human Development two or three times every year. In this introductory course for master's candidates, she helps students recognize their own growth and development. She becomes known among the faculty for helping students improve even their graduate level writing.

Dawn and her husband live in Salt Lake City. Between them, they have nine children and twelve grandchildren. Three of her children have taken the family international: one son-in-law from Switzerland, French-Swiss; a daughter-in-law from Brazil; and another son-in-law from Ukraine, an ethnic Russian. Half of her grandkids are bilingual in French, Portuguese, or Russian. Her husband's family carries a military tradition: a great grandfather was a large animal veterinarian in the Civil War; an uncle was a flying ace in WWI; his father was second wave at Omaha Beach, going ashore with the 1st Infantry Division, the Big Red One; her husband is a Vietnam combat veteran, going in country as an infantry private and coming home as a sergeant; his twin sons are military, one Army and one Marines, and a son-in-law is Navy.

CPSIA information can be obtained
at www.ICGtesting.com
Printed in the USA
BVHW042317070622
639018BV00005B/4